The Faber Pocket Guide to Bach

Nicholas Kenyon has been Managing Director of the Barbican Centre since 2007. He was Director of the BBC Proms from 1996 to 2007, and Controller, BBC Radio 3, from 1992 to 1998. He read History at Balliol College, Oxford, and his first post was with the English Bach Festival 1973–6. He was a music critic for *The New Yorker*, *The Times*, and the *Observer*, and has written the history of the BBC Symphony Orchestra, the biography of Simon Rattle, edited the influential volume *Authenticity and Early Music*, and co-edited *The Proms: A New History*. He is a member of the boards of English National Opera and Sage Gateshead, a Trustee of Dartington Hall and a member of Arts Council England.

THE FABER POCKET GUIDE TO
Bach

Nicholas Kenyon

ff

FABER & FABER

First published in 2011
by Faber & Faber Limited
Bloomsbury House
74–77 Great Russell Street
London WC1B 3DA

Typeset by Donald Sommerville
Printed and bound by
CPI Group (UK) Ltd, Croydon, CR0 4YY

A CIP record for this book
is available from the British Library

ISBN 978–0–571–23327–4

In memory of
George Malcolm (1917–1997),

Lina Lalandi (1920–2012)
founder and director of the English Bach Festival,

and for all those performers who bring Bach's music to life.

Contents

Foreword

Bach's music has been part of my life for as long as I can remember. I had to perform his work as a young chorister at St Paul's Cathedral in London, although it was inevitable that my experience in the choir would be limited to his sacred, rather than his secular, music. I can still recall distinctly the feelings of elation, satisfaction and tiredness as I sang in the final, consolatory chorus of the St Matthew Passion at the end of our annual performance of that overwhelming work. Other, later memories are equally sharp: hearing for the first time the great slow movement of the Concerto for two violins as my father drove my family across Europe at the beginning of our summer holiday; or wading through a prelude and fugue from *The Well-tempered Clavier* when I was a teenager and realising, in a sudden, exhilarating flash, that playing the piano could actually be fun.

I have continued to listen to and play Bach's music throughout my adult life, aware that, given his enormous output, there will always be new works to discover and to study. With this marvellous guide, Nicholas Kenyon has offered people like me a great gift. Listening to Bach can be demanding – think of the complexities of *The Musical Offering* or the Goldberg Variations – and Kenyon takes care to acknowledge this. As a compensation, he offers us a friendly hand and clear, unpretentious analysis. With his help, music that can seem daunting will yield great rewards. This book – a long labour of love – is about a miracle. It tells the story of how a man from an ordinary family, with a thorough but unexceptional education, a man who wrote dazzling music that summons up the sensual, everyday pleasures of the world around us, could then push himself to produce work that touches the face of God. That is a journey that anyone who loves music would be eager to trace. With this book in their hand, their task will be a simple pleasure.

Simon Russell Beale
October 2010

Introduction

Bach's music was nourished by the past and feeds the
future.
   Friedrich Blume

'Who needs Bach?' 'You, me, everybody else, civilisation,
and the Jacques Loussier Trio.'
   Bernard Levin, *The Times*, 31 July 1975

Let's face it, Bach can be daunting. He does not give up his
secrets easily. He is one of the most mysterious of Western
composers. Mozart is one of us, a person whose feelings we
can recognise; Beethoven asserts our common humanity, and
declares our common fate; Handel articulates our basic human
emotions, and cuts to the heart, while Wagner extends those
primeval emotions on the grandest scale. But with Bach, there
is always something more, something veiled. He is 'the other':
his vision and aspiration carries us far beyond ourselves, and we
can find his transcendental idealism very difficult to penetrate.

Like all cultural icons, Bach has been made to serve every
prevailing ideological tendency: in one view he is the spiritual hero of German music who spent his life writing sacred
cantatas to the greater glory of God; in another, the cantanker-
ous artist forever complaining at employers and disgruntled
with patrons; in yet another, more recent, he has become the
first great entrepreneur of the classical music scene, selling his
own goods and services and acting as an agent for published
music and pianos around the courts and cities of Germany
in the eighteenth-century equivalent of e-commerce. He was
even a financial investor: as this book went to press in December 2010, a new discovery of documents revealed that in the
1740s Bach bought shares in a Saxon silver mine.

All great artists have a perpetually fluctuating relationship
to posterity, but in Bach's case this is especially so because

what we know about his personal life is limited and even the facts we do know have shifted so much in recent years. There is no rich body of correspondence (we have far less than from Mozart or even from Monteverdi). We have plenty of information about which organs he examined, which pupils he recommended, and why he fell out with his superiors, but this does not add up to a rounded picture of his personality. Hence it has been easy for successive generations to impose on Bach their own ideas of his character and motivations.

Perhaps this does not matter at all to the listener who wants to put the essence of Bach's astounding music in his or her pocket. But it provides the context for scholarly work that is far from being complete. The story of Bach is an ever-changing narrative, for there are advances being made all the time and every scholarly step forward requires a reassessment of the balance of Bach's work. Just in the last few years there have been the discovery of the very first autograph manuscripts in Bach's hand, written when he was around fifteen, the identification of an unknown aria from Weimar (now BWV 1127), and the rediscovery of the Old Bach Archive which resurfaced as part of the Sing-Akademie library in Kiev in the Ukraine and has now come back to Berlin. Bach's copy of the Calov Bible with his revealing marginal markings turned up in a barn in Michigan; Gerhard Herz tells the story of an autograph flute part of Cantata 9 being mysteriously found among the rubble on a New York building site in 1971. Cantata libretti from 1727 have recently turned up in St Petersburg. Is there a lost Bach Passion waiting to be found in an organ loft?

There is a vast amount that can now be understood about Bach's political and social background in order to put him in context: Ulrich Siegele has written about Bach's relationship to the complex cultural politics of Leipzig and Saxony, John Butt about his relation to the philosophy of his time, while Robin Leaver is a distinguished recent interpreter of Bach's understanding of Luther's theology and liturgy. Equally, musicians and scholars have explored radically new ways to understand his music: Robert Marshall has tried to disentangle how Bach actually composed, what his scores show about his mental processes; John Butt surveyed all his articulation marks. Particularly suggestive have been Laurence Dreyfus's explorations of Bach's patterns of invention, while a whole strand of analysing and understanding Bach's critical stance towards the musical conventions of his time has been explored by Dreyfus, Michael Marissen and Eric Chafe. Relevant documents are still being turned up as near to home as Leipzig, by sharp-eyed scholars such as Andreas Glöckner, Uwe Wolf and Peter Wollny. A recent course at King's College, London, suggests that

> various scholars have begun to challenge [Bach's] transcendent status more seriously, opening up a number of compelling alternative perspectives on the composer and his world. Others, meanwhile, continue to seek new answers to the baffling question of how this provincial cantor's music could have become such a dominant force in Western cultural life.

Perhaps most striking, for those of us who are primarily listeners to Bach, has been the revolutionary reinvention of the sounds and textures of his music over the last half-century of historical performance practice, which has reinvigorated our understanding of Bach's genius. From the epoch-making Bach cantata cycle of Nikolaus Harnoncourt and Gustav Leonhardt, which I would unhesitatingly call the most important recording project of my lifetime (others might give this accolade to the Solti *Ring* cycle), there has flowed a sea-change in our understanding of baroque music in general and Bach in particular. In this context, the still-simmering arguments highlighted by Joshua Rifkin and Andrew Parrott (which will be referred to later), about whether his 'choral' music should be performed with one singer to a part or more, continue to resonate throughout the world of performance. Bach cantata cycles on CD are still being released; John Eliot Gardiner's was completed in November 2010.

This process has ensured the continuing relevance of Bach's music for a wide public. Constant reinterpretation and reinvention have guaranteed that it continues to resonate throughout our musical world. Bach was central to the sound of the Swinging Sixties, when Jacques Loussier, the Swingle Singers and the Moog synthesizer all made us listen to the classics in a new way. Stokowski's film *Fantasia*, with its abstract dramatisation of the Toccata and Fugue in D minor, was not a total success when it appeared in wartime in 1940, but it took off in the 1960s and influenced a generation. The Moog synthesizer 'Switched-on Bach' was the first LP based on classical music ever to sell over half a million copies, and the 'Air on the G string' made people buy cigars called Hamlet. As noted below, Bach's music has been continually used (and misused) in a wide range of films and media from *Truly, Madly, Deeply* to *Rollerball*. Few contemporary composers, from Andriessen to Kagel, from Birtwistle to Henze, have been untouched by exposure to and admiration for Bach's music.

His impact continues: when BBC Radio 3 devoted its entire schedule over Christmas 2005 to the complete works of Johann Sebastian Bach, the response was extraordinary. At a time when high culture was supposedly undervalued, listeners wrote, phoned and e-mailed to testify to the power this music from a quarter of a millennium ago had over them. Bach's appeal shows no signs of diminishing in the twenty-first century. He is now a postmodern resource for creative artists. Herbert Wernicke's innovative theatre piece *Actus Tragicus* uses music from Bach's cantatas to illustrate the obsessive repetitiveness of daily life in a never-changing landscape. In 2009, meanwhile, the architect Zaha Hadid conceived the 'J. S. Bach Music Hall' for performances of the solo violin and keyboard music at the Manchester International Festival: an installation of a 'voluminous ribbon', which 'swirls within the room, carving out a spatial and visual response to the intricate relationships of Bach's harmonies', surrounded performer and audience. The continuing, infinitely varied reception of Bach's music gives us the confidence to believe that music can indeed transcend its original cultural context and speak across time.

*

There is really nothing original in this book, except a personal response to Bach's music based on my years of listening. I have acknowledged, in the Further Reading and in the text itself, the many writers and scholars on whose work I have directly drawn to create this latest summary of Bach's life and music. This book does try some new and different approaches: for all the surveys of Bach's cantatas that exist, for example, I think none so far has tried to illustrate Bach's development of this form by presenting the cantatas in the order in which they were most likely composed – rather than by the days of the liturgical year for which they were written, which is the most usual approach, or by BWV number, which recent research has rendered outdated. More risky, because more uncertain, is a broadly chronological approach to the keyboard and organ music, acknowledging that these two genres, although separated here into secular and sacred music, do often overlap.

Bach's output is vast, and I have risked ignoring some minor works while first drawing attention to many favourites, as the new listener may require some guidance as to where to begin: the 'Top 50' (or so) Bach works I list at the start are my personal preferences. The book is not designed to be read straight through, but to be used as a resource. It aims to complement, for example, the life-and-works narrative of the late Malcolm Boyd's excellent Master Musicians volume on Bach by providing separate information on as many works and movements as possible within the format. In the same way as my *Faber Pocket Guide to Mozart*, this book aims to assimilate some recent scholarship and make its insights as accessible as possible; the unfinished debate is reflected in these pages by the overuse of the words 'perhaps', 'surely' and 'probably' – in the knowledge that we shall never feel that we have penetrated to the heart of one of the most mysterious, accomplished, and protean creative geniuses our civilisation has ever produced. As Malcolm Boyd put it, 'the difficulty of writing anything on Bach remotely worthy of its subject remains'.

A note on numbering Bach's works

One of the most problematical aspects of organising Bach's output is that the great catalogue of his music by Wolfgang Schmieder, *Thematisch-systematisches Verzeichnis der Werke Johann Sebastian Bachs*, which gave its name to the BWV *Bach-Werke-Verzeichnis* system (unlike other more egotistical cataloguers of composers, Schmieder did not want his own name used as an abbreviation), is not chronologically ordered. Its sequence of cantatas from BWV 1 onwards bears no relationship to the order of composition; other numberings are equally outdated by modern research, and in any case are organised by type rather than by date. My ancient red-bound volume of Schmieder, already battered when I bought it second-hand many years ago, has steadily collapsed during the writing of this book.

The second edition of the BWV catalogue attempted to remedy some of these faults, and a smaller *Kleine Ausgabe*, edited by Alfred Dürr and Yoshitake Kobayashi, appeared in 1998: in addition to being bright blue, which helps, it is the most practical current catalogue, even though thinking has subsequently moved on. A third edition of the full BWV catalogue, reflecting the latest research, is awaited. A recent project, the *Bach Compendium*, was begun under the editorship of Christoph Wolff and Hans-Joachim Schulze in 1985, but publication is as yet confined to four volumes on the choral works; while its numberings extend further, to the organ and keyboard works, their logic is not yet explained, and thus they have not yet become established in the popular mind. Though they are listed in the second edition of *The New Grove Dictionary of Music and Musicians* (2001) alongside BWV numbers, they are not used, for example, in Wolff's own biography of Bach (2000).

The most easily available current listings of Bach's works are those in Malcolm Boyd's *Bach* (third edition, 2000) and *The New Grove Bach Family* (edited by Christoph Wolff), but the latter has since been updated in the second edition of *New*

Grove and on *Grove Music Online* (now part of *Oxford Music Online*); there still remain many uncertainties. It is chastening to know, for instance, that there is no currently reliable and detailed listing of all Bach's works in chronological order: compiling this would at the moment be an impossible task, given the stylistic world of his earliest music, as many datings are uncertain within a wide range of possibilities. Quite a few familiar Bach works are in doubt: the most famous of all is the Toccata and Fugue in D minor BWV 565 (is it for organ? is it by Bach?), but also the well-known single-movement *Nun ist das Heil uns die Kraft*, Cantata 50, and the solo *Amore traditore*, Cantata 203, as well as a wide range of possible early works. Moreover, fixing a date precisely, which is sometimes possible, might tell us only about a single version of a work: it might be a revision of a previous version or the subject of future revision. A recent commentator on Bach's early works, the English scholar Richard Jones, points out that the process of establishing dates is fraught with difficulty: 'The kind of analytical studies that lead to observations on Bach's stylistic development must also be used to try to establish approximate composition dates in the first place. The scope for circular argument is obvious, and the whole situation is intellectually unsatisfying.'

Throughout the book 'Bach' refers to Johann Sebastian, rather than to any other member of the extensive family. In references to keys, 'Suite No. 1 in C' means in C major, whereas the Suite No. 2 is referred to as 'in B minor'. All references to Bach works are to the BWV catalogue in the version of 1998, and its various appendices (Anhang). Cantatas are as usual referred to by their BWV numbers, but I refer simply to 'Cantata 106', for example, rather than 'Cantata BWV 106'. I have not given BWV numbers for individual preludes and fugues within *The Well-tempered Clavier*, or individual chorale preludes within the *Orgelbüchlein*: the keys of the former and the titles of the latter clearly distinguish which piece is being referred to, but readers who require more detailed information will find it in the work-lists in *New Grove* and elsewhere.

I have used the well-known shorthand of the '48' to refer to the two books of *The Well-tempered Clavier*. The recording recommendations doubtless reflect my own preferences for recent period-instrument performance, but there are some historic recordings as well: there are many more available and discussed at www.bach-cantatas.com.

I would like to thank Belinda Matthews of Faber, for persuading me that this undertaking was ever a realistic proposition, and for enthusiastically supporting the lengthy process, the excellent editing, setting and proof-reading team at Faber for their support, John Carewe for the overlong loan of many of his *Neue Bach Ausgabe* volumes, Martin Randall of Martin Randall Travel for squeezing me into his fine Bach Tour of 2010, Amy Blier-Carruthers for much research and checking, and Hester Furman for invaluable work on the discographies. Vikram Seth kindly gave permission for the quotation from *An Equal Music*. I thank Jonathan Freeman-Attwood, John Butt, Martin Neary, Stephen Roe and my wife Ghislaine for their close reading and thoughtful comments on parts of the manuscript. In particular I must thank Richard D. P. Jones, whose rich knowledge and careful checking saved me from signal errors. Finally I thank those very many Bach performers and scholars who over the years have provided fascinating conversations and insights. They cannot be blamed for any of what follows.

NK
21 March 2010 (325th anniversary of Bach's birth) –
28 July 2010 (260th anniversary of Bach's death)

For corrections in this reprint I thank especially Margaret Steinitz and Pekka Sipilä.

September 2013

The Bach 'Top 10'

The popular image of Bach, as on countless compilation CDs:

> Toccata and Fugue in D minor (but is it by Bach?)
> 'Air on the G string' (arr. from Orchestral Suite No. 3)
> 'Jesu, joy of man's desiring' (from Cantata 147)
> 'Sheep may safely graze' (from Cantata 208)
> *Ave Maria* (arr. Gounod, from Prelude in C, Book 1 of the '48')
> Brandenburg Concerto No. 3
> Largo from Concerto for two violins
> 'Sleepers, wake!' (from Cantata 140)
> Prelude from Violin Partita in E
> Badinerie from Orchestral Suite No. 2

What a limited list this is! Based around the idea of Bach as a master of the memorable melody, some in later arrangements, few of these pieces involve Bach's greatest strengths. But they are the pieces repeatedly featured on 'Bach's Greatest Hits', 'Essential Bach', 'Chill Out to Bach', 'Magical Wedding Music' and 'Bach for My Baby' . . .

My Top 50 (or so) Bach

A very personal selection: these are some of the pieces that I return to over and over again in my listening to Bach and have come to value most highly over the years – just the tip of a wonderful iceberg.

The Art of Fugue BWV 1080, Nos. 4, 10, 14
Ascension Oratorio BWV 11
Brandenburg Concertos Nos. 3, 4, 5, BWV 1048, 1049, 1050
Cantata 34 *O ewiges Feuer*
Cantata 45 *Es ist dir gesagt, Mensch*
Cantata 54 *Widerstehe doch der Sünde*
Cantata 61 *Nun komm, der Heiden Heiland*
Cantata 62 *Nun komm, der Heiden Heiland*
Cantata 67 *Halt im Gedächtnis Jesum Christ*
Cantata 78 *Jesu, der du meine Seele*
Cantata 79 *Gott, der Herr, ist Sonn und Schild*
Cantata 82 *Ich habe genug*
Cantata 106 *Gottes Zeit ist die allerbeste Zeit*
Cantata 197 *Gott ist unsre Zuversicht*
Cantata 202 *Weichet nur, betrübte Schatten*
Christmas Oratorio BWV 248
Concerto in D minor for two violins BWV 1043
Concerto in C for two harpsichords BWV 1061
Concerto in A minor for four harpsichords BWV 1065
Fantasia and Fugue in A minor for keyboard BWV 904
Fantasia and Fugue in G minor for organ BWV 542
Goldberg Variations BWV 988
In dir ist Freude, prelude for organ BWV 615
Komm, Jesu, Komm, motet BWV 229
Kyrie, Gott heiliger Geist, prelude for organ BWV 671
Jesu, meine Freude, motet BWV 227
Magnificat in D BWV 243
Mass in B minor BWV 232

The Musical Offering BWV 1079
O Jesu Christ, mein Leben Licht BWV 118
Orchestral Suites Nos. 1–4 BWV 1066–9
Partitas for keyboard Nos. 2, 3, 4, 6, BWV 826, 827, 828, 830
Prelude and Fugue in E flat for organ, 'St Anne' BWV 552
Preludes and Fugues from the '48', BWV 846–93
Sonata in B minor for flute and keyboard BWV 1030
St Matthew Passion BWV 244
St John Passion BWV 245
Toccata and Fugue in D minor for organ, 'Dorian' BWV 538
Trio Sonatas for organ BWV 525–30
Violin solo Partitas in D minor, E BWV 1004, 1006
Violin solo Sonatas in G minor, C BWV 1001, 1005
Wir glauben all an einen Gott, prelude for organ BWV 680

If one had to choose a single work of Bach's that most completely expressed his genius, would it be the B minor Mass or
the Goldberg Variations . . . ? Fortunately, we have both.

Bach in sound and number

Bach was conscious that he had been born into one of the great musical families of his time. He was also aware that his name had meaning: both as sound, as a melodic fragment, and, more controversially, as a number.

B (=B flat) – **A** (A natural) – **C** (C natural) – **H** (=B natural)
This sequence of notes occurs at critical points in several late Bach works, and in a host of works by other composers written as a tribute to him. J. G. Walther first pointed out the musical nature of this theme in his *Musicalisches Lexicon* of 1732, and it was used by others of the Bach family; it then appears clearly in Bach's own Canonic Variations and the (possible) final fugue of *The Art of Fugue*, and has been found lurking elsewhere. Beethoven planned an overture on it which he never completed, Schumann used it in fugues, Liszt created his dramatic *Preludium und Fugue über den namen BACH*, Schoenberg embedded it in his *Variations for Orchestra* Op. 31, Rimsky-Korsakov, Casella, Bartók, Honegger, Wellesz and countless others have utilised it, often to mark Bach anniversaries.

BACH = 14 and J. S. BACH = 41

Among the much debated and disputed number alphabets extant in Bach's time, it is unarguable that Bach was aware of one formula and regarded it as significant, building it into significant moments of his music, especially in his late works. This is the system in which A = 1, B = 2, C = 3, D = 4, E = 5, F = 6, G = 7, H = 8, etc., meaning that the letters in BACH add up to 14, while the letters in J. S. BACH add up to 41. Further than this it might be unwise to go, though many have, in wildly counting and attributing importance to word symbolisms, bar numbers, and other 'hidden messages' in Bach's works. Beware.

Bonae
Artis
Cultorem
Habeas
'You have someone who cultivates good art'

From an inscription to a canon, 1 March 1749

VIVAT: JSB

BACH	theurer Bach!	Beloved Bach
G G# F F#	ruffet, ach!	call out, ah
E D# D C#	hofft auf leben	hopes for life
So di innen nur kanst geben		Which only you can give
Drum erhör ihr sehnlich ach!		Thus grant our wish, alas
Theurer BACH Bach		Beloved BACH Bach

Inscription on the Bach Goblet, c.1735, Bach-Museum
Eisenach

Tortoise: . . . Now getting back to Bach's melodic name,
did you know that the melody B–A–C–H, if played upside
down and backwards, is exactly the same as the original?

Achilles: How can anything be played upside down? Backwards, I can see, but upside down? You must be pulling my
leg . . .

Tortoise: . . . Let me just go and fetch my fiddle . . . let's see
now . . . here's the last Contrapunctus, and here's the last
theme . . .

*The Tortoise begins to play B–A–C – but as he bows the final H,
suddenly, without warning, a shattering sound rudely interrupts
his performance. Both he and Achilles spin round, just in time
to catch a glimpse of the myriad fragments of glass tinkling to
the floor from the shelf where Goblet G had stood, only moments
before. And then . . . dead silence.*

Douglas Hofstadter, *Gödel, Escher, Bach, an Eternal Braid*

Things people said about Bach

JOHANN KIRNBERGER 1781
The great J. Sebastian Bach used to say 'Everything must be possible', and he would never hear of anything being not feasible.

JOHANN FRIEDRICH REICHARDT 1782
Had Bach possessed the high integrity and deep expressive feeling that inspired Handel he would have been much greater even than Handel; but as it is he was only more painstakingly and technically skilful.

CHRISTIAN FRIEDRICH DANIEL SCHUBART 1784
Without doubt the Orpheus of the Germans! Immortal in himself, and immortal through his great sons ... His spirit was so original, so vast, that centuries would be needed to measure up to it ... His hand was gigantic. He would reach a twelfth with the left hand and fill it in with the middle fingers. He performed passages on the pedal with the greatest accuracy. He used the stops with such subtle variety that the listener was overcome by the power of his magic ... What Newton was as a sage of nature, Bach was as a musician.

CHARLES BURNEY 1789
He was so fond of full harmony that, besides a constant and active use of the pedals, he is said to have put down such keys with a stick in his mouth as neither hands nor feet could reach.

JOHANN KARL FRIEDRICH TRIEST 1801
What joy for a patriotic resident of our Fatherland to know that the greatest, most profound harmonist of all previous time, who exceeds everything that Italy, France, England had done for pure music, who moved his musical world – which surely was accustomed to learned works – to amazement, and passed on to posterity still unequalled models, which would be considered like mysteries ... this man, I say was German!

Proud and majestic shines the name of Johann Sebastian Bach before all German composers of the first half of the preceding century. He grasped with Newton's spirit everything that had been thought about and established as example, probed the depths so fully and successfully that he is considered to this day the rule-giver of authentic harmony.

ATTRIB. LUDWIG VAN BEETHOVEN 1801
The immortal god of harmony.

JOHANN WOLFGANG VON GOETHE 1827
His works are an invaluable national patrimony with which no other nation has anything to be compared.

CARL FRIEDRICH ZELTER 1827 (TO GOETHE)
Could I let you hear some happy day one of Sebastian Bach's motets, you would feel yourself at the centre of the world as a man like you ought to be. I hear the works for the many hundredth time, and am not finished with them yet, and never will be.

FRIEDRICH ROCHLITZ
[Bach is] . . . the Albrecht Dürer of German music, since he attains great expression by the profound development and inexhaustible combination of simple ideas.

WILHELM LOEBELL 1829
Sebastian is certainly austere and grave, but in such a way that even among the lamentations, grief, repentance and penance, the cheerfulness and joy of existence still breaks through in the most wonderful manner, indeed grows directly out of those emotions and flourishes. I must tell you that I think I have found in Bach the composer I have sought for so long, a musician who may be compared with Shakespeare.

FELIX MENDELSSOHN 1831
. . . here I have found a proper registration to play Seb. Bach's 'Schmücke dich, o liebe Seele'. It is as if it were made for it, and sounds so moving, that every time I start to play it, I shudder all over . . . this imbues the chorale with a peaceful sound,

as though they were far-off human voices, singing the chorale from the bottom of their hearts.

ROBERT SCHUMANN 1836 (TO MENDELSSOHN)

... then you Felix Meritis ... played one of the chorales ... gilded garlands hang about the *cantus firmus*, and you poured such blissfulness and joy into it, that you confessed to me yourself 'if life were to rob you of every hope and belief this one chorale would restore them all to you'.

Play the fugues of the great masters, above all Johann Sebastian Bach. Let *The Well-tempered Clavier* become your daily bread. Then you will become a solid musician.

GEORG WILHELM FRIEDRICH HEGEL, PUBLISHED 1838

A grand, truly Protestant, robust and, so to speak, erudite genius which we have only recently learned again to appreciate at its full value.

FRIEDRICH NIETZSCHE 1878

In Bach there is too much crude Christianity, crude Germanism, crude scholasticism. He stands at the threshold of modern European music, but he is always looking back towards the Middle Ages.

PYOTR ILYICH TCHAIKOVSKY 1888

I would add that I like playing Bach because it is interesting to play a good fugue, but I do not regard him, as some do, as a great genius.

CAMILLE SAINT-SAËNS 1899 (ON BERLIOZ)

I always remember his astonishment and delight at hearing a chorus of Sebastian Bach that I played him one day. He couldn't get over the idea that the great Sebastian had written things like that; he told me that he had always taken him for a sort of colossus of learning, grinding out scholarly fugues but devoid of poetry or charm. The truth was, he didn't know him.

RICHARD WAGNER 1865
... the almost unexplainably puzzling phenomenon of the
musical miracle man ... this master, a wretched cantor and
organist wandering from one little Thuringian village to
another, hardly known even by name, dragging out his existence in miserably paid posts, remaining so unknown that it
took a century for his works to be rescued from oblivion; even
in music finding an art form already in existence that was
externally the perfect picture of its time – dry, stiff, pedantic,
like a wig and pigtail portrayed in notes. And now see what
a world the inconceivably great Sebastian constructed out of
these elements ...

GEORGE BERNARD SHAW 1898/1923
Bach's method was unattainable: his compositions are wonderful webs of exquisitely beautiful Gothic traceries in sound,
quite beyond all human talent. Beethoven of blunter craft
was thoroughly popular and practicable: not to save his soul
could he have drawn one long Gothic line in sound as Bach
could, much less have woven several of them together with
so apt a harmony that even when the composer is unmoved
its progressions saturate themselves with their emotion which
springs as warmly from our delicately touched admiration as
from our sympathies ...

FERRUCCIO BUSONI 1923
I have to thank my father for the good fortune that kept me
strictly to the study of Bach in my childhood, and that in a
time and in a country in which the master was rated little
higher than a Carl Czerny ... How did such a man in his
ambition for a child's career come to hit upon the one very
thing that was right?

ALFRED BURGARTZ 1931
Bach's fugues and Frederick [the Great]'s battle plans are
spiritually united.

ROGER FRY
Bach almost persuades me to be a Christian.

ARNOLD SCHOENBERG 1950

I used to say 'Bach was the first composer with twelve tones'. This was a joke of course. I did not even know whether somebody before him might not have deserved this title. But the truth on which this statement is based is that the Fugue of No. 24 of the first volume of *The Well-Tempered Clavier*, in B minor, begins with a subject in which all twelve tones appear.

ANTON VON WEBERN

You find everything in Bach: the development of cyclic forms, the conquest of the realm of tonality – the attempt at a summation of the highest order.

ERNEST NEWMAN 1946

Here is Bach, a poor boy self-educated in music, with the minimum of culture even in his own domain, who never read a book on musical aesthetics or musical form in his life, for such things did not exist in his day, but who somehow managed, for all that, to demonstrate in his works all the architectonic possibilities of the flow and combination of any given set of musical sounds. Yet while achieving this wonder his mind was not merely working like a superlative machine; his genius for permutation and combination went hand in hand with an inexhaustible power of artistic creation of the most varied kind, each purely technical problem being solved not as it is in the books, by means of a portmanteau formula, but in the terms of the particular aesthetic of the case in hand.

RALPH VAUGHAN WILLIAMS 1950

We unmusical have taken John Sebastian Bach to our hearts. A young exquisite once said to me 'I don't like Bach, he is so bourgeois' to which I probably answered that being bourgeois myself I considered Bach the greatest of all composers. It is Bach's intense humanity that endears him to me and my fellow bourgeois. The proletarians (if there were any in this country) would be too much occupied with their wrongs, and the 'governing classes' (if indeed they existed outside the imagination of the *New Statesman*) would be too much occupied with preserving their rights to have time to be human. The warm human sentiments are reserved for the bourgeois; therefore of all Bach's works it is those great choral expressions of his personal and anthropomorphic religion which appeal most to us country and small-towns folk.

PAUL HINDEMITH 1950

A shadow seems to have fallen upon his creativeness, the shadow of melancholy ... What can a man do, who technically and spiritually has climbed to the highest rung of artistic production attainable by mankind? He can climb no higher, for he is only a man. Is he serenely to continue his former work, forcing it by mere rearrangement into apparently new forms? ... he has arrived at the end, he stands as the old Persian poem says, before the curtain that nobody will ever draw aside. For this ultimate attainment he must pay a dear price: melancholy, the grief of having been bereft of all former imperfections and with them of the possibility of proceeding further.

THEODOR W. ADORNO 1951 (TRANS. 1967)

The view of Bach which prevails today in musicological circles corresponds to the role assigned to him by the stagnation and industriousness of a resurrected culture ... Bach is degraded by impotent nostalgia to the very church composer against whose office his music rebelled and which he filled only with great conflict ... Bach was the first to crystallise the idea of the rationally constituted work, of the aesthetic domination of nature ... Perhaps Bach's most innermost truth is that in him the social trend which has dominated the bourgeois era to this very day is not merely preserved but, by being reflected in images, is reconciled with the voice of humanity which in reality was stifled by that trend at the moment of its inception.

SUSAN MCCLARY 1987

I participated during 1985 in several Bach Year celebrations ... to my overwhelming joy (as paranoid confronted with worst-possible scenarios) I was told outright by prominent scholars that Bach (unlike 'second-rate' composers such as Telemann) had *nothing* to do with his time and place, that he was 'divinely inspired', that his music works in accordance with perfect universal order and truth. One is permitted in other words to deal with music in its social context, but only if one agrees to leave figures such as Bach alone . . .

HANS WERNER HENZE 1976

There are things said in this music [Cantata 77] which up until this point no one had ever dared say with sounds, had ever been able to say, or ever even tried to say. With unparalleled realism, here we have the birth of a universal language, a plain language, and through its help and mediation, human emotions and conditions are revealed in which – and only now can we see and think of it this way – not just the traditional Christian bourgeois audience sees itself, but also the modern, lonely, doubting human being, who has lost faith, who has no firm foothold in society, and whose life must primarily be spent (like Büchner's Woyzeck), "without the church's blessing".

BERNARD LEVIN 1975

The truth of the matter is that I am not at all sure I like Bach, and quite certain that I do not understand him . . . to my ears almost everything he wrote sounds as though it is in the minor key . . . practically all Bach sounds as if it was written to make me feel unhappy . . . I know that Bach was one of the greatest geniuses ever to adorn the human race, and that he wrote some of the most sublime music in all history. But he leaves me, literally, cold.

DOUGLAS R. HOFSTADTER 1979

The Musical Offering is a fugue of fugues, a tangled hierarchy like those of Gödel and Escher, an intellectual construction which reminds me, in ways I cannot express, of the beautiful many-voiced fugue of the human mind.

LOUIS ANDRIESSEN 1989

Apart from Stravinsky, Bach is the composer I study all the time. Every day in fact. It's very strange and it's getting worse.

EDWARD SAID 2000

Like a mathematician with a rare insight into the heart of natural numbers, what their basic properties are, the way they cohere, combine and behave in groups, Bach saw into the tonal system, discerning its potential for concentration, expansion, expression and elaboration, its harmonic as well as its melodic capacities, the rhythmical and logical compatibilities of notes, as well as the articulation of inherently beautiful phrases taken from a huge number of possibilities. No one else in musical history has had that power to such a degree.

NINA SIMONE

Bach made me dedicate my life to music.

MICHAEL TORKE

Why waste money on psychotherapy when you can listen to the B minor Mass?

MARK MORRIS

Bach is God's favourite composer.

Bach: the performers' view

PABLO CASALS

For the past eighty years I have started each day in the same manner. It is not a mechanical routine but essential to my daily life. I go to the piano and I play two preludes and fugues of Bach. I cannot think of doing otherwise. It is a sort of benediction on the house. But that is not its only meaning for me. It is a rediscovery of the works of which I have the joy of being a part. It fills me with awareness of the wonder of life, with a feeling of the incredible marvel of being a human being. The music is never the same for me, never. Each day it is something new, fantastic and unbelievable. That is Bach – like nature, a miracle! [*Joys and Sorrows*]

WANDA LANDOWSKA

Everything is close to Bach, and everything in Bach's music is close to us, is part of our own life of misery, despair or bliss. Bach never climbs on a pedestal to preach or admonish ... there is something eternal in Bach's music, something that makes us wish to hear again what has just been played. This renewal gives us a glimpse of eternity.

LEOPOLD STOKOWSKI

In the character of the man who so revolutionised the music of his own time and so influenced that of centuries to come was a remarkable balance between the heart, head and hand. From his heart came the intensity of expression and from his head came his superb mastery of counterpoint, fugue and every other form of polyphonic music. His dexterity of hand amazed all those of his contemporaries who were capable of understanding his technical mastery.

YEHUDI MENUHIN

A crystalline logic underlies all of Bach's work, which is one reason why he is so often the favourite composer of mathematicians and scientists. But his music also throbs with a living pulse; his rhythms and harmonic modulations, however controlled, evolve with seeming spontaneity. His endlessly inventive melodies, however they neatly fit into a scheme, rise and fall and intertwine with a lyrical life of their own. The most solid of his constructions are nevertheless charged with energy and intensity.

DANIEL BARENBOIM

I was reared on Bach. My father was virtually my only teacher and attached great importance to my growing up with Bach's keyboard music ... in my childhood I played practically all the Preludes and Fugues from *The Well-tempered Clavier* and many other pieces by Bach. That was my basis. At the age of twelve I moved to Paris to study harmony and counterpoint with Nadia Boulanger. When I arrived for my first lesson, *The Well-tempered Clavier* was on the music stand of the grand piano . . . she settled on the Prelude in E minor from Book 1 and said, 'Right my boy now play it for me in A minor.' She held a wooden ruler in her hand and every time my fingers played a wrong note she tapped them with it.

KURT MASUR

A crucial musical experience of my childhood was directly connected with Bach. I was twelve years old when I first heard *The Art of Fugue* played on the famous Engler organ in St Nicholas' Church in my home town of Brieg in Silesia by the organist Max Drischner and my first piano teacher, Katharina Hartmann. The experience was simply overwhelming. This piano teacher transmitted to me one of the guiding principles of my later conducting career: in interpreting a work of music, one must work with humility and uncompromising respect for the music itself.

THOMAS BEECHAM

Too much counterpoint; what is worse, Protestant counterpoint.

STEPHEN HOUGH

I'm quite embarrassed about this, but I don't like Bach. I admire him enormously, of course – who couldn't? Every bar he wrote is extraordinary. I hear people talking about the 'universality' of it, and the 'deep spirituality of it' and the expression and the romanticism, but it just doesn't reach through to me. I feel like a priest who's lost his faith. I really am meant to believe this, but somehow I don't. Occasionally I put the B minor Mass on in the car thinking: 'This is the greatest Mass ever written, get on with it,' but within a couple of minutes my mind starts to wander . . . There's clearly some important screw missing in my musical mechanism.

NIGEL KENNEDY

Bach? Jazz cats love the geezer!

Bach: the biographers' view

JOHANN NIKOLAUS FORKEL 1802

He laboured for himself, like every true genius; he fulfilled his own wish, satisfied his own taste, chose his subjects according to his own opinion, and lastly, derived the most pleasure from his own approbation ... He believed the artist could form the public, but that the public could not form the artist ... This man, the greatest musical poet and the greatest musical orator that ever existed, and probably ever will exist, was a German. Let his country be proud of him, let it be proud but be worthy of him too ...

PHILIPP SPITTA 1873–80

Bach's nature was above all grave and earnest, and with all his politeness and consideration for his fellow men his demeanour was dignified and commanded respect. If we may judge the portraits which remain of him his appearance answered perfectly to this. To judge from them he must have been of a powerful, broad and stalwart build, with a full but vigorous and marked face, a wide brow, strongly arched eyebrows, and a stern or even sinister line between them. In the nose and mouth, on the contrary, we find an expression of easy humour; the eyes are keen and eager, but in his youth he was somewhat short-sighted. All his actions were based on a genuine piety which was not the outcome of any mental struggle, but inborn and natural; and he clung to the tenets of his fathers. He was fond of reading theological and edifying books, and his library included eighty-three volumes of that class at his death.

ALBERT SCHWEITZER 1911

He did not ask the world for the recognition of that part of his work which was not of his age, and in which his deepest emotions found expression. It did not even occur to him that he should or could expect this from the epoch. He did nothing to make his cantatas and Passions known, and nothing to preserve them. It is not his fault if they have survived to our day ... Bach himself was not conscious of the extraordinary greatness of his work. He was aware only of his admitted mastery of the organ and clavier and counterpoint. But he never dreamt that his works alone, not those of the men all round him, would remain visible to the coming generations ... No one was less conscious than he that his work was ahead of his epoch. In this respect he stands, perhaps, highest among all creative artists; his immense strength functioned without self-consciousness, like the forces of nature; and for that reason it is as cosmic and copious as these.

C. S. TERRY 1933
Bach's opus disproves the illusion that he was a cold mathematical precisionist. Rather it reveals him as one of the tenderest and most emotional of men – with a poet's unshakeable soul and a technical skill that was miraculous.

CHARLES HUBERT PARRY 1934
I would be hard put to strike up a friendship with Beethoven ... But with Bach, I would sit down comfortably and quaff a stein of beer.

EVA MARY AND SYDNEY GREW 1947
The revival is not yet complete, since the music still waits for the discovery of the right way to perform it. But there are English music-lovers who were caught up in the spirit by it in their first days, when they did not know how to pronounce the composer's name, and could not have said whether he was alive or dead. They have lived with it unbrokenly all their lives (but in private, not in public), finding more and more contentment in it as the years pass, until in their old age, when so many things fade, it becomes very nearly all they want in the way of music, and is certainly the kind they hope to discover in whatever next world they may be destined for.

DENIS ARNOLD 1984
Bach may have been a mystic, an ecstatic – but that view may shed more light on Schweitzer's mentality than his subject's. He may have been a convinced Lutheran who sought his salvation in writing music and persuading others to virtue.

He may be considered the last of the medieval craftsmen in music, the product of a Germany which missed the Renaissance. All this is speculation. What is not is that he was a thoroughly professional musician, doing his job day in, day out, sometimes so short of time that he had to use up formerly invented materials, sometimes in a mood for brilliant improvising, sometimes content to set himself and solve puzzles . . . One of the missing facets of human experience in Bach is any sense of nostalgia. Bach never looks back. There has never been a Golden Age. He faces new problems to the end.

ROBERT MARSHALL 1972

A composer like Beethoven enjoyed a 'luxury of time' which allowed him to experiment with and assemble a large number of ideas from which he would ultimately choose the best one. Bach and his contemporaries had to invent or 'discover' their ideas quickly. The hectic pace of production obviously did not tolerate passive reliance on the unpredictable arrival of Inspiration.

MARTIN GECK 2000

Bach's music, though rationally planned, sometimes seems an impenetrable, unsolvable myth, touching pre-linguistic levels of meaning, where experience is not worked through but simply got through. When this occurs, what counts is not the argument but shock and awe, those emotions that take hold and move precisely those listeners who are incapable of decoding complex structure. The result can be laughter as well as tears: laughter over the infinitude of creation, and tears at one's own insignificance.

CHRISTOPH WOLFF 2000

Bach's concentrated approach to his work, to reach what was possible in his art, pertained to all aspects of music, from theory to composition and from performance to physiology and the technology of instruments. In the final analysis this approach provides the key to understanding his never-ending musical empiricism, which deliberately tied theoretical knowledge to practical experience. Most notably, Bach's compositions, as the exceedingly careful musical elaborations that they are, may epitomise nothing less than the difficult task of finding for himself an argument for the existence of God – perhaps the ultimate goal of his musical science.

Bach in the media

The use of Bach in popular culture is a tribute to his staying power, and to the emotional associations of his music. The wealth of references to, and uses of, Bach's music in films of all dates and kinds reflects his extraordinary appeal.

Some of these uses are just mood music, evoking fear, pity, terror or beauty. Some associate Bach with unbearably poignant human moments (*Breaking the Waves*, Bergman's *Autumn Sonata*, *Cries and Whispers*) while others (the superb *Truly, Madly, Deeply*; the dreadful *Hilary and Jackie*) are in the context of films actually about musicians. The first in this list, the classic abstract realisation of the Toccata and Fugue in D minor in Disney's *Fantasia*, did more to establish Bach in the popular mind for the post-war generation than anything until Jacques Loussier, the Swingle Singers and the Moog synthesizer.

Surely the most purely intense and musical use of Bach in a wholly appropriate context is Pasolini's classic film of *The Gospel According to St Matthew*. This stylised and ritualised telling of the Gospel story, reduced to its barest essentials, is clothed in long silences and broken by Bach's music. Extracts from the St Matthew Passion, especially the final chorus and the violin obbligato to the aria 'Erbarme dich', are hypnotically and repeatedly used to highlight moments of drama, and Bach's music is juxtaposed with spirituals, folksong, and the exuberant *Missa Luba* to create a uniquely resonant score.

There is one famous film that puts Bach's music in the foreground rather than the background: *The Chronicle of Anna Magdalena Bach* by Jean-Marie Straub, a 1967 essay featuring Gustav Leonhardt playing Bach in Leipzig, and the crowded organ loft of the Thomaskirche serving as the scene of his Passions. The approach was literal and static, using music as Straub put it 'not as accompaniment or commentary but as aesthetic material'; the film critic John Russell Taylor thought 'music-making has never been so movingly captured ... it should be obligatory viewing', while Penelope Gilliatt in *The New Yorker* wrote, 'I came out blessing the film for letting me listen to Bach.' The music includes extracts from the Fifth Brandenburg Concerto, the Magnificat, Cantata 205, the *Trauer Ode*, the St Matthew Passion, the B minor Mass, Cantata 215, the Ascension Oratorio, and ends with *The Musical Offering*, *The Art of Fugue* and the 'deathbed chorale'.

Toccata and Fugue in D minor	*Fantasia*
	Rollerball
	Gremlins II
	Sunset Boulevard
Air from Orchestral Suite No. 3	*Beyond Utopia*
	Moll Flanders
	One Night Stand
	Seven
	The Runaway Bride
	Devil's Advocate
	The Spy Who Loved Me
Goldberg Variations: Aria	*Silence of the Lambs*
	The English Patient
	The Day the Earth Stood Still
	Hannibal
Concerto for two violins: Largo	*Children of a Lesser God*
first movement	*Hannah and Her Sisters*
Sonata for viola da gamba No. 3	*Truly, Madly, Deeply*
Keyboard concerto No. 5: Largo	*Hannah and Her Sisters*
	Slaughterhouse Five
	Portrait of a Lady
St Matthew Passion	*The Gospel According to St Matthew*
Brandenburg Concerto No. 5	*The American President*
	Tamara Drewe
Cello Suite No. 1	*Antonia's Line*
	Hilary and Jackie

Cello Suite No. 3	*Hilary and Jackie*
Cello Suite No. 4	*Autumn Sonata*
Cello Suite No. 5: Sarabande	*Cries and Whispers*
Cello Suite No. 6	*Another Woman*
	Hilary and Jackie
Violin Partita No. 3: Prelude	*The Truth about Cats*
Concerto for four harpsichords	*Dangerous Liaisons*
Flute Sonata BWV 1031: Siciliano	*Breaking the Waves*
	The White Ribbon
Italian Concerto	*The Talented Mr Ripley*
'Mache dich' from St Matthew Passion	*The Talented Mr Ripley*
Toccata, Adagio and Fugue: Adagio	*Sour Grapes*
Passacaglia in C minor	*White Nights*
Brandenburg Concerto No. 4: Presto	*Slaughterhouse Five*
English Suite No. 2: Bourrée	*Schindler's List*
Suite No. 2: Minuet and Badinerie	*Father of the Bride*
Mass in B minor: Et resurrexit	*Man Trouble*
Goldberg Variations: Variation 25	*Maurice*
	Before Sunrise
Brandenburg Concerto No. 3: first movement	*Moll Flanders*
	Die Hard
	Hannibal
	Truly, Madly, Deeply
Violin Concerto in A minor	*Portrait of a Lady*
Ave Maria (Bach–Gounod)	*Mad Dogs and Englishmen*
'Jesu, joy of man's desiring'	*Boogie Nights*
	Flubber
	Paradise Road
	Picture Perfect
Ich ruf zu dir	*Solaris*

And not forgetting . . . by far the most memorable use of Bach in the media in the UK for a certain generation of TV viewers, now outdated by our politically correct age: the advert 'Happiness is a cigar called Hamlet', with the Air from the

Suite No. 3 distinctively arranged by the Jacques Loussier Trio. (A distant second is 'Sleepers, wake!' in a Lloyds Bank ad.)

A famous use – homage or plagiarism? – of Bach in popular music is recalled in this 2009 news story: 'Procol Harum borrowed from Bach's Suite No. 3 for their international 1960s hit, "A Whiter Shade of Pale". Gary Brooker of Procol Harum told *Uncut* magazine: "If you trace the chordal element, it does a bar or two of Bach's *Air on a G String* before it veers off. That spark was all it took. I wasn't consciously combining Rock with Classical, it's just that Bach's music was in me." Nearly forty years after this song was released, Matthew Fisher, who played the organ in the recording, filed a lawsuit claiming that he deserved songwriting royalties for his contributions. After his claim was heard, dismissed and appealed against, on 30 July 2009 the Law Lords unanimously ruled in the organist's favour, pointing out that there were no time limits to copyright claims under English law.'

But what about Bach? Could he have sued?

In 1977 Carl Sagan was advised by a Dr Lewis Thomas on choosing music to include in the Voyager space shuttle, in case it could be heard by aliens. The first track was by Bach. Sagan said: 'I would vote for Bach, all of Bach, streamed out into space over and over again. We would be bragging, of course, but it is surely excusable to put on the best possible face at the beginning of such an acquaintance. Any species capable of producing the music of Johann Sebastian Bach cannot be all bad.'

Meanwhile the misuse of Bach in the media produced this outburst in 2010 from the *Guardian*'s music critic Tom Service in the last days of a tennis tournament:

> The worlds of library music and TV sports montage combined yesterday to conjure the single most nauseating, tasteless, and limb-gnawingly idiotic musical experience I can remember . . . What those of us unfortunate enough

to have tuned in actually heard was something that
crossed all known limits of postmodern genre-busting,
the last chorus from the Matthew Passion, with the addition of a lazily loungey drum-track. I don't just mean
the tune, I don't just mean the harmonic progression – I
mean the words, the orchestration, the whole thing. And
yes, yes, I know, the original Bach is still there, it's just a
different context, who cares, nobody owns the Matthew
Passion, only a tiny percentage of those watching would
have recognised this musical horror show for what it was,
it's just music to be sampled and used in new ways, etc. All
true – but not, for the love of Bach, music, and even God,
like this!

Bach from 1750 to 2010

Leipzig, March 2010

On the 325th anniversary of Bach's birth, one of those cheap flights that take off at the crack of dawn and land in a field in the middle of nowhere. A coach drives towards Leipzig, through the endless woods and fields of Thuringia, the dry, flat region of the Bach family, passing villages and farms, here isolated garages, there a burnt-out car, a few local shops. This is the former East Germany, and the echoes of its previous regime are still strong – not much affluence, some industry, predominately rural. Then a sudden burst along a new (European-funded) motorway and, touching Saxony, we are in Leipzig, not Bach's birthplace but the city where he spent the majority of his working life. The Bach Museum in Leipzig is to be reopened in a ceremony attended by the German president Horst Köhler and attended by many local dignitaries – perhaps the descendants of those Leipzig worthies who were reluctant to appoint Bach in the first place, reviled him in his lifetime, complained about his music, and then auditioned for his replacement before he was on his deathbed. But now atonement has been made in the form of a superbly appointed museum based around the Bach Archiv Leipzig, where many of Bach's manuscripts are kept.

The museum is directly opposite the Thomaskirche where Bach worked and taught; while the house at Thomaskirchhof 16 in which it is sited has no direct connection with the composer, its owners, the Bose family, were contemporaries and friends of the Bachs. The new museum has not been short of investment or expertise provided by the leading scholars of the Bach world. Although it is traditional in form, in content it is superb. Here are some of the most precious autograph scores of Bach's time in Leipzig, newly displayed and explained. Here is the organ console of an instrument examined by Bach himself in 1743 from the former Johanniskirche church, a casket with curious relics supposed to be from Bach's tomb, and an impressive heavy cash box, with the Bach monogram, which was recently discovered among the property of the Bach family. There is a room devoted to baroque instruments, and another where one can listen to Bach recordings from Mengelberg to the present day.

All this is but one aspect of the extensive work of the Bach Archiv Leipzig, which is busy putting all Bach's autograph material in a digital online database so that it can be studied from afar; it is re-editing and supplementing the hundred-and-more volumes of the *Neue Bach Ausgabe* (New Bach Edition), which was completed only in 2007, with a range of new volumes reflecting scholarly advances (starting with the B minor Mass, and then different versions of the St John Passion, Weimar cantatas, motets, organ works, the violin sonatas and the cello suites). Scholars, encouraged by recent discoveries, are carrying out an exhaustive archive search of German libraries for new material relating to the Bach family.

Thuringia, June 2010

The new Bach Museum in Leipzig is in one respect an act of blatant rivalry, an attempt to recapture the Bach heritage for the place where he spent most of his life. For in the town where he was born, the much less accessible Eisenach in mid-Thuringia, there has been a tradition for more than a century of Bach commemoration and homage, based around the Bachhaus. Though this is one of the oldest houses in the town, it was not where the composer was born. (His birthplace further up the Lutherstrasse is unmarked, torn down many years ago, though there is a touching extant house nearby where his father lived for a while.) The Bachhaus embarked a few years ago on a major contemporary extension designed by a pupil of Frank Gehry, which is a dramatic addition to the landscape and houses a new, deliberately instructive Bach exhibition. Here you can follow the progress of one Bach autograph (they don't have so many here, but they have made the most of it) from score to editions, from the Bach Gesellschaft to the *NBA*, and hear its realisation in different forms. Here you can compare, at a single console, recordings of Cantata 61 by interpreters from Karl Richter to John Eliot Gardiner, Helmut Rilling to Philippe Herreweghe, and a bold multimedia installation has the same directly educational intent. This may not be Bach's house, but it brings you much closer to Bach's music.

Only thirty kilometres from Eisenach is Mühlhausen, where Bach worked early in his life, a wonderfully well-preserved, lovingly maintained town of half-timbered houses surrounded by a medieval wall that is still intact. There is a tangible sense of municipal pride – you can see why this Council would have gone to the trouble of printing and publishing their celebratory cantata by the new organist (this and its lost successor were the only cantatas of Bach's to be published in his lifetime). In the St Blasius Church where he was organist, the whole Bach family tradition springs to life: the intensity with which he and his relatives must have lived their lives and felt their calling to be musicians, within this tiny, concentrated geographical framework.

There is quite a contest for possession of Bach going on, now that the former East is open and attracting tourists. Nearby Weimar, with its unrivalled artistic and cultural heritage ranging from Goethe and Schiller to Liszt and Bach, boasts the renovated Schloss where Bach performed (though where he worked burned down long ago); a plaque stands marking his house and the birthplace of Wilhelm Friedemann and Carl Philipp Emanuel, and there is now a plan to build a Bach exhibition in a cellar under a car park of a nearby hotel, claiming this as a definitely authentic site of his work.

Has any great composer been subject to such radical reappraisal over the last half-century as Johann Sebastian Bach? Scholars who have subjected the source material to new scrutiny have come to conclusions that completely alter the accepted view of Bach's life and pattern of work. And performers, experimenting with the instruments and playing techniques of the past, have produced startlingly new realisations of his music, which challenge old assumptions about how it ought to sound. These two processes, though not necessarily related, have gone hand in hand, defamiliarising Bach in our minds and moulding him to the temper of our times.

No scholarly change has been more startling than that, proved by laborious work on the manuscripts and handwriting of the cantatas in the 1950s, which redated the bulk of Bach's Leipzig cantatas to his first few years in that post. Traditional scholarship, led by the pioneering biographer Spitta, pictured Bach as preoccupied with church music almost to the end of his life, developing the genre through the twenty years he was active in Leipzig to produce the great chorale cantatas in the 1740s: an appropriate and logical culmination of his work. In fact these works were written in the mid-1720s, in an enormous first flood of enthusiasm for his work at Leipzig. He accumulated a body of cantatas that could be drawn upon for weekly use, performed the work of others, and shifted his preoccupations into other areas, notably the Collegium Musicum during the 1730s. It was the forensic work of the scholars Alfred Dürr, who as early as 1951 established a new chronology for the Weimar cantatas, and Georg von Dadelsen, culminating in work they both published in 1957–8, that really shook the foundations of Bach scholarship to their roots. Bach's creative effort in cantata writing was shown to be concentrated in the first three years of his time in Leipzig (possibly extending to the first five years, depending on whether one believed that there were further cantatas now lost from that second two-year period). This research was very quickly and widely accepted, and began to change the view of Bach's entire output. (Ironically, Spitta was advanced in his use of watermark evidence, and usually correct in his analysis. Hence his datings were generally accepted. But only those watermarks which were related to dated works could be relied on: all his other datings were hypothetical.)

When it came, the reaction to the new chronology was extreme and radical: a leading Protestant scholar, Friedrich Blume, seemed to conclude that Bach had virtually given up his faith, had become disillusioned with his service of God, and turned to more worldly matters. It was an understandably exaggerated reaction, and one can see the pendulum swinging, more wildly than it needed to, against the notion of Bach as lifelong Lutheran and proselytiser for the faith. Blume spoke at the International Bach Society in Mainz in June 1962 and his paper was published a year later in *Music and Letters*. Blume attributed the Lutheranisation of Bach, his elevation to the status of the 'Fifth Evangelist', to nineteenth-century sentimentality, to the biographers Bitter and Spitta, and claimed it was completely absent in Forkel's earlier view of the composer. Not content with reflecting on the changed chronology of the cantatas, Blume also laid into the idea that Bach was particularly linked to the organ, arguing that he had no 'ancestral connection' to the instrument or to church music. 'Did Bach have a special liking for church work? Was it a spiritual necessity for him? Hardly. There is at any rate no evidence that it was. Bach the supreme cantor, the creative servant of the Word of God, the staunch Lutheran, is a legend. It will have to be buried along with all the other traditional and beloved romantic illusions.'

This was going too far, especially since another discovery of the time was Bach's copy of the Calov Bible, obviously read with great care and annotated with religious awareness. The reaction against Blume was swift. Another Lutheran scholar, Friedrich Smend, tried to correct what Blume called an avalanche by referring to it as no more than 'a little breeze'. That was certainly an underestimate of its effect. Rereading Blume's portrait of Bach now, it seems more balanced than his critics gave him credit for: he was trying to contrast the elements in Bach's life, not denying any of them, reasonably pointing out that our picture of Bach must not be distorted by the works that happen to have survived: 'What has come to down to us is merely a part of Bach's total output, and circumstances have brought it about that far more of the ecclesiastical part has survived than of the secular.'

Then the assumption that Bach's instrumental and chamber music dated largely from his time at the court of Cöthen was suddenly undermined by Christoph Wolff's suggestion that great pieces, including the Concerto for two violins, might date instead from his mature Leipzig years. George Stauffer has begun to explore the repertory of the Leipzig Collegium Musicum in Bach's time, opening up the fascinating hypothesis that Bach might have performed up-to-date repertory such as Handel opera arias. The accepted chronology of Bach's last years was effectively rewritten by the demonstration by the Japanese scholar Yoshitake Kobayashi, from a close study of the autograph scores and handwriting, that *The Art of Fugue*, far from being his last work left incomplete on his death, was essentially finished some years earlier; it was the Mass in B minor that occupied Bach's final creative phrase.

Bach scholarship, which had concentrated first on the music and then on matters of chronology, was opened up to a whole new range of documentary evidence after the Berlin Wall came down, and East German archives that had previously been inaccessible were opened up to scholars. These explorations may yet yield further discoveries. Bringing the many divergent views into a harmonious whole, or at least a harmonious counterpoint, has been a major undertaking of recent Bach biography. The straightforward approach of Malcolm Boyd was refreshingly unpartisan, while Peter Williams has gone back to the source of the Obituary of Bach, analysing its implications in detail. It has been left to the leading Bach scholar of our generation, Christoph Wolff, to achieve a complete synthesis with his biography published in Bach's 250th anniversary year, 2000, and its implications are still only just being explored. Wolff's characterisation of Bach's world-view is highly significant, and he has yet to write a companion volume on the music itself.

The process by which performances of Bach's music have been transformed in recent times is dealt with below, pp. 119–27. But one scholarly debate of recent years, argued on a very public battlefield through recordings and performances, has been among the most fraught areas of recent research. Joshua Rifkin's dramatic assertion, unveiled to the world in an American Musicological Society conference paper and performance of the B minor Mass in Boston in 1981, and a subsequent recording, was that Bach's normal practice was to use only one singer on each vocal part in his sacred music. However one views the extremely complex evidence (which can be assessed and interpreted in many ways), the shock that Rifkin administered to the system was a wholly positive one, and even if its only effect were to have offered a corrective to the idea that large-scale choral performances are the best way to hear Bach's vocal music, it would have been beneficial.

The most thoroughgoing expositions of these theories, paradoxically, have come not from Rifkin himself – he has never published the book-length justification that was promised – but from the English conductor and scholar Andrew Parrott. In *The Essential Bach Choir*, Parrott spells out with daunting detail the basis for the revolutionary view, drawing on a wealth of knowledge of performance practice before Bach, as well as a forensic examination of what Bach actually meant by his famous document of 1730 arguing for a well-appointed church music. The opposing, traditional view of Bach's resources is still expressed by most conductors of the 'choral' tradition, even in its new guise with small-scale forces and period instruments, as well as by Bach scholars such as Boyd and Wolff (who does not mention Rifkin once in his Bach biography of 2000, even though Rifkin's crucial redating of the St Matthew Passion has been accepted). This is, to over-simplify, that Bach was able to draw on various singers and players as 'externi' from the town's other resources, but that he did not mention these in his document because it might have undermined his case for more good singers as part of his basic establishment.

Rifkin's important theory, looked at over the perspective of a quarter of a century, now seems to fit with uncanny exactness into both the developing view of Bach performance practice and the altered view of Bach's creative personality: for what better way to disengage Bach singing from the traditions of yesteryear than to whisk him out of the choral tradition altogether, and what better way to move away from a vision of Bach as the great Lutheran preacher than to imbue his deepest and most profound music with transparent lightness and dance-like grace? Also, of course, the textures that Rifkin, Parrott, Paul McCreesh and most recently John Butt advocate take to an extreme the taste of the times for small-scale performances: is this just a matter of our contemporary performance styles matching the style of our era; is it a reflection of the practicality (and economy) of soloist-led performance, or is it a richer and subtler interaction between past evidence and present taste?

Perhaps, as in many of these cases of historical judgement, extreme positions are giving way to a more flexible approach that may be regarded by the purists as compromise, but which is actually the most creative response to the evidence in the changed conditions of today's performances. (However, the scholarly debate seems to have become even more entrenched in the 2010 issues of *Early Music*.) In the case of Bach's vocal music, the controversy has alerted us to the vitally important fact that these performances did not *oppose* choral singers and soloists, but grew out of a tradition of consort-scale, ensemble-led performance driven by skilled soloists. This is another revolution in our understanding of Bach's music.

The perception that Bach was rediscovered only in the nineteenth century was encouraged by the statement as recently as *The New Grove* that 'Bach was known only to a small circle of pupils and devotees until the Romantic movement stimulated a growing interest in his art'. But this will really not stand up to scrutiny. Long ago it was established by Gerhard Herz, Ludwig Finscher, Hans-Joachim Schulze and others that Bach's sons and pupils kept his music alive after his death, and more and more fascinating details are emerging of the

Bach legacy that was cultivated in the later eighteenth century. True, it was a partial legacy, which did not impact on the wider public consciousness until later, but it prepared the ground for that popular revival – in much the same way as those who revived old instruments in the early twentieth century from Arnold Dolmetsch onwards prepared the way for the popular period-instrument revival of the last fifty years.

The main impetus for the performance of Bach's music after his death was the activity of his pupils, and in particular his sons Wilhelm Friedemann in Halle and Carl Philipp Emanuel in Hamburg (and perhaps also J. C. F. Bach as a keyboard player), who presented his works in concert. Friedemann Bach's biographer Falck mentions performances of some cantatas. In line with the temper of the times they adapted the music for their forces: Carl Philipp Emanuel in Hamburg took portions of his father's Passions for his own settings, and later adapted two cantatas. Friedemann added trumpets and timpani to Cantata 80, and Emanuel Bach revised the score of the Credo of the B minor Mass by altering his father's own manuscript in a way that has made it very difficult to disentangle what he wrote and what his father wrote (even the most recent scientific spectroscope analysis undertaken by Uwe Wolf for the latest facsimile edition of the Mass has been disputed by Rifkin in 2010). The Credo was performed in Hamburg in 1786 and Emanuel wrote an introduction to be played before the piece. Bach's sons kept alive keyboard works, and the motets continued in the repertory of the Thomanerchor in Leipzig – this is evidenced by the famous Rochlitz anecdote of Mozart hearing a Bach motet when he visited Leipzig in 1786.

Mozart was interested in Bach through the agency of Baron van Swieten, who had a well-known appetite for the music of the past. Either Mozart or members of his circle arranged Bach fugues for string trio in the 1780s and added some preludes of their own, and the influence of Bach can be heard in many places in Mozart's later music, in the chorale of the armed men in *The Magic Flute* and in some keyboard pieces.

It has been suggested that the Viennese interest in Bach was stimulated by a revival in Berlin, where some of Bach's sons and pupils had lived, and a recent investigation of the Berlin harpsichordist Sara Levy and her musical soirées has revealed the extent to which the music of the Bach family was heard there towards the end of the century.

There was a continual fascination with Bach's music through the second half of the eighteenth century, but its preservation and transmission depended on who took most care of the manuscripts they acquired on Bach's death. It is known that Wilhelm Friedemann, for instance, acquired a great deal but sold much of it; C. P. E. Bach acquired the larger vocal pieces including the B minor Mass, but Forkel claimed that Wilhelm Friedemann had the largest share, in which case what may have been lost? Even before the end of the eighteenth century, copies of Bach's music were listed for sale in the publisher's catalogue of Johann Traeg in Vienna: Peter Wollny of the Bach Archiv Leipzig suggests these copies may have originated with Baron van Swieten himself. Beethoven's patron Count Lichnowsky also owned copies of Bach's music, perhaps through contact with Forkel. Beethoven studied the '48' with his teacher Neefe – who said in a letter from Leipzig in 1776 that Passion music by Bach was to be performed there. Max Schneider found many Bach works in the Breitkopf catalogues of the 1760s and 1770s, especially the '48', but also the Chromatic Fantasy and sacred and secular cantatas. Haydn owned a rare copy of the B minor Mass. Johann Philipp Kirnberger, a Bach pupil and theoretician, was the curator of the music library of Frederick the Great's sister, Princess Anna Amalia, and this was another vital source keeping Bach's music alive, through many copies as well as his publication of a major collection of chorale harmonisations. Forkel learned much from this collection for his first Bach biography, and after his death the library went to Berlin, where Zelter used it for his early Bach choral revivals.

Carl Friedrich Zelter, a minor composer but a major figure in the Bach revival, was the key link between those connoisseurs and enthusiasts and the next wave of Bach popularisation. He too made arrangements, such as the E major Fugue from Book 2 of the '48' for string quartet, and performed the Harpsichord Concerto in D minor in 1807 and Brandenburg No. 5 in 1808. Armed with Kirnberger's copies from Anna Amalia's library, and also with Bach manuscripts he had himself collected from C. P. E. Bach's legacy, he set out to rehearse the most ambitious works of Bach's output, including (incredibly for the time) the two Passions, the B minor Mass and many cantatas. He tried the Kyrie of the B minor Mass in 1811, the A major Missa and a cantata in 1812, and the whole B minor Mass in 1813: these were essentially private sing-throughs, but enormously influential none the less; in 1815 he tackled parts of the St John and St Matthew Passions. (We can take with a grain of salt the claim by Adolf Bernhard Marx that Zelter 'obtained the score of that immortal work [the Matthew Passion] from a cheese shop, where it was being used as wrapping paper' – but it shows the desire to claim the evolution of Bach's reputation as a radical rediscovery; Marx led a concerted press campaign on behalf of Mendelssohn's activity.)

All this led directly to Mendelssohn's famous performance of the St Matthew Passion in 1829. That was, of course, a signal moment in the reception of Bach's music, but it is better to see it not as a revolution from the blue but as the culmination of a long process of cultivation and revival for which the ground had been well prepared over previous years: Zelter had encouraged Mendelssohn and the singer Edward Devrient, both his pupils. The performance was certainly a great event, and even impressed Goethe from afar: 'The news of the successful performance of the great old masterpiece . . . makes me think. It seems to be as if I heard the ocean roaring from afar. I offer congratulations upon such a complete attainment of the virtually inconceivable.' There were three performances in Berlin in 1829, and more followed; but it reached Leipzig under Mendelssohn only in 1841.

Our authenticist approach to history is now so odd that not only do we perform Bach's St Matthew Passion, we also revive

Mendelssohn's version of Bach's St Matthew Passion and present it as a separate art-work in its own right, performing it
and publishing it. It is of course fascinating to know the alterations, cuts and reorchestrations that Mendelssohn for reasons
of contemporary taste and practicality felt it necessary to
make, but are we able to enter into its spirit? Is that a scholarly
exercise or can it make a musical experience? Mendelssohn's
revival evidently sparked off a series of performances of the
choral music on a wide scale around Germany, and the Bach
revival in the public sphere had begun. Extensive publication
programmes followed: Bach's 'Oeuvres complètes' had been
planned by the Leipzig firm Hoffmeister and Kühnel, but it
was only with the launch of the complete Bach Gesellschaft in
1850, the centenary of Bach's death, that the entire output of
Bach's work was made available, and Brahms was able to say
that he felt the mission of the Bach-Gesamtausgabe was one
of the most important experiences of his musical life. Spitta's
great Bach biography was published in two volumes in 1873
and 1880 and was translated into English as early as 1883–5 by
Clara Bell and J. A. Fuller-Maitland. By then the Bach revival
was already well established, and his position in the repertory
assured.

The intense impact that Bach's music made on creative
figures led to reinterpretation and reworking of his music in
the nineteenth century – partly to make it performable, as
Mendelssohn did, partly to make it available, but also attempting to interpret it for a new generation. Brahms, with his total
dedication to the music of the past, understood better than
most the origins of the Bach style as it developed from Schütz
and Gabrieli, for he edited their work and performed it in his
own concerts, as he did Mozart's Requiem and Beethoven's
Missa solemnis. As the Bach Gesellschaft edition appeared,
he performed cantatas and the Christmas Oratorio, and his
music increasingly shows the influence of Bach – in his organ
preludes, some of the late chamber music, and most prominently in the great passacaglia finale of the Fourth Symphony,

where a ground bass of Bach's from the early Cantata 150 is extrapolated on the largest scale.

But contrast Brahms's extremely pure arrangement, for piano left hand, of the famous Chaconne from the Violin Partita in D minor – an utterly un-self-advertising and understanding transcription – with the virtuoso showpiece that Ferruccio Busoni made of the same movement half a century later. What had happened? Both Mendelssohn and Schumann had arranged the same Chaconne, Mendelssohn more freely. Mendelssohn also gave unaccompanied violin pieces a piano accompaniment for Ferdinand David's recitals. Schumann brought the solo violin and cello works to the attention of a wider public by providing them with accompaniments because without them they might not have been heard, but at the same time he subtly draws them into a new musical world of explicit richness and romanticism, whereas in Bach the harmonic elaboration is only implied. (Schumann's piano-accompanied version of the famous Prelude from the E major violin Partita is arguably less imaginative than Bach's own rescoring for ensemble in Cantata 29.) Ignaz Moscheles added cello obbligato parts to the '48'. Growing out of this tradition was Gounod's legendary addition of a melody to the first Prelude from the '48' to make his famous *Ave Maria*. (I must add here the glorious explanation of that piece from a nineteenth-century periodical unearthed by Charles Cudworth: 'This immortal melody was composed by Bach on his deathbed, and with his dying breath he entrusted the accompaniment to Gounod.')

Then Franz Liszt, with his virtuosic pianistic style, used Bach not so much as a subject for faithful transcription but as a jumping-off point for musical elaboration. While his early versions of organ preludes and fugues are quite literal, by the time one reaches his fantasias on *Weinen, Klagen*, rewriting the cantata movement of that name and the 'Crucifixus' of the B minor Mass, we are into very different territory: independent composition stimulated by a far-distant original. As a concert pianist, Liszt performed major works such as the Goldberg

Variations and the Chromatic Fantasy, but he increasingly moves to making the music his own – with the *Preludium und Fugue über den Namen BACH* for organ at the most extreme end of the spectrum of co-ownership. It is interesting, though, to note that these two interpretative approaches – transcription and recomposition – are not totally separate, but rather part of a gradual continuum, encapsulating the somewhat modern idea that any approach to, or reading of, a text is essentially an individual interpretation.

Directly influenced by Liszt's Bach were Busoni's Bach and Reger's Bach – both concepts from which we find ourselves today at pretty much the opposite pole, though who is to say that they will not return to the centre of our taste? Busoni's engagement with Bach, as Martin Zenck has put it, 'lasted his entire life as a presence that often threatened to be all-consuming'. He thought of staging the St Matthew Passion; he planned extensive editions of Bach's keyboard works, and made a 'practical' edition of the Goldberg Variations which eliminated some of the canonic movements and reduced the variations from thirty to twenty. In the case of the Chaconne, Busoni was using it as a source for his own imaginative flights of fancy – and this is surely far more successful. It is a Bach transformation that remains absolutely identifiable: Busoni is precisely mirroring Bach's stretching of the potential of the eighteenth-century violin to the maximum of its powers, with the stretching of the twentieth-century concert grand to the very edges of its technical capability. Busoni went further in his later works related to Bach, such as the massive *Fantasia contrappuntistica* which mixes chorales, variations, and fugues using material from *The Art of Fugue* in a phantasmagorical sequence. Yet his transcriptions remain distinctive: in the organ chorale *Ich ruf zu dir*, as soon as you make the first chord in the left hand an eloquent minor tenth (rather than separating it as in the organ original into pedal and left hand) you have changed the piece and it becomes a pianistic original. Reger's Bach is more glutinous, in the style of Mahler's rescorings of movements from the Orchestral Suites, and his transcriptions of the Brandenburgs and the Suites as piano duets are pretty impenetrable. He made organ trios out of the three-part Inventions. Much more fun (though even more difficult) are the chromatic touches that Rachmaninov added to his own version of movements from the Violin Partita in E major: naughty but nice.

It is typical of our time that, as in the twentieth century Bach interpretation strove to become more faithful to the perceived originals, transcriptions too reverted to a form that was more recognisably Bachian. Which is not to say that they were literal: Schoenberg's overwhelming 1928 orchestration of the 'St Anne' Prelude and Fugue (which may have been inspired by Busoni's version 'for the pianoforte for concert use') uses the full resources of the modern symphony orchestra to create an effect that reveals how he heard the music, with full organ colours. Schoenberg's versions of organ chorale preludes are more restrained but equally rich. They make a strong impression today, as does Elgar's reworking of the Fantasia and Fugue in C minor with its hilarious xylophone writing at the climax. Fantasy reigned in Percy Grainger's piano transcriptions, notably *Blithe Bells*, his wandering, chromatically lush mediation around 'Sheep may safely graze'. Respighi added weighty orchestration to the organ Passacaglia in C minor. The greatest Bach orchestration of the twentieth century is surely Anton Webern's version of the six-part Ricercar from *The Musical Offering*: laid out like a patient on a table, every strand of Bach's marvellous contrapuntal concept is coolly exposed and dislocated between instruments in a way that forces us to listen, and then reassembles the music to wonderful effect.

Bach was especially important to the whole neo-classical revival, and it is no surprise that Stravinsky and Paul Hindemith were particularly influenced by him. At the very end of his life Stravinsky was arranging music from the '48', and those transcriptions have only recently been performed for the first time; better known are his versions of the Canonic Variations on 'Vom Himmel hoch', a more or less literal analysis of Bach's original (though with the chorale melody sung). Bartók's Sonata for solo violin was inspired by Bach; Schoenberg's *Variations for Orchestra* Op. 31 quotes the B–A–C–H theme, and most famously Berg's Violin Concerto uses the chorale setting 'Es ist genug' from Cantata 60, a setting which the contemporary composer Magnus Lindberg has also arranged. The maverick composer Maurizio Kagel celebrated the Bach anniversary of 1985 by creating the *Sankt-Bach Passion*, a powerfully surreal piece which used the genre it aimed to deconstruct, creating a Passion story based on Bach's own life and documents. The influence of the strong Bach choral tradition in England is powerfully felt in Michael Tippett's *A Child of Our Time*, with its use of spirituals as quasi-chorales, recitatives and a Passion-like structure with direct references to Bach's St John Passion. On the other side of the globe, the Brazilian Heitor Villa-Lobos wrote transcriptions of Bach preludes and fugues for an orchestra of cellos, and then his nine *Bachianas Brasileiras* of 1930–45 after Bach's Brandenburg Concertos: 'inspired by the musical ambience of Bach, a universal folkloric source, rich and profound, an intermediary for all peoples'; among them No. 5 is well known with its combination of eight cellos and soprano voice.

Many composers have continued to arrange Bach's music and to derive inspiration from it, as in Lukas Foss's *Baroque Variations* and Robin Holloway's two-piano *Gilded Goldbergs* – which began, as the composer says, as a version 'to be able to play and relish their ingenuities with ease and clarity, but slowly and shyly entered further and further reaches of fantasy . . . "shyly" is an understatement. I felt guilty and ashamed. But desire knows no curb.' John Tavener conceived his huge and visionary religious work about St John of the Cross, *Ultimos Ritos* (premiered in 1974), as a piece that was completely derived from, and finally dissolved into a recording of, the 'Crucifixus' from Bach's B minor Mass. The most beautiful and touching Bach transcriptions today are the utterly simple piano-duet versions by the Hungarian composer György Kurtág, which he plays with his wife on their recording *Játékok* (Games). Trio sonata movements for organ are transcribed with one line transposed up an octave; most memorable is the introductory Sinfonia to the funeral Cantata 106, *Gottes Zeit*: the Kurtágs played this on an upright piano at the 2006 funeral of their compatriot, György Ligeti.

In the 1960s the appropriation of Bach by popular culture seems to symbolise a moment of openness, of a coming-together between pop and classical music, that held out much hope for the future. Was Bach essentially trivialised by the Moog synthesizer and the Swingle Singers? The Moog with its gloriously crude technicolours certainly enabled Bach to be played with a virtuosity beyond purely human endeavour, but to listen to it today is to be reminded of its strong links with sewing-machine neo-classical inflexibility: the Prelude of the E major violin Partita (or rather its transcription in Cantata 29) sounds relentlessly driven. The Swingles, on the other hand, are far freer and more fanciful in their rather sweet and sentimental approach to the repertory, especially in the F minor Prelude from Book 2 of the '48' or the Badinerie from the Orchestral Suite No. 2. Jacques Loussier made a huge impression with his jazzed-up Bach as early as 1959, offering relaxed, sophisticated and often intricate responses to the music, and has continued to work in this vein for many years. Bach's harmonic framework seems to suit the process of improvisation, a benefit recently discovered by the newest of the Bach improvisers, Gabriela Montero, who plays Bach on the piano and then improvises her own music around it.

There could be no greater demonstration of Bach's integral, accepted place in our culture than the number of parodies and references his music has produced. It started long ago: when Sullivan wanted a reference to 'masses, fugues and ops by Bach interwoven with Spohr and Beethoven' in *The Mikado*, he just slipped the perky subject of the G minor Fugue for organ into the accompaniment (and assumed everyone would recognise it!). Peter Schickele's newly invented Bach son P. D. Q. Bach became an industry in itself in America, a portmanteau device for parodying all classical music genres, spawning phenomena like the Baroque Beatles (their hits rearranged in an all-purpose sub-Bach idiom), or Peter Ustinov's glorious impersonation of a cellist playing a Bach suite (without a cello). From 'Bach Goes Bossa' to Bud Powell's *Bud on Bach* (actually an improvisation around C. P. E. Bach's *Solfeggietto*) to classically trained Nina Simone's 'Love Me or Leave Me', Bach has infused popular culture. The jazz composer Alec Templeton produced a little classic in *Bach Goes to Town*, described as 'an effectively suburban idea about what a gently swung Bach prelude and fugue might be like'; it was recorded by Larry Adler among many others and stimulated Steeleye Span's *Bach Goes to Limerick*. When the pioneering harpsichordist George Malcolm was going to record the Templeton on the harpsichord for a 78rpm disc, he sat up the night before and composed a companion piece for the B side, *Bach Before the Mast*, a witty baroque-isation of the sailors' hornpipe. (When he got to the studio the next morning he found he couldn't play it very well. 'Because you were very tired?' asked an interviewer. Malcolm replied testily: 'No, it's actually a really rather difficult piece.')

Salzburg, Easter 2010

The Salzburg Easter Festival 2010: in the Karajan-inspired grandeur of the Grosses Festspielhaus and its elegant and overblown halls, a lavish parade of dresses, formal evening wear, Austrian national costume and plastic surgery. This is an event whose existence has been threatened by administrative corruption, money-laundering and political in-fighting, and the short (but horrendously expensive) festival is in the course of a rescue by the English manager Peter Alward. The artistic direction has traditionally been in the hands of the conductor of the Berlin Philharmonic: first Herbert von Karajan, now Sir Simon Rattle.

It is a curious and unlikely setting for a spiritual revelation. But in the middle of all this, a performance of riveting intensity and power of Bach's St Matthew Passion, newly re-imagined for the twenty-first century: Simon Rattle and the Berlin Philharmonic are joined by the director Peter Sellars to take apart the jigsaw pieces of this work and put them back together. It is not the first time Bach's Passion has been staged – Jonathan Miller's effective concert staging in London, mingling singers and players, was successfully televised some years ago – but it is surely the most radical rethinking of it. Sellars has separated the two choirs and orchestras out around the stage in the most disrupting way, to create a large open central space, with one choir at the left front facing sideways, and an orchestra behind it facing forwards, one choir at the right back facing forward, with an orchestra in front of it facing opposite – and the pairs of orchestras and choirs are not the ones you might expect, but match each other across the open space. Even Rattle as the conductor has to commute across stage for those numbers with separate orchestras. In the central space, a few wooden blocks, which can be a seat, a table, an altar, and finally a grave. In this space Mark Padmore's Evangelist begins to speak, his back to us, and his eloquent narration gradually draws in other commentators – as the soloists appear for their meditative arias, the instrumental obbligato players come to the centre of the stage and form beautifully constructed groupings where solo singer and solo players can look into each other's eyes. It is an extraordinarily powerful experience, as if a great stone monument, familiar across the ages, has been deconstructed and torn apart, to reveal a beating human heart within.

What this St Matthew Passion really proves is that Bach will never die. He will just go on being recreated. From his own lifetime across the centuries his music has been ignored, vilified, misrepresented, used for political ends and commercially exploited, but it has always survived. Which does not mean that just any performance will do: there is no music so demanding to realise in sound, and so quick to reveal a lack of understanding or a lack of integrity in approaching it.

*

Why was Bach so good at what he did? In his book *Outliers*, Malcolm Gladwell has some penetrating observations on the nature of creativity and genius. One of his key observations is that those who accomplish great things need to be born in the right time and right place, and need to be able to practise their craft – that applies as much to computer programmers as it does to sportsmen and musicians. As a teenager Bill Gates had access to a mainframe computer for thousands of hours. Anyone who has studied music knows how much practice it takes to make even the most innately talented musician great; we do not know how many possibly great musicians did not develop because they did not practise their craft or recognise their talent.

There is a central fact here about Bach: he spent hundreds of thousands of hours on the task of conceiving music. From his earliest days he was surrounded by music at home, was taught music, played music, and probably wrote music as soon as he was able – most likely every day of his life he either wrote down, or thought out, or made up music. And from every one of those hours he learnt. The comparison with others is not that he wrote more (Telemann, Graupner and other contemporaries produced far more music) but that he learnt so productively from what he did. As his Obituary stresses, thanks to his own efforts (and the writers were interestingly eager to stress the element of his being self-instructed), he got better at what he did. Bach shows every sign, in the continual improvements he made to his scores, his frequent reuse of material which he strove to perfect, of having acquired a quite exceptional level of self-criticism and self-awareness as to what needed to be changed and improved. This chimes precisely with what Forkel wrote in his biography: 'I have often felt both surprise and delight at the means he employed to make, little by little, the faulty good, the good better, and the better perfect.' Bach was never content. Even after his music was published he was tinkering with it, correcting it and adding to it. Whether or not one accepts that the final fugue of *The Art of Fugue* was unfinished at his death, there is a mythic truth in the idea that he was always searching for something better and greater. As Wolff writes, 'When Bach set his indefatigably self-critical hand in motion, there seemed to be no such thing as an "untouchable" text, whether manuscript or print.'

Bach is thus the apotheosis not only of our idea of the composer as craftsman, as worker, as inexhaustibly active; but also of our idea of the composer as idealist, as spiritual striver for something that lies beyond. Rarely do these two characteristics come together in such perfect balance as they do with Bach: they cannot be separated because the work, whether in the realm of sacred music or secular music, is the spiritual quest. He challenges us to do better.

BACH: THE LIFE

We know all too little of Bach compared with the lives of some other great composers; there are many uncertainties of chronology and activity in his career, especially around the dating of his works, and while there is plenty of information about him, he left few personal letters or documents. Only a very few incidents bring him to life as a person, such as his youthful fight with a bassoonist he despised (as Ernest Newman wrote in a nice aside, 'the thought of the future composer of the St Matthew Passion and *The Art of Fugue* trying to put an end to a bassoonist with a knife is one that appeals to all that is best in human nature').

One of Bach's most famous statements was his 'Short but Most Necessary Draft' of his needs for performers at Leipzig, over which scholars have argued endlessly. Here by analogy is my own version . . .

A 'Short but Most Necessary Draft' for a biography of the composer

Johann Sebastian Bach, the youngest son of Johann Ambrosius Bach, town musician of Eisenach and descendant of a Thuringian family of musicians, was born on 21 March 1685. At the age of eight he began to attend the Lateinschule in Eisenach. His mother died in 1694 and his father in 1695; with his brother Jakob he went to Ohrdruf, where their eldest brother Johann Christoph was organist, and there attended the Gymnasium for five years as well as having instruction from Johann Christoph. In 1700, perhaps because of lack of funds, Bach sought employment. Both he and Georg Erdmann found places as treble singers in the Mettenchor in Lüneburg. Here he came into contact with the organist Georg Böhm, and travelled to hear Reincken in Hamburg. His earliest surviving music manuscript, written out (in tablature) in Böhm's house in 1700, is a copy of two organ fantasias by Buxtehude and Reincken. In 1703 he spent a few months as a 'lackey' in Weimar, as court violinist to Duke Johann Ernst of Saxe-Weimar, but was offered the post of organist in Arnstadt after examining the organ there in July 1703.

Bach came into conflict with his superiors in Arnstadt: there are records that he was rebuked for the strangeness of his chorale harmonisations and preludes; that he neglected concerted music because he felt that the students were inadequate; and that he was involved in a street brawl with a bassoonist. In 1705–6 he spent some four months in Lübeck, listening to Buxtehude play the organ and attending the Abendmusik series of concerts, and on his return he was rebuked by the council for the length of his absence. In December 1706 Ahle, the organist at St Blasius, Mühlhausen, died. Bach was offered the post and left Arnstadt the following year. He was installed as organist on 15 June, and on

17 October married his relative Maria Barbara in the small nearby town of Dornheim. Some of Bach's earliest keyboard works were transcribed by his eldest brother Johann Christoph in two valuable manuscripts, the Möller Manuscript of 1703–*c*.1707 and the Andreas Bach Book of 1708–*c*.1713, which show his early works (some of which have previously been doubted) as well as the range of keyboard music to which he was exposed in his early years.

Bach's stay in Mühlhausen brought him into contact and conflict with the Pietist and orthodox strains in Lutheranism. He found his employer at St Blasius, J. A. Frohne, unsympathetic to the concerted music he wished to perform; this met a readier reception at the Marienkirche, for which Bach wrote the very early Cantata 131 *Aus der Tiefen* at the request of the orthodox Pastor G. C. Eilmar. He wrote the Cantata 71 *Gott ist mein König* for the inauguration of the Town Council in 1707 and this appeared as his first published work (and, apart from its successor, which is lost, the only cantata to be published in his lifetime). In 1708 he requested his dismissal on the grounds that it had been impossible for him to realise his aim of a well-regulated church music, and because he had been offered a post at the Weimar court.

As Court Organist to Duke Wilhelm Ernst of Saxe-Weimar (brother of Bach's previous temporary employer, Johann Ernst), Bach had to play not only the organ but also the harpsichord in the court ensemble. From this period dates Bach's exploration and transcription of concertos by Vivaldi and other Italian composers for both solo harpsichord and organ, stimulated by manuscripts which Prince Johann Ernst brought back from Amsterdam. By 1713 Bach's activities outside the Weimar court were increasing: he visited the court of Weissenfels, where Cantata 208 *Was mir behagt* was performed for the Duke. Later the same year his request to succeed Zachow as organist in Halle was granted. But Bach apparently refused the post and at about the same time was made Konzertmeister at Weimar, in addition to his other duties. Now he had to write instrumental music and cantatas for monthly performance. Though famous as an organist and increasingly as a composer, he was passed over in 1717 when the post of Kapellmeister at Weimar fell vacant. However, he secured the post of Kapellmeister in Cöthen, having probably met Prince Leopold of Anhalt-Cöthen the previous year at a wedding for which Bach provided the music. In November 1717 he attempted to leave Weimar, but was imprisoned for 'stubbornly forcing the issue of his dismissal'; he was dishonourably discharged a month later.

In Cöthen Bach had a sympathetic and musical employer in Prince Leopold, and a small, highly skilled group of players for whom he wrote instrumental and chamber music, though it is not certain whether the superb set of Six Concertos that Bach sent to the Margrave of Brandenburg in 1721 were written originally for Cöthen forces: they are works of the utmost instrumental diversity and variety. At this time he was beginning to compile keyboard collections: early versions of the Preludes from the '48', the two- and three-part Inventions, as well as other keyboard works were entered into the *Clavierbüchlein* for his son Wilhelm Friedemann (then nine) from 22 January 1720.

Later in 1720 Bach's wife Maria Barbara died, and the following year he married Anna Magdalena, the daughter of a trumpeter in the orchestra of the Duke of Saxe-Weissenfels, and herself a singer at the Cöthen court. In 1722 the Weimar Duke married again and Bach later wrote that the Prince's musical inclinations cooled from this point. Bach had applied in 1720 for the post of organist at Hamburg, where there was a particularly fine organ; then in 1723 he applied for the post of Cantor at the Thomaskirche in Leipzig in succession to Kuhnau. Telemann was offered the post but declined it, and Graupner had his salary increased at the court of Darmstadt. So the Leipzig town council reluctantly appointed Bach.

Bach's position in Leipzig was described as 'Thomascantor and Director musices'. He was responsible for the musical education of the boys in the Thomasschule, under the supervision of the rector; for the music in all four principal churches of Leipzig, under their clergy; and for the musical aspects of the municipal celebrations, under the town council. Bach used the resources provided for church music to the full: in the first years of his appointment from the First Sunday of Trinity, 30 May 1723, he wrote a cantata for most of the Sundays and major feast-days of the church's year. He wrote the St John Passion and the St Matthew Passion for performances on Good Friday. Subsequently he made increasing use of the cantatas and passions of other composers, and recent research has revealed a wide variety of sacred music used by him during the 1730s.

In 1730, in the middle of a dispute about his teaching obligations, for which he was being censured by the town council, Bach made a long protest to the council that the facilities provided for church music were now inadequate: 'The state of music is quite different from what it was . . . taste has changed astonishingly . . . considerable help is therefore all the more needed.' But the permanent forces remained unchanged, and Bach continued to depend on help from university students and others to realise his most elaborate music. In the same year Bach wrote to his old schoolfriend Georg Erdmann, now in Danzig, about the possibilities of employment there.

Instead of moving, during the 1730s Bach widened the scope of his activities while remaining in Leipzig. In 1729 he took over the direction of the Leipzig Collegium Musicum, which gave regular concerts in the coffee-house of Zimmermann in the Catherinestrasse. This stimulated the production of a new series of secular works. It is possible that some of Bach's greatest instrumental works – for example, the Violin Concerto in A minor and the Concerto for two violins in D minor – were newly composed for the early years of the Collegium Musicum; these were not necessarily works with earlier versions. The innovative harpsichord concertos for one, two, three and four instruments, which Bach probably wrote to feature himself and his sons as performers, were all based on earlier models.

In 1733 the Elector of Saxony, Augustus the Strong, died, and Bach sent his successor Augustus II (later also crowned Augustus III, King of Poland) the elaborate Missa BWV 232 which later became the Kyrie and Gloria of the Mass in B minor. Bach hoped to be appointed Court Composer (an honorary, non-resident appointment); the new Elector visited Leipzig a year later and a *Cantata Gratulatoria* was performed in his honour, but Bach did not receive his appointment until 1736 when he went to Dresden and played the organ for 'many persons of rank'.

In 1734 a period of good relationships with his superior at the Thomasschule came to an end when the rector J. M. Gesner (who left a vivid account of Bach's playing and conducting) took up a post in Göttingen. His successor was Johann August Ernesti (no relation of the Ernesti who was rector until 1729). By 1736 Bach and Ernesti were in conflict about the appointment of the school's prefects. During the two-year conflict Bach appealed first to the town council and then to the Elector, who seems to have ruled in Bach's favour. Meanwhile Bach was giving his attention to preparing some of his work for publication and sale. The first part of the *Clavierübung*, the six Partitas, had been issued singly from 1726 and the whole set (though originally planned as a set of seven) appeared in 1731. Further volumes of keyboard music followed in 1734 (*Clavierübung II*, the Italian Concerto and Overture in the French Style), 1739 (*Clavierübung III* for organ based around chorales from the liturgy and catechism), and in autumn 1741, the so-called Goldberg Variations. He also compiled a second set of 24 Preludes and Fugues and made some arrangements for Schemelli's Hymn Book of 1736.

His contributions to the liturgy did not cease in the 1730s, but moved towards set-pieces for the major feasts: the lost St Mark Passion of 1731, the set of six cantatas known as the Christmas Oratorio, largely adapted from secular models, and complemented by an Easter and Ascension Oratorio. Recent discoveries suggest that music he performed during these years included Passions and cantatas by Stölzel, Telemann and others. His own compositional preoccupations turned to fugue and canon, while he also made an effort in works such as the Peasant Cantata and the Goldberg Variations to keep abreast of the latest musical developments. As a result of a visit to the court of Frederick the Great in 1747, *The Musical Offering* was written and published within a few months. The King reportedly asked Bach to improvise on a subject that he provided, and Bach's dedication of the finished work to the King says that he 'determined to work out many possibilities of the Royal Theme and then issue it to the world'. This he did in a mixture of intricate old-style learned canons, new-style keyboard improvisation suitable for the fortepiano, an expressively galant trio sonata, and a six-part Ricercar he never surpassed.

Bach's preoccupations during this period were reflected in the fact that in 1747 he finally joined (as its fourteenth member) the Society for Musical Sciences, which had been in existence for many years in Leipzig, and was run by his former pupil Lorenz Christoph Mizler. He wrote for the Society a set of canonic variations on the hymn 'Vom Himmel hoch', which introduces his musical signature, B–A–C–H, and had engraved for them the Canon triplex which is also seen in his portrait by Haussmann of 1746, and which in its fourteen notes above the bass line seems to symbolise the letters of Bach's name. The canon is also one of a set of fourteen (discovered only in 1976) which Bach added to his own copy of the Goldberg Variations.

In the early 1740s Bach planned a publication later called *The Art of Fugue*, a guide to the art of counterpoint for keyboard, which underwent various transformations before it was sent to the printer in 1749. The other major project of the late 1740s was the compilation and revision of the Mass in B minor in 1748–9, adding further movements to the Missa of 1733, which involved parody adaptations and substantial new work on the Credo, his last completed work. Increasing blindness hampered Bach's ability to work and he had ceased to write by the end of 1749; Bach was unsuccessfully operated on for his blindness in March and April by John Taylor, the same English surgeon who treated Handel. He seems to have supervised the St John Passion again on Good Friday 1749, and as late as May 1750 to have had a pupil, Johann Gottfried Muthel, arrange one of his family's pieces: the motet *Lieber Herr Gott* by his relative Johann Christoph – possibly as a funeral motet.

At Pentecost 1750 Bach fell ill; a newly discovered document shows that his duties were transferred to a prefect, Johann Adam Franck. Though *The Art of Fugue* was not finished, it was printed with a note by his son C. P. E. Bach, including a final chorale arrangement which, it was said, Bach had 'dictated on the spur of the moment to the pen of a friend'. It is a version of an earlier chorale prelude, revised (and it is difficult to believe this is a coincidence) so that the first line contains fourteen and the whole melody forty-one notes. Bach died after a stroke on 28 July 1750 and was buried on 31 July in the graveyard of the Johanniskirche. His remains were exhumed and identified in 1894; in 1950 they were reburied in the Thomaskirche, where a bold and simple grave marks their presence.

The Bach family

Veit Bach, a white-bread maker in Hungary in the
sixteenth century, was compelled to escape from Hungary
because of his Lutheran faith. After converting his
property into money, as far as this could be done, he
went to Germany, and finding security for his religion
in Thuringia, settled at Wechmar near Gotha, and
continued his trade there. What he most delighted in
was his little cittern which he used to take with him to
work to play while the mill was grinding. A pretty noise
the pair of them must have made! However, it taught
him to keep time, and that apparently is how music first
came into our family.

Thus begins the *Ursprung der musicalisch-Bachischen Familie*
which Johann Sebastian Bach either wrote, or copied out and
updated, in 1735, the year that he turned fifty. It was an act of
homage, and the account of his ancestor as a wandering musician also has a deeply symbolic dimension, bringing the exile
to rest in the area of Thuringia which was to be the homeland
of the entire family. As an introduction to Bach's understanding of his place in the family one cannot do better than quote
the Obituary begun by Mizler in Walter Emery's eloquent
translation:

Johann Sebastian Bach belonged to a family whose every
member seems to have had, as a natural gift, a fondness
for music and ability in its practice. At least it is certain
that, from the founder of the family (Veit Bach) to the
descendants of the seventh and present generation, all
the Bachs have been devoted to music; and further, with
one or two possible exceptions, they have all made it their
profession. This Veit was exiled from Hungary in the
sixteenth century for religious reasons; he later settled in

Thuringia, in which province a number of his descendants also have made their homes.

It is also worth stressing the self-contained nature of the Bach dynasty, as the Obituary, having mentioned several outstanding members of the family, continues:

> It would seem strange that men so worthy should have remained so little known outside their own province, did we not remember that these honest Thuringians were so content with their fatherland and circumstances that never once would they venture upon following their fortune far away. The applause of noblemen in whose domain they were born, and that of a host of their simple-hearted fellow-countrymen, was theirs already; and this they greatly preferred to the encomiums, to be won (if at all) only with difficulty and expense, of strangers fewer in number and most probably envious.

One possible way of understanding the essential relationships of the very complex Bach family – there are eighty-three members listed in the full family tree – is to go back to the origins of 1735, and trace the musical line forward. The numbers here are those used to identify the musicians in Bach's family tree as published in 1823 (and in *The New Bach Reader*).

1 **Veit Bach** (d. 8 March 1619)

He had three sons, two of whom were musicians:

2 **Johannes** (d. 1626), town musician in Gotha and Wechmar 'The Wechmar Bach' and originator of that pedigree.

3 **Caspar** (d. *c.*1642), also a carpet maker.

Johannes (2) had three sons:

4 **Johann** (1604–1673)
Town musician, organist and composer in Suhl, Schweinfurt and Erfurt.

5 Christoph (1613–1661)
Town musician in Weimar, Erfurt, and Arnstadt.

6 Heinrich (1615–1692)
Town musician, organist and composer in Schweinfurt, Erfurt and Arnstadt.

Johann (4) had three sons:

7 Johann Christian (1640–1682)
Town musician in Eisenach and Erfurt.

8 Johann Aegidius (1645–1716)
Town musician and organist in Erfurt.

9 Johann Nicolaus (1653–1682)
Town musician in Erfurt.

Christoph (5) had three sons:

10 Georg Christoph (1642–1697)
Cantor and composer in Themar and Schweinfurt.

11 Johann Ambrosius (1645–1695)
Town musician and court musician in Erfurt and Eisenach.

12 Johann Christoph (1645–1693)
Town and court musician in Erfurt and Arnstadt.

(Ambrosius, JSB's father, and Christoph were twins, and impossible to tell apart.)

And Heinrich (6) had three sons:

13 Johann Christoph (i) (1642–1703)
Organist, court musician and a much praised composer whom Bach described as 'profound', to which C. P. E. Bach added 'this is the great and expressive composer'. Bach later performed his music, including motets in Leipzig in the 1740s.

14 Johann Michael (1648–1694)

Organist and composer in Arnstadt and Gehren. A 'capable composer' whose music included works for double chorus in the tradition of Schütz and more modern arias with violin solo.

15 Johann Gunther (1653–1683)

Organist, instrument maker in Arnstadt.

All these fifteen were distinguished professional musicians.

Then among the many other children and branches of the family:

Johann Ambrosius (*11*) had three musical sons among his eight children:

24 Johann Christoph (ii) (1671–1721)

Organist in Erfurt; his two younger brothers came to live with him after their father's death and he must have taught Sebastian the keyboard and composition.

25 Johann Jacob (1682–1722)

who grew up with his younger brother:

26 Johann Sebastian (1685–1750)

Our composer, and undoubtedly the greatest of the family.

The other family composers with whom Sebastian was in contact were:

18 Johann Bernhard (1676–1749),

Son of Johann Aegidius (*8*) who worked in Erfurt and Magdeburg, and then Eisenach. He wrote orchestral suites which Bach used at the Collegium Musicum in Leipzig in the 1730s.

27 Johann Nicolaus (1669–1753)

Son of Johann Christoph (i) (*13*) who declined to move to Eisenach to succeed his father. Settled in Jena. 'Present senior of all the Bachs still living,' wrote Bach in the family tree; he was to outlive even Sebastian. He was credited by Walther with first using the letters B–A–C–H as a musical melody.

64 Johann Ludwig Bach (1677–1731)

From Caspar's (3) side of the family. Bach performed his cantatas and two masses extensively in Leipzig in 1726 and then in the 1740s, copying certain devices such as using strings to clothe the words of Christ.

Bach's own children who became musicians were:

45 Wilhelm Friedemann (1710–1784)

His eldest son with his first wife; organist in Halle and then living in Berlin; highly talented as a composer but never fulfilled his promise; received the largest share of his father's manuscripts but sold them.

46 Carl Philipp Emanuel (1714–1788)

Bach's fifth child with his first wife; studied law in Leipzig and Frankfurt; worked for Frederick the Great and in Hamburg; the most original composer among Bach's sons, writing especially vivid and intense symphonies and keyboard music reflecting the 'Sturm und Drang' movement of the mid-eighteenth century.

47 Johann Gottfried Bernhard (1715–1739)

The black sheep of the family? Organist at Mühlhausen and Sangerhausen, but died early with many debts.

48 Gottfried Heinrich (1724–1763)

The first son with Anna Magdalena. He 'showed great genius which failed to develop', according to C. P. E. Bach.

49 Johann Christoph Friedrich (1732–1795)

A talented composer of symphonies, keyboard and chamber music, who worked in Bückeberg, serving the court assiduously, and visiting London at least once. Some of his music was published, but much has been lost: a shadowy figure who seems to have suffered from depression.

50 Johann Christian (1735–1782)

The last surviving son of Bach and his second wife Anna Magdalena. Went to Italy, became a Catholic, came to London and settled there in the service of Queen Charlotte. Is there is a tinge of disapproval or just of brotherly envy in C. P. E.'s concluding note at the end of the family tree: 'among us, he has managed differently from honest old Veit!'

The sense of belonging to the family, and carrying on a continuous tradition in their work, has been movingly demonstrated by the rediscovery of the Alt-Bachischen Archiv, part of the collection of the Berlin Singakademie, known before the Second World War but lost during that conflict. In the past decade it has resurfaced in Kiev, in the Ukraine, and is now being comprehensively edited and documented. A couple of early finds illustrated in Wolff's Bach biography show how close was the sense of family. Firstly, there is a wedding cantata by Sebastian's relative Johann Christoph, with a title page newly written out by Sebastian around 1740, but a violin part written by his father Johann Ambrosius before 1695. Then at the very end of his life, Bach wrote out the title and headed some instrumental parts for J. C. Bach's *Lieber Herr Gott, wecke uns auf*: Bach had a score that dated back to December 1672, and added these instrumental parts as late as 1749–50. One does not need to believe that this was intended by Bach for his own funeral (which would surely in its way be as sentimental a theory as that of the chorale dictated on his deathbed) for it to be an very touching signal of the respect in which Bach held the earlier creations of his family.

Another testimony is Forkel's no doubt colourful, but genuine, later account of the family gatherings of the Bachs:

> The different members of this family had a very great attachment to each other. As it was impossible for them to live in one place, they resolved at least to see each other once a year, and fixed a certain day, upon which they were all to appear at an appointed place. Even after the family had become much more numerous, and many of the members had been obliged to settle outside Thuringia, in different places of Upper and Lower Saxony, and

Franconia, they continued their annual meetings, which
generally took place in Erfurt, Eisenach or Arnstadt.
Their amusements, during the time of their meeting,
were entirely musical.

Since the company consisted of none but cantors,
organists and town musicians, all of whom had to do with
the church, first of all, when all were assembled, a chorale
was sung. From this devotional opening they proceeded to
jesting, often in strong contrast to it. For now they would
sing folksongs, the contents of which were partly comic
and partly indelicate, all together and extempore, but in
such a way that the several improvised parts made up a
kind of harmony . . . they called this a quodlibet . . . and
enjoyed a hearty laugh at it.

The Quodlibet preserved as BWV 524 is a lively example
of this form, and though Bach copied it out it is not certain
whether he made the arrangement.

Some Bach family recordings

𝆕 *Die Familie Bach vor Johann Sebastian* Rheinische Kantorei,
Musica Antiqua Köln/Goebel
Archiv 419253-2
𝆕 *Bachiana: music by the Bach family* Musica Antiqua Köln/
Goebel
Archiv 471 150-2
𝆕 *Kantaten aus dem Altbachischen Archiv* Capella Fidicinia/
Grüss
Capriccio 10029
𝆕 *Altbachisches Archiv: les Archives de J. S. Bach* Cantus Cölln,
Concerto Palatino/Junghänel
HMC 901782.84
𝆕 *The Bach Family* Bach Ensemble/Helmut Rilling
Hänssler Classics CD98.614 (3 CDs)

A chronology, 1685–1750

A more detailed chronology of Bach's life than the brief biography above is made difficult by the fact that although many events are precisely documented (and for those, *The New Bach Reader* is an indispensable guide), much else about his work and his compositions remains in a state of flux. We can identify the occasions on which many cantatas and secular works were performed, but except in the case of publication (and very few of Bach's works were published during his lifetime) we cannot be at all sure of the dates of composition and revision of some of his music. This chronology gives reliable dates, in the context of other musical, cultural and social landmarks.

1685

21 March: Johann Sebastian Bach is born in Eisenach, Thuringia, the capital of the Duchy of Saxe-Weimar. He is the last of eight children of Ambrosius and Elisabeth Bach.

23 March: Bach is baptised in the Georgenkirche, which still stands. His godparents are Sebastian Nagel and the forester Johann Georg Koch, but his mother is not present due to the strict Levitican rules that she cannot enter a church until she is purified six weeks after the birth.

- Birth of Domenico Scarlatti
- Birth of Georg Frideric Handel
- Death of King Charles II
- Accession of King James II
- Playford's *The Division Violin* published

1686

As town musician since October 1671, his father Ambrosius arranged music-making twice a day in the town square, and performed as required in Sunday services and extra civic services, receiving extra payments for ducal court music.

3 May: Bach's sister Johanna Juditha dies at the age of six and is buried.

- Benedetto Marcello born
- Legrenzi appointed to St Mark's Venice
- Marais's first *Pièces de violes* published in Paris
- League of Augsburg formed against Louis XIV

1687

Bach's house, misidentified in the nineteenth century, was at No. 35 Fleischgasse (now Lutherstrasse), but has been demolished: the Bach Museum is down the road at No. 21 Frauenplan, formerly thought to be his birthplace and one of the oldest extant houses in the town.

- Francesco Geminiani born
- Jean-Baptiste Lully dies
- Newton's *Principia Mathematica* published

1688

Bach's elder brother Balthasar, who was fifteen at this time, becomes apprenticed to his father as a violinist.

- Frederick III becomes Elector of Brandenburg
- Frederick William I of Prussia born
- Glorious Revolution in England
- Charpentier, *David et Jonathas*

1689

Bach is perhaps attending the church where he was baptised, and hearing its rich repertory of traditional sacred music.

- William and Mary assume English throne
- Peter the Great deposes his sister and takes Russian throne
- Jacobite Rebellions begin
- D'Anglebert, *Pièces de clavecin* (with table of ornaments that Bach later copied)

1690

Bach turns five. He begins to attend a German school in Eisenach.

- Death of Legrenzi
- Battle of the Boyne, in which William III defeats James II
- Couperin, *Pièces d'orgue*
- Locke, *Essay Concerning Human Understanding*

1691

We know from his Obituary that Bach had an 'uncommonly fine treble voice', which would now have been beginning to develop. His brother Johann Balthazar dies.

- Plymouth Colony becomes part of Massachusetts Bay colony
- Purcell, *King Arthur*
- Fleury, *Histoire ecclésiastique*

1692

Bach enters the Lateinschule in Eisenach, in the building of the Dominican church cloister, probably in the spring after his birthday, where he studies Latin grammar, mathematics, history, and religious education.

Johann Jacob, a cousin who had worked with Ambrosius for a decade, dies.

- Birth of Tartini
- Salem witch trials
- Purcell, *The Fairy Queen*
- Maximilian II, Elector of Bavaria, becomes governor of the Spanish Netherlands

1693

At Easter Bach is forty-seventh out of eighty-one in the fifth class at the Lateinschule, but has been absent for ninety-six sessions.

His father's identical twin, Johann Christoph, dies.

- Kerll dies

- Opera house in Leipzig opens
- Charpentier, *Médée*
- Halley works on distances from the sun

1694

Bach rises to fourteenth of seventy-four at the Lateinschule, having been absent for fifty-nine sessions and entered a higher class. Johann Michael Bach dies this year.

1 May: death of his mother, Elisabeth, at the age of fifty; buried 3 May.

23 October: wedding of his brother Johann Christoph, at which Pachelbel and Bach's father perform.

27 November: his father marries again, to Barbara Margharetha, whose first husband had been a musician and instrument builder in Arnstadt.

- Bank of England founded
- Campra becomes *maître de musique* at Notre Dame, Paris
- Corelli Op. 4 published
- Death of Queen Mary; Purcell, *Funeral Music for Queen Mary*
- Congreve, *The Double Dealer*

1695

Bach turns ten.

20 February: only three months after remarrying, his father dies at the age of forty-nine and is buried on 24 February.

At Easter he is ranked twenty-third of forty-five in the fourth class, but had been absent for 103 sessions, just above his brother Jacob.

Soon after Easter he leaves Eisenach and travels to Ohrdruf, capital of the small area of Gleichen, with his brother Johann Jacob, to live with his eldest brother Johann Christoph, a decisive move for him.

July: enters the third class at the Lyceum in Ohrdruf in July.

- Purcell, *The Indian Queen*; Purcell dies 21 November
- Congreve, *Love for Love*

- Locatelli born
- Pachelbel organist at Nuremberg
- Georg Muffat, *Florilegium primum*

1696

Bach is studying with his eldest brother Johann Christoph, who had learnt from Pachelbel in Erfurt. Was he already writing music?

20 July: fourth in the class and first among the new boys.

- Bononcini, *Il trionfo di Camilla*
- Death of John III, King of Poland
- Vanbrugh, *The Relapse*

1697

The Obituary records that 'in a short time he had fully mastered all the pieces his brother had willingly given him to learn'.

19 July: he was first of twenty-one students in the class and promoted to the second class.

- August II of Saxony elected to Polish throne
- Death of Charles XI of Sweden; his son Charles XII succeeds
- Birth of Quantz
- Leclair born
- Campra, *L'Europe galante*
- Keiser joins Hamburg opera
- Roger's music publishing firm in Amsterdam opens

1698

18 July: Bach is fifth in class. It is around this time that his Obituary tells a famous story of a music manuscript which his brother Johann Christoph kept in a locked cupboard with a lattice door. Bach was able to stretch through the lattice by night and take the manuscript to copy it. When Christoph discovered this he removed the manuscript and forbade the young boy to look at it again.

- Russian peasant revolt

- The future George I becomes Elector of Hanover
- Fux court composer to Leopold I in Vienna
- Torelli, *Concerti musicali* Op. 6
- Muffat, *Florilegium secundum*

1699

24 July: Bach is second of eleven in class, promoted to first class when fourteen years and four months old. He is beginning to copy out and learn from the many keyboard works around him in Johann Christoph's possession, so that as the Obituary says, Bach 'really showed the first fruits of his application to the art of organ playing and to composition and learned chiefly by the observation of the works of the most famous and proficient composers of his day and by the fruits of his own reflection upon them'.

- Fénelon, *Télémaque* published
- Birth of Hasse
- Treaty of Karlowitz
- Caldara *maestro di cappella* in Mantua

1700

Bach turns fifteen.

15 March: he is fourth in the first class.

He leaves for Lüneburg, a major move; as a reason the school register says 'ob defectum hospitiorum', probably meaning 'in the absence of free board'.

April: he is a choral scholar at St Michael's School Lüneburg, singing in the fifteen-strong Mettenchor (which entitled him to free lodging) and he receives money in May for his work. Bach arrives soon after one of the most notorious episodes in Lüneburg's history, the desecration and looting of a precious panel in St Michael's Church, for which those responsible were gorily executed. It has been wondered whether this event made an impression on the young Bach and affected his attitude to death.

Bach's earliest music manuscript to have survived is a

tablature transcription of two major chorale preludes by Buxtehude and Reincken – the latter copied out, a note in Bach's handwriting confirms, at the house of Georg Böhm in 1700, on paper owned by Böhm.

- Congreve, *The Way of the World* published
- Great Northern War until 1721
- Berlin Academy of Sciences founded by Leibniz
- Charles II of Spain dies; Leaves inheritance to Dauphin of France
- Philip V becomes King of Spain
- Great Northern War begins
- John Blow Composer of the Chapel Royal
- Kuhnau, *Biblical Stories* published
- Corelli, Op. 5 Violin Sonatas published

1701

By now Bach's voice has probably broken and so he may not have continued in the choir, but in the absence of records we do not know how soon after his arrival in Lüneburg this occurred. Some suggest he continued in the choir as a bass (Spitta thought he might have been employed as an instrumentalist, but this is less likely).

- Frederick III becomes King of Prussia
- War of Spanish Succession: Britain, Netherlands and Austria against France
- Prussia becomes a kingdom
- Kuhnau Kantor of Thomaskirche Leipzig

1702

Travels to Hamburg to see Reincken. Bach had a cousin in the city who would have been able to show him around: did he hear his first opera at this time, perhaps something by Reinhard Keiser? Another well-worn story (relayed by Marpurg in 1786) shows how important these journeys were to Bach: staying outside an inn because he had no money, a pair of herring heads were thrown out of a window, and Bach found two ducats in them, enabling him to visit Reincken again.

April: graduation from St Michael's School and return to Ohrdruf.

9 July: Gottfried Christoph Gräffenhayn, organist at St Jacobi Sangerhausen, dies; Bach applies for the position. He is examined and offered the post, but the Duke chooses another applicant, J. A. Kobelius.

- Death of William III; Queen Anne succeeds
- Britain, Holland and Austria–Hungary in war against France
- The first regular English-language newspaper, *The Daily Courant*, published
- Telemann director of the Leipzig opera
- Royal Danish Opera House opens in Copenhagen

1703

In January to March, and April to June, we hear of Bach in his first professional post, albeit temporarily, as a 'lackey' at Weimar, probably playing the violin; this was a stop-gap until he found a post as organist.

July: examines new organ at Neue Kirche in Arnstadt

9 August: Bach is appointed organist at Arnstadt, where many of his ancient family had been active since Caspar, a bassoonist, in the early seventeenth century.

- Brossard, *Dictionary of Music*
- Johann Gottlieb Graun born
- Portugal and Savoy join alliance against France
- Archduke Charles proclaimed King of Spain
- Peter the Great lays foundations of Sternberg
- Sir Isaac Newton becomes chairman of the Royal Society

1704

It is to this year that Bach's *Capriccio on the departure [absence] of his beloved brother* is dated, but there is nothing to suppose that this was actually for Bach's brother Jacob (who more likely left in 1706); the departure of his close friend Georg Erdmann might have been a more likely circumstance for the piece.

- Biber dies
- Charpentier dies
- Carl Heinrich Graun born
- Battle of Blenheim
- Newton publishes *Optics*
- Jonathan Swift, *The Battle of the Books*, *A Tale of a Tub*

1705

Bach turns twenty. In August he is in trouble at Arnstadt over a dispute in August with bassoonist Johann Heinrich Geyersbach. In one of the very rare incidents that cast light on Bach's character, he is accused of fighting him and calling him a 'Zippel Fagottist', a 'nanny-goat' (or supply your own adjective) bassoonist. A late-night and perhaps drunken exchange led to Geyersbach striking Bach with a stick, and Bach drawing his sword; the two of them fought until the students who were with them separated them so that Bach could go home. The town's accusation is that Bach 'had a reputation for not getting along with the students, and of claiming that he was engaged only for simple chorale music, and not for concerted pieces which was wrong, for he must help out in all music making' (see Newman, p. 56).

November: Bach leaves for Lübeck on four weeks' leave of absence to see and hear Dietrich Buxtehude. We are told he walked, but did he really make the 260-mile journey on foot, or is that the stuff of legend? He did not go to Lübeck only to hear Buxtehude play but to experience the Abendmusik series that the composer presented, which took place that year between 15 November and 20 December.

- Handel, *Almira* premiered in Hamburg
- Halley predicts comet of 1758
- Leopold I dies, Joseph I becomes Emperor
- Benjamin Franklin born

1706

7 February: Bach returns to Arnstadt. The consistory complains about his absence, but in an early example of not suffering fools or employers gladly, Bach dismisses their reasonable complaints.

November: Bach is reproached for bringing a strange woman into the organ loft – presumably his second cousin and soon-to-be wife, Maria Barbara. Bach's defence is that he had permission and she was there only to practise with his accompaniment.

2 December: death (at age fifty-five) of the organist Ahle in Mühlhausen.

- Pachelbel dies
- Rameau, *Pièces de clavecin*
- Handel travels to Italy
- Marlborough conquers Spanish Netherlands

1707

24 April: Bach auditions for the post of organist at St Blasius, Mühlhausen (as well as playing the organ, a cantata had to be performed, perhaps Cantata 4).

14–15 June: he is appointed organist; asks for a contract including fifty-four bushels of grain, two cords of wood, six times threescore faggots, delivered to the door. Salary eighty-five gulden.

29 June: leaves Arnstadt, returns organ keys. Assigns remaining salary to his cousin Johann Ernst Bach.

10 August: Tobias Lämmerhirt, Bach's uncle, dies in Erfurt. Possibly Cantata 106 is performed at his funeral on the 14th (but did Bach really have time to write and rehearse this great masterpiece in those three days?)

Bach arrives in Mühlhausen, an imperial free city governed only by the Emperor. He begins to teach: J. M. Schubart and J. C. Vogler were his first pupils.

17 October: Marriage to Maria Barbara, aged twenty-three, daughter of Johann Michael Bach of Gehren, at the small church of Dornheim, east of Arnstadt.

- Buxtehude dies
- Handel, *Il trionfo del Tempo e del Disinganno* and *Rodrigo*
- Act of Union between England and Scotland
- Alliance between Prussia and Sweden

1708

4 February: performance of Cantata 71 for the changing of the town council – *Gott ist mein König* becomes the first of his cantatas to be published in a handsome score. Bach has better relationships with the rector of the other Mühlhausen church, Eilmar (who was godfather to Bach's daughter Catharina), than with his own rector Frohne.

25 June: Bach requests dismissal as he has been appointed organist and chamber musician in Weimar: his request refers to his 'long-time goal of a well-appointed church music' and how difficult that was to achieve in Mühlhausen.

July: moves to Weimar where he is to receive 150 florins in cash (more than his predecessor Effler), eighteen bushels of grain, twelve bushels of barley, four cords of wood and thirty pails of beer. His successor Schubart was paid 130 florins – a testimony to Bach's status, or his negotiating skills?

29 December: first child, daughter Catharina Dorothea, baptised

- Blow dies
- Jesuits expelled from Holland
- Handel, *La resurrezione*
- Charles XII invades Ukraine
- Stahl, *Theoria medica vera*

1709

4 February: another cantata performed in Mühlhausen and Bach's travel expenses from Weimar paid. The work is lost, but this too was published.

13 March: Bach and his family are living in Weimar with the master of the pages, who became a godfather to Carl Philipp Emanuel. He made extra money from repairing harpsichords. He made the friendship of Johann Walther, one of his cousins,

who wrote the first German-language musical dictionary (*Musicalisches Lexicon*, published in 1732).

- Cristofori's first piano
- F. Benda born
- Torelli dies
- Charles XII defeated by Peter the Great at Poltava
- Great Plague in Russia
- Steffani Apostolic Vicar in Hanover

1710

Bach turns twenty-five. His salary is now 150 florins plus 'some wood and coal to tide the court organist over the winter'.

4 February: possible third Mühlhausen cantata and visit to the town.

26 October: organ inspection in Traubach.

22 November: his first son Wilhelm Friedemann Bach born, baptised on 24 November.

- Pergolesi born
- Arne born
- Pasquini dies
- English conquer French colony at Nova Scotia
- Handel in Hanover and London
- Campra, *Les fêtes venitiennes*
- Berkeley *A Treatise Concerning the Nature of Human Knowledge*

1711

3 June: the Prince increases his salary and allowances to 200 florins. He teaches the Duke's page as well, receiving more timber for doing so.

- Boyce born
- David Hume born
- Handel, *Rinaldo* in London
- Vivaldi, *L'estro armonico* Op. 3 published

- Death of Emperor Joseph I; Charles VI succeeds him
- *The Spectator* founded

1712

27 September: baptism of the son of Weimar organist Walther, with Bach as godfather. A story from much later is that Bach gave a large number of pieces to Walther, who teased Bach because of his claim that he could play anything at sight, and tricked him by leaving a deliberately unplayable piece for Bach to try.

- John Arbuthnot creates John Bull to symbolise Britain
- Handel in London
- Alexander Pope, *The Rape of the Lock*

1713

In February Bach visits Weissenfels for birthday of Duke Christian: Cantata 208, the Hunting Cantata, performed there.

23 February: twins are born but one, Johann Christoph, dies after birth.

15 March: the other twin, Maria Sophia, dies.

July: Johann Ernst of Weimar brings concertos including Vivaldi Op. 3 back from Netherlands: bills for binding and shelving the music.

2 August: Bach inscribes a canon BWV 1073 in an autograph book.

7 September: baptism of his brother Johann Christoph's son Johann Sebastian in Ohrdruf.

28 November: he is invited to apply for the post of organist in Halle.

13 December: he is elected and contract offered dated 14 December. He stays at the Inn of the Golden Ring, and his expenses are paid – receipt 15 December.

- Corelli dies
- Death of Frederick I; Frederick William I becomes Elector
- Mattheson, *Das neu-eröffnete Orchestre*

- Maria Grimani, *Pallade e Marte* in Vienna
- Treaty of Utrecht; all states except Austria make peace with France
- Charles VI's Pragmatic Sanction
- Philip V King of Spain
- Nova Scotia and Newfoundland ceded to Britain

1714

14 January: Bach writes a letter putting off a decision about the Halle post, citing that he had not been released from Weimar and asking questions about the salary. At some later point he decides against accepting.

19 March: writes another letter to Halle expressing surprise that they were surprised he declined the offer.

2 March: promoted to Konzertmeister at Weimar, writing monthly cantatas. Duke raises his salary to 250 florins.

8 March: son Carl Philipp Emanuel born; one of his godfathers is Telemann.

25 March: Palm Sunday: Cantata 182 performed, the first Weimar church cantata written after his new appointment.

- Gluck born
- Domenico Scarlatti becomes maestro of the Capella Giulia
- War of the Spanish Succession ends/Peace of Rastatt
- George I first Hanoverian King of England
- Peter the Great conquers Finland
- Fahrenheit invents thermometer

1715

Bach turns thirty.

March: his salary is increased again 'to receive the portion of a capellmeister'.

11 May: son Johann Gottfried Bernhard born, baptised on 12th.

9 July: a bill of 13 florins 15 groschen was paid for two reams of writing paper and twelve reams of printing (or copying) paper for the church cantatas.

1 August: Duke Johann Ernst dies in Frankfurt, aged only nineteen.

- Agenesis born
- Louis XIV dies; Louis XV succeeds under regency of Duc d'Orléans
- Jacobite risings suppressed in Scotland
- Fux Hofkapellmeister in Vienna
- First Three Choirs Festival in England

1716

April: celebration of the marriage of Duke Ernst to Eleonore, sister of the Prince of Cöthen. They have a Weimar residence where Bach may well have met the princess's brother, Prince Leopold of Anhalt-Cöthen.

28 April: travels to Halle to examine their new organ by Christoph Cuntzius, in the company of Johann Kuhnau.

31 July: examines the organ in Erfurt.

1 December: death of court Kapellmeister Drese. Bach passed over in favour of Drese's son. Bach has cultivated Johann Ernst's elder brother Ernst August, but there is severe jealousy between the two branches of the family.

- Opéra Comique opens in Paris
- Pagodenburg built by Joseph Effner in the Nymphenburg, Munich

1717

Bach is referred to in Mattheson's *Das beschützte Orchestre* as 'the famous Weimar organist'.

26 March: performance of lost Passion in Gotha on Good Friday.

5 August: accepts post of Kapellmeister in Cöthen and requests to leave Weimar, but that is not granted and the Duke keeps him at work until the end of the year.

Visits Dresden for competition with Louis Marchand: the story goes that Marchand fled the city because 'the famous Frenchman found his talents too weak to withstand the powerful assaults of his expert and valiant opponent'. (This is a much later retelling of the occasion by Bach's pupil, Birnbaum.) Two contests are planned, one on the harpsichord and one on the organ, but it seems only the harpsichord one may have taken place.

6 November: detained for 'too stubbornly forcing the issue of his dismissal' until 2 December, when he left in disgrace.

10 December: arrives in Cöthen in time to celebrate Prince Leopold's birthday.

16 December: organ examination in University Church, Leipzig.

- The Mississippi Scheme leads to increased settlement in Louisiana
- Handel, *Water Music*
- Francoeur leader of the Vingt-Quatre Violons
- Watteau, *The Embarkation of Cythera* sent to Académie
- Prince Eugene and the Battle of Belgrade

1718

Bach is earning about 450 thalers a year compared with around 250 in Weimar, and receives an extra fifty for moving expenses. He begins as a tenant in Stiftstrasse 11.

May–July: with Prince Leopold in Carlsbad, with six musicians from the Kapelle; the servants were paid to help carry the princely harpsichord.

15 November: seventh child, Leopold Augustus, born; the Prince and other nobility stand as godparents.

10 December: birthday of Prince Leopold: performance of Cantata 66a.

- Voltaire imprisoned for criticising the French aristocracy
- Maurice Greene organist of St Paul's
- Handel, *Acis and Galatea* and *Esther*
- Peace of Passarowitz; end of the Austro-Turkish war
- Death of Charles XII of Sweden; succeeded by his sister

1719

March: Bach visits Berlin and purchases harpsichord by Michael Mietke for the court, which possibly stimulates the

composition of the Fifth Brandenburg Concerto. At this time in Berlin he may have met the Margrave of Brandenburg, brother of the deceased King and youngest son of the Elector.
14 May: attempts to meet Handel but fails.
28 September: death of son Leopold Augustus.

• Leopold Mozart born
• Daniel Defoe, *Robinson Crusoe*
• Lotti, *Giove in Argo* opens Dresden court theatre
• Breitkopf publishing firm opens in Leipzig

1720

Bach turns thirty-five. During this year he visits the aged Reincken and improvises on the chorale *An Wasserflüssen Babylon*.
22 January: start of *Clavierbüchlein* for Wilhelm Friedemann.
7 July: wife Maria Barbara dies, aged nearly thirty-six, while Bach is with Leopold in Carlsbad.
November: auditions for the post of organist at St Jacobi in Hamburg but on 23 November is summoned to return home; Mattheson says that the job was sold to the highest bidder and Bach was ignored.

• Agricola born
• Altnickol born
• Marcello, *Il teatro alla moda*
• Leipzig opera closes
• The South Sea Company Act and the South Sea Bubble in Great Britain
• First opera season at the Royal Academy in London: Handel, *Radamisto*
• Peace with Spain, with settlement on Italian succession
• Spain occupies Texas

1721

22 February: death of Bach's elder brother Johann Christoph at forty-nine.
24 March: dedication of score of Brandenburg Concertos to

Monseigneur Christian Ludwig, Margrave of Brandenburg.

August: performs in Schleiz for Count Reussstays at the Inn of the Blue Angel.

15 June: Anna Magdalena is mentioned for the first time in the register of communicants; she is a godmother later in the year.

3 December: marries Anna Magdalena Wülcken (also called Wilcke or Wilken), aged twenty, singer at the court and daughter of a court trumpeter at Weissenfels; she is subsequently employed by the court at a salary of 200 thaler, half that of Bach. Her elder brother is a trumpeter in Zerbst.

11 December: marriage of Prince Leopold to Frederica of Anhalt-Bernburg, who disliked music.

• Great Northern War ends with division between Sweden and Russia
• Clement XI dies; Innocent XIII becomes Pope
• Robert Walpole becomes First Lord of Treasury
• Telemann Cantor in Hamburg

1722

16 April: death of Bach's brother Johann Jacob in Stockholm.

9 August: performance in Zerbst for the birthday of Prince Johann August of Anhalt-Zerbst.

Start of *Clavierbüchlein* for Anna Magdalena – she wrote the title page and he wrote the music, prefacing a shared effort that was to be constant across the years.

Completion of the first book of the '48', with the title-page: 'preludes and fugues through all the tones and semitones . . . for the use and profit of the musical youth desirous of learning as well as for the pastime of those already skilled in this study'. (The end point of the collection is given as 1732, though this refers to corrections in the copy.)

March: inherits money from the Lämmerhirt estate in Erfurt; asks town council to find in his favour if proceedings were begun for the money by others.

5 June: Johann Kuhnau dies in Leipzig, opening a new possibility for Bach, in line with his desire to be musical director

of a large city. Telemann is the preferred candidate, but by 22 November he has refused.

23 November: the Leipzig councillors reconvene and Councillor Platz says that Telemann is no loss, since they need a teacher rather than a Kapellmeister.

21 December: another meeting of the council, by which time Graupner and Bach have applied for the post. (A third candidate Fasch is eliminated because he cannot teach.) Graupner had studied law in Leipzig and is a graduate of the Thomasschule, so is well known to many in Leipzig.

- Georg Benda born
- Reincken dies
- Daniel Defoe, *Moll Flanders*
- Charles VI founds Dutch East India Company
- Peter the Great gains access to the Black Sea
- Rameau, *Traité de l'harmonie*
- Mattheson, *Critica musica*
- Work begins on James Gibbs's church, St Martin-in-the-Fields, in London

1723

January 1723: Graupner (composer of some 1,418 cantatas) auditions for the Leipzig post: he is approved providing he can secure his dismissal.

22 March: Graupner, offered more money by his employers in Darmstadt, declines the Leipzig post, leaving the field open for Bach to be considered alongside two other candidates: Georg Friedrich Kauffmann, from Merseburg, and Georg Balthasar Schott, from the new church in Leipzig.

7 February: Bach auditions in Leipzig, with performances of Cantatas 22 and 23; a newspaper report refers to 'the music of the same having been amply praised on that occasion by all knowledgeable persons'.

?Spring: daughter Sophia Henrietta born.

13 April: is granted dismissal from Cöthen with regret by Prince Leopold.

19 April: signs his provisional contract in Leipzig.

22 April: elected in Leipzig; one of the council says 'he should make compositions that are not theatrical'.

5 May: signs contract in Leipzig with undertakings as to his behaviour: 'in order to preserve the good order in the churches, so arrange the music that it shall not last too long, and shall be of such a nature as not to make an operatic impression, but rather incite the listeners to devotion'.

8 May: takes theology examination to ensure his Lutheran creed.

15 May: paid by Leipzig for the first time.

16 May: Cantata 59 perhaps performed at the Paulinerkirche.

22 May: the family arrives in Leipzig with 'four wagons loaded with household goods'; apartment at the Thomasschule newly renovated.

30 May: Bach's first new Cantata 75, perhaps already composed at Cöthen, performed at the Nikolaikirche 'with much applause'.

1 June: the chief Town Clerk describes the slight breach of protocol by one Weiss in introducing the new Cantor, rather than the superintendent doing so.

14 June: W. F. and C. P. E. accepted into Thomasschule.

September: he begins wrangles with the university over responsibility for the services.

25 December: the first performance of the Magnificat, the version in E flat with interpolations of Christmas hymns. The D major Sanctus BWV 238 might also have been written at this time: there was extensive music-making between Christmas Day and the Epiphany on 6 January, with several new cantatas.

- Christopher Wren dies
- Coronation of Charles VI: Fux, *Costanza e Fortezza* performed
- Turkey attacks Persia
- Louis XV comes of age
- Voltaire, *La Henriade*

1724

Bach's energetic pursuit of the aims of his new post continues unabated, with a stream of new cantatas. During Lent, when there are no cantatas, he completes work on his St John Passion. 26 February: son Gottfried Heinrich born.

7 April, Good Friday: first performance of the St John Passion in the Nikolaikirche. Bach had planned the performance for the Thomaskirche, but was told that the Passion performances alternated annually between churches. He makes some objections because the harpsichord in the Nikolaikirche needs repairing and the space allocated is not large enough (perhaps indicating that he intended to bring in the other choir from the Thomaskirche to join in this performance); these were attended to and the performance took place there.

11 June: on the first Sunday after Trinity, a new cantata cycle begins with Cantata 20. This is a more thoroughly planned cycle, based around the relevant chorales of the liturgical year which would underpin the music of each cantata.

25 June: he undertakes an organ examination in Johannis-kirche, Gera.

July: he returns to give a guest performance in Cöthen with Anna Magdalena.

- Immanuel Kant born
- Birth of Klopstock
- Swift, *Drapier's Letters*
- Philip V abdicates
- Treaty of Constantinople: Russia and Turkey divide Persia
- Handel, *Giulio Cesare in Egitto*
- Metastasio, libretto for *Didone abbandonata*

1725

Bach turns forty. His most intense period of creativity continues through this year, leading up to Easter: all the new cantatas are based on chorales (with libretti perhaps written by Andreas Stübel of the Thomasschule, who died in January 1725), but then after Easter he moves on to a different kind of libretto with texts by Marianne von Ziegler.

23 February: guest performance in Weissenfels for birthday of Duke Christian; Cantata 249a, the Pastoral Cantata, is the first product of a lengthy collaboration with the librettist and poet Picander (Christian Friedrich Henrici).

30 March: second version of the St John Passion is performed on Good Friday; significant revisions are made including the replacement of the opening chorus.

14 April: son Christian Gottlieb baptised.

June: the third Leipzig cantata cycle begins but is fully sustained only until the turn of the year.

14 September: petition to Elector of Saxony about responsibilities for university church services. At the start of 1726 the King gives his judgement and Bach fails to expand his responsibilities for the university, though he maintained some involvement.

19/20 September: organ recitals in Dresden.

15 December: visits Cöthen.

- Alessandro Scarlatti dies
- Fux, *Gradus ad parnassum*
- Peter the Great dies: Catherine I becomes Tsarina, founds St Petersburg Academy
- Casanova born
- Louis XV marries Polish wife Marie-Leszczynska instead of Spanish infanta
- Congress of Cambrai dissolves Treaty of Vienna

1726

During this year Bach's productivity suddenly declines, and between February and September he performs eighteen cantatas by his cousin Johann Ludwig Bach. He does not write a Passion of his own for Good Friday but revives a St Mark Passion at one time attributed to Keiser.

5 April: daughter Elisabeth Juliana Frederica baptised.

19 April: anonymous St Mark Passion with additions performed on Good Friday.

29 June: daughter Christiana Sophia Henrietta dies aged three
June: continues series of new cantatas for the Sundays after
Trinity
1 November: announcement of *Clavierübung* series and first
instalment published, the B flat Partita; Bach sends one to his
old home at Cöthen with a poem of dedication to a newly
born prince.

- Lalande dies
- Vivaldi, *Four Seasons*
- Voltaire exiled from France to England
- Swift, *Gulliver's Travels*
- The Academy of Vocal Music founded, London

1727

It was thought that Bach's creativity in this year was concen-
trated onto the creation of a single large work, the St Matthew
Passion, but it is now clear that there were new cantatas for
Whitsun and Trinity as well.
11 April: St Matthew Passion probably first performed on
Good Friday.
12 May: celebration and procession for the birthday of King
August II at which BWV Anh. 9 (now lost) was performed.
The audience includes Prince Leopold of Cöthen and Duke
Christian of Weissenfels.
Whitsun: the latest research suggests that Bach originates
new cantatas for the three Whit feast days and Trinity Sunday,
filling a gap that has puzzled scholars. Cantatas 34, 173 and
129 are performed alongside a revival of Cantata 184.
18 August: writes canon BWV 1074 for Houdemann.
5 September: death of Electress of Saxony; dispute over the
funeral commission.
17 October: *Trauer-Ode* Cantata 198 for memorial service for
Electress of Saxony. This is a major undertaking during the
period of mourning within which no regular church music is
performed.
30 October: son Ernestus Augustus baptised; dies two days
later.

- Edmund Burke born
- Bordoni and Cuzzoni rivalry in London
- George I dies; George II succeeds
- Tiepolo creates fresco cycle for Udine
- Last witch burning in Scotland

1728

Picander publishes this year a cycle of cantata texts: Bach's Obituary claims that he wrote five cantata cycles, so if the new discoveries relating to 1727 were part of a fourth cycle, the Picander sequence of 1727–8 could be the fifth referred to. (Fragments of possible settings of Picander's texts survive in the chorale harmonisations later published by C. P. E. Bach and Kirnberger.)

New Year's Day: Guest performance in Cöthen for festivities.

September: dispute with sub-deacon of Nikolaikirche, Dr Salomon Deyling, over choice of hymns: Bach is overruled.

21 September: son Christian Gottlieb dies aged three.

10 October: daughter Regina Johanna baptised.

19 (or 23) November: death of Prince Leopold of Anhalt-Cöthen at thirty-three.

27 December: his sister Maria Salome dies at fifty-one and is buried in Erfurt.

- Steffani dies
- Marais dies
- Piccinni born
- James Cook born
- Johann Mattheson retires from Hamburg Cathedral
- Gay's and Pepusch's *The Beggar's Opera* opens and runs for sixty-two performances

1729

12 January: Duke Christian of Weissenfels visits Leipzig: Cantata 210a performed.

23 February: Bach visits Weissenfels and receives honorary, non-resident post as Kapellmeister.

23/24 March: visits Cöthen for funeral cantata for Leopold, Cantata 244a.

April: Becomes agent for Heinichen and Walther publications.

15 April, Good Friday: St Matthew Passion performed again.

Spring (before the third Sunday after Easter in April): takes over Leipzig Collegium Musicum after three weeks away in March.

6 June: Cantata 174 with its Sinfonia based on a much-elaborated version of Brandenburg Concerto No. 3 surely demonstrates that he now had access to the resources of the Collegium, including their brass players.

29 June: another attempt to invite Handel, as Bach sends Wilhelm Friedemann to Halle.

20 October: funeral of rector Johann August Ernesti, at which motet *Der geist hilft* BWV 226 is sung. Gesner succeeds Ernesti as Rector of the Thomasschule.

By 1729 Bach has a stock of musical publications he is involved in distributing.

- Heinichen dies
- La Guerre dies
- Handel and Heidegger launch second Royal Academy of Music
- Lessing born
- Jonathan Swift, *A Modest Proposal* published
- North and South Carolina British colonies
- Treaty of Seville

1730

Bach turns forty-five: this is a time of conflict with the Leipzig authorities.

1 January: daughter Christiana Benedicta baptised.

4 January: Christiana Benedicta dies.

7 April: a St Luke Passion is performed, with some additions by Bach.

August: the most serious dispute yet with the town council erupts over the teaching of the lower classes, where Bach is said to be inactive (one said the Cantor was incorrigible); councillors argue that someone else should be put in charge of the lower classes and the Bachs' income restricted.

23 August: against this background of dispute Bach produces his famous 'short but most necessary draft for a well-appointed church music, with certain modest reflections on the decline of the same'. Bach does not feel he has enough skilled singers or players to perform church music well enough. Interestingly he seems even more concerned about players than singers, saying that he lacks violins and flutes, which have to be supplied by the university or alumni of the school.

28 October: writes a letter to schoolfriend Georg Erdmann enquiring about possibilities in Danzig. He says that his present post is not as lucrative as he supposed, he has failed to obtain fees pertaining to the office, the place is very expensive, and the authorities are 'very odd and little interested in music, so that I must live among almost continuous vexation, envy, and persecution'. He adds that he can form a vocal and instrumental ensemble from within his family. It does not seem that any answer to this imploring letter was received.

- Hasse, *Artaserse*
- Grandi dies
- Vinci dies
- Clement XII becomes Pope
- Peter II dies; Anna becomes Tsarina
- Death of Frederick IV of Denmark, succeeded by Christian VI

1731

Publication of the six Partitas *Clavierübung 1* in one set; Bach describes himself as Kapellmeister to the court of Weissenfels before that of *Directore Chori Musici Lipsiensis*. It is published as his Opus 1.

Perhaps one Passion and three cantatas are newly written this year, including the famous Cantata 140 *Wachet auf*.

18 March: daughter Christiana Dorothea baptised.

23 March: Good Friday performance of St Mark Passion (BWV 247, music lost).

13 September: probably attends premiere of Hasse's opera *Cleofide*, giving highly praised organ recital the next day.

1 October: matriculation of C. P. E. from university.

- Cannabich born
- Hasse marries Bordoni
- Second treaty of Vienna averts European war
- *The Gentlemen's Magazine* begun in London

1732

4 February: Bach undertakes organ examination in Stöntzch.

5 June: dedication of renovated St Thomas School; Cantata Anh. 18 (music lost).

21 June: sixteenth child, son Johann Christoph Friedrich born.

31 August: daughter Christiana Dorothea dies.

September: travels to Kassel with Anna Magdalena for organ examination and recital (28th) probably including the Dorian Toccata and Fugue.

Walther's *Musicalisches Lexicon* published, describing Bach as 'Sachsen-Weissenfelsischer Capell-Meister'.

- Haydn born
- Marchand dies
- Pergolesi, *Lo frate innamorato*
- Handel, *Ezio* and *Sosarme*
- Protestants from Salzburg go to Prussia

1733

1 February: death of Elector Friedrich Augustus I and beginning of a five-month period of mourning, during which Bach works on the Missa for Dresden.

21 April: Ceremony at Nikolaikirche for loyalty to Friedrich Augustus II.

25 April: Regina Johanna dies aged four.

7 June: Wilhelm Friedemann applies for organist post in Dresden; appointed 23 June.

27 July: Dedication of the Missa BWV 232 to the new Elector of Saxony, Friedrich Augustus II. Bach visits Dresden at the end of July; possibly the Missa was performed in the Sophien-kirche there. He applies for the title of court composer, complaining in his request that he 'has innocently had to suffer one injury or another, and in addition also a diminution of the fees accruing to me in this office'.

3 August: Bach starts a series of secular cantatas in honour of the Elector and his family.

5 November: son Johann August Abraham born; dies the next day.

8 December: Cantata 214 performed.

Acquires Calov Bible and annotates it: for example he writes in the margin of 2 Chronicles: 'In devotional music God is always present in his grace.'

- Böhm dies
- Couperin dies
- Pergolesi, *La serva padrona*
- Rameau, *Hippolyte et Aricie*
- Handel, *Orlando, Arianna in Creta*
- War of the Polish Succession
- Excise Crisis in Britain
- Pope begins *Essay on Man*

1734

17–19 January: Celebrations for the coronation of Friedrich Augustus II continue.

March: Franz Benda visits Leipzig.

June: Lorenz Mizler presents his thesis to Bach and other composers: 'Your instruction in practical music, dear Bach, I have used with great profit.'

3 August: 'solemn music with trumpets and timpani' (identity not known) for the Elector's high name day.

9 September: C. P. E. Bach matriculates from Frankfurt university.

4 October: Rector Gesner leaves Leipzig for Göttingen.

5 October: Cantata 215 performed for the Elector at the Michaelmas Fair.

21 November: Ernesti installed as new rector of the Thomas-schule (Cantata Anh. 19).

25/26/27 December: First performances of parts 1–3 of Christmas Oratorio.

- Gossec born
- Handel, Concerti grossi Op. 3 published
- Voltaire *Lettres philosophiques*
- Hogarth, *The Rake's Progress* begun

1735

Bach turns fifty. He draws up his family tree showing six generations of his musical family, and annotates a family genealogy to accompany the tree: 'Origin of the Bach family of musicians' (see pp. 64–70).

1/2/6 January: parts 4–6 of Christmas Oratorio given first performances.

Clavierübung II published, reinforcing Bach's status as a composer and publisher of keyboard works.

19 May: Ascension Oratorio performed.

June: visits Mühlhausen; examines organ. Johann Gottfried Bernhard Bach appointed organist.

5 September: Johann Christian Bach born.

- Rameau, *Les Indes galantes*
- Eccles dies; Greene Master of the King's Musick
- Handel, *Ariodante*, *Alcina*
- Treaty of Vienna

1736

30 March, Good Friday: revised version of St Matthew Passion performed. A copy of the new version was also written out at this time, with its careful use of different coloured inks.

Easter: provision of new tunes and arrangements for Schemelli's *Musicalisches Gesangbuch*.

July: dispute over the appointment of prefects begins, absorbing a large amount of time.

7 October: Birthday cantata for Friedrich Augustus II, Cantata 206.

19 November: Bach finally achieves his ambition of being made court composer by Augustus, a communication given him by Count Keyserlinck, a friend of the family. This is an honorary, non-resident post.

1 December: Organ recital in the Dresden Frauenkirche on the Silbermann organ.

• Pergolesi, *Stabat mater*; dies same year
• Caldara dies
• Handel, *Atalanta*, *Alexander's Feast*
• James Watt born
• Russo-Turkish War
• Butler, *Analogy of Religion*
• Stanislaus I of Poland abdicates
• Clement XII condemns freemasonry
• Statutes against witchcraft repealed in England

1737
14 January: Johann Gottfried Bernhard appointed organist in Sangerhausen.

4 March: Bach temporarily resigns as director of the Collegium Musicum.

Preparation of *Clavierübung III* for organ.

Nephew Johann Elias comes to live with the family, acting as correspondent and secretary for Bach.

10 April: town council gives opinion on the appointment of prefects.

14 May: Johann Adolf Scheibe's attack on Bach appears. 'This great man is not particularly well up in the sciences that are especially required of a learned composer. How can one be quite without blemishes in his musical work who has not, by

knowledge of the world, qualified himself to investigate and understanding the forces of nature and reason?' This attack on the complexity and bombastic nature of Bach's writing was not altogether unexpected or unusual, but nevertheless seems to have upset Bach considerably. A rather feeble reply the following year by the Leipzig academic Johann Abraham Birnbaum does not seem to have improved matters.

30 October: daughter Johanna Carolina baptised.

12 December: Elector intervenes on Bach's behalf in prefects' dispute.

- Stradivarius dies
- Monteclair dies
- Teatro San Carlo opens in Naples
- Edward Gibbon born
- Salon established in Paris
- Grand Duke of Tuscany dies
- Foundation of Richmond, Virginia

1738

8 January: Birnbaum's defence of Bach against Scheibe.

Spring: C. P. E. appointed harpsichordist to the Crown Prince.

27 or 28 April: *Dramma per musica* performed for betrothal of King and Princess Amalia.

May: visits Dresden.

Johann Gottfried Bernhard amasses debts and absconds.

- Domenico Scarlatti, *Esercizi* published
- John Wesley begins Methodism revival
- Third Treaty of Vienna
- Fund for the support of Decayed Musicians founded in London
- Handel, *Israel in Egypt*, *Saul*

1739

Second book of '48' worked on.

28 January: son Johann Gottfried Bernhard matriculates at Jena University.

Good Friday: Passion performance cancelled in dispute with Council.

> I have gone to Mr. Bach here and have pointed out to the same that the music he intends to perform on the coming Good Friday is to be omitted until regular permission for the same is received. Whereupon he answered: it had always been done so, he did not care for he got nothing out of it anyway, and it was only a burden . . . if an objection were made on account of the text, it had already been performed several times.

27 May: Johann Gottfried Bach dies at twenty-four.
August: Wilhelm Friedemann visits Leipzig and gives concerts with Weiss.
September: organ examination and recital in Altenburg.
Michaelmas Fair: publication of part III of *Clavierübung*.
October: takes over as director of Collegium Musicum again.
In Zedler's Lexicon of 1739 it is said: 'In Leipzig, the Bachian Collegium Musicum is more famous than all the others.'
November: goes to Weissenfels with Anna Magdalena for an undocumented visit and also gives a recital in Altenburg.

- Keiser dies
- Marcello dies
- Dittersdorf born
- Mattheson, *Der vollkommene Capellmeister*
- Rameau, *Dardanus, Les fêtes d'Hébé*
- Moravians established in America
- War of Jenkins' Ear between Britain and Spain
- Hume, *A Treatise on Human Nature*

1740

Bach turns fifty-five. It is perhaps strange that so little is known of Bach's day-to-day activities during his last decade. From this year we have only two written documents. We can deduce that his preoccupation with canon and fugue was building steadily: he probably worked during this year on the second book of the

'48', on the Goldberg Variations, published as *Clavierübung*, and also on early ideas for *The Art of Fugue*.

18 January: a report on three candidates for the assistant's post at the Thomasschule.

24 February: a testimonial on behalf of Schemelli.

17 April: visits Halle.

3 August: Cantata for the name day of Friedrich Augustus II.

- Frederick II of Prussia accedes
- War of the Austrian Succession: Austria and England against France, Prussia and Bavaria
- Pope Clement XII dies; Benedict XIV succeeds
- Paisiello born
- Handel, Concerti grossi Op. 6 published
- First Silesian War; Frederick II of Prussia conquers Austrian province of Silesia

1741

January: a letter from Johann Elias Bach about a score of a bass solo cantata and some canons. Bach solves a puzzle canon by Ricci around this time.

August: trip to the Berlin–Potsdam court of Frederick the Great where C. P. E. has been appointed harpsichord player; he writes the Flute Sonata in E BWV 1035 for the King's Chamberlain.

August: Anna Magdalena falls ill and Johann Elias has to warn Bach to hasten his journey.

30 May: death of Zimmermann, patron of the Collegium Musicum; Bach withdraws from the organisation.

September: publication of *Clavierübung*, nicknamed the Goldberg Variations, at the time of the Michaelmas Fair.

17 November: returns from journey to Berlin with Count Keyserlinck. Perhaps this is the truth of the link between him and the Goldberg Variations: that Bach (not the young Goldberg) played variations from the newly published print to amuse the count on this trip. Sometime after the publication of the Goldbergs, Bach corrects some details in his copy and adds fourteen canons on a back page.

- Fux dies
- Grétry born
- Vivaldi dies
- Quantz to Berlin
- Gluck, *Artaserse*
- Handel, *Deidamia*
- Empress Elizabeth takes over the Russian throne
- Anders Celsius develops a centigrade thermometer scale

1742

22 February: Bach's daughter Regina Susanna baptised.

May: state mourning for Empress Maria Amalia.

30 August: to Kleinzschocher for performance of the Peasant Cantata 212 in homage to Count Heinrich von Dieskau: a rare instance of Bach demonstrating an up-to-date light-hearted musical style.

Works on *The Art of Fugue*; completion of '48' book II.

September: acquires seven volumes of Luther's collected writings in an auction.

31 October: Johann Elias Bach leaves Leipzig.

- Edmund Halley born
- Handel, *Messiah*
- Henry Fielding, *Joseph Andrews*
- Treaty of Berlin
- New opera house at Sanssouci
- C. P. E. Bach Prussian sonatas published
- Hogarth, *Marriage à la Mode*
- Charles VI elected Holy Roman Emperor

1743

All that was thought to survive from Bach's life this year is one liquor tax receipt and one recommendation for a student, Wunsch, in December. But Andreas Glöckner recently found an interesting recommendation signed by Bach for one of the school prefects, Christian Beck, on 18 April. This suggests that there was a scholarship fund for needy students set up by

Mathern Hammer, a native of Bohemia, in 1591, providing endowment funds for four or five years of study. Similar documents survive from 1745 and 1748 for Christian Gottlob Fleckeisen and Johann Wilhelm Cunis; Bach's involvement in this was not previously known.

A group of musical enthusiasts in Leipzig found and sponsor the Grosse Concert, a successor to the Collegium but seemingly less professional.

December: organ examination at the Johanniskirche Leipzig.

- Treaty of Worms between Great Britain, Austria, and Sardinia
- Maria Theresa Queen of Bohemia
- Battle of Dettingen, with George II leading troops
- Boccherini born
- Copenhagen Academy of Science founded

1744

Little is known of Bach's activities during the year, but the Russian scholar Tatiana Shabalina has recently discovered a printed libretto, dated 1744 in Bach's hand, for a revival of the St Mark Passion at the Thomaskirche, in a revised version with two new arias. (The music of this Passion is lost and, it was previously thought, had never been revived after its first performance.)

C. P. E. Bach marries Johanna Maria Dannemann in Berlin.

- Mohammed Ibn Saud founds first Saudi State
- Herder born
- Campra dies
- C. P. E. Bach, Württemberg Sonatas published
- Frederick the Great invades Saxony
- Berkeley, *Siris*

1745

Bach turns sixty. He is a sales agent for his son W. F. Bach's Sonata in D

24 July: Bach reports on the town piper, Pfaffe, who can play all the instruments acceptably.

30 November–25 December: Occupation of Leipzig by Prussian troops.

30 November: first grandchild, Johann August, born.

- Zelenka dies
- Forqueray dies
- Rameau, *La princesse de Navarre*
- Jacobite Rebellions begin
- Death of Charles VII of Bavaria
- Maria Theresa's husband elected Holy Roman Emperor

1746

16 April: Wilhelm Friedemann becomes organist of the Marktkirche in Halle.

7 August: Bach reports on the new organ in Zschortau by Johann Scheibe.

24 September: with Gottfried Silbermann, reports on organ in Naumburg.

- Battle of Culloden, Charles Edward Stuart defeated
- Goya born
- Dresden opera house opens
- Philip V dies; Ferdinand VI becomes King of Spain
- Christian VI of Denmark–Norway dies; succeeded by Frederick V

1747

7–8 May: the most famous encounter of Bach's life takes place in Berlin, see below p. 427 under *The Musical Offering*. It was probably arranged through Keyserlinck. The King's welcome – 'Gentlemen, old Bach is here' – stresses how aged he now was (while not old by our standards, he had already outlived his siblings by some way). Bach returns, fired to produce, in time for the Michaelmas fair, a *Musical Offering* consisting of two fugues, and also canons and a trio sonata in quasi-rococo style.

May: testimonial for Altnickol, performing sometimes as violinist, sometimes cellist, but mostly as vocal bass.

June: finally joins Lorenz Mizler's Corresponding Society of the Musical Sciences. Telemann and Graun were fellow members. He has put this off for some time; one reason might be because he wanted to be the fourteenth member. His Canonic Variations on *Vom Himmel hoch* including his B–A–C–H musical signature, were his contribution to the Society.

7 July: Dedication of *The Musical Offering*.

September: *The Musical Offering* published in unusual format with separate sheets and different sizes for the various sections, in time for the Michaelmas Fair.

October: leases a clavier to Eugen Wenzel.

15 October: the chromatic canon BWV 1077 from the Goldberg set is dedicated to Fulde.

November: organ examination at Thomaskirche Leipzig after restoration.

- First venereal disease clinic opened at London Lock Hospital
- British naval victory at Belle-Isle
- Ahmad Khan founds kingdom of Afghanistan
- Gray, 'Ode on Eton College'
- Franklin, *Plain Truth*
- Bononcini dies
- Handel, *Judas Maccabeus* performed
- Johnson begins his English *Dictionary*

1748

Bach writes recommendations for Altnickol, and Cuntzius, organ builder and instrument maker in Halle.

Publication of Schübler Chorales.

20 March: urgently requests a harpsichord from Martius.

Sales agent for W. F. Bach Sonata in E flat

26 September: son of C. P. E. called Johann Sebastian, baptised in Berlin.

November: letter to his cousin complaining about a cask of wine he sent which got damaged en route.

December: Bach auditions town musicians.

- J. G. Walther dies

- Rameau, *Zaïs*, *Pygmalion*
- Holywell Music Room in Oxford opens
- Cimarosa born
- Treaty of Aix-la-Chapelle ends War of Austrian Succession
- Pompeii rediscovered

1749

Supervises the printing of *The Art of Fugue*; completes B minor Mass.

20 January: Bach's daughter Elisabeth Juliana Frederica, aged twenty-three, marries Johann Christoph Altnickol, aged twenty-nine, in Leipzig.

1 March: canon BWV 1078 for Benjamin Gottlob Faber, a medical student at Leipzig University, using acrostics for FABER and BACH; copied by Kirnberger.

4 April: performance of St John Passion.

6 May: sells a fortepiano to Count Branitzky of Poland.

Bach becomes involved in supporting a musician in Nordhausen against his rector, who was downgrading the position of music in schools.

May: Bach has sudden illness: eye trouble and cataracts.

8 June: Gottlob Harrer given audition for Bach's Leipzig post.

6 October: grandson Johann Sebastian Altnickol baptised; dies and buried 21 December.

30 November: W. F. Bach performs a cantata composed by himself in Leipzig on the First Sunday of Advent.

- Goethe born
- Clérambault dies
- Rameau, *Naïs*, *Zoroastre*
- Handel, *Susanna*, *Solomon*
- Maria Theresa unites Austria and Bohemia

1750

Bach turns sixty-five.

January: son Johann Christoph Friedrich is appointed court musician in Bückeburg.

2 February or 25 March: C. P. E. Bach's Magnificat performed in Leipzig.

28 March/5 April: Bach has eye operations performed by the English surgeon John Taylor, who lectures in Leipzig at the same time. He later also operated on Handel.

4 May: Bach's last pupil, Johann Gottfried Müthel, arrives in Leipzig.

Pentecost: according to a very recent discovery, Bach falls ill and his duties are taken over by the prefect of the first choir, Johann Adam Franck.

22 July: Bach has a stroke and receives last communion.

28 July: Bach dies at 'just after a quarter past eight, in the sixty-sixth year of his life'.

31 July: Bach is buried in the graveyard of the Johanniskirche.

- Cleland, *Memoirs of a Woman of Pleasure* (*Fanny Hill*)
- Frederick the Great, *Oeuvres du Philosophe de Sanssouci*
- Rousseau, *Discours sur les arts et les sciences*
- John V of Portugal dies; Joseph I succeeds
- Göttingen Academy of Science founded

If ever a composer displayed the full power of polyphony, and made artistic use of the most hidden mysteries of harmony, then certainly Bach did; none other has infused such imaginative and various life into these otherwise dry-seeming artifices. He had but to hear a theme to realise instantly how it could be subjected to artistic treatment. His melodies were certainly peculiar; but always different, full of invention, and unlike those of any other composer. His serious temperament inclined him chiefly to laborious, serious, and profound music; yet he could also condescend, when necessary, to a light and jocular manner, especially in his playing . . .

Obituary by C. P. E. Bach and Agricola, trs. Walter Emery

Composers important to Bach

A brief account of some composers whose music Bach worked with, copied out, arranged, or was influenced by.

CARL FRIEDRICH ABEL (1723–1787)
His father Christian Ferdinand was a viol player whom Bach came to know when in the service of Prince Leopold of Cöthen. The sonatas for viola da gamba may have been written for the son, as Carl Friedrich is said by Burney to have been a pupil of Bach's in Leipzig. He later became a close friend of J. C. Bach's in London, where they founded an important concert series together.

TOMMASO ALBINONI (1671–1751)
A composer of popular concertos (and of the small fragment on which the infamous Adagio is based), Albinoni's music was closely studied by Bach, who borrowed some of his fugue subjects and wrote out some of his music – an early example of his interaction with the Italian idiom, before his involvement with Vivaldi's concertos. Bach also apparently used Albinoni's violin works to teach his pupils figured bass.

ELIAS AMMERBACH (c.1530–1597)
One of Bach's predecessors at the Thomaskirche in Leipzig; Bach owned his published volume of organ music, written in tablature, and Bach's earliest organ manuscript is known to follow in this notational tradition.

GIOVANNI BASSANI (c.1657–1716)
Who knows why Bach became interested in the church music of this minor Italian composer? He not only had several Masses of Bassani's copied out, but very late in life wrote a short setting of the words 'Credo in unum Deum' for one of them, using the same plainsong as in the Credo of the B minor Mass, perhaps then being planned.

GEORG BÖHM (1661–1733)

A key influence on Bach's early music, Böhm was organist in Lüneburg where Bach went to school, and (though C. P. E. Bach changed the text of the Obituary to omit the suggestion) surely taught him; the recently discovered earliest manuscript of Bach's was written at Böhm's house in 1700, so he may also have lodged there. Böhm's strongly profiled preludes and chorale partitas influenced Bach's organ style.

NICOLAUS BRUHNS (1665–1697)

A pupil of Buxtehude, Bruhns wrote attractive and vivid organ music in the north German tradition that Bach knew. Mattheson claimed he could play the organ and the violin at the same time . . .

DIETRICH BUXTEHUDE (c.1637–1707)

The most famous story of Bach's youth is of his walking on foot to Lübeck in 1705 to hear Buxtehude play the organ; it is probable however that he also wished to hear (and maybe participate in) the traditional series of Abendmusik concerts that took place in Lübeck in November and December each year. Buxtehude's immensely dramatic organ music was a major influence on the young Bach, and his vocal music too must have made a strong impression. Bach owned much music by Buxtehude in his library and was an important route for the transmission of Buxtehude's works.

ANTONIO CALDARA (c.1670–1736)

As part of Bach's involvement with old-style church music, perhaps in preparation for the B minor Mass, he copied out a Magnificat by this leading Italian composer and added violin parts to one of the movements, presumably for performance in Leipzig. C. P. E. Bach includes Caldara in his list of composers Bach admired.

ARCANGELO CORELLI (1653–1713)

Bach must have known some of the famous Italian composer's published music, but seems to have used it only once, basing an organ fugue on a subject he found in Corelli's Op. 3 No. 4

trio sonata. He is, however, increasingly regarded as a major influence on Bach's early music.

FRANÇOIS COUPERIN (1668–1733)

Traces of a relationship between the Bach family and Couperin are found in a couple of pieces included in Anna Magdalena's keyboard book, and we know that Bach esteemed Couperin's music, remote in style and feeling though it is from his own.

CHARLES DIEUPART (c.1667–c.1740)

A minor French composer who worked in London; Bach copied out his Suites of 1701 some years later, and modelled his own keyboard suites on the sequence of dance-forms that Dieupart used.

JOHANN FRIEDRICH FASCH (1688–1758)

Fasch and Bach just missed each other in Leipzig: Fasch had been educated there and applied for the post of Cantor; he left the city for Zerbst where he worked until he died. It seems that music by Fasch was in the repertory of the Leipzig Collegium Musicum, and at least one arrangement for organ of Fasch's music was formerly thought to be by Bach.

GIROLAMO FRESCOBALDI (1583–1643)

In 1714 Bach made a copy of Frescobaldi's *Fiori musicali*, a famous collection of keyboard music which influenced Bach's own settings for the liturgy; he studied Frescobaldi's music early in life, providing, as Wolff says, 'evidence of his continuing interest in the great keyboard masters of the more distant past'.

JOHANN JACOB FROBERGER (1616–1667)

Among the keyboard music that first made an impression on the young Bach was that of Froberger, whose works were included in the manuscript belonging to his brother that Bach tried to copy, incurring his brother's wrath. Pachelbel taught Froberger's music both to Johann Christoph Bach and to Johann Valentin Eckelt, so it was valued in Middle German circles – for its fugal writing in particular.

JOHANN JOSEPH FUX (1660–1741)

C. P. E. Bach claimed that Bach admired Fux as a composer, but it was as a theorist that he surely had the greatest influence, as his famous treatise *Gradus ad parnassum* was the teaching manual that formed the basis of Bach's interaction with old-style counterpoint. He wrote a Mass with a set of canons that might have influenced the Goldberg Variations.

CARL HEINRICH GRAUN (c.1703–1759)

Both Graun and his brother Johann Gottlieb (c.1702–1771) were highly regarded by Bach in his last years, according to his son C. P. E., and Johann Gottlieb taught Wilhelm Friedemann Bach the violin. One suspects that C. P. E. Bach was closer to them, as Carl Heinrich worked for Frederick the Great: perhaps his music was heard on Bach's famous visit to the court of 1747. Graun's *Der Tod Jesu* became an enormously popular Passion oratorio, in a style far sweeter than Bach's.

NICOLAS DE GRIGNY (1672–1703)

Among the French composers whom Bach admired, de Grigny has assumed importance because Bach copied out his *Premier Livre d'orgue* of 1699. Bach's music echoes his style in its use of rich five-part textures. The British composer George Benjamin has orchestrated one of the de Grigny pieces that Bach copied.

GEORG FRIDERIC HANDEL (1685–1759)

The other outstanding composer of the high baroque, Handel carved out an almost diametrically opposed career to Bach's, concentrating on opera and dramatic oratorio, genres that Bach did not explore. Bach attempted to meet Handel a couple of times, but it never happened (they were linked in their last years by the fact that the dubious English eye surgeon, John Taylor, operated on them both). In their separate ways they synthesised the musical styles of their time to permanent and glorious effect.

JOHANN ADOLF HASSE (1699–1783)

A leading operatic composer in Dresden, Hasse has the distinction of being the only composer whose operatic music we know Bach certainly heard: his opera *Cleofide* was given in September 1731 when Bach was in the city, and Hasse and wife (the famous singer Faustina Bordoni) returned the compliment and attended Bach's organ recital in the city. There is one keyboard piece by Hasse in the Anna Magdalena Bach *Clavierbüchlein*, a Polonaise.

REINHARD KEISER (1674–1739)

Bach performed in Leipzig a St Mark Passion he had used in Weimar, which was at one time attributed to Keiser but now seems unlikely to be by him. Keiser had been a pupil at the Thomasschule in Leipzig and then worked in Hamburg as opera director, where Bach might well have heard his music, but Keiser is not mentioned in Bach's Obituary as an influence.

JOHANN CASPAR KERLL (1627–1693)

One of the composers whom C. P. E. Bach said his father most admired, and also one of those included in the famous anthology that the young Bach tried to copy from his brother's manuscript. At the very end of his life, Bach returned to Kerll's music, adapting the Sanctus from his *Missa superba* as he planned the B minor Mass.

JOHANN KUHNAU (1660–1722)

Bach's immediate predecessor as Thomaskantor in Leipzig was an important precursor of his in various idioms: cantatas, organ music, and what he called *Clavier-Übung*, a form Bach followed. Kuhnau's important *Biblical Stories*, programmatic and narrative keyboard pieces, must have been known to the Bach family. Kuhnau, highly skilled as a lawyer as well as a musician, apparently also showed an interest in numerology, linking Bach to this controversial field.

GIOVANNI LEGRENZI (1626–1690)

Maestro di cappella at St Mark's, Venice, from 1685 to 1690, and an important figure of the Italian baroque. An early organ fugue by Bach, BWV 574, draws on themes from one of his trio sonatas, and though the attribution has been questioned, the definite statement in the Andreas Bach Book is 'Thema Legrenzianum. Elaboratum per Joan Seb. Bach.'

ANTONIO LOTTI (c. 1667–1740)

Lotti is most famous for his eight-part Miserere, and was the well-paid head of the Dresden opera from 1717. Among the Italian compositions whose work Bach studied and copied while in Leipzig, Lotti's *Missa sapientia* was copied by Bach – presumably for performance. Bach might have encountered Lotti or his music while in Dresden for the planned competition with Marchand.

ALESSANDRO MARCELLO (1669–1747)
AND BENEDETTO MARCELLO (1686–1739)

The two Marcello brothers were active in Venice and Bach took one concerto from each of them to arrange for solo keyboard, at the time he was studying and learning from the concerto methods of Vivaldi and his contemporaries.

JOHANN PACHELBEL (1653–1706)

Of all the composers from whom Bach learned, and who also influenced those by whom he was taught, Pachelbel increasingly emerges as crucial, because he was a significant teacher as well as a major composer of the time, with a large body of published work. In him, all the strands of South and Central German keyboard music converge, and Bach's early chorale preludes and chorale partitas appear strongly influenced by Pachelbel's models. He certainly taught Bach's elder brother Johann Christoph, so it is logical that his music is mentioned as having been in the manuscript that the young Bach tried to copy; it is also in the Andreas Bach Book. Bach and he could have met at a family wedding.

GIOVANNI PIERLUIGI DA PALESTRINA (c. 1525–1594)

The classic Renaissance harmoniousness of Palestrina's output would seem to be far away from Bach's idiom. Yet in about 1742 Bach became fascinated by this old style, and wrote accompaniments for the *Missa sine nomine* for bass and continuo, effectively bringing the work up to date for performance: parts were written out for the Kyrie and Gloria, implying it was performed in the Lutheran liturgy, a rather surprising development. A further arrangement of the *Missa Ecce Sacerdos Magnus*, performed around 1745, has been identified by Barbara Wiermann.

GIOVANNI BATTISTA PERGOLESI (1710–1736)

Pergolesi represented the new galant, advanced style of Bach's time, and was most famous for his little opera *La serva padrona*. Bach clearly felt the need to work with this new style: nevertheless it is remarkable to find him during the 1740s transcribing a complete work of Pergolesi's, the famous *Stabat mater* (which had not travelled north of the Alps at this time), and reworking it as a composition with a German psalm text *Tilge, Höchster, meine Stunden*. The arrangement is faithful to a work that mixes old and new styles, with interesting small additions.

JOHANN JOACHIM QUANTZ (1697–1773)

A well-known member of the court of Frederick the Great from 1741, Quantz had earlier been a musician at the Dresden court, where he may well have met Bach and had an impact on Bach's adoption of a more modern, galant style in some of his flute music.

JOHANN ADAM REINCKEN (?1643–1722)

One of the most important influences on the young Bach, Reincken is supposed to have lived until he was nearly a hundred, though recent scholarship has queried his date of birth, thought to be 1623 but more likely 1643. He wrote some of the most ambitious North German keyboard music; in particular, his massive chorale fantasia on *An Wasserflüssen Babylon* must have been known to Bach, who improvised on the same chorale when he met Reincken. Wolff has closely studied the process by which the young Bach took models by Reincken and transformed them into his own early sonatas and fugues.

GOTTFRIED HEINRICH STÖLZEL (1690–1749)

A prolific composer who worked mainly in Gotha; his links with Bach seem increasingly significant: there is a pleasant Partita included in Bach's book for his son Wilhelm Friedemann, and we have now recovered from the shock that one of Bach's best-loved melodies, 'Bist du mei mir', is actually by Stölzel. It now appears that Bach performed a Passion-oratorio by him in 1734 and a cantata cycle in 1735–6.

GEORG PHILIP TELEMANN (1681–1767)

The worlds of Bach and Telemann, a successful and hugely prolific composer, intersected very closely: Telemann studied in Leipzig and in 1702 founded the Collegium Musicum there, which Bach subsequently ran. Telemann then worked in Bach's birthplace, Eisenach, near where Bach was working in Weimar, and C. P. E. Bach later wrote of his father that 'in his younger years he was often with Telemann, who also held me at my baptism' (i.e. was his godparent). Some of Telemann's many cantatas were attributed to Bach in the old Bach edition, but though their styles and genres overlapped at many points the content of their music is quite different. Telemann wrote a touching verse tribute on Bach's death.

GIUSEPPE TORELLI (1658–1709)

An Italian composer of concertos whom Bach studied: he transcribed one of his concertos for harpsichord (BWV 979), though it has also been attributed to Vivaldi. Torelli's concerto style, alongside that of Albinoni and Vivaldi, played an important part in Bach's compositional development.

ANTONIO VIVALDI (1678–1741)

One of the most important and influential composers of the baroque, Vivaldi's status has risen rapidly in recent years, often outstripping Bach's in popular consciousness through works such as the *Four Seasons*. His concertos made an impression on Bach when at Weimar, and it seems likely that Prince Johann Ernst brought copies with him back from Amsterdam. Bach arranged several for solo harpsichord and organ, and learnt much from their style. Later, for the Leipzig Collegium Musicum, he transcribed Vivaldi's fine B minor Concerto for four violins for the unusual combination of four harpsichords.

JOHANN GOTTFRIED WALTHER (1684–1748)

A distant relative of Bach, he was invited to compete for the post at Mühlhausen taken by Bach, but instead became organist in Weimar and teacher of the young Prince Johann Ernst. He wrote about Bach briefly in his *Musicalisches Lexicon* of 1732, for which Bach acted as sales agent.

SILVIUS LEOPOLD WEISS (1687–1750)

One of the most famous lute players and composers of his day, Weiss was in Leipzig in 1739 and visited Bach regularly. We learn that 'very special' music was made at his home during this period, and Bach may have written his lute works with Weiss in mind. Wolff has shown that Bach's Suite in A major for violin and harpsichord BWV 1025 is actually an arrangement of a work by Weiss.

JOHANN PAUL VON WESTHOFF (1656–1705)

A violinist at the Weimar court when Bach first worked there, and a precursor of Bach's in writing music for unaccompanied violin: he published six partitas in 1696, nowhere near as complex as Bach's, but a significant model.

JAN DISMAS ZELENKA (1679–1745)

A fascinating and neglected composer who worked at the Dresden court, he was one of the few baroque composers to produce music of a rugged individuality to rival Bach's. One imagines that Bach would have been in sympathy with the chromatic counterpoint of his trio sonatas for oboes and bassoon, and his vocal Lamentations. His choral music, some of which has been recorded, is less unusual, but still strong and effective. Bach and Zelenka would have been in touch around the time that Bach was writing the 1733 Missa for Dresden, and Bach acquired material from Zelenka's extensive music library.

Performing Bach today:
an autobiography in sound

> In conducting, he was very accurate, and extremely sure in
> the tempo, which he generally took very briskly.

Obituary of Bach by C. P. E. Bach and Agricola

> Bach never dreamed of a performance of the Gloria, the
> Et resurrexit and the Osanna of his B minor Mass by three
> or four hundred voices; nevertheless we may venture to
> perform it in this way, and it has been done successfully.
> We ought to recognise, however that it is all a matter of
> chance. Even with a choir of a hundred and fifty there is
> a danger of lines of the vocal polyphony coming out too
> thickly and heavily in a way directly opposed to the nature
> of Bach's music.

Albert Schweitzer, trans Ernest Newman 1911

> No one who knows Bach intimately will need to be told
> that our plan of compensating for the absence of some ten
> or eleven skilful and sympathetic singers by substituting
> ten or eleven hundred stolid and maladroit ones will not
> answer with his music, however strong-lunged the ten or
> eleven hundred may be.

George Bernard Shaw, *The World*, 1891

> Today we are prepared to accept only the composition
> itself as our source and to represent it on its own merits.
> In particular, we must attempt to hear and to play the
> masterpieces of Bach as if they had never been interpreted,
> as if they had never been shaped or distorted in perfor-
> mance.

Nikolaus Harnoncourt, *The Musical Dialogue*, 1984

Changing styles of Bach performance in recent decades have been a microcosm of the revolution in performance generally. No music lover has been untouched by the seismic changes in our approach to the composer over the last fifty years, and no one who has lived through that period can have failed to be affected by the new perspectives on performance that have opened up during that time – even if to some, as the enlightened Bach scholar Robert Marshall honestly admitted, 'like so many new and unfamiliar experiences, they take a lot of getting used to'.

The stirrings of dissatisfaction with a style of Bach performance that assimilated his music into the conventions of the prevailing mainstream go back at least a century; but they took half a century and more to break through to the wider public. Everyone will have their own story of the evolving reappraisal of what Bach could sound like: we have moved from massive St Matthew Passions by choral societies such as Leith Hill conducted by Vaughan Williams to the airy 'B minor Madrigal' of Joshua Rifkin with a handful of voices, from weighty Brandenburg Concertos by Furtwängler and Karajan to speedy ones by Musica Antiqua Cologne and Il giardino armonico, from Bach on the piano by Myra Hess and Dinu Lipatti and Rosalyn Tureck to Bach on the harpsichord by Wanda Landowska, Ralph Kirkpatrick and Gustav Leonhardt – and then back again to Bach on the piano by András Schiff and Murray Perahia. The pendulum has swung, sometimes gently, sometimes violently, but we now appear to be reaching a more inclusive, more open-minded attitude to performance styles.

The experience can only be essentially personal: Bach on the piano was and is an essential feature of any musician's training: the Minuet in G from the Anna Magdalena Book (which has turned out not to be by Bach!), the Little Preludes in the Associated Board edition, then some of the easier Preludes and Fugues from the '48'. One was taught to create a shapely legato line, with long phrases and sustained sound. The pieces were also object lessons in perfectly formed short compositions, with a luminous sense of rise and fall, activity and repose. Bach featured regularly in the examinations of the Associated Board, usually in vastly over-prescriptive editions. For piano Grade 8 I played some movements from the English Suite No. 3 in G minor, supreme music to encounter – but still presented and articulated as piano music.

It felt odd even then: for me, a revelation at the age of ten or eleven had been hearing George Malcolm play the Gold-berg Variations in Manchester, and encountering a whole different rhetoric which came from the sound of the harpsi-chord (however modern that sounded with Malcolm's pow-erful Goble instrument and his vividly orchestral changes of registration). From then on, I sought out every opportunity to hear that music on the radio and on record: that led back to Wanda Landowska, who performed the Goldbergs on her clanking Pleyel with *da capo* repeats of the first few bars of some canons; Gustav Leonhardt, sober and utterly musical on the harpsichord; and the maverick and wholly individual Glenn Gould on the piano in his innovative, and by then famous, 1955 recording.

I was probably rather behind the times as a northerner in the late 1960s, because although the harpsichord was a fasci-nation, the new world of orchestras of period instruments had not yet begun to penetrate: for me the familiar performances of the Brandenburgs, the Orchestral Suites and the concertos were not symphonic, but modern chamber-orchestra versions by Karl Münchinger with the Stuttgart Chamber Orchestra, Raymond Leppard and the English Chamber Orchestra, or the Academy of St Martin-in-the-Fields and Neville Marriner. Choral thrills on record were more reliably to be gained from the hard-hitting, metrically regular German performances of Karl Richter with his Munich Bach forces: his old 1958 recording of the St Matthew Passion was a benchmark, with Ernst Haefliger and Dietrich Fischer-Dieskau among the soloists. Richter's new recordings of the cantatas in the 1970s were revealing this music even as performance styles were swirling and changing radically around him.

Smaller-scale Bach performances had been gaining ground rapidly: for example, John Tobin's Passions in the 1950s, billed as 'in the chamber-music style of Bach's own performances', and Paul Steinitz's magnificent, pioneering work with the London Bach Society. Even major conductors moved away from the large-scale sound: Otto Klemperer's recording of the B minor Mass used the small forces of the BBC Singers and a slimmed-down Philharmonia. It was at almost the same time that Nikolaus Harnoncourt's seminal B minor Mass, with period instruments and all-male choral voices, appeared on record in 1968. Still, when I arrived in Oxford at the end of the 1960s, the famous Oxford Bach Choir under Sydney Watson was still giving the opportunity for a choir of hundreds to participate in the B minor Mass – and there lay a fundamental paradox, for it was through those large and inclusive amateur performances (open even to those of us whose singing was very limited), that generations came to love the Passions and the Mass. (Watson, I recall, did insist that the huge choir sang softly enough in the 'Qui tollis' of the Mass to allow the pair of solo flutes to be heard, a rare concession to Bach's instrumental balance.)

The 1970s were the years when everything began to shift, and the winds of change blew through performance styles. In Oxford, the redoubtable Lina Lalandi of the English Bach Festival was reflecting changing taste. At first she brought Wolfgang Gönnenwein and Helmut Rilling with their fine Passion performances with traditional forces, but small in number and superbly disciplined. (A Rilling performance of the St Matthew Passion in the beautiful but not soundproof Sheldonian Theatre was interrupted at the height of the second part by the bizarre sound of a brass band processing down the street outside; the conductor had to stop the performance for a few minutes of baffled contemplation.) Roger Norrington directed the B minor Mass with the modern instruments of the Bournemouth Sinfonietta with matchless liveliness; the young James Bowman sang solo cantatas with New College Choir with supreme eloquence. A vital background was sketched into our understanding of Bach by the revivals of the music of his predecessors, notably on the BBC and in concerts by the Schütz Choir under Norrington and the Monteverdi Choir under John Eliot Gardiner.

Then we began to hear what was going on in Europe. The new series of Bach cantata recordings jointly undertaken for Telefunken under Gustav Leonhardt and Nikolaus Harnoncourt from 1971 onwards made a radical impact, and a whole new world was opened up of transparent sounds and dancing textures, skating strings, quirky oboes and burbling bassoons, with boys' voices that were sometimes insecure but always pungent and beautiful. A revolution had begun. Some of the very first recordings in that series represented a coming-together with the English cathedral tradition, and used the Choir of King's College, Cambridge, with whom Leonhardt had collaborated earlier on the music of Purcell. Later recordings moved to the Tölz Boys Choir, with their throaty continental sound, or the Collegium Vocale of Ghent, a light-voiced mixed choir. Reviewers and listeners struggled with the idiosyncrasies of the Harnoncourt–Leonhardt series, and some traditionalists such as Paul Henry Lang denounced their eccentricities, but as they progressed the cantata releases (LPs in sturdy boxes with the huge benefit of complete orchestral scores as well as booklets) became highlights of each year.

The impact of these recordings was all the greater because, although Harnoncourt and Leonhardt had by then been active for almost forty years in the baroque repertory, they had had far too little presence in Britain. Very early in the 1950s, even before the formation of Concentus Musicus and the Leonhardt Consort, the two musicians and their two wives had joined forces with the English counter-tenor Alfred Deller in a recording of the Agnus Dei from the B minor Mass and Cantata 54. This was part of the important initiative of The Bach Guild, which followed the Vienna celebrations of Bach in 1950 by creating pioneering recordings of the choral works. Harnoncourt's recording of the Brandenburgs appeared as early as 1964, and then there were versions by the Collegium Aureum and Leonhardt. Adventurous concert promoters brought over some of those pioneers in my first years in London in the early 1970s: I can recall some of those moments as if they were yesterday – Gustav Leonhardt and Sigiswald Kuijken playing Bach (and Kuijken alone the unearthly Biber Chaconne for solo violin) in St John's Smith Square; the counter-tenor René Jacobs and flautist Barthold Kuijken duetting in the Purcell Room, Leonhardt joined by Frans Brüggen on flute and recorder in sonatas and suites. These few individual events – there will equally have been many more for others – were the ones that persuaded me that a new rhetoric, a new sound and a whole new approach to Bach's music could pay rich dividends.

Lina Lalandi was among the first to respond to these new waves of performance style and quickly imported some of the leading lights to her English Bach Festival in both Oxford and London. Ton Koopman and Philippe Herreweghe shared the direction of a couple of memorable St John Passions, with Herreweghe conducting the choruses and Koopman directing the arias from the keyboard (before they went their own ways and became rivals rather than collaborators). Both went on to record Bach cantatas very distinctively with their own forces: Koopman began a complete cycle on Erato which then continued on Challenge Classics, full of fire and incisiveness; Herreweghe's more mellow and lyrical accounts flourished on Harmonia Mundi, where they were planned around the seasons of the liturgical year.

It was a pity that more collaborations were not established at this time between the continental pioneers and English forces, though I recall a single Leonhardt concert of Bach cantatas with the Schola Cantorum of Oxford in the Spitalfields Festival that hinted at a possible new, flexible style. The mid-1970s saw the establishment of the baroque orchestras in Britain that would take Bach into new realms. Trevor Pinnock and the English Concert were at the forefront of Bach performance and recorded the Brandenburgs, the Suites and Concertos. John Eliot Gardiner recorded the Orchestral Suites, while Christopher Hogwood traversed the concertos, and by this time the revolution was here to stay.

Experimentation with an appropriate choral sound to match the innovations brought by period instruments was more tricky. In 1975 Roger Norrington, always a pioneer in this area, gave the St Matthew Passion in St Andrew's Holborn in London – a revelatory small-scale performance using baroque strings but modern wind instruments, with the voices of the Schütz Choir. He followed this up and first gave the St John Passion with boys' voices and period instruments two years later, in the Church of St Bartholomew-the-Great. Martin Neary, at Winchester Cathedral, gave the first complete period-instrument St Matthew Passion. Andrew Parrott and his Taverner Choir and Consort became expert in the small-scale performance of the B minor Mass, which they later recorded using solo voices that matched, rather than contrasted with, the timbre of the choir: an exemplary lesson in balance and sound that others were slow to learn.

The English reaction to Joshua Rifkin's radical theories of Bach performance has been mixed. On the one hand, given that the principle of small-scale performance had been well established here, a move to strictly one-to-a-part performance was not as revolutionary for us as for others. Parrott embraced it; Paul McCreesh followed with a solo-led recorded St Matthew Passion. Others have maintained a less radical approach. The 250th anniversary of Bach's death in 2000 stimulated the huge undertaking of John Eliot Gardiner's Bach Pilgrimage, performing the cantatas on their appropriate liturgical Sundays in European churches, including many associated with Bach himself: a vast and quixotic undertaking that stretched the resources of his organisation to the utmost, but has resulted in a permanent legacy of memorable, well-documented performances on disc. He maintained a three- or four-to-a-part basis for his chorus, achieving results of great clarity and expressiveness within the choral tradition.

In the 1980s and 1990s the period-instrument movement moved so rapidly into Beethoven and beyond that the task

of reinterpreting great baroque masterpieces had less prominence. In recent years, as in all areas of the historical performance movement, there has been a more flexible approach to
performance style. Harnoncourt has re-recorded major works
and some cantatas with a quite large, mixed-voice Arnold
Schoenberg Choir alongside his Concentus Musicus Vienna.
Sigiswald Kuijken with his Petite Bande has made one-to-a-
part cantata recordings, as has Christophe Coin. There are
beautiful, intimate, small-scale recordings of Bach and his
predecessors by the lutenist Konrad Junghänel and his Cantus
Cölln. Some of the liveliest new entrants in the field have been
the Italian baroque groups, Il Giardino Armonico with their
highly praised Brandenburgs, and Rinaldo Alessandrini with
his Concerto Italiano in versions of *The Art of Fugue* and *The
Musical Offering*. The most recent distinctive vocal recordings
have been those by the Dunedin Consort under the leading
British Bach scholar John Butt, whose St Matthew Passion
and B minor Mass (2010) have won high praise.

In the field of keyboard recordings there has been a balance between the harpsichord and the piano, with a predomi-
nant feeling that the piano, for so long outlawed by the more
dogmatic areas of the historical performance movement, was
now coming back into its own. When artists as outstanding as
András Schiff and Murray Perahia take up the Partitas, and
Maurizio Pollini and Daniel Barenboim *The Well-tempered
Clavier*, they make music on their own terms. That rapproche-
ment has also taken place to a lesser extent in orchestral performance: that Simon Rattle should tackle the St John Passion
and the St Matthew Passion with the Berlin Philharmonic
(see above) is a sign of the times, and Riccardo Chailly as
the new music director of the Leipzig Gewandhaus in Bach's
own city has embarked on a major exploration of Bach. Two
hundred and sixty years after the composer's death, Bach performance seems to grant equal status to modern and period-
style performances: in the Bach Festival Leipzig in 2010 a new
orchestration of the Goldberg Variations was performed by
the Leipzig Gewandhaus Orchestra, and Harrison Birtwistle

unveiled a major new work inspired by Bach, *Angelfighter*. The BBC Proms in the summer of 2010 gave a Bach day that ranged from John Eliot Gardiner's Brandenburg Concertos on period instruments, an organ recital with original works and transcriptions, and Andrew Litton conducting the technicolour arrangements of Bach by Stokowski, Respighi, Wood, Sargent and Bantock, to new reflections on the string music of Bach from young composers Tarik O'Regan and Alissa Firsova.

Inspired by Bach: some transcriptions

♫ *Bach Transcribed by Busoni, Liszt, Berners, Hess, Kempff, Rachmaninov* Gordon Fergus-Thompson (piano)
ASV DCA 759

♫ *Bach Organ Transcriptions* Percy Grainger (piano)
Biddulph LHW 010

♫ *Bach Arrangements* Angela Hewitt (piano)
Hyperion CDA 67309

♫ *Bach Piano Transcriptions* Piers Lane (piano)
Hyperion CDA 67344

♫ *Stokowski's Symphonic Bach* BBC Philharmonic/Bamert
Chandos 9259

♫ *Bach Transcriptions by Elgar, Mahler, Schoenberg, Stokowski, Webern* LA Philharmonic/Salonen
Sony Sk89012

♫ *Bach Transcriptions by Respighi, Bantock, Honegger, Reger, Vaughan Williams, Raff, Holst, Schoenberg* BBC Philharmonic/Slatkin
Chandos 9835

♫ *Twentieth-century Bach: Virtuoso Orchestral Transcriptions*
Boston SO/Ozawa
Philips 432 092-2

♫ *Jazz Sebastian Bach* The Swingle Singers
Philips 824 703-2

♫ *Kurtág: Játékok* György and Márta Kurtág (piano)
ECM 1619

BACH: THE MUSIC

The criterion for inclusion in this part of the book is essentially that listeners are likely to find the work performed and recorded under Bach's name. Works that are currently of doubtful authenticity are listed with a question mark, and many minor works are omitted. The problems of authenticity, particularly for Bach's early works, are very great: the circumstances from which he emerged make it difficult to distinguish between his early work and that of his colleagues. There was a period in which dubious works were ruthlessly excluded by scholars from the canon, and anything that could not be shown to be by Bach was relegated to the Anhang (appendix) of his catalogue. Recent scholarship has tended to be more inclusive, and to ask questions about Bach's possible authorship rather than deciding the answers. This may well have been a reaction to a couple of the discoveries outlined below, where works once thought not to be by Bach have turned up in his autograph or that of his close relations, with reliable attributions.

Bach's music encompassed such an encyclopedic variety of genres and styles that it is a challenge for listeners to orientate themselves among the wealth of compositions. The only significant area of music that he did not cultivate was opera, and some argue that his output was limited by that. Others respond, however, that a work like the St Matthew Passion covers an even greater range of expressive styles and genres than the opera of the time.

To help to orientate us, though at the risk of over-simplifying vastly, here is a chronological approach to Bach's changing preoccupations in his music, which are partly but not totally related to his places of work:

BACH: A MUSICAL TIMELINE OF GENRES

Keyboard music ➤ Organ chorales
*c.*1695–1705

As Bach begins to study the keyboard, his earliest works are chorale-based pieces for harpsichord or organ, early suites, and some free toccata-type compositions.

Keyboard music ➤ Cantatas ➤ Organ collections
*c.*1705–16

Bach develops his keyboard skills with extensive keyboard compositions, and begins to write cantatas for special occasions. After the move to Weimar in 1708, organ music dominates, and following his promotion there in 1714 he begins to write monthly cantatas. His first attempt at a major collection is the *Orgelbüchlein*, a collection for the liturgical year that remains unfinished around 1713–16.

Virtuoso instruments ➤ Solo suites ➤ Keyboard collections
*c.*1716–23

This is the first period of instrumental virtuosity: with the forces at his disposal in Cöthen he compiles or composes the Brandenburg Concertos, and explores the highest reaches of individual accomplishment in the suites for solo violin and solo cello. Organ music becomes more virtuosic. Cantatas recede in importance in Cöthen. He continues to work on keyboard music: the French and English Suites and the first book of the '48'.

Cantatas ➤ Passions ➤ Keyboard instruction ➤ Publications
*c.*1723–9

Having arrived in Leipzig in 1723, he is now at the height of his commitment to the cantata, writing one weekly and producing several cantata cycles and the St John and St Matthew Passions. He is beginning to work on teaching materials for his children, and on the Six Partitas and the *Clavierübung* Part II, collections of keyboard works for publication.

Instrumental works ➤ Church music collections
*c.*1729–39
A change of direction is signalled by the move of his activities to the Collegium Musicum, and the cultivation of new and newly arranged instrumental music for those concerts: virtuosity but now within an orchestral context. He continues to assemble church compositions in the lost St Mark Passion of 1731, the Missa of 1733 and the Oratorios of 1734 onwards for Christmas, Easter and Ascension, and revises the St Matthew Passion in 1736.

Keyboard collections ➤ Fugue and canon
*c.*1739–46
The publication of *Clavierübung III* for organ and the Goldberg Variations for two-manual harpsichord; completion of Book 2 of the '48'. This leads to an increasing fascination with canon and fugue, with the compilation of the early version of *The Art of Fugue*, later expanded.

Counterpoint ➤ Mass
*c.*1745–50
The writing of *The Musical Offering*, and reworking *The Art of Fugue* for publication; the study of older music and editing works by the Bach family for performance; and finally the compilation of the B minor Mass.

[Admire] . . . how with both hands, and using all his fingers, he plays the clavier . . . or that instrument of instruments, whose innumerable pipes are animated by bellows; how he flies over the keys this way with both hands, and that way with his nimble feet and, unaided, calls forth a plurality of quite different passages that yet harmonise with each other . . . [he] keeps thirty or forty musicians in order, one by a nod, another by stamping time with his foot, and a third with a warning finger, and joins in with his own voice now in a high part, now in a lower one, and again in a middle one; and how he alone, when they are all working together at their loudest – although he has the hardest task of all – yet at once notices when and where something is wrong, and keeps them all together, and watches everything, and if there is any hesitation restores certainty; how rhythm is in every limb of him; how his quick ear grasps every harmony, and he himself reproduces each voice within the small compass of his own.

From a note to Johann Matthias Gesner's version of *Institutiones variae* of Quintilian, 1738

SACRED MUSIC

Church music

Mass in B minor BWV 232

To begin at the end, the so-called Mass in B minor is one of the most mysterious, and at the same time one of the most universal, of Bach's creations. Its ultimate purpose is veiled yet it is exultantly direct in its communication. We cannot be sure why, in the last decade of his life, Bach devoted so much time and effort to bringing together a collection of music that precisely matches the needs of the Roman Catholic Ordinary of the Mass. He had drawn together the Kyrie and Gloria as a Missa – that is, a short Mass, consisting of those two movements alone, as included in the Lutheran liturgy – for Dresden in 1733, and had maintained good relations with such composers there as Jan Dismas Zelenka. So it must be possible that he was hoping that the full work might be taken up in Dresden. (Bach calls his Credo the 'Symbolum Nicenum', which was also a description of the text that Zelenka used.) What were the opportunities for its performance? None of the theories seems quite convincing: it is surely too restricting to suggest a specific event such as the dedication of the Hofkirche (eventually opened after Bach's death, in 1751) or the St Cecilia Day's celebrations. There has been some recent excitement about the possibility if a Viennese connection to the origins of the B minor Mass. In March 1749, Count Johann Adam von Questenberg, who had his court in Moravia, was in contact with Bach; he had been a member of a 'Musical Congregation', founded in 1725, a kind of Viennese brotherhood whose members consisted mainly of wealthy music patrons (such as the princes of Esterházy) and a large section of the imperial court orchestra. The society met in St Stephen's Cathedral in Vienna every year on St Cecilia's Day, 22 November, to celebrate a musical High Mass. Contemporary accounts tell us that this always lasted several hours and was performed by the most famous virtuosos. A work like Bach's Mass in B minor could have fitted well, and there was at least one Mass by a Viennese composer performed by the Society in the early 1740s which displays formal parallels with Bach's Mass. But this remains highly speculative.

The B minor Mass has had a remarkably bad press from those who regard it as a confusing and inconsistent work: Denis Arnold went so far as to exclaim, 'What a ragbag! It is also an impractical ragbag.' Yet we can be absolutely sure from the surviving material that Bach did not intend this as a merely abstract work, but as a collection of music for performance, and he made changes in the material as he revised (changing the voice parts in the Sanctus, for example). Nor should the Catholic aspects of this compilation be over-emphasised at the expense of the Lutheran: there was a strong continuing presence of Latin texts (or Greek in the case of the Kyrie) in the Lutheran liturgy, and both the Kyrie and Gloria 'Missa' texts, as well as the Sanctus, were used in Leipzig. Up until the 1730s, however, Bach had preferred to direct his energies in Leipzig into cantatas rather than masses: the only Latin work he set beside a couple of Sanctuses was the Magnificat, written for Vespers.

For all the splendour and variety of Bach's annual cantatas, Bach had not until the 1730s assembled any major collection of his sacred music. He had gathered keyboard music in the '48' and the *Clavierübung*, he was to gather chamber music in *The Musical Offering*, and was working on the collection of contrapuntal material in *The Art of Fugue*. He created three sacred Oratorios, for Christmas, Easter and Ascension in the 1730s. The assembly of a major testament for performance in the field of sacred vocal music must have been a priority for him as he entered his last decade. It is surely most persuasive to regard the B minor Mass as Bach's last bringing-together of his achievements in sacred music, in the most tangible form that was available to him: that of the Catholic liturgy.

We have to agree that Friedrich Smend, who produced the much criticised edition of the work as the initial volume of the

Neue Bach Ausgabe, was correct in saying that Bach never called this work a Mass or gave it any overall title: his beautifully copied manuscripts have four sections, numbered and titled separately. These groupings are of special interest because they show that Bach's love of symmetry and logical grouping was more important than faithfulness to the liturgical function of the text. Indeed, by separating out the Sanctus from the following sequence of 'Osanna, Benedictus, Agnus Dei and Dona nobis pacem', Bach was respecting the Lutheran nature of the Sanctus as a text on its own. To break the work after the Sanctus, regrouping the six-part choir as an eight-part choir, is perfectly logical in musical if not in liturgical terms.

However, other aspects of Smend's work were suspect. He came from a family of Lutheran theologians and rejected any implication that Bach could here have been writing a work for the Catholic liturgy. He ignored the Dresden connections, excluding the dedication of the original 1733 Missa and the interesting variants of the performing parts in that version (of which the most notable are the galant rhythms in some instrumental parts of the 'Domine Deus'). In the end, the *Neue Bach Ausgabe* has admitted the inadequacy of Smend's single view by publishing in 2005 the 1733 version of the Missa from the Dresden sources, as well as earlier versions of the Sanctus and the curious discovery of the start of the Credo written out in G major rather than A, by Bach's pupil Altnickol. It is now planning a new edition as part of the revised *NBA*.

As George Stauffer has pointed out, it was specifically the aspects of the Mass that took it beyond the Lutheran tradition – its Latin text and liturgical elements – that ensured that it travelled far and wide and was one of the first choral works to become established internationally. As Christoph Wolff reminds us, this Mass more than any other piece of Bach's 'provides an instance of the case that the questions posed by a work are simultaneously a reflection of the many levels of complexity in the creator's artistic intentions'.

John Butt points out that C. P. E. Bach's Magnificat was performed in Leipzig in 1749, and refers directly to the Mass

– does this point to the Mass itself having been performed, or to the opposite, a family tribute making use of unperformed material? In either case Emanuel clearly valued the Credo of the B minor Mass, because he altered it in the manuscript (giving rise to plenty of confusion for subsequent editors) and performed it in 1786 at a concert in Hamburg. The Mass was highly valued by those who came after Bach: Christoph Nichelmann printed the opening bars with an admiring commentary as early as 1755 in a treatise. Others copied and studied the work: one of those copies from the circle of Johann Philipp Kirnberger, the Bach pupil, came to Charles Burney and thus to England, creating a new family of manuscripts which Yo Tomita has studied. Baron van Swieten had a copy in Vienna, as did Haydn, and Beethoven tried to acquire a copy unsuccessfully. Clearly the fame of the 'Great Mass' went before it, and when Nägeli announced its publication (which he did not achieve until 1833), it was proclaimed as 'the greatest musical work of all times and peoples', a verdict that has proved surprisingly resilient.

The tonal structure of the Mass essentially moves from B minor to D major, moving around those twin poles:

Missa
Kyrie: B minor – D – F sharp minor
Gloria: D – A – D – G – B minor – D
Symbolum Nicenum
Credo: A – G – B minor – E minor – D – A –
                        F sharp minor – D
Sanctus
Sanctus: D
Osanna, Benedictus, Agnus Dei et Dona nobis pacem
Osanna etc: D – B minor – D – G minor – D

Missa

Bach wrote this most elaborate of his settings of the Lutheran Mass texts in Latin as an offering to the Elector of Saxony in 1733: he hoped to obtain the post of court composer, and an honorary title was eventually granted to him in 1736. The period of writing probably coincided with the death of Augustus the Strong at the start of 1733, followed as it was by five months of mourning in which musical performances were forbidden.

For many there is no more arresting opening in all music than the beginning of Bach's Kyrie, a solemn call based directly on Luther's own melodic formulation of the Kyrie in his *Deutsche Mass* of 1526 – and so a gesture that immediately places the work in the context of Lutheran history. Robert Marshall thinks this introduction was added after the fugue, based on some earlier source, was completed. Wolff has pointed out the similarities of the first Kyrie to a Mass by the obscure composer Johann Hugo von Wilderer, which was composed in 1729–31 and which Bach copied out, and it is also clear that the chromaticism in the Kyrie's winding subject is similar to that in a Mass by his Dresden colleague Zelenka. But these links only serve to emphasise how superbly Bach develops his own theme: Wilderer follows the repeated notes on 'Kyrie' with four more repeated notes on 'eleison', whereas Bach takes the four initial notes as a jumping-off point for his expressive chromatic theme.

The first Kyrie with five-part choir builds its entries starting with the tenor, and then reverses the process, building up from the bass. The winding line of the subject unfolds inexorably, with a perfect arc shape. Listen out in the central orchestral interlude for a lovely entry of the theme in shining D major in the second violins. The 'Christe eleison' brings two soloists to picture the more human side of the appeal for mercy in florid figuration. Here there seems to be a conscious attempt to reflect the latest galant musical styles fashionable in Dresden, flowing and harmonious with roulades and flattened sevenths.

Then there is a conscious reversion to the *stile antico* in the second Kyrie fugue, in F sharp minor: a chromatic subject doubled by instruments but not elaborated. The shape of the fugue subject seems visually to trace the outline of a cross, a device that will recur at the start of the St John Passion. The F sharp major close leads straight to the opening of the Gloria, a 3/8 Vivace with trumpets, derived from an earlier piece: Smend suggested a concerto but there is no reason why it should not have been a secular cantata. One of the most extraordinary passages – fully present in 1733 but very forward-looking – is the transition to 'Et in terra pax', the vocal theme emerging like lapping waves from the texture, then leaving the instruments to develop the material so that the vocal fugue, when it finally arrives, seems the most natural thing in the world, rhapsodic and beautifully shaped. After instrumental interruptions the vocal fugue returns reinforced by instruments – are more voices called for here? The movement is not long, but perfectly paced.

The symmetrical structure of the Gloria has been differently described by commentators, but Robin Leaver with his close knowledge of the Lutheran liturgy suggests that the opening linked movements are a Lutheran biblical hymn, and the following movements are a liturgical hymn arranged symmetrically:

Laudamus te	soprano 2 solo with violin
Gratias agimus	chorus
Domine Deus	soprano 1/tenor duet with flute
Qui tollis	Chorus
Qui sedes	alto solo with oboe d'amore
Quoniam tu solus sanctus	bass solo with horn
Cum sancto spiritu	chorus

It is surely deliberate and symbolic that each voice has a role in this setting: soprano 1, soprano 2, tenor, alto and bass, while each area of the orchestra provides an obbligato instrument (the exposed horn line in the 'Quoniam tu solus sanctus' poses a notorious challenge to players). The 'Laudamus te' has the most elaborate and decorative obbligato in line with the up-to-date galant style in Dresden; then the 'Gratias agimus', reworking a movement from Cantata 29 of 1731, is one of Bach's most powerful fugues: the four-part texture is at first doubled by the instruments, with the trumpet reserved for the soprano line, but then in a heart-stopping moment the two trumpets enter with independent lines over the top of the vocal texture and resume this stratospheric duetting as the movement reaches its climax.

The next movement is the duet 'Domine Deus', which shows the most evidence of Dresden habits with its much discussed unequal notes in the flute solo which were ignored by Smend (it was Gerhard Herz who found them in the orchestral parts of other sections of the movement too). The lilting, rocking, harmonious thirds in this music are entirely consistent with Bach's attempts at progressive style. As the Gloria linked to the 'Et in terra pax', so this movement leads directly into the 'Qui tollis', at the centre of the symmetrical scheme, where two flutes duet in semiquavers over the falling lines in the choral parts; this movement is based on the opening movement of Cantata 46 of 1723, but with careful revisions. The 'Qui sedes' brings the oboe d'amore to the fore, and then (marked *sequitur* in the score) the most unusual 'Quoniam tu solus' with its unique complement of solo horn with two bassoons at the top of their register. What the origins of this remarkable aria are it's difficult to say, but William Scheide has been trawling the sources for pieces with texts that might fit, and suggests a link for this (and the 'Laudamus te') in the lost wedding cantata BWV Anh. I 14. From the 'Quoniam tu solus' the music races seamlessly into the final 'Cum sancto spiritu' with a sense of concentrated excitement rarely equalled in Bach's output. The first section closes, and then the tenor intones a leaping fugue subject with rising sequences which is subject to ever closer overlapping entries as the movement reaches its abrupt end; the trumpets, generally kept in reserve, suddenly burst into life in the final bars, and the timpani are saved until very late too: an utterly thrilling management of musical resources. (The material of this Gloria was also reused in the shorter Cantata 191 which was assembled for performance in Leipzig during Christmas Vespers between 1743 and 1746, probably the first stage of the revision that led to the Mass.)

Symbolum Nicenum

The Bach scholar Yoshitake Kobayashi says that the writing of the Credo and the following movements in the manuscript comes from the period August 1748 to September 1749, which is at the very end of Bach's creative life. Yet his sense of innovation continues: Bach had presumably never written a Credo before, though there must have been some pre-history to the music of this movement, and a recent discovery of a version of the first movement written out in G rather than A confirms this. Bach also experimented with other composers' settings: he provided a Credo intonation to a Mass by Bassani in 1747 or 1748. There is every reason to suppose that Bach regarded this Credo as a personal statement of the highest importance to him.

There is a fascinating question raised by the autograph score at the end of the 'Patrem omnipotentem' where Bach notes the number of bars in the movement, eighty-four. It has often been wondered how consciously Bach incorporated both his own name B–A–C–H and his own number symbolism BACH = 14 into his music. Eighty-four is fourteen times six. Though many doubts have been cast on the wilder conclusions of number symbolism by the scholarly work of Ruth Tatlow, not all of this hypothesis can be excluded, even if it is in the end not important. It may indicate something of what Bach intended to express: in the same number alphabet (not the only one that was used at the time), CREDO = 43, and there are precisely forty-three repetitions of the word Credo in the first movement; the first two movements together have 129 bars (43 x 3), as does the 'Et exspecto' through to the end of the Credo – perhaps expressing the Trinitarian belief in one God, and the association of Bach the composer with that fundamental truth.

Whether or not one accepts the literal symbolism, the evident design of the symmetry is very striking. Bach originally planned three groups of movements:

Credo in unum Deum
Patrem omnipotentem

Et in unum Dominum
Crucifixus
Et resurrexit

Et in spiritum sanctum
Confiteor
Et exspecto

But then he decided at a very late stage to interpolate another movement, removing the words 'Et incarnatus est' from the end of the 'Et in unum Dominum' and setting them in a separate movement. This created a new symmetrical structure:

Credo in unum Deum	chorus fugue in *stile antico*
Patrem omnipotentem	chorus (concerted)
Et in unum Dominum	duet
Et incarnatus est	chorus
Crucifixus	chorus
Et resurrexit	chorus
Et in spiritum sanctum	solo
Confiteor	chorus fugue in *stile antico*
Et exspecto	chorus (concerted)

This revision also implies that the new movement 'Et incarnatus', whether or not it draws on an adaptation of an earlier work, must be among the very last things Bach completed. It is indeed highly original, and striking confirmation that it is late in style is given by the radical way in which the subject changes on its different appearances (see below).

Under the inexorable tread of the continuo bass, the plainsong Credo is intoned by all five voices in imitation, to which the two violins then add their own independent entries (as the trumpets did in the 'Gratias agimus'), intensifying the texture in the final bars. The 'Patrem omnipotentem' is derived from Cantata 171 of 1729, where the text is analogous, but there are considerable revisions. The energy and drive are superbly paced: the trumpet is given another high independent solo part, with second trumpet and drums joining only at the end.

The 'Et in unum Dominum' in its final form (not, confusingly, the one Smend included in the main text of his edition, but found in an appendix) is a duet at very close imitation, with a contrast of articulations: the first violins and oboe d'amore have a phrase marked staccato, followed by the second and oboe d'amore with the same figure slurred. This pair of articulations also occurs in the famous Largo of the Concerto for two violins, where – as is surely the case here – there is a deliberately symbolic demonstration of the creation of unity from diversity. The last section of the movement is quite different, with a falling figure that was clearly written (or adapted) to represent the words 'Et incarnatus est' with a slide into E flat at 'Et homo factus est'. But Bach, perhaps because of his very unfamiliarity with setting these crucial words, recognised that they were inadequate for this text. So he added the new movement and (restless as ever in the quest for perfection) took the opportunity to revise the old one, adding a glorious high A for the soprano on the word 'Jesus' that does not appear in the other version.

The inner symmetry of the Credo begins with the added 'Et incarnatus', with the imitative entries over a sighing orchestral texture (which Wolff thinks might have been suggested by Bach's work on adapting Pergolesi's *Stabat mater* in 1746–7). The vocal entries are of a new modulating kind: the first spanning an octave, the second a seventh, and the third (the soprano entry) an expressive diminished seventh. (This very new idea late in the life of the counterpoint is exactly mirrored in the Contrapunctus 4 that Bach added late to *The Art of Fugue*, with its modulating entries.) It achieves a piercing emotional effect as the sopranos rise to an entry on

G sharp, the highest vocal note in the movement. 'Et homo factus' is set off at the end as a separate cluster of brief and eloquent entries. The heart of the Credo is the 'Crucifixus', the triple time of the 'Et incarnatus' maintained but over a throbbing chromatic bass line. Astonishingly, this is the oldest music identified in the piece, the first chorus of Cantata 12 from the Weimar years of 1714. Bach may have recalled it because it contained a cross motif, and the text 'Weinen, Klagen' was perfectly apposite to its new circumstances. The bass line is a common currency used by Vivaldi and many others, and Bach is here paying homage to his seventeenth-century predecessors, but the expressiveness goes further. The choir is now reduced to four parts and the chromatic final bars, 'Et sepultus est', are unaccompanied except by continuo.

The 'Et resurrexit' bursts like sunlight on the scene; the immediate choral outburst (a concerto introduction has surely been dropped in favour of this immediacy) is taken up by the instruments and then developed upwards from the bass line in acclamatory style. This movement must be a parody, but it is so well done we cannot quite tell whether it is an instrumental sinfonia or perhaps a secular cantata that has provided the model (some favour the cantata for Augustus I, BWV Anh. 9). Certainly the word-setting is odd in places: the setting of 'Et ascendit' cannot have been written for this text, rising to its peak at 'dexteram Dei Patris'. There is a brilliant and isolated bass passage of great virtuosity, before the ritornello returns set to 'cujus regni non erit finis' – at which point Bach allows himself a fully instrumental conclusion. 'Et in spiritum sanctum' is set as a lilting 6/8 movement for a pair of oboes d'amore, and though the word-setting here has also been criticised, and was revised by C. P. E. Bach, the affect of the music suits the serene mood of the text. (But for Schweitzer, reflecting an older tradition, it was 'perfunctory and quite nonsensical'.)

The 'Confiteor', the second movement in *stile antico*, must have been conceived especially for this setting. The choir creates a tapestry of strict counterpoint over a walking bass (like an organ chorale prelude before the melody enters) until – first almost unnoticeably in the bass – the 'Confiteor' plainsong creeps in, answered by the altos, and then declaimed by the tenors in ever bolder, longer chant. Suddenly the music collapses, all certainty gone, in bars that are the most dramatically forward-looking Bach ever wrote. The last 'peccatorum' becomes a diminished seventh, and 'Et exspecto' reaches into the wilderness beyond harmony, as if the moment of waiting for the Resurrection is to last an eternity. Haydn's 'Representation of Chaos' here meets Mozart's 'Dissonance' Quartet, with an almost Mahlerian intensity. A semitone clash between sopranos underlies the unbearable tension, but then the music resolves onto a downwards scale of D and the timpani and trumpet fanfares of a renewed and now exultant 'Et exspecto' blast in to take over. This is a disturbing and unique passage which takes Bach right into the nineteenth century (and which provides one of the great moments on Karajan's first recording).

'Et exspecto' is now reworked as rising fourths, confident and bold (derived from an earlier group of cantatas, BWV 120, 120a and 120b, which are lost) – wonderfully concentrated and shorn of all unnecessary material. Butt aptly praises the 'impression of a work which seems to contain twice the amount of music that its duration would normally allow'. The end, as with the Gloria, is rapid and pungent, the accumulated intensity released with a dramatic flourish.

Sanctus

The Sanctus was originally composed in Leipzig for Christmas Day 1724 and uses a six-part choir. It makes extensive use of triplets, three voices, and groups of three instruments so that the Trinitarian symbolism is impossible to overlook: even the succeeding 'Pleni sunt coeli' section is in triple time. The Lutheran origin is confirmed by the final word: 'Terra gloria *eius*', rather than the 'tua' heard in all Catholic mass settings. There is something overwhelming about this music from the very first moment, sweeping us along with relentless impetus and intensity. Donald Tovey described the 'swinging censers' of the three-part writing, marked by the powerful descending bass line and repeated fanfares on the first two notes of the bar; a fine performance will highlight the climactic moment where the first trumpet breaks into triplets just before the end. The 'Pleni sunt coeli' fugue, by contrast, is a romp. There are three oboes needed for the first time, which would have been played by those who played oboes d'amore earlier.

Osanna, Benedictus, Agnus Dei et Dona nobis pacem

This final grouping of the Mass is the most controversial: although these movements would have appeared in this order, they are not linked in this way liturgically. In the Catholic liturgy the 'Osanna' and 'Benedictus' (plus its 'Osanna' repeat) follow directly on from the Sanctus (though concerted settings of the 'Benedictus' were usually separated out and sung after the Consecration in the Canon of the Mass), while the 'Agnus Dei' is a three-part text of which the refrain for the first two parts is 'Miserere nobis' and only for the third is 'Dona nobis pacem'. But Bach creates a different and simple symmetrical structure:

Osanna	chorus
Benedictus	solo
Osanna	chorus
Agnus Dei	solo
Dona nobis pacem	chorus

Now there are eight voices needed, as if by deliberate expansion of the textures, and a full complement of instruments: the voices begin in unison, a most unusual device (recently traced by Daniel Melamed through other Bach works, such as the opening of the Christmas Oratorio and the phrase 'Ich bin Gottes Sohn' in the St Matthew Passion). The structure maintains double-choir writing with one choir interpolating in unison. Presumably here Bach was trying to demonstrate the greatest variety in his sacred music, including double-choir writing. The 'Benedictus', for which Bach did not (or forgot to) specify a solo instrument, is presumed by most but not all to be a parody adaptation – there is a sketch underneath the finished autograph. The obbligato works best on flute, but can also be played on the violin. It is in galant style, so may indeed have its origins in a lost work of the late 1730s or 1740s, with elaborate triplets reminiscent of *The Musical Offering*'s trio sonata.

The Agnus Dei, for strings and solo alto, is familiar because it is adapted from the aria 'Ach bleibe doch' in the Ascension Oratorio BWV 11, or rather its earlier model, a lost wedding cantata of 1725 (BWV Anh. I 196). Here, unusually, the music is simplified, as if Bach were here paring down the music to its essentials, shorn of all elaboration and *da capo*. This is a supremely great creation, the wide leaps of the violin's line at first contrasted with and then taken over by the singer, and expanding in the final instrumental coda to over two octaves within two bars. The final chorus repeats the 'Gratias agimus' to the new text 'Dona nobis pacem', a device some have found uncomfortable, but which feels completely right – whether simply because long use has accustomed us to it, or for some deeper reason, we shall never know. Throughout this extraordinary work, it is not the details of the word-setting that are important, but the meaning of what is expounded, and here Bach is inspired in his choice of a movement that recapitulates the essence of the work, including the moment when this sober four-part fugue is transformed, as the two solitary trumpets take wing and create a six-part texture that rises high above the voices in confident supplication.

🎧 *Mass in B minor* Hansmann, Iiyama, Watts, Equiluz/ Wiener Sängerknaben, Chorus Viennensis/Concentus Musicus Wien/Gillesberger, Harnoncourt
Teldec 4509-95517-2

🎧 *Mass in B minor* Kirkby, van Evera, Iconomou, Covey-Crump, Thomas, Tölz Boys Choir Soloists/Taverner Consort and Players/Parrott
EMI 561998-2

🎧 *Mass in B minor* Gens, Zomer, Scholl, Prégardien, Kooy,
Müller-Brachmann/Collegium Vocale/Herreweghe
Harmonia Mundi 5901614

🎧 *Mass in B minor* Osmond, Hamilton, Hobbs, Oitzinger,
Brook/Dunedin Consort and Players/Butt
Linn 354

🎧 *Mass in B minor* Sampson, Nicholls, Blaze, Türk, Kooy/
Bach Collegium Japan/Suzuki
BIS 1701

🎧 *Mass in B minor* Schwarzkopf, Höffgen, Gedda, Rehfuss/
Choir and Orchestra of the Gesellschaft der Musikfreunde
Vienna/Karajan
EMI References Mono CHS 7 63505 2

Other Missas and Mass movements

Missa in F BWV 233
Missa in A BWV 234
Missa in G minor BWV 235
Missa in G BWV 236

Bach's four short Missas, consisting of settings of the Kyrie
and Gloria (and thus suitable for use in the Lutheran liturgy)
constitute one of the most unfairly neglected areas of his
output. These works should be far better known and more often
performed: paradoxically they were highly rated in the years after
Bach's death, but then disappeared under the puritanical eyes of
those who disapproved of parody. No convincing explanation for
why they were written has yet been found, and they have been
overlooked partly because they are based entirely on earlier
music, as if reused music is necessarily secondary. But looked
at the other way round, these Missas bring together some of
Bach's 'greatest hits' from his cantatas, and every movement is
a winner. They are short, taut demonstrations of his greatness.

After some inconsistency – at one stage *The New Grove*
article on Bach said that they 'probably date from the mid-
1720s' (unlikely when Bach was in the middle of his most

intense cantata-writing period) while the worklist gave
the commonly accepted 'late 1730s' – there is now greater
though not total agreement: the article gives 'about 1738'
while the worklist gives '1738–9 or later'. It feels logical to
regard these Missas as the product of the period after the
Oratorios of the mid-1730s (for which see below), when Bach
is moving towards compilations in his output, and maybe
even already contemplating the notion of a large-scale Mass –
realised in the 1740s with the Mass in B minor. Arnold Schering made the ingenious suggestion that these earlier Missas
were written for the Bohemian nobleman, Count Anton von
Sporck. He was a Catholic much preoccupied with reconcil-
ing opposed religious practices, well known in Leipzig as a
patron of the arts, who also helped to introduce Italian opera
into his native Bohemia. Schering's hypothesis was based on
no firmer fact than that Bach wrote a note on his Sanctus
of 1724 (the piece that ended up in the B minor Mass) that
Sporck had borrowed the parts. All one can say is that Sporck
had both the resources and the interest to perform Bach's
Latin music for the Ordinary of the Mass.

These Missas show Bach trying to move towards a greater
universality in his appeal: perhaps recognising the limited
nature of his cantatas with their German text and Pietistic
sentiments, he used more universal texts and was not limited
by the days of the liturgical year for which the cantatas were
intended. One of the great puzzles of Bach scholarship is how
many cantatas from Leipzig and other periods have been lost
to us. Some have drawn a hypothesis from the number of Bach
chorale harmonisations, surviving in later publications, that
cannot be found in the cantatas. Here is another clue: almost
all the cantatas used in these Missas were written between
July 1723 and January 1727. We do not know the origin of
four out of their twenty-four movements, which is one-sixth.
Could this bear some rough relation to the proportion of lost
cantatas from this period?

The Missa in F BWV 233, perhaps from 1738, begins with
a Kyrie with three successive strict fugues (there is surely

a link here to the organ *Clavierübung* of 1739), based on the presentation of the Lutheran 'Christe du lamm Gottes' and the Gregorian Kyrie, as if in a conscious attempt to reconcile the two traditions. (It is derived from the Kyrie BWV 233a.) Spitta admired it greatly. The Gloria, whose origin is not known, sounds like an anticipation of that in the B minor Mass – with triple time and syncopations – but it is, unusually, in *da capo* form. The 'Domine Deus' is a bass solo, perhaps based on the lost cantata *Froher Tag* BWV Anh. 18, and the *da capo* is omitted, leading straight to the 'Qui tollis', adapted from Cantata 102 – a striking example of Bach's revising tendency. The melody is quite radically altered and moved from alto to soprano, showing the influence of the secular music Bach was performing for the Collegium musicum. The same cantata provided the 'Quoniam tu solus' for alto and violin, and the horn-dominated 'Cum sancto spiritu' is adapted from Cantata 40 for the day after Christmas. Never content to let matters rest, however, Bach alters the fugue subject near the end, and is then inspired to an exhilarating stretto which combines the fugal entries in new complexity.

The Missa in A BWV 234 is probably also from around 1738; there are no horns. Here the models are missing for the Kyrie, which is a flowing triple-time movement of an almost pastoral nature; indeed this whole Missa has a light and galant feel to it. The Gloria is from Cantata 67, adapted from one of Bach's most dramatic movements – it is a stroke of genius to have remembered that the opposition there between the Vivace opening and the gentle, swinging continuation would be perfect for the contrasted words 'Gloria in excelsis . . . Et in terra pax' (here marked *adagio e piano*). We don't know the original of the bass solo 'Domine Deus' with violin, but then the 'Qui tollis' for soprano is from Cantata 179, the 'Quoniam tu solus' is from Cantata 79 (which Bach was to plunder again in the G major Missa) and the 'Cum sancto spiritu' returns to the triple-time exuberance of the opening with the opening chorus of Cantata 136.

The Missa in G minor BWV 235 is on an even higher level of achievement, and could be slightly later. The scoring is for strings and oboes. The opening Kyrie reworks one of Bach's finest cantata choruses, the opening of Cantata 102, with a swirling, swinging gait that belies its minor mode, and the 'Christe eleison' section maintains the momentum over a staccato bass line. The Gloria, from Cantata 72, feels like an instrumental work in origin – in its G minor relentless semi-quaver activity it is reminiscent of Handel's *Dixit Dominus*, a piece Bach could hardly have known. Then there follows an unusual set of four movements all adapted from the same Cantata 187, though they appear in a different order: a severe 'Gratias agimus', a lilting 'Domine Deus' for alto, an eloquent dotted rhythm 'Qui tollis' for tenor and oboe, and then the 'Cum sancto spiritu' which is taken from the cantata's opening movement, in C minor over a walking bass.

The Missa in G major BWV 236 is my personal favourite of these four, especially as it reuses two of Bach's very best cantata choruses. Horns are again prominent, suggesting the hypothetical link with Count von Sporck. The autograph survives, showing the fluency with which Bach conceived these adaptations, making alterations and modifications even as he copied. First there is a severe fugal Kyrie from Cantata 179, and then the wonderful Gloria drawn from Cantata 79: a superbly mature work which is adapted with a masterstroke, the voices immediately being given the horn parts from the cantata. The piled-up entries in the centre of this movement are as excitingly dense here as in the original. (Robin Leaver, whose theological understanding is usually second to none, suggests that the Missa might have been planned deliberately to complement a performance of Cantata 79 on Reformation Sunday. However, the evidence suggests that when Bach reworked material – Brandenburg Concertos from Cöthen for Leipzig cantatas, or secular cantatas for sacred works – they were usually intended for different audiences.) The ' Gratias agimus' is for bass, from Cantata 138; the 'Domine Deus' a duet for soprano and alto which reverts to Cantata 79. The expressive 'Quoniam tu solus' (an unusual treatment of the text) is for tenor solo and oboe, and leads to the 'Cum sancto spiritu': here newly added block chords lead to a jovial fugue from Cantata 17, above a bouncy walking bass, which show Bach's ability to create a perfectly arched long line and then to combine it magically in contrapuntal elaboration.

🎧 *Missas BWV 234, 235* Gritton, Blaze, Padmore, Harvey/ Purcell Quartet
Chandos CHAN0642
🎧 *Missas BWV 233, 236, BWV 529* Argenta, Chance, Padmore, Harvey/Purcell Quartet
Chandos CHAN0653
🎧 *Missas BWV 233–236* Soloists, Cantus Cölln/Junghänel
Harmonia Mundi HMC 901939.40
🎧 *Missas BWV 233–236, Sanctus BWV 238* Collegium Vocale Gent/Herreweghe
Virgin Veritas 6 28481
🎧 *Missas BWV 233–236, Sanctus BWV 232, Cantata 191, Magnificat* Zomer, Bartosz, Dürmüller, Mertens/Amsterdam Baroque Orchestra and Choir/Koopman
Challenge 72188

Sanctus in C BWV 237
Sanctus in D BWV 238
?Sanctus in D minor BWV 239
?Sanctus in G BWV 240
Sanctus after Johann Caspar Kerll BWV 241
'Christe eleison' for Mass by Durante BWV 242
Kyrie and Gloria after Palestrina
Credo intonation for Mass by Bassani BWV 1081
Suscepit Israel **after Antonio Caldara BWV 1082**
Alleluia from cantata *Languet anima mea* **by Conti**
Tilge, Höchster, meine Sünden **(arr. of Pergolesi**
Stabat mater) **BWV 1083**

Bach wrote some isolated settings of Latin and other texts for liturgical use: the Sanctus in C was written in 1723, and the

Sanctus in D the same year, perhaps for Christmas Day. The Sanctus in D minor BWV 239 and in G BWV 240 were certainly performed later in the 1730s (perhaps linked to Bach's early thinking about the Mass in B minor), but are probably not by him, while the Sanctus in D BWV 241 preserved in his hand is definitely an arrangement from the *Missa superba* by Johann Caspar Kerll, performed towards the end of Bach's life in 1747/8, and shows him working with eight-voice choir.

This and other copies and versions of sacred works are a fascinating workbench of fragments, showing Bach's interaction with the music of his contemporaries towards the end of his life. In the 1730s he inserted a new 'Christe eleison' in a Mass by Francesco Durante, a flowing duet for soprano and alto in 12/16 time. (He might also have been toying with a Missa in C minor at this time; a fragment survives as BWV Anh. 29.) The *Neue Bach Ausgabe* includes Bach's scoring of a Kyrie and Gloria by Palestrina, which is not in BWV, a Credo intonation for a Mass by Bassani, and a version of the 'Suscepit Israel' for a Magnificat by Caldara where he adds new violin parts to the texture, as well as an Alleluia by Conti (not in BWV). A further Palestrina transcription of the *Missa Ecce Sacerdos Magnus*, performed around 1745, has recently been identified.

To this list of arrangements we should add Bach's complete version of Pergolesi's famous *Stabat mater*, rewritten as a German psalm setting of Psalm 51, adding a viola part at some points rather like an inner continuo realisation that we know Bach himself added when performing. Bach's engagement with this highly popular work (of which he acquired one of the first copies to travel north of the Alps) is an important indication of his wish to keep ahead with the latest taste in sacred as well as secular music. All these show the essential fluidity and continuing development of Bach's approach to his art even in his last years.

Magnificat

Magnificat in D BWV 243
Magnificat in E flat BWV 243a

There are two versions of the Magnificat: it is the greatest
and most glorious of Bach's shorter choral works, in which
the exuberance of his invention shines through a form
that is totally concentrated, and not a note is wasted. The
Magnificat is the hymn of Mary on being told that she is to
be the mother of Christ: 'My soul rejoices in God my saviour,
all generations will call me blessed.' Traditionally it has been
sung at the service of Vespers. We are told that the version in
E flat, which contains four extra movements for Christmas,
is the original version of the work, first performed at Vespers
on Christmas Day 1723, which survives in Bach's composing
score. The much more familiar D major version is a revision
of the 1730s. We can accept that as the order of events, but
the added Christmas movements are of such a different
musical character (not to mention the fact that their texts do
not belong to the Magnificat) that to regard them as integral
to the work feels plain wrong. The interpolations appear at
the end of the manuscript of the E flat work, with indications
as to where they should be inserted, so they can hardly be
thought to be indispensable. In the Thomaskirche Leipzig
they were performed from the 'swallow's nest' organ loft in
the east of the church, by a separate group of performers.

It was previously thought there were no occasions other
than Christmas, Easter and Pentecost on which a Magnificat
was performed in the Lutheran liturgy, but the research
of Robert Cammarota shows that there were numerous
opportunities in the liturgy for Magnificat settings – and
that Bach and his copyists had many such settings, so he
could have performed his own on several occasions. The E
flat Magnificat belongs to the first creative burst of activity
in Leipzig in 1723; even if it was first performed with the
Christmas interpolations, they were surely a second thought
and an optional addition (in which Bach was following a

Leipzig tradition of his predecessor Johann Kuhnau in his cantata *Vom Himmel hoch* of 1721). The D major version sounds much more natural for the trumpets and drums (are there Leipzig cantata movements using trumpets and drums in E flat?).

A great performance of the Magnificat takes the listener from start to finish in a single breath. Every movement is condensed to its essence and leads directly to the next. It is already a compendium of Bach's styles. It is scored in five vocal parts, with a solo for each (and successful performances can be given with only one singer to a part, in spite of the elaborate orchestration). The opening Magnificat with rushing figures in D is energetic, but over it the trumpet outlines the plainchant *tonus peregrinus* to which the text was sung on non-feast days. The bass line strides and leaps in octaves; the wholly natural word-setting of 'Magnificat' produces a dotted rhythm of great forward impetus. The 'Et exsultavit' is for second soprano and strings, dancing in triple-time over a lightly descending bass figure; 'Quia respexit' brings the first soprano and oboe d'amore in B minor in an adagio, and then the chorus interrupts with the final words 'Omnes generationes' in F sharp minor (this may have been observed in an Albinoni setting of the Magnificat), repeating 'omnes' obsessively over a powerfully descending bass line. The upper voices are allowed a moment of their own before the basses crash in again. (The earlier version is a little rawer here: the dissonance is resolved in the D major version.)

The 'Quia fecit' is set for bass and continuo, and then the flowing pastoral duet of 'Et misericordia' for alto and tenor with the haunting sound of strings and flutes provides another moment of repose before the chorus pile in with 'Fecit potentiam'. Here the tenors take the lead in the middle of the texture, and the frenetic activity comes to a striking halt with the massive chords of 'mente cordis sui' overlaid by the trumpets. The tenor with unison violins depicts 'Deposuit potentes' with fiercely descending lines, and then the alto with a pair of recorders (replaced by flutes in the 1730s version) sings 'Esurientes', with a nicely programmatic moment at the end when the rich are sent empty away and the music evaporates, leaving a single bass note. The *tonus peregrinus*, alluded to earlier, is now made specific in the 'Suscepit Israel', intoned by oboes (the early version had a solo trumpet) over the three upper voices. There is a deliberately old-style fugue for 'Sicut locutus est', possibly derived from Telemann's use of the same device in his setting to refer to ancestral forefathers. The 'Gloria patri' starts with a moment of great power: block chords for the word 'Gloria' followed by triplets that grow up from the dark depths of the basses (echoed by Beethoven in the solo vocal writing in his Ninth Symphony?); the device occurs twice, the second falling where the first rose. It leads to a 'Sicut erat in principio' which Bach takes literally to mean 'as it was in the beginning': he returns to the thrillingly appropriate music of the opening.

The four interpolated movements in the E flat version are mixed-language Laudes, German and Latin texts of praise: 'Vom Himmel hoch', the angel's appearance to the shepherds; 'Freut euch und jubilieret', the angel's message; 'Gloria in excelsis', the subsequent singing of the heavenly host; and 'Virga Jesse floruit', joy at the birth of Christ. They are distinctively simpler than the main movements, in a more homely style suited to the Christmas celebration. But they are not the essence of Bach's great Magnificat.

⋒ *Magnificat in D BWV 243, Missas BWV 233–236, Sanctus BWV 232, Cantata 191* Magnus-Harnoncourt, Larsson, Bartosz, Türk, Mertens/Amsterdam Baroque Orchestra and Choir/Koopman
Challenge 72188
⋒ *Magnificat in D BWV 243, BWV 1082, 1083, 1088, 246/40a* Schäfer, Verebics, Danz, J. Taylor, Quasthoff/ Gächinger Kantorei, Stuttgart Bach Collegium and Choir/ Rilling
Hänssler 92073

🎧 *Magnificat in E flat BWV 243a, BWV 238, 63* Agnew,
Bott, George, King, Robson, Scholl/New London Consort/
Pickett
Decca 4767 863
🎧 *Magnificat in E flat BWV 243a, BWV 63, 133, 121, 91*
Sampson, Danz, Padmore, Noack/Collegium Vocale Gent/
Herreweghe
Harmonia Mundi 901781/82 (2 CDs)
🎧 *Magnificat in D BWV 243, BWV 235, 733, 541* Keohane,
Zander, Mena, Mammel, MacLeod, Jacob/Ricerar Consort/
Pierlot
Mirare MIR102

Passions
St John Passion BWV 245

Of Bach's two extant Passion settings, the St John Passion is
the shorter, more dramatic, more concentrated, and has in the
past suffered in public esteem compared to the more expansive, more humane and more famous St Matthew. In recent
years, thanks to a wide variety of performances using histori-
cally based forces, the St John Passion has been revealed as
an equally affecting and powerful work, and has leapt up in
popular estimation.

The Passion setting as experienced in Leipzig had grown
out of the tradition of the Oratorio-Passion, which was rather
new to Leipzig: Johann Kuhnau's St Mark Passion, heard
in 1721 and 1722 shortly before Bach's arrival, was the first
example there, combining free-flowing reflection on the
Passion story with the Evangelist's narrative. (The Passion-
Oratorio, on the other hand, does not have biblical narration.)

We know that the St John Passion was performed in the
Nikolaikirche Leipzig on Good Friday, 7 April 1724, and
it is believed that this was its first performance. More than
that, as so often these days with Bach scholarship, it might
be unwise to assume. There is no original score; that has

disappeared, though there is a set of performing parts, and there is a beautifully written score in Bach's own hand from later revivals. There are strong hints of a pre-history for the work, with incomplete parts that date back further, but whether they date back prior to Bach's arrival in Leipzig in 1723 it is difficult to say. The most logical view is that Bach wrote the Passion in the first flush of enthusiasm for his post in Leipzig, when cantatas sprang weekly from him. The work became a constant challenge for him, and was revised in several different versions. There was already a conflict around the 1724 performance, because it was the tradition to hold the Passion performances (which took place during afternoon Vespers) alternately in the main church and in the second church. In 1724 it was the turn of the Nikolaikirche, but Bach's published libretto advertised the Thomaskirche as the venue. When this was queried he said that there was no room in the organ loft for all the performers, and that the harpsichord needed repairing – both interesting sidelights on the performing forces. The necessary work was done and the performance was given in the Nikolaikirche, and then Bach repeated the work in the Thomaskirche a year later, making some quite substantial changes. It is fascinating to consider whether these changes were the result of circumstance and necessity, or from the idea of improving the work and bringing it to perfection.

How long might it have taken Bach to write such a thoroughly conceived and possibly totally original piece? We know from a note on the score that Mattheson wrote his St John Passion, *Das Lied des Lammes*, in eighteen days. Alfred Dürr suggests six weeks, with some preliminary planning of the texts – a not unreasonable time-frame. The texts, once thought to be possibly by Bach himself (it is now believed that he did not write any of his own texts), have been shown to derive from extant models, especially by Brockes, in a text of 1712, and the St John Passion by Postel of around 1700. Bach imposes his own symmetrical logic on the forward-moving narration of the Passion, creating a quite remarkable sense of unity in the second half of the piece (the concerted numbers below are separated by recitative sections):

27		chorale
29, 31–32, 34		chorus–solo–chorus
36		'crucify' chorus
38		fugal chorus
	40	central chorale
42		fugal chorus
44		'crucify' chorus
46, 48, 50		chorus–solo–chorus
52		chorale

In the Roman Catholic tradition, the liturgy of Good Friday stresses very strongly the triumph of the cross: Christ's death is but a prelude to the Resurrection on the third day. This too was the perspective of orthodox Lutheranism (though that became altered over time, producing the sort of indulgent personal misery that bears little relation to the biblical proclamation of events). There is a tension, however, between on the one hand viewing Christ's death as the central event, with the Resurrection as its consequence, and on the other viewing the Easter period as one which, having passed through the darkness of Tenebrae and Good Friday, culminates in triumph. In this Passion we are invited to identify closely with the suffering of Christ through the arias, but the sentiments they express are those of the universal Christ; Peter's remorse is our remorse; it is we who sin, but are set free by Christ's suffering. This is why the culmination of the St John Passion is so remarkably different from that of the St Matthew: affirming, confident, and looking forward to the life beyond.

The Passion opens with a unique movement in which, over a relentless bass line (marked *con bassono grosso*) violins swirl menacingly, and oboes draw out the visual picture of the cross in piercing suspensions. Just before the voices enter the second oboe traces a chromatic descent including the notes B–A–C–H (but not in that order). The voices cry 'Herr, unser Herrscher' in block chords before taking up the turbulent movement of the violins. There is little relief in this unremitting fresco as the central section develops the opening and then returns to it. The pace of this passion is unrelenting: no sooner has the Evangelist begun the story than the chorus interrupt twice with 'Jesum von Nazareth'. Two chorales lead to the first aria for alto with two strictly imitative oboes and continuo – 'My Saviour is being bound to set me free' – and then almost immediately the flowing aria for flute and soprano, 'I follow with joyful steps', again associating us personally with Christ's suffering. Then comes the episode of Peter's betrayal, and Bach's graphic portrayal of Peter's weeping, elaborated over a rising and falling chromatic bass line. The tenor aria is despairing: 'O my senses, where will you end?' A final chorale laments Peter's denial and asks for forgiveness when we too have done ill. This first part is extremely concentrated, and passes as if in a single breath.

The second part, originally performed after the sermon, begins dramatically with a sturdy chorale which returns us to the narration of Christ's suffering. The intensity of the setting is ratcheted up as the *turba* chorus sings 'It is not lawful for us to put any man to death', set to insistent chromaticisms driven by increasingly frenetic flutes; the confrontation between Jesus and Pilate ensues, and the crowd's plea for Barabbas to be released ends with the graphic portrayal of Jesus's scourging by the Evangelist. A serene bass arioso for two violas d'amore (a part for lute in some performances was later replaced by keyboard) leads straight to a tenor aria which again uses the viola d'amore to contemplate Jesus's suffering. This long aria with *da capo* seems to conclude the first section.

Bach begins the central kernel of the work with a chorus of sarcasm: 'Hail king of the Jews', and the violent rejoinder 'Crucify him', where once again the cross motif of the opening recurs with its associated dissonances. 'We have a law and by that law he should die' is intoned legalistically in strict imitation, and then the Passion reaches its symmetrical heart with the chorale 'Durch dein Gefängnis' ('through your prison, freedom has come to us ... if you had not suffered imprisonment, our slavery would be everlasting') with a particularly expressively harmonised last line. The music spools back, with another fugue on 'If you let this man go, you are not Caesar's friend' and repeated calls for Pilate to crucify him with a doubled dissonance between soprano/alto and tenor/bass, before the musical symmetry is carried forward with the chorus 'We have no king but Caesar'. This combination of advancing narrative and musical recapitulation is startlingly close to the beginnings of symphonic form.

The final part of the Passion is the road to Golgotha, announced by the running strings and the bass aria which is interrupted by the voices asking 'Where, whither?' The last chorus that forms part of the symmetrical framework is 'Write not the King of the Jews'. Pilate, given the benefit of the doubt in St John's account of events, answers that what he has written, he has written, after which comes one of Bach's most resolute chorales, with widely sprung lines: 'Deep in my heart your name alone will shine'. The Evangelist narrates the moment when the soldiers divide his garments among them, giving rise to a weirdly jaunty male chorus, in which the music, like the garment, is seamless. Another chorale leads to the moment of Jesus's death, where the Evangelist's phrase 'Es ist vollbracht' ('It is finished') is taken up by the alto, as the beginning of an aria with solo viola da gamba. This has a stirring central section ('The hero from Judah has triumphed') before the gamba resumes and the alto repeats the Evangelist's phrase. Now the bass solo over continuo takes up the individual's view of this narrative. It is striking that in both the St John and the St Matthew the bass soloist has an aria after the point in the narrative when Christ has died. If we accept that all the music for bass including the part of Christ was sung by the same singer, this is a very direct way of linking our response to Christ's death directly to him. The lilting aria in 12/8 is a plea that asks whether, now Jesus is dead, the rest of humanity have been saved. The chorus add a gentle chorale in common time.

Here Bach briefly departs from St John's narrative by interpolating the dramatic passage from St Matthew about the veil
of the temple being rent in two, and after an arioso there is
one of the most affecting moments in the work: the soprano aria 'Zerfliesse mein Herze' ('Melt my heart in floods of
tears'), with the unusual combination of flute and oboe da caccia solo – a very difficult piece to sing with a sustained high
register. Did Bach have a boy soloist equal to the demands of
this aria? The long final narration is broken by a chorale of
resolve – 'Help us through your bitter suffering to be faithful to you' – and Jesus's body is laid to rest. The chorus sing
the elegiac lament, 'Ruht wohl' ('Rest in peace'). But (unlike
in the St Matthew) this valedictory lament is not the end of
the Passion. In line with the strong character this setting has
demonstrated showing belief in Christ's conquering death,
the final number is a triumphant chorale of hope, that when
our end comes we shall be carried away to Abraham's bosom
and at Judgement Day will glimpse the son of God. The magnificent harmonisation of this final hymn takes the tonal arch
of the Passion from G minor to E flat major, with a vision of
eternity that awaits.

The following year Bach created a second version for 30
March 1725, with major changes: some movements were
added, possibly based on an earlier St Matthew Passion from
Weimar. In the most substantial change, the opening chorus
was replaced: I wonder whether Bach found the original was
actually too difficult to perform? (It has significantly more
challenges than many cantata opening movements of this
period.) The new opening is the magnificent setting which
Bach later took to conclude the first part of the St Matthew
Passion. The new movements were replaced in the third
version of 1732, bringing the Passion back closer to the form
we know.

𝄞 *St John Passion* Türk, Urano, Schmithüsen, Hida, Mera,
Sakurada, Kooy/Bach Collegium Japan/Suzuki
BIS 921/922

🎧 *St John Passion* van der Meel, Stumphius, Bowman,
Prégardien, Sigmundsson, Kooy/Netherlands Chamber
Choir, Orchestra of the Eighteenth Century/Brüggen
Philips 434905
🎧 *St John Passion* Covey-Crump, Thomas, Bonner, van
Evera, Revor/Taverner Consort and Players/Parrott
Virgin Veritas 5 45096 2
🎧 *St John Passion* (*1725 version*) Padmore, Vole, Rubens,
Scholl, Noack/Collegium Vocale/Herreweghe
Harmonia Mundi 901749

St Matthew Passion BWV 244

Occasionally a great work of music stands outside time to such
an extent that its origin seems to recede into unimportance.
In the case of Bach's 'great passion', described on its title
page as 'Passio Domini nostri J. C. secundum Evangelisten
Matthaeum', its origin and its transcendence of those origins
are equally remarkable. The work grows directly out of its
liturgical and cultural context and is fully grounded in it,
yet it seems to reach beyond that context, beyond narrow
sectarianism and even beyond religious observance, to say
something to the whole of humanity.

The most monumental of Bach's works, and for many
the peak of his output, was almost certainly first performed
in Leipzig on Good Friday, 11 April 1727. (For many years
it was assumed that the first performance was in 1729, but
Joshua Rifkin has established that 1727 is the more likely
date. So the music which Bach wrote for his funeral music for
Prince Leopold of Anhalt-Cöthen in November 1728, which
was performed in March 1729, derives from the Passion,
rather than the Passion being derived from it.)

There are few more moving musical autographs than the
fair copy of the St Matthew Passion that Bach prepared in
1736, written out with great care with two colours of ink: red
for the Evangelist, opening choral melody, and some rubrics,
and dark ink for the rest. It is evidence of the great importance

that Bach attached to this unprecedented work, and his continual wish to perfect it, that he should have copied and revised the entire work some years after its first performance. It seems likely that it was performed again that year, and in 1742, and there is a later copy of part of the work from around 1744-8 in the hand of Altnickol, which could have served as a basis for a performance late in Bach's life. The most major change in the 1736 version is the incorporation of the large-scale chorale fantasia that concludes the first part: this had been written as the opening movement in the second version of the St John Passion but was then brought in here when the original opening of the St John was restored.

We should not assume that the monumentality of the St Matthew Passion, as we perceive it, means that it was performed with monumental resources. Far from it: it is clear from the surviving performing parts that the Passion in its 1736 version could have been performed by eleven singers: four each in the two 'choirs' and three extra singers for additional (and some very small) parts. That it could have been performed this way is not quite the same as saying that it was, and saying that it was is not the same as saying that it should be (see Daniel Melamed's book *Hearing Bach's Passions* for a very clear treatment of these issues). What is worth emphasising is that as the parts are laid out, the Evangelist, Christus and the singers of the arias were the tenor, bass and soloists of choir one, and so took part in *all* the music assigned to that group. The parts are described as follows:

CHORI I
Soprano Chori 1
Alto 1 Chori
Tenor 1 Chori Evangelista
Basso 1 Chori Jesus
plus
Soprano (Maid 1, Maid 2, Pilate's wife)
Basso (Judas, Priest 1)
Basso (Peter, Priest 2, Pilate)

CHORI II
Soprano Chori 2
Alto Chori 2 (Witness 1)
Tenor Chori 2 (Witness 2)
Basso Chori 2

and

Soprano in ripieno (belonging to neither choir)

Because the Good Friday liturgy was sung in only one of the Leipzig churches, it is clear that Bach had more forces at his disposal than usual. Most performances these days have two choirs of equal size and one solo singer for each voice-part. But the separated two-choir structure, each with its own continuo group, is a product only of the 1736 revision; the earlier version had one continuo group for all. In each instrumental group there are two flutes, two oboes, doubling oboe d'amore (and in group 1 oboe da caccia), strings, and a viola da gamba. What is rarely reflected today is that the second 'choir' is always subsidiary, and functions more in the nature of a ripieno group, albeit in this case with music of its own. This is emphasised if you look at the careful disposal of the solo arias – some of the less ambitious ones for the singers of Choir 2 (though not all are easy), and the big ones for the soloists of Choir 1. John Butt has observed that when we reach the end of the work, the bass of Choir 1 comes into his own as an aria singer – after Christus is dead: this identification of the solo singer with us and with the part he has been playing is a particularly significant one.

Eric Chafe's magisterial analysis of the theological background to the composition of the Passion alerts us to one other important fact: it was not very likely to have been composed, like the cantatas, straight through from first number to last. There needed to be a plan – theological, musical, structural – into which Bach might have inserted arias, chorales, and narrative, in accordance with keys, instrumental resources and so on. More than the St John Passion, which is driven by its biblical narration with some interpolations, the structure of the St Matthew is derived from the non-biblical poetry of Picander,

Christian Friedrich Henrici, who wrote the libretto. Several of the arias are based on the sermons of Heinrich Müller, whose preachings Bach owned, so he may have had a hand in directing Picander towards them. Picander published some Passion libretti in 1725, and it may be that work on the plan for a Passion began around then (he published the finished libretto in 1729). How much Bach had to do with the selection and shaping of the text, it is impossible to say, but it seems likely that he was an active partner in the treatment of the material. John Butt has demonstrated how Bach combines from the start the closed form of the chorale-based chorus with a forward-moving narrative; Bach sets up this tension throughout his two Passions, using symmetrical and balanced forms which nevertheless deliver a continuously advancing dramatic narrative, and this tension is extremely productive. Karol Berger's recent analysis of the opening chorus of the St Matthew in the context of his consideration of the change from circular forms to linear narration in eighteenth-century music (in *Bach's Cycle, Mozart's Arrow*) offers another perspective on this rich subject.

One could present the complex structure of the St Matthew Passion in many ways, but there is a strong tendency to symmetry in its sixty-eight movements:

[PART I]
1 Opening Chorus
    2–16 Last supper
        17 Chorale
    18–28 Arrest
29 Chorus
[PART II]
        30–39 Interrogation I
           40 central chorale
        41–53 Interrogation 2
54 chorale with two verses
    55–61 Execution
        62 chorale
    63–67 At the sepulchre
68 Final chorus

In this analysis chorale No. 40 becomes the central symmetrical point. This does not quite reflect what we feel in
performance: there the unique aria 'Aus Liebe' (No. 49) is
felt to be more central, because of its absence of continuo
bass: it creates a wholly distinctive sound-world. Around that
is the literal repeat of the music for the chorus 'Let him be
crucified'. Looking at the symmetry of Part II alone, Friedrich
Smend proposed this shape:

36b/d Chorus 1+2
   37 chorale
  38 Chorus 2
    39 Aria 'Erbarme dich'
  41b chorus 1+2
    45b chorus 1+2 'Lass ihn kreuzigen'
      46 Chorale
      49 Aria 'Aus Liebe'
    50b chorus 1+2 'Lass ihn kreuzigen'
  50d chorus
    52 Aria 'Können Tränen'
  53b Chorus
   54 Chorale
58a/d Chorus 1+2

Alfred Dürr, following Martin Dibelius, adds the perspective
that the threefold sequence of narrative (Evangelist) comment
(Arioso) and prayer (Aria) regularly articulates the structure of
the Passion.

PART I

1 The opening chorus, with its inexorable tread based on
repeated notes in the bass and gradually rising patterns in
the other parts, is balanced between the world of E minor in
the ever-unfolding instrumental and vocal dialogue, and the
world of G major tonality in the affirmative chorale setting
that the ripieno sopranos sing supported by the organ. To
the first choir's invitation, 'Come, you daughters, help me
lament', the second choir responds with its single-word

questions, 'Whom, how, what?': the human dimensions of the work are established with our summons to be involved in the story of Christ's Passion, and the chorale continues to sound above the dialogue. The broad slurred phrases of the first section are contrasted with a staccato central section where the voices and instruments move into B minor while the chorale still remains in G; when the first section returns and the last line of the chorale has concluded, the music turns to a final forward-looking and hopeful cadence with a sharpened third in E major, setting the tone of eschatological hope which pervades the Passion.

2–6 The Evangelist's story begins with the moment when Christ foretells his crucifixion, and the strings clothe his words, highlighting the cross-shaped depiction of 'kreuziget'. Immediately a chorale associates us with his suffering: 'What have you done wrong that they have pronounced this sentence?' The Evangelist takes us into the heart of the debate with the high priest and the elders, deciding whether to capture Jesus, and the first of an extraordinary series of *turba* choruses begins with a double-choir outburst. There is nothing in the pre-history of the Passion to prepare us for the richness and impact of these extraordinary moments: if this really was originally a single-choir work, this rewriting has been most skilfully done. The second outburst is for Choir 1 (here representing the disciples) complaining at the waste of precious ointment. Christ replies in expressively chromatic lines praising the devotion of those who serve him. There is a pattern repeated during the Passion where the first human reflection on the story is a linked recitative (more like what we would call an arioso) and a following aria, here for alto and two flutes. The text associates us with the woman ('May I with tears streaming from my eyes pour water on your head'), with weeping flutes in B minor. The aria for the same forces, in F sharp minor, develops the theme of penance and remorse, with a vivid depiction of tears falling from the eyes.

7–10 The Evangelist tells of Judas's betrayal, and an aria for soprano in B minor says that the heart must bleed at the thought of the betrayal. The first flute of group 2 doubles the voice throughout, even in the complex roulades of the middle section – did Bach's treble soloist from the second choir need support here? The narrative leads to the Passover meal, Choir 1 asking in an open G major where to gather. Jesus says that one of the twelve will betray him, and Chorus 1 ask in F minor: 'Lord, is it I?' In the later version there are eleven phrases beginning 'Herr bin ichs?' – is this an example of Bach's number symbolism, or is it a coincidence? (Hans-Joachim Schulze recently observed that this could not be central to the work because in the early version there are not eleven entries, but surely the point is that when Bach later revised it he changed it to make this explicit allusion.) The following chorale for both choirs links us to the betrayal: 'It is I who should atone.'

11–18 The narration moves to the Last Supper. Jesus identifies Judas as his betrayer, but rather regretfully, with falling string figures. The institution of the Eucharist, the giving of Christ's body blood, is set in triple time, which to our ears can sound almost jaunty, but accumulates eloquent power as the continuo bass sweeps down to a conclusion. A different sound (it is striking how very rarely Bach repeats the instrumentation of any aria) brings two oboes d'amore with rolling triplets to join the soprano for a recitative in which sadness at Christ's departure is linked to happiness at his legacy of giving himself to us. That finishes in C major, and the optimism is taken up in the aria that follows in G major, where the two oboes d'amore pursue each other in canon and the soprano gives the heart to God. The narration takes Christ to the Mount of Olives, depicted by a simple rising scale; Jesus's words about the shepherd being smitten and his sheep scattered are given even more vivid pictorial illustration in the strings. The first appearance of the famous Passion Chorale is in E major: 'Know me my keeper, my shepherd take me to you.' Peter's declaration that he will stand by Christ, which Jesus questions, is followed by a repeat of the same chorale, now in E flat.

18–25 The agony in the garden, in which Jesus says his soul is sorrowful unto death. Jesus asks the disciples to watch with him, and the following recitative section in F minor juxtaposes the tenor from Choir 1, expressing the trembling of the anxious heart over a repeated bass note, with Choir 2 singing a quiet chorale, 'What is the cause of all these woes?' The tenor continues, this time with oboe obbligato, with a substantial C minor aria ('I will watch beside my Jesus'), to which the chorus interpolates its reflection 'so then our sins go to sleep': the lovely rocking phrases on 'schlafen' conjure up the baroque pastoral image of sleep. There are wonderful moments of intensification as the chorus extends this word chromatically over a walking bass line. Jesus prays to be saved from his suffering, and the bass, accompanied by strings, meditates on the fact that the suffering of Christ saves man, with falling string figures; in an aria he resolves to take up the cross himself. This triple-time aria in G minor, driven across the bar lines by suspended notes, moves the action forward, unusually for an aria: Jesus returns to find the disciples asleep. A chorale then simply and powerfully proclaims our need to do God's will so that he will not forsake us, echoing Christ's words: 'Thy will be done.'

26–29 This major tableau opens with Jesus returning to find the disciples again asleep. He upbraids them, and the multitude arrives with Judas, who betrays Jesus. The drama here is downplayed, described not illustrated, and Jesus's reply to Judas is quietly reproachful. Then unfolds one of the great scenes of this Passion, a duet in E minor for the soprano and alto of Choir 1 begun without continuo bass, the strings in unison (*un poco p*) counterpointing pairs of flutes and oboes with the tense feeling of events unfolding relentlessly. 'So is my Jesus captured now', they sing, while Choir 2 interpolates 'Leave him, bind him not', even as the duet continues its anguished imitative course. (Ornaments in the instrumental parts are not marked in the vocal parts but should surely be copied.) The duet is suddenly interrupted by both choirs in unison in B minor: 'Have lightning and thunder vanished in the clouds?' This explosive chorus has been called by Karl Geiringer 'one of the most violent and grandiose descriptions of unloosed passion produced in the baroque era'. The music accumulates tremendous force, with phrases thrown between the two groups, and finishes with both together denouncing 'the false betrayer, the murderous blood'. The narration takes us to the arrival at the palace of the High Priest: Jesus remarks that he sat daily teaching in the temple and had never been arrested, and the disciples flee in terror. The final chorale of Part I was originally another simple chorale verse, but in his 1736 revision Bach introduced the magnificent chorale fantasia 'O Mensch bewein' dein Sünde gross' which he had written (or perhaps adapted from earlier material) for the second version of the St John Passion. (This alteration means that in the 1736 version of the St Matthew there are now fourteen simple chorales, Bach signing his own name to the communal hymns.) This giant fresco is in E major, giving a luminous brightness to the end of the first part, once again highlighting a contrast between slurred legato material and sharp staccato chords. Two flutes and two oboes d'amore bring together the two choirs, and there is again a soprano ripieno group hymning the melody 'O Man, bewail your great sin'; at the close the music just evaporates as the apostles scatter.

PART II
['PASSIONIS D. N. J. C. SECUNDUM MATTHEUM A DUE CORI. PARTE SECONDA']
30–35 Part II opens with an impassioned aria for alto in B minor with Orchestra 1, 'Ah now is my Jesus gone', answered by Choir 2 in gentle imitative writing in D major, 'Whither then is my friend gone?' The dialogue continues, the choir reassuring the anxious soloist, but seems unfinished as it ends with a question on a dominant cadence. The Evangelist takes up the story: Jesus is brought before Caiphas the High Priest and the chorus identifies with him: 'The world has judged me with lies and false utterance.' The false witnesses come forward from Choir 2, singing in canon, a device used by Schütz.

Jesus remains silent, and the tenor explains (34) 'My Jesus holds his peace before false lies', with the oboes and viola da gamba (in the later version) of Orchestra 2, in A minor. Then the tenor from Choir 2 urges 'patience even when false tongues sting me', as the gamba jerks angrily through a dotted rhythm bass line (which is not copied by the singer).

36–40 The confrontation between Jesus and the High Priest takes place, with Jesus's ringing assertion that they will see the Son of God sitting upon the clouds, wreathed by the strings in the recitative. The high priests say he is guilty of death (a chorus of only five bars with eight-part imitation between the two choirs). The crowds taunt Jesus, and another double chorus reinforces this with phrases tossed between them. Immediately a chorale for both choirs follows, as the singers now become the present-day observers who question 'who has buffeted you so . . . you are not a sinner'. Peter makes his first and second betrayals of Jesus, and Chorus 2 adds 'surely you were one of them'. The third betrayal is more violent, and the Evangelist's chromatic phrase shows Peter's bitter weeping (more concisely than in the St John Passion). Immediately follows one of the most memorable and deeply felt arias Bach ever wrote: 'Erbarme dich', for the group 1 forces, alto solo, solo violin, strings and pizzicato bass line in B minor. It demands great resources from the solo violinist (in the same elaborate style, though worlds away in emotional language, as the 'Laudamus te' of the B minor Mass). The emotional charge generated by the soloist's continually rising and falling lines is huge, and the violin's elaboration intensifies it: 'Have mercy my God . . . Heart and eyes weep bitterly before you'. The scene is completed by a chorale in A major: 'Although I have strayed from you, yet I have returned again.'

41–44 The scene moves to the next day: Jesus is being delivered by the High Priest and the elders to Pontius Pilate. Judas repents, but it is too late and he is dismissed (in a brief double chorus): he goes and hangs himself. Two priests pontificate on the fate of the silver pieces, 'the price of blood'. The bass from Choir 2, with a different violin solo and supporting strings, has a magnificent aria in a completely different style from 'Erbarme dich': diatonic where that was chromatic, in G major where that was in B minor, and boldly open in style where the previous one was introverted and closed. 'Give me back my Jesus, see the money the wages of murder thrown down at your feet.' The Evangelist narrates the story of the spending of the tainted money, and Jesus is brought before the Governor, but remains silent. Once again the Passion chorale, now in D major, concludes the tableau: 'Commend your way to Jesus and whatever troubles your heart trust to him.'

45–50 The narration shifts to Pilate's confrontation with Jesus and the crowd. Pilate asks whether the crowd wishes him to release Jesus or the man called Barabbas, and on a sudden diminished-seventh chord the two choirs cry 'Barabbas'. When Pilate asks what he should do with Jesus, the two groups shout 'Let him be crucified', with angular chromaticisms and accents – and then revert to present-day penitents, singing the expressively harmonised chorale, 'The good shepherd suffers for his sheep'. Pilate asks 'Why, what evil has he done?' and this is reinforced by the soprano of Choir 1, with two oboes da caccia, singing that 'he has done good to all'. Then in what feels like the heart of the work, a most beautiful soprano aria in A minor for flute and two oboes da caccia unsupported by continuo, proclaiming the central assertion of the Passion that 'out of love my Saviour is willing to die'. The effect of this unique aria, unlike anything else in the work, with a high voice intertwining with the higher-pitched instruments without bass support, is unearthly and poignant. But as if unmoved by this plea, the remote calm is shattered and the double chorus repeats its cry for Jesus to be crucified. The Evangelist records Pilate's declaration of innocence, washing his hands. And the two choruses join again to declare 'his blood be upon us and our children', moving from B minor to D major. Pilate releases Barabbas, and delivers Jesus to be crucified.

51–57 The alto of Choir 2, with the Orchestra 2 strings, in an arioso asks God to have mercy, and pleads with the tormentors to stop their torture. Then in a strongly dotted-rhythm G minor aria with the strings, she sings 'If my tears can achieve nothing, take my heart'. The Evangelist takes up the story of the soldiers mocking Christ, and singing 'Hail King of the Jews' – another taut double chorus. Now the two choirs join together for the Passion chorale, this time in F major with two verses, giving it especial weight at this point in the structure. Christ is led out to be crucified – the word again specially coloured by the vocal and continuo lines. The bass from Choir 1 with the two flutes and viola da gamba associates himself with the carrying of the Cross ('gladly is the flesh and blood in us compelled to the cross'), and an elaborate dotted-rhythm gamba solo with huge leaps and flourishes accompanies the bass as he sings 'Come sweet cross. My Jesus let me carry it.'

58–63 They reach Golgotha, where Christ is crucified and his garments divided. The two thieves crucified with him mock him and challenge him to save himself (this is set not as two solos but as a double chorus, and goes up to an unusual high B): 'He trusted in God; let him deliver him now.' It ends with an emphatic hollow unison – 'Ich bin Gottes Sohn'. The alto with two oboes da caccia now takes up the cry, with a low, despairing texture with pizzicato cello in A flat: 'Alas Golgotha.' The following aria, over a striding bass line, uses the same combination to great effect, but now in E flat major ('see Jesus has his hand stretched out to greet us'), and the Choir 2 answers, just as in the opening chorus, 'Whither? Where?' The scene of Christ's death is powerfully understated. His cry of 'Eli eli lama asabthani' is translated by the Evangelist, and a pair of tiny choruses, first for Choir 1 and then for Choir 2 (as if in separated sound, an almost cinematic device), show Christ calling on Elias. In the briefest of recitatives, Christ dies, and the Passion Chorale returns with a feeling of closure and an elongated cadence. The veil of the temple is rent, with the most dramatic irruption in the continuo bass line, and then the Evangelist tells of the centurion standing by the cross. He lifts the narration from G minor high into A flat major and the two choirs, marked *due chori in unisono*, utter the amazed acclamation 'Wahrlich dieser ist Gottes Sohn gewesen' (' Truly this was the Son of God'). Bach turns this brief phrase into a confessional moment of transcendent power, a single arching phrase with a perfect curve, rising and subsiding to create a proclamation of faith that echoes across the generations. With poignant effect it starts in the top three voices, the bass joining to reinforce the message (and in the 1736 version, Bach slightly revised the bass line so that it contains fourteen notes, surely a personal signature at the critical point in the work.) The evangelist then tells of Joseph of Arimathea asking Pilate for the body, which was given him.

64–68 A mood of intense wistfulness and mourning falls over the final section of the Passion. Over slurred strings in G minor and a sustained single bass line without continuo chords, the bass sings of the cool evening and the beautiful hour when peace is now made with God, rising and falling over an octave and a half of expressive cantilena. Then for the bass aria the strings are doubled by the oboes da caccia, and the tonality moves into B flat major, with a strength and confidence informed by a lilting pastoral feeling: 'Cleanse yourself, my heart, I will myself entomb Jesus for he shall for ever take his sweet rest.' The Evangelist takes on the story of Joseph placing the body in its tomb, and the High Priests and the Pharisees telling Pilate to ensure the security of the tomb – this last powerful crowd chorus has a finality and power quite beyond the meaning of the words, as the two groups of voices come together and twist the music from its opening assertive E flat into D major. Pilate dismisses their pleas, and the final tableau unfolds around the tomb. In the only arioso for all the voices, the four voices of Choir 1 take it in turns to lay their Lord to rest, and Choir 2 has a drooping refrain, 'My Jesus, good night', each entry led by a different voice. Then the groups of voices and instruments join together in the final chorus, a massive and moving Sarabande (there is a similar movement in an early keyboard suite), mostly unanimous but splitting for some antiphonal moments. In his final version Bach marks this movement precisely with *piano* and *pianissimo* echoes. From C minor the music moves to a warm E flat major, chromatically back to C minor before subsiding onto a C minor chord on which the flutes impose a dissonant B natural (in German, this note is 'H' – significantly the last letter of Bach's name?) which resolves onto the final C.

Can it be a coincidence that Bach, ever more interested in the question of his own identity, as expressed in the equation BACH = 14, J. S. BACH = 41, seems to embed this in the work in the 1736 revision? There are fourteen recitatives that include Christ, and forty-one separate recitatives in all. There are fourteen solo arias and fourteen chorales included, which added to the other movements makes forty-one movements added to the biblical narration. As pointed out above, it is only in the 1736 revision that the phrase 'Wahrlich, dieser ist Gottes Sohn gewesen' has the bottom line revised to contain fourteen notes. The afterlife of the St Matthew Passion, from Mendelssohn's famous revival in 1829 (on what was then believed to be the centenary of the work) to the most recent staging by Peter Sellars, merits a book of its own. It has led the choral revival of Bach's works, being regarded by composers and practitioners alike as one of the greatest pieces of music of all time. Yet it still remains mysterious and difficult to fathom, a perpetual challenge to our ability to penetrate and understand Bach's musical and theological mind.

🎧 *St Matthew Passion* Haefliger, Engen, Seefried, Töpper, Fischer-Dieskau, Proebstl/Munich Bach Choir and Orchestra/Richter
DG Originals E 4636352
🎧 *St Matthew Passion* Bostridge, Selig, Rubens, Scholl, Güra, Henschel/Cantate Domino Schola Cantorum, Collegium Vocale, Collegium Vocale Orchestra/Herreweghe
Harmonia Mundi HML5908376/78
🎧 *St Matthew Passion* Prégardien, Goerne, Schäfer, Röschmann, Fink, von Magnus, Henschel/Concentus Musicus Wien, Arnold Schoenberg Choir, Wiener Sängerknaben/Harnoncourt
Warner Classics 2564643472

🎧 *St Matthew Passion* Padmore, Harvey, York, Gooding, Kozená, Bickley, Gilchrist, Loges/Gabrieli Consort/ McCreesh
DG Archiv 474 200
🎧 *St Matthew Passion* Mulroy, Brook, Hamilton, Osmond, Wilkinson, Gill, Bennett, Bannatyne-Scott/Dunedin Consort and Players/Butt
Linn CKD 313
🎧 *St Matthew Passion, Mass in B minor, St John Passion, Christmas Oratorio* Argenta, Bonney, Holton, von Otter, Chance, Crook, Rolfe-Johnson, Blochwitz, Bär, Schmidt, Hauptmann, Varcoe/Monteverdi Choir, English Baroque Soloists/Gardiner
DG Archiv Collectors Edition 4697692 (9 CDs)
🎧 *St Matthew Passion: the Leith Hill Festival performance of 1958* Greene, Clinton, Evans, Brown, Carol Case/Vaughan Williams
Pearl GEMS 0079
🎧 *St Matthew Passion: Six excerpts illustrating performance practice* Mengelberg (1939), Furtwängler (1954), Richter (1958), Solti (1987), Koopman (1992), Spering (Mendelssohn arrangement, 1992)
Teldec 3984-28176-2 (part of Bach 2000)
🎧 *St Matthew Passion (Concertgebouw 1939)* soloists, Concertgebouw/Mengelberg
Naxos 8.110880-82

St Mark Passion BWV 247
?'Aus der Tiefen' BWV 246/40a for anonymous St Luke Passion
Chorales for anonymous St Mark Passion BWV 500a, 1084

The Obituary of Bach published soon after his death claimed that he composed five Passions, of which one was for double chorus. The latter must refer to the St Matthew Passion, and the St John Passion survives: what of the others? Only one can be identified with certainty, and that is the St Mark Passion for which the poetic text survives by Picander. It was performed on Good Friday, 23 March 1731, and the music has disappeared, as has the Gospel narrative. But the likelihood is that the music drew on the *Trauer Ode* and other cantatas, and that has led several editors and performers to attempt to reconstruct it – none, it must be said, with enough success to ensure it a regular place in the repertory. The first movement, for example, draws on the opening movement of the *Trauer Ode*, which had already been adapted for the first movement of the funeral music for Count Leopold of Anhalt-Cöthen (BWV 244a in 1729, which also drew heavily on the St Matthew Passion). The third movement of the *Trauer Ode* provides another aria. Other movements can be traced to Cantata 54 and there is one movement which reappears in the fifth cantata of the Christmas Oratorio, so was perhaps later adapted. It was thought that the work was never revived; however, a recent discovery in St Petersburg by the Russian scholar Tatiana Shabalina has shown that Bach did revise the St Mark Passion, adding two new arias for a performance in Leipzig in 1744. Present-day versions range from those of Andor Gomme and Simon Heighes, which use narrative from an anonymous St Mark Passion previously supposed to be by Keiser that Bach adapted and performed (see below), to that of Ton Koopman, which strangely ignores the *Trauer Ode* as a source and instead uses other cantata movements and contains newly written recitatives. A couple of recordings use spoken narration.

A setting of the St Luke Passion, written out in Bach's own hand, was maybe performed in Leipzig at some point, but it has an uncertain history. It was known in the nineteenth century, but Mendelssohn said crisply, 'If that is by Sebastian I'll be hanged.' Yet it was published as Bach's work, extensively discussed by Spitta as authentic, and listed by Schmieder as BWV 246, ensuring it a degree of status it does not deserve. It has now been relegated as inauthentic, but one movement revised in score by Bach, 'Aus der Tiefen', turned up in Japan in the 1960s. Daniel Melamed in *Hearing Bach's Passions* tells the instructive story of how this work has drifted in and out of the Bach canon over the years.

Bach also arranged a St Mark Passion doubtfully attributed to Reinhard Keiser, which he had already given in Weimar in 1713, for performance in Leipzig in 1726, but the work was extensively altered and modified; Bach added at least two extra chorales, BWV 500a and 1084. When this St Mark Passion was performed again in Bach's lifetime in Leipzig during the 1740s, major changes were made, including the incorporation of movements from Handel's *Brockes Passion*. Towards the end of his life other Passion settings were heard in Leipzig that were pasticcios involving music by Handel, Keiser, Graun and others, but what Bach's involvement was is not clear, and Christoph Wolff adds the enigmatic footnote that these were 'possibly concert hall performances' – perhaps because they were Passion-Oratorios. Other than that, what happened to Bach's other Passions remains a mystery.

🎧 *St Mark Passion* Horwitz, Amarcord/Kölner Akademie/
Alexander Willens
Carus 83.244
🎧 *St Mark Passion (Koopman reconstruction)* Rubens,
Agnew, Mertens Kooy, Landauer, Prégardien/Amsterdam
Baroque Orchestra, Amsterdam Baroque Choir, Cappella
Breda Boys/Koopman
Erato 80221
🎧 *(Anon.) St. Luke Passion* Spägele, Van Berne,
Schreckenberger, Iven , Müller Sandmann/Alsfeld Vocal
Ensemble, Bremen Baroque Orchestra/Helbich
CPO 999293

Oratorios

Christmas Oratorio BWV 248

There is no more life-giving, joy-enhancing experience in Bach's music than a great performance of the Christmas Oratorio; it is nevertheless another puzzle among his works, for though he titled it 'Oratorio', he would not have expected it to be performed at one sitting. In the 1730s Bach began to turn away from the composition of single works towards the compilation of works into cycles. This coincided with his withdrawal from the pressure of weekly new composition for the Leipzig liturgy. This should not be taken as an indication that he had lost interest in sacred music: the major undertaking of the Missa for Dresden was a product of 1733, and in 1734 he turned towards the creation of a major new project in sacred music, the compilation of six cantatas – perhaps better described as an oratorio in six parts – spanning the two weeks of Christmas and the New Year. They would be performed on the first, second and third days of Christmas, then on New Year's Day, the Sunday following, and finally the feast of the Epiphany, 6 January. Unusually, there is a dated libretto from 1734 for the series.

Unity across the time-frame for performance is provided by a strong tonal thread to the six parts, moving as they do in their basic keys from D to G to D, and back from F to A to D. As became typical at this time (see the Missa settings discussed above), Bach drew heavily on existing work to create such a large amount of music in so short a space of time. In this case the models were very near at hand: the *dramma per musica*, Cantata 213 *Lasst uns sorgen*, the 'Hercules Cantata' for Friedrich Christian of Saxony, performed on 5 September 1733, and Cantata 214 *Tönet ihr Pauken!* for the birthday of Maria Josepha on 8 December 1733. It is tempting to think that Bach might already have had a sacred adaptation in mind when he composed the secular pieces, but that would be to fall into the sentimental view that for him the sacred always had to come first. In this case it definitely came second chronologically, but as with all his other parodies, the process of selection and revision enabled him to come up with music that was absolutely out of his top drawer. And as Robin Leaver has nicely observed, 'when Bach and his contemporaries celebrated the earthly majesty of their ruler they did so with the understanding that such dignity is God-given, and that, however imperfectly the ruler may exercise his office, it is the office as embodied by the person, rather than the person alone, that is being celebrated. From Bach's point of view the celebration of the birthday of a prince is also a celebration of the majesty of God . . . ' And in fact, the reuse of the material gives it a greater universality and a greater permanence.

So the first part of the Christmas Oratorio can begin without embarrassment with an upbeat chorus in D that hailed Maria Josepha, the specific imprecations to 'Tönet, ihr Pauken' changed to the more general exhortation to 'Jauchzet frohlocket', but with the timpani still retaining their unusually prominent role. The Christmas narrative extends through the cantata cycle, and the second aria for alto solo in A minor is from the earlier *dramma per musica*, here reworked as 'Bereite dich Zion' ('Prepare yourself Zion with tender affection'). After the chorale usually associated with the Passion but here with a text alluding to the imminent birth of Christ, there is a beautiful and probably new recitative with an interleaved chorale setting as an arioso for soprano and bass. Then the tremendous trumpet solo aria, which hailed the outstanding woman Maria, now hails the 'Grosser Herr' who has been born: the mighty Lord who little heeds any earthly pomp (an ironic reversal of the original text). The music here is an object lesson in Bach's ability to use syncopation and rhythm to propel his music forward. The first cantata ends with a simple chorale most effectively decorated with ringing trumpet fanfares between the lines (a fine rationalisation and simplification of the wild improvisations that Bach the young organist might have interpolated).

The second part begins with a pastoral symphony with the exquisite sonority of two oboes and two oboes da caccia. The announcement by angels to the shepherd in the fields leads to the outburst of the chorale 'Brich an, o schönes Morgenlicht' ('Shine forth oh heavenly light'), and thence to a tenor aria and further chorale. A little added narrative to the biblical story urges the shepherds to sing the newborn child to sleep, leading to the beautiful aria 'Schlafe mein Liebster', with a rocking motif derived from the earlier secular model (this is in G, that was in B flat). 'And suddenly there was with the angels a multitude of the heavenly host, praising God and singing': a busy chorus for the rejoicing angels 'Ehre sei Gott' leads to the final chorale which is linked to the opening pastoral symphony by being gently swung in triple time, welcoming the long desired guest into the world.

The third part opens with the final chorus of BWV 214, the tenors leading a bright triple-time fugue praising the 'Herrscher des Himmels' ('Lord of the heavens'). Then the lightly tripping chorus go up to Bethlehem, and after a central chorale the soprano and bass have a duet ('Your mercy, your forgiveness sets us free') of the genre linking Christ with his church that Bach had explored in a recent new Cantata 140, *Wachet auf*. A darker mood pervades the alto solo with violin, 'Keep this miracle safe within your faith', before a pair of final chorales as the shepherds return home.

The fourth part brings horns into the instrumental equation, and the opening hunting-type triple-time chorus is an effective parody of the opening of BWV 213. The soprano solo with echo is also from that cantata, but fits well here as the singer questions how they should feel on the arrival of Christ, with the echoing answers 'yes' and 'no'; the superb tenor aria with duetting violins is also adapted from that work. How did Bach conceive these marvellously natural figures – a leaping octave, a run up to repeated notes, and then winding figures leading to the second entry? The solo vocal line is very instrumental in nature, giving no time to breathe; the singer certainly needs all the strength of will referred to in the text. The final chorale maintains the horn-dominated mood of this cantata with a swinging triple-time prayer to Jesus to guide us.

In the fifth part, the horns are no longer present, but two oboes d'amore are added, and the cantata bounds into life in bright A major with one of Bach's most inspiring, fleet-of-foot choruses, newly written for this piece, with ideas bounced around between strings and wind and pairs of voices, exhilarating and uplifting. This cantata narrates the arrival of the three wise men; their enquiry as to where the newborn king can be found seems to have been drawn from the lost St Mark Passion. The bass solo with oboe d'amore leads to one of Bach's most sublime movements: the Terzetto for soprano, alto and tenor with violin solo. It is the nearest Bach ever came to a serious operatic ensemble, in the same musical family as Handel's ensembles in *Acis and Galatea*, *Semele* and *Jephtha*, and even Mozart's quartet in *Idomeneo*. Here the duetting of soprano and bass is interrupted by the questioning of the alto ('When will the time appear? Hark, he is already here. Jesus, then come to me'): there is something deeply mysterious and other-worldly about this movement, which must contain rich hidden symbolism. The final chorale is a simple setting, saying how unworthy is the human heart for Christ, preparing the way for the opening of the sixth cantata with its bright three trumpets and timpani.

As far as we can tell, this whole sixth part is based on a lost model for which some incomplete parts survive: recent thinking suggests a lost Michaelmas cantata for 29 September 1734. It lifts the sequence of cantatas onto an appropriately extrovert final level, with the exuberance of the opening chorus carried forward into the completion of the story. The story of Herod's enquiry of the wise men is narrated, with a soprano aria with oboe d'amore, and chorale, and then a tenor aria with the two oboes d'amore saying that whatever happens he will remain loyal to Jesus. The narration goes as far as the moment when the family must leave for Egypt, but stops short of the story of the murder of the innocents. Instead, as in the St Matthew Passion, the four voices come together in the final recitative, explaining that the world and sin can do no harm to those who rest in Jesus. The sequence ends with a superbly imaginative scoring of the well-known Passion chorale, but here surrounded with trumpet roulades and imitative wind and string passages, praising Christ for avenging death, and taking the hopefulness of Christmas onto the highest level of exultation. (If Bach devised this brilliant trumpet line for his favourite trumpeter Gottfried Reiche, he was to be disappointed, as Reiche died from over-exertion in October, just three months before this first performance, after playing Cantata 215 outdoors and inhaling too much smoke.) Wolff makes a good point about the outstanding clarity and sophistication of the chorale harmonisations in this piece: 'Having harmonised over the years hundreds of chorales and having taught the skill to scores of students, Bach still found it possible to break through even his own conventions . . . they reveal a new degree of polyphonic sophistication, elegance of voice leading, and immediacy of expression.'

⋒ *Christmas Oratorio* Altmeyer, Buchhierl, Stein, McDaniel/ Collegium Aureum, Tölzer Knabenchor/Schmidt-Gaden
EMI 7 49119 8 (3 CDs)
⋒ *Christmas Oratorio* Schäfer, Fink, Güra, Finley, Gerhaher/ Concentus Musicus Wien, Arnold Schoenberg Choir/ Harnoncourt
DHM 88697333212 (3 CDs)
⋒ *Christmas Oratorio* Röschmann, Scholl, Güra, Häger/RIAS Chamber Choir, Akademie für Alte Musik Berlin/Jacobs
Harmonia Mundi HMX2901630/31
⋒ *Christmas Oratorio* Lattke, Sampson, Lehmkuhl, Lattke, Wolff/Gewandhaus Orchestra, Dresden Kammerchor/ Chailly
Decca 47822714

Ascension Oratorio: *Lobet Gott in seinen Reichen* BWV 11
Easter Oratorio BWV 249

Though included in the BWV listings and in the old Bach edition as a Cantata, Bach's treatment of the Ascension story is described by the composer as 'Oratorium Festo Ascensionis Christi', and forms part of his collection of sacred oratorios of the mid-1730s. It is outstanding among them, once again rescuing some great music from other sources and using it freshly. It was probably first performed on 19 May 1735; not only does the autograph score survive, but the parts recently turned up in Krakow, enabling the *Neue Bach Ausgabe* to produce in 1983 a second edition of the work. The instrumentation brings trumpets and timpani alongside flutes and oboes, giving a distinctive richness of sound. The D major opening chorus is thought to derive from an earlier cantata: Bach's mastery of the simple line and phrase is now outstanding, as the gestures of the opening trumpet melody prove, and the chorus enters with a contrasting phrase before picking up on the trumpet line which functions as a cadence: 'Praise God in his kingdoms.' The story of the Ascension is narrated though a mixture of different Gospel texts, and is much telescoped. The outlines are recognisable: the first recitative tells of Christ lifting up his hands to bless the disciples, the bass accepts the blessing and the alto aria then pleads with Christ not to leave so soon. The first aria is immediately obvious as the one that later became the 'Agnus Dei' of the Mass in B minor, though it is considerably longer here. Then Jesus is lifted up and departs: after the central chorale a sequence of recitatives shows the disciples gazing after Christ and being joined by the two men in white robes, who say that he will come again. In a recitative the alto responds to that promise with gladness, and the soprano has an exquisite aria without continuo, 'Jesu, deine Gnadenblicke' ('Jesus, your glances of grace I can see constantly'): it is set for unison strings on the bottom line, with two flutes and one oboe intertwining with the soprano part. Then the final chorus looks forward to Christ's return: it is another superb, dynamic movement in D, and features the chorale melody 'Von Gott will ich nicht lassen' as a *cantus firmus*. (This is surely a new piece, for even Bach might have been challenged to introduce a sacred chorale into a pre-existing concerto or secular cantata.) 'When will it come about that I shall see him in his glory . . . Come, appear!'

The Easter Oratorio, a later adaptation from around 1738 of the pastoral Cantata 249, has not established itself so firmly; Bach clearly liked it, as he performed it at the end of his life, between 1743 and 1746 and again in April 1749. I have never managed to feel so enthusiastic about it, partly because the pietistic sentiments of the text, which tells the story of the Resurrection through the words of Peter, Mary and Mary Magdalene, are less strong than those of Bach's predecessors, especially Heinrich Schütz in his fine *Resurrection Story*. (Even Alfred Dürr seems less than convinced by Peter's exclamation that possessing Christ's napkin will be a consolation to him.) The music, though on the grandest scale, does not always convince in its new form. The original was a cantata for Duke Christian of Weissenfels on 23 February 1725, quickly reused for a sacred cantata on 1 April 1725. Then it was reworked again in secular form on 25 August 1726 for another birthday, this time of a military governor. Picander wrote both secular texts, so must have adapted it for Bach. The Oratorio opens unusually with two instrumental movements, Sinfonia and Adagio, recently argued by Rifkin and others to be newly written, and then a chorus (which in the first version was a duet): 'Come hasten, come running.' The narrative is told not through an Evangelist but through the poetic words of the trio, first lamenting Jesus's loss, then searching for him at the sepulchre, and then discovering the empty tomb from which he has disappeared. Alberto Basso has pointed out the great similarity of this sequence of vocal movements to an orchestral suite, with a minuet as the soprano aria, a bourrée as the tenor aria (albeit of rather dark and reposeful nature), a gavotte as the alto aria, and a sprightly gigue as the final chorus. This could be thought to link to Bach's exploration of the dance forms in his orchestral suites. The short final chorus has the two-part structure of the D major Sanctus that Bach had recently written.

🎧 *Easter Oratorio, Magnificat*, McCord, Gooding, Blaze, Agnew, Davies/Gabrieli Players/Paul McCreesh
DG Archiv 469 531-2

🎧 *Ascension Oratorio, Easter Oratorio, BWV 6, 43, 44, 2, 20, 176*, Schlick, Patriasz, Prégardien, Kooy, Wessel, Taylor, Zomer, Danz, Kobow/Collegium Vocale/Herreweghe
Harmonia Mundi HML5908354/56 (3 CDs)

♫ *Ascension Oratorio, Easter Oratorio, Magnificat, BWV 4, 50*
Van Evera, Tubb, Trevor, Crook, Grant, Daniels, Thomas,
Kirkby, Jochens, Charlesworth/Taverner Consort and
Players/Parrott
Virgin 5616472

Motets

Ich lasse dich nicht **BWV Anh. 159**
Fürchte dich nicht **BWV 228**
?Lobet den Herrn, alle Heiden **BWV 230**
Der Geist hilft unser Schwachheit auf **BWV 226**
Singet dem Herrn ein neues Lied **BWV 225**
Jesu, meine Freude **BWV 227**
Komm, Jesu, komm **BWV 229**
O Jesu Christ, mein Lebens Licht **BWV 118**
?Der Gerechte kommt um (after Kuhnau)
?Jauchzet dem Herrn, alle Welt **BWV Anh. 160**

Among the various bodies of Bach's music, few are so perfect, and so gem-like as his motets. They are at the centre of his work, for though it was the chorales that lay at the heart of his work for the Lutheran liturgy, it was the motets that lay at the heart of his work as a teacher and choir-trainer. This was the repertory that all his pupils were expected to sing and to master, and even the weaker boys (of whose abilities he complained) should have been able to join in with these works. Some of them require double-choir writing, and show the impetus that lay behind the use of those forces in the St Matthew Passion. These were the works that remained in the repertory of the Thomasschule after Bach was dead and his cantatas nearly forgotten; it was a Bach motet that so excited Mozart when he visited Leipzig in 1789. They were some of the first works of Bach's to be published in the nineteenth century.

Equally, these were the works in which Bach looked backwards most strongly to his local and family tradition: Thuringia had been a place where the Bach family had cultivated the form of the motet for many years, and one of the most touching records of Bach's involvement in his family's music is his supervision right at the end of his life of a motet *Lieber Herr Gott* by his ancestor Johann Christoph Bach, for which Bach's own hand can be seen in the performing material. (Wolff even suggests that Bach might have had it prepared for his own forthcoming funeral.)

It has often been said that the motets were all written for funeral or memorial services, but though some were certainly performed on such occasions, this is an unnecessarily limited view. The motet was an essential part of the Lutheran liturgy, and there were many opportunities for their performance at the beginning of services; these were frequently chosen from old collections rather than being newly written. Bach may well have conceived his wonderful pieces as instruction works for training his boys, enabling them to grasp the main techniques such as fugues, chorale settings and the kind of concerto-type writing that they would need when they came to grapple with the demands of his cantatas. At any rate, most of the thoughts about the origins of these pieces are pure guesswork, as are attempts to establish their chronology. Instrumental doubling was frequently employed, though this was not preserved in the nineteenth-century revival of these works, where, as Andreas Holschneider has noted, the *a cappella* unaccompanied concept became the basis for the purist aesthetic view of choral music in Catholic and Lutheran traditions alike.

Ich lasse dich nicht had been relegated by scholars to the Bach Anhang, but Daniel Melamed has recently single-handedly rescued it and demonstrated that it could be an early work of Bach's, written before September 1713. The other early work is likely to be *Fürchte dich nicht* BWV 228, for eight-part choir, whose heavy chromaticisms suggest both a funeral context and a link to the Weimar period. *Lobet den Herrn* BWV 230 is still in doubt as a work of Bach's but regularly recorded as such. *Der Geist hilft* is known to have performed at the burial of the Rector of the Thomasschule in October 1729, but might have been written earlier. It is also in eight parts, a concerto-like first section leading to a strict fugue, and a final chorale. Parts survive doubling the voices with instruments (strings for one choir, woodwind for the other), which would have provided support for the boys' voices.

The remaining motets are unqualified masterpieces. *Singet dem Herrn* BWV 225 was the one Mozart heard, crying 'Here is something from which one can learn!' New Year 1727 has been suggested as an occasion for its composition and performance. The text is based on Psalm 149, and the complex layering of the opening movement – Choir 1 with a pedal bass note and chiming imitative entries, while Choir 2 interpolate block chords, is unequalled in his output. That leads to a chorale for Choir 2, with a line marked Aria for Choir 1. One of Bach's happiest melodies then takes over on the words 'Lobet den Herrn in seinen Taten' and soars above the texture, and the two choirs come together in unison for the final four-part fugue, 'Alles was Odem hat' ('All that have voice, praise the Lord!)

Jesu, meine Freude is for five-part choir, and is tentatively assigned to before 1735 because of some copies – but it may well be based on earlier material because of slight inconsistencies between the versions of the chorale melody used. It is one of Bach's most perfectly realised symmetrical structures, but as so often this may derive from skilful revision rather than from the original concept. This motet could be seen as one of Bach's first attempts at a compilation, a form that was going to be so important to his later life.

1 Chorale a 4	Jesu meine Freude
2 Five voices	Es ist nun nichts
3 Chorale a 5	Unter deinem Schirmen
4 Trio S1/2 A	Denn das Gesetz
5 Chorus w chorale	Trotz dem allen
6 Fugue	Ihr aber seid nicht fleischlich
7 Chorale	Weg mit allen Schätzen
8 Trio ATB	So aber Christus
9 Quartet w chorale	Gute Nacht
10 Five voices	So nun der Geist
11 Chorale a 4	Weicht ihr Trauergeister

Some of the symmetries are perfect: the outer movements match, as do the second and the tenth; the two trios are followed by freer treatments of the chorale (though it has been noted that 'Gute Nacht' features a different version of the chorale melody, suggesting an earlier origin). Most impressive of all is the perfect balance and contrast of the work, and its intense spirituality. Even to those who may feel that Bach's world in the cantatas is too remote from our needs, this motet speaks directly.

Komm, Jesu, komm, for eight voices, must have been completed before 1732 as it was copied then by a pupil, and might have been for the funeral of the Leipzig professor Johann Schmid in June 1731. The original text was written for a funeral of the Rector of the Thomasschule in 1684, and Bach would have known it from a collection he owned. It starts arrestingly with cries of 'Komm' thrown between the two choirs, and a new imitative motive is used for every phrase of the text. The final section is described as an aria but is a simple chorale, expressively harmonised, in which the chorale-like poem is treated line by line as if it were a biblical text.

Included among the motets, though they have independent instrumental accompaniment, should be the two versions of *O Jesu Christ*, described as 'Trauermusik' and included in BWV as Cantata 118. This is one of the most sublimely restrained and deep of all Bach's works, and only because of its strange orchestration is it so little performed. In its first version of around 1736 it was scored for two litui (special trumpets), cornetto and three trombones, suitable for being played during a funeral procession. A later version from the end of Bach's life in 1746–7 retained the litui but added strings and three oboes. The way that this music unfolds through dissonance over a pulsating bass line is immediately reminiscent of the Sinfonia to Bach's very earliest funeral piece, the cantata *Gottes Zeit*. There could be no greater demonstration of how his art developed than the transformation of the variety and sectional nature of that first piece into a serene and gently unfolding single texture here. It could go on for ever, and seems to stretch into eternity.

Dating perhaps from around the same time as the 1740s reworking is one final, beautiful piece which has recently begun to find favour: the setting attributed to Bach's predecessor Johann Kuhnau of the Latin text *Tristis est anima mea* was reworked by Bach with a German text, *Der Gerechte kommt um*. This may, however, be not an independent work but an insertion into a Graun Passion. No matter: if it is not Bach's it is exceptionally mature, and fits well with Bach's exploration in his last decade of the work of his contemporaries and predecessors. The reworking is an act of homage, using the same gentle offbeat accompaniments, treading bass line and slowly moving vocal parts as *O Jesu Christ*, but expressively pungent and powerful on its own terms. A small masterpiece.

As a postscript, *Jauchzet dem herrn, alle Welt* BWV Anh. 160 does have some original Bach nestling between a rather effective Telemann movement which Bach touched up, a central chorale arranged from Cantata 28 and a finale, 'Amen', which seems to have been added later by Bach's successor as Leipzig Kantor Gottlob Harrer. With its lively instrumental writing, this is definitely worth hearing. Less impressive, but also sometimes recorded, are several works that have only a tangential connection with Bach: *Unser Wandel ist im Himmel* BWV Anh. 165 is by Johann Ernst Bach, in a grave old style; the much livelier *Nun danket alle Gott* Anh. 164 is by Bach's pupil Altnickol (this was performed by Bach in 1748 and is very much in the master's idiom, for five voices); *Merk auf, mein Herz* Anh. 163 is by some member of the Bach family described as 'di Eisenach'; and *Lob und Ehre* Anh. 162 is by another Bach pupil, Georg Gottfried Wagner, though it was published under Bach's name in the nineteenth century.

♎ *Motets BWV 225–230* Regensburger Domspatzen/Schneidt DG Archiv 427 117
♎ *Motets BWV 225–230, Anh. 159* The Hilliard Ensemble ECM 4765776
♎ *Motets BWV 225–230, Anh. 159* Sette Voci/Kooij Ramee RAM 0906

🎧 *Motets BWV 225–230* Rubens, Kiehr, Fink, Türk Kooy/
RIAS Chamber Choir, Akademie für Alte Musik Berlin/
Jacobs
Harmonia Mundi HMC901589
🎧 *Motet BWV 118b O Jesu Christ, mein Lebens Licht,
BWV 106, 198* Argenta, Chance, Rolfe Johnson, Varcoe/
Monteverdi Choir, English Baroque Soloists/Gardiner
Archiv 463 581
🎧 *The Apocryphal Bach Motets BWV Anh. 159–165*
Alsfelder Vokalensemble/Helbich
CPO 999 235

**Chorales, sacred songs and arias BWV 253–438
(from 186 chorales)**
Schemelli Gesangbuch BWV 439–507
Notenbüchlein fur Anna Magdalena BWV 508–518

The chorale was central to Bach's life and work; in addition to
the many movements in his cantatas based on chorales, there
are organ chorale preludes, and countless smaller works based
on the melodies that were fundamental to Lutheran liturgy.
Some of those melodies derived from plainsong hymns and
were adapted by Luther himself, so have great antiquity:
'Veni redemptor gentium' became 'Nun komm der Heiden
Heiland', and 'Veni creator Spiritus' became 'Komm, Gott
Schöpfer', and 'A solis ortus cardine' became 'Christum wir
sollen loben schon', arranged by Luther. These chorales
became an integral part of the liturgy and a repertory of
particular melodies became established, one that is fully
reflected both in Bach's cantata cycles and in his organ works.
Lutheran hymns were provided to substitute for the Ordinary
of the Mass: this created a real difference of character between
Catholic and Lutheran liturgies, for where in the Catholic
tradition the elaborate concerted movements had always set
the Ordinary of the Mass, Kyrie, Gloria, Credo and so on,
in the Lutheran tradition elaboration became focused on the
cantata.

Bach wrote very many chorale settings, and they have been of the highest importance for the teaching of harmony across the years, since his skill at supporting the melodies and writing logical and harmonious inner parts was unequalled. The chorale harmonisations were first collected in four volumes published by Breitkopf between 1784 and 1787, edited by Johann Philipp Kirnberger and C. P. E. Bach. These chorales, excluding those already known from cantatas, were listed as BWV 253–438, and are a remarkable repository of the chorale harmonisation tradition that has proved valuable to generations of students. Indeed, when Albert Riemenschneider published his famous edition of 371 chorale settings by Bach, he claimed that 'probably no music publication in existence today has enjoyed so long a period of continued popularity and usefulness as the present one'. An interesting question is how many of these 180 chorales derive from cantatas or passions by Bach that have been lost: if all of them, it would show that the descriptions in the Obituary of several cantata cycles is true or an underestimate; if fewer, it shows that Bach made vocal harmonisations of chorales for separate purposes, for teaching at the Thomasschule as well as for composition lessons. (Three further chorales for a wedding are preserved as BWV 250–252. There are four chorales preserved by Johann Ludwig Dietel BWV 1122–1125, and a couple in the recently discovered Penzel collection that Bach may have composed, BWV 1089 and 1126.)

In 1736 Bach edited the Schemelli Gesangbuch of sacred melodies, all of them in freer, more lyrical form than Lutheran chorales, and presented as arias with bass line rather than worked out with inner parts. These sacred Lieder are BWV 439–507, and Bach probably composed about twenty of them himself.

Finally in the two volumes of *Clavierbüchlein* for Anna Magdalena begun in 1722 and 1725, there are some vocal pieces, including the very famous 'Bist du bei mir' BWV 508, which turns out to be by Gottfried Heinrich Stölzel, who had studied in Leipzig and worked in Gotha; it was doubtless a well-known aria of the time. The central aria of Cantata 82 is also

here, suggesting it was a favourite work for domestic performance. Other vocal pieces are either traditional, like the *Aria
di Giovannini* BWV 518, or arranged by Bach, possibly from
other family members such as Gottfried Heinrich Bach. It is
significant that we cannot always tie down what is by Bach and
what he just adopted and arranged for his family use.

⋒ *'Ein Choralbuch' Chorale-Settings for Johann Sebastian,*
Vols. 1–8 Schmidt, Prégardien, Danz, Taylor, Gnann/
Gächinger Kantorei, Stuttgart Choir, Stuttgart Bach
Collegium Orchestra/Rilling
Hänssler 92078-92085 Johann Sebastian Bach Edition
⋒ *BWV 509–511, 513–518, 121, 132, 299, 82, etc.* Lawrence-
King, Stubbs, Headley, van Evera, Potter/Tragicomedia/
Stubbs
Teldec 91183
⋒ *Music in the Bach Household* Schreier/Capella Fidicinia/
Grüss
Capriccio 10 031

Cantatas

There are those who can sit and listen to Bach's cantatas
for two hours at a stretch and say that they enjoy it and do
not grow tired of it. They are either incorrigible pedants
or unmitigated dissemblers.

Eugen d'Albert, a member of the Bach Gesellschaft (1906)

Before the war there were things [on the BBC] like a series
of Bach Cantata broadcasts. With only one wavelength
available to cater for all tastes, they were not universally
popular; one orchestral player told the story of being
picked up by a taxi, asked what his work was, and after
confessing that he was on his way to take part in another
Bach cantata, being summarily expelled from the vehicle.

Leo Black, *BBC Music in the Glock Era and After* (2010)

One day I hope to start [writing] again, because it was one
of the big aesthetic experiences of my life, like getting into
the Bach cantatas.

Clive James, *The Blaze of Obscurity* (2009)

Is there any body of music so rich, varied and impressive
as Bach's cantatas? Yes, we have Mozart's piano concertos,
Wagner's music dramas, Bartók's string quartets – but there
are over two hundred Bach cantatas, each of them completely
individual, and many more that are lost. Each one of them
is a unique piece of text-setting and theological reflection,
offering some solution to the formal and musical problems
of the text, aiming to expound a spiritual and doctrinal truth.
These cantatas are the product of a Lutheran liturgy in which
scripture was read and chorales were sung: Bach's works
reflect this with a density and complexity that must often, we
can surmise, have been too great for his congregation.

Were they also too challenging for his performers? This
touches on the argument about whether Bach was an idealist, writing for eternity, and ignoring the limitations of his
forces. Yet time and again in the cantatas we shall hear him
picking up on the skills of available performers, in the wind
obbligati of the Weimar cantatas, or the individual vocal
lines of the Leipzig solo cantatas, or the emergence of the
flute or the organ as an obbligato instrument. It is my firm
belief that Bach would not have written music he knew stood
no chance of being performed properly. Certainly he may
have been repeatedly dissatisfied with the standards reached
within the short rehearsal period that he had available for the
weekly cantata; as we know from vivid accounts by Gesner
(see p. 134) and others, he had to direct the performances
with continually vigorous involvement, giving cues, singing
parts, and beating time.

His famous document of 1730 arguing to the Leipzig Town
Council for a well-appointed church music shows how he felt
that the forces available to him were inadequate (in terms of
their skills, not just in the numbers of singers and instruments

available). If we are to take seriously recent research into the forces he expected for his cantatas, it becomes clear that a very small number of skilled performers could deliver these works adequately – mostly just four good singers and a small instrumental ensemble. In the chorale cantatas the elaboration in the writing is often confined to the lower three parts, so that the most complex of opening movements could have been delivered with a boy or boys on the upper line who had to sing only a sustained chorale melody.

Bach did not call many of these pieces 'Cantata'. They are usually described on the surviving scores as 'Concerto', meaning a piece for voices and instruments together. The cantata was part of the Sunday service and had taken on the role, formerly fulfilled by the motet, of drawing out the message of the Gospel of the day; it was therefore entirely grounded in the liturgical action of that Sunday's reading, and its purpose was to provide an elaborate meditation on the themes of the Gospel. It was Erdmann Neumeister who set this trend as a poet and theologian, and many of Bach's libretti conform to this model. An opening chorus quotes the Gospel or Epistle, a recitative and aria meditates on it, a further recitative and aria draws out the moral for us, and a final chorale associates the entire congregation with those sentiments. As Robert Marshall has put it, 'Bach's cantatas were conceived and should be regarded not as concert pieces at all but as musical sermons; and they were incorporated as such in the regular Sunday church services.' Indeed, they were not only incorporated but were an essential part of that service.

When Bach noted down the order of service for the First Sunday of Advent 1723 on his score of Cantata 61, at the beginning of the liturgical year, he was summarising a slightly untypical liturgy because this was Advent. It included, for example, the Litany, but not the Gloria. He was clearly outlining for himself in Leipzig the circumstances in which this cantata (first given in Weimar) would be performed. He writes:

1 Preluding
2 Motetta
3 Preluding on the Kyrie which is wholly concerted
4 Intoning before the altar
5 Epistle reading
6 Litany sung
7 Preluding on the chorale
8 Gospel reading
9 Preluding on the 'principal music'
10 The creed is sung
11 The sermon
12 After the sermon, various verses from a hymn
13 Verba institutionis
14 Preluding on the music. And after which alternating preluding and singing of chorales until communion is ended & sic porro

This is a slightly curious description of the order of events, and one possibility is that its purpose may be to clarify (for Bach's own benefit?) the role in the proceedings of the organ. Thus there are several (useful) references to preluding, where the organist improvises before the item in question. Oddly, the cantata itself is buried in 9 as the 'principal music', but there is a clear indication that this was prefaced by organ music – maybe to enable the instruments to tune. The other main pieces of music were the opening Motet, the Kyrie and Gloria (treated as one item), the Litany which was sung only in Advent and Lent, the chorale before the Gospel, the congregational Creed followed by the sermon and the words of institution, and the communion hymns or second half of the cantata, usually ending with the German version of the Agnus Dei. Given that on feast days the *Verba institutionis* began with a Preface and the Sanctus, the closeness of the Lutheran liturgy to the pre-Reformation Catholic tradition is clear, and the amount of Latin (or in the case of the Kyrie, Greek) in the service is significant.

By the time he reached Leipzig and embarked on a punishing weekly schedule of writing and preparing cantatas, how did Bach work alongside the unforgiving deadline of the weekly liturgical and teaching activity at the Thomasschule? There is a sober assessment of this question by Christoph Wolff, and a more colourful account by Gerhard Herz based on his investigation of the parts for Cantata 140.

The outline of work was clear, according to Wolff:

- select texts, which were published in advance in booklets, around twelve a year
- compose choruses, arias, recitatives, chorales usually in that order
- organise and supervise the copying of parts
- check the performance materials, add performance marks
- rehearse on Saturday
- perform on Sunday

Robert Marshall, at the end in his magnificent study of Bach's compositional processes, attempts to reconcile the demands of Bach's week, as outlined by Arnold Schering's survey of the Thomasschule timetable, and speculates as to whether Bach might have been writing a week in advance, to allow time for copying and instruction of the singers – but this seems inherently unlikely. Having selected the text some while in advance, he might be thinking about his treatment of it, but did he actually start to write it down before the previous week's cantata was out of the way on Sunday and a few beers had been quaffed in celebration?

The pressures on the copyists, and on those preparing the work, let alone on the performers, must have been intense. Herz takes a late cantata, 140, to recreate the process, and suggests that Bach entrusted copying of the parts to his pupils, in this case Krebs, even before the autograph score was complete. 'He could have given him the opening chorus to get going on before the rest was complete, so that the singers might be able to start learning the extended opening chorus.' Three other copyists were involved, and Bach him-self got involved later as mistakes started to be made through haste:

'then copyist 3 decided to do more than he was supposed
to . . . not realising that thereby he bestowed the first violin
part upon the viola player. Krebs caught this mistake,
scratched out these two wrong lines (with what good Saxon
oaths we can only imagine) and wrote out the correct viola
recitative himself. Bach then seems to have been drawn
into this squabble . . . he took the part away from Krebs
and wrote out the final chorale himself, squeezing it onto
this page only by the addition of a hand-drawn staff at the
very bottom. (Sometimes Bach wrote in the final chorale
himself because it had not yet been chosen when the rest
was being copied.)'

This is gripping stuff, which brings us vividly into Bach's
composing laboratory, and colourfully demonstrates the practical chaos that must have surrounded the creation of some of
Bach's very greatest music.

This survey attempts to list the cantatas not in the usual
way, liturgically by season, or by BWV catalogue number,
but chronologically according to the latest research into their
dating. One result is that Bach's development of the genre can
be followed, and also the pacing, which shows that some periods
of his life are crowded with such works, while other periods are
empty. Eric Chafe has shown how astonishingly the earliest
cantatas, for example Cantata 106 *Gottes Zeit*, prefigure the
richness of response and understanding of Lutheran theology
demonstrated in the later works. What becomes clear from a
chronology is the innovative nature of the earlier works, however
much they are rooted in tradition; the broadening of musical
scope and sheer virtuosity in the Weimar cantatas; the blazing
excitement and exuberance of the early Leipzig cycles, and after
a period of less activity the immense maturity and wisdom that
underlies the few late new works including Cantata 140.

Each cantata is treated on its earliest appearance for which
material survives: i.e. the first performance, unless that version
is lost, in which case the occasion on which it was revised and
revived. The accounts owe much to the magisterial work of

Alfred Dürr as translated and annotated by Richard Jones in *The Cantatas of J. S. Bach*, as well as the entries by Nicholas Anderson and others in the *Oxford Composer Companions J. S. Bach* (edited by Malcolm Boyd), updated by some recent research.

COMPLETE CANTATA RECORDINGS

See the end of this section for a list of recordings of cycles and collections of cantatas. While both the pioneering Harnoncourt–Leonhardt cycle and the now complete Gardiner cycle are both indispensable, the first was recorded in strict (and now meaningless) BWV order, while the Gardiner cycle is logically grouped by liturgical use, reflecting his performances on the Bach Pilgrimage. For those who prefer modern-instrument performances, Helmut Rilling's cycle with his Bach Ensemble is on Hänssler Classics. The continuing cycle that most nearly reflects the chronology of composition is that by Masaaki Suzuki and the Bach Collegium Japan, so the relevant volumes that have been released so far are inserted below; however they inevitably do not precisely match the groups of works discussed.

EARLIEST CANTATAS

Cantata 150 *Nach dir, Herr, verlanget mich*
Cantata 131 *Aus der Tiefen rufe ich, Herr, zu dir*
Cantata 106 *Gottes Zeit ist die allerbeste Zeit*
Cantata 4 *Christ lag in Todes Banden*
Cantata 71 *Gott ist mein König*
Cantata 196 *Der Herr denkt an uns*

Bach's earliest cantatas were written in his years in Arnstadt and Mühlhausen, for occasions of which little is known. Cantata 150 was once thought to be inauthentic because the sources are late, but Andreas Glöckner has now suggested both that it is authentic, and that it is in fact Bach's earliest surviving cantata. It is undeniably an uneven piece, but there is great inventiveness in the choral writing: especially impressive is the ensemble in the centre of the cantata where a single line on the words 'lead me' rises up the scale from the bass line to the top of the first violin register in the course of the movement. The opening Sinfonia is an expressive piece in what was to become an important key for Bach, B minor, and the opening chorus 'Unto you Lord will I lift up my soul' moves through short sections, as in several of these early cantatas, illustrating words like 'trust' and 'confounded'. The last movement is an unusual Chaconne which anticipates Cantata 12 *Weinen, Klagen* and gave Brahms the theme he transformed in the finale of his Fourth Symphony. (Spitta mentions in his Bach biography that he showed this cantata to Brahms, who suggested some harmonic changes!) The last four lines of text are an acrostic, the lines starting with the letters BACH – coincidence, or proof of his authorship?

With Cantata 131 we are immediately on firm ground with a beautiful work that sounds wholly characteristic of early Bach. The autograph survives, and explains that the work was written at the request of Dr Eilmar, pastor of the Marienkirche in Mühlhausen, and a supporter of Bach's work in the city, so it must date from 1707–8. The text combines Psalm 130 with a penitential hymn, and Alfred Dürr believes the cantata may have been for a memorial service, perhaps as a result of the fire that wrecked the town soon after Bach arrived. A serious, lilting triple-time chorus with solo oboe, 'Out of the depths, Lord, I cry to you', leads to a more urgent section, 'Lord, hear my voice', which dies away into a bass solo with treble solo chorale: 'If you would mark our sins, Lord, who would survive?' The centrepiece is very powerful: in block chords with solo flourishes, the singers proclaim 'I wait for the Lord', out of which emerges an aching sequence of suspensions for the singers with oboe and violin duetting mournfully above. As in much early Bach, the passage is perhaps over-extended; then there is a matching tenor solo with treble chorale, and the symmetrical form is completed with a full-scale chorale fugue, 'Israel hope in the Lord'. The continuity of the whole cantata and the Bible-based text give it the feeling of an expressive and expansive motet.

Cantata 106, a funeral cantata known as the *Actus Tragicus*, is the masterpiece of this group: it is an amazingly mature reflection on death for a composer who cannot have been more than twenty-two (but had already seen his mother, father and several family members die). Although Bach went on to write grander, more brilliant cantatas, he never surpassed the interior drama of this concentrated piece. The scoring is unusual, with two recorders paired with two gambas, creating an unearthly overlapping sonority with repeated dissonances in the exquisite opening Sonatina. The structure is symmetrical, the solos emerging seamlessly from the choral sections (with the light scoring, a performance by solo singers is entirely convincing), and the text moving from the Old Testament to the New again combines biblical texts with hymn movements. The central fugal section in F minor uses a winding, expressive subject over a walking bass line which, as the soprano calls on Jesus, completely evaporates, leaving the singer alone in space – or as Spitta put it, 'wandering in mist'. There is a balancing duet and the final chorale-based ensemble reunites the recorders and viols which, after the imitative Amens, close the cantata with an ethereal cadence marked *piano*. Bach never wrote anything quite like this again: there is no autograph score. It was one of the first cantatas to be revived and revered in the nineteenth century.

Cantata 4 is the most famous of Bach's early cantatas, and he revived it frequently; it takes the form of a strict chorale cantata in which every movement treats a verse of the hymn in an ingeniously different way, giving it strong links with the early chorale partitas for organ. It is for Easter Sunday, for which only one later cantata survives (as Bach generally put great effort into the preparation of Passions for the previous liturgical period). Alfred Dürr calls it 'a masterpiece of baroque textual interpretation', since the changing character of the music is well suited to the changing text. Only a certain stiffness perhaps marks it out as early Bach; the imitative counterpoint flows with little sense of culmination, though the first movement 'Christ lay in the bonds of death' reaches a climax with its Alleluias. The structure is symmetrical: the second verse is a duet in which the singers can be doubled, the third a tenor solo with racing violins, the central section a motet-like chorus with the chorale in the alto part (an early example of Bach's skill at combining an imitative tag drawn from the chorale melody with melody itself in longer notes), the fifth another solo (for bass with all the strings) and the sixth another duet. A simple chorale concludes the cantata, though it is possible that the earliest version started with a repeat of the first movement to new words.

Cantata 71 was an important work for Bach: it was written in Mühlhausen for the celebrations of the new Town Council following the elections, and was performed on 4 February 1708. (He also wrote one in 1709, but this has disappeared, and possibly also one for 1710.) It was published in a small edition, and was thus the first of Bach's works to be printed. (The lost work of 1709 was also printed.) As with all the early works, biblical texts predominate: here Psalm 74, with additions perhaps by Eilmar. The orchestra is divided into four groups, echoing the polychoral practices of Buxtehude and others: trumpets and drums, strings, oboes and bassoon, recorders and (high) cello. There are two groups of singers, the second used as ripieni to strengthen the soloists at climaxes, and an interesting feature is the use of obbligato organ in a couple of movements – did Bach perhaps not trust his players to cope? He certainly makes more demands of his singers in the second-movement fugue, while the bass in the fourth movement has a virtuosic little riff at the mention of the land's borders. The trumpets fanfare as the alto sings of 'mighty power', and after an over-extended chorale movement (which asks a lot of the cellist), the finale is an elaborate North-German-type movement in several sections with a sudden little burst from the solo organ. Bach was learning to be grand, but had still to become more flexible.

Cantata 196 is a short and lively piece which was formerly thought to be intended for a wedding; though it was doubted as Bach's by some scholars, Dürr feels it is authentic and that is now the prevailing view. (Occasionally Cantata 15 *Denn du wirst meine Seele* is still seen mentioned as an early cantata, but William Scheide showed that it was by the cousin Johann Ludwig Bach. Cantata 143 *Lobe den Herrn, meine Seele*, is a work of uncertain authenticity which might be an early pre-Weimar work; it includes three horns in the instrumentation, but even Alfred Dürr says it is 'perhaps a little colourless in invention'.)

☊ *Cantatas Vol. 1: 4, 150, 196*
Cantatas Vol. 2: 71, 131, 106
Soloists/Bach Collegium Japan/Suzuki
BIS CD 751, 781

EARLY WEIMAR CANTATAS

Cantata 182 *Himmelskönig, sei willkommen*
Cantata 12 *Weinen, Klagen, Sorgen, Zagen*
Cantata 172 *Erschallet, ihr Lieder, erklinget ihr Saiten*
Cantata 21 *Ich hatte viel Bekümmernis*
Cantata 199 *Mein Herze schwimmt im Blut*

There is a gap in Bach's cantata writing following his move to Weimar, where he was not at first required to compose cantatas. Then Bach was promoted to Konzertmeister in Weimar during March 1714 and immediately set to work: Cantata 182 was first performed on Palm Sunday, 25 March. As Christ enters Jerusalem the words of the cantata make that sentiment personal: 'Enter! You have ravished our hearts.' In the opening Sonata, over a detached bass and pizzicato strings, a solo recorder and violin duet, an effect beautifully intensified at the close as the bass line picks up their dotted rhythms under sustained lines. The opening chorus in G major is a perky dancing fugue, with a contrasted central section: while strings double the voices, the recorder adds its own supple high-lying contrapuntal part (as trumpets were later to do in Cantata 29 and the B minor Mass). Unusually there are then three arias, for bass with strings, alto with recorder, and tenor, followed by a chorale in the style of a motet with the melody ringing out from sopranos, violins and recorder. Instead of this being the end, there is then a joyous gigue-like final movement (of the type that reaches its apotheosis in the Gloria of the B minor Mass) led off by the solitary recorder: 'Then let us go in to the Salem of joy . . . he goes before us and opens the way.' The whole cantata has a young person's exuberance and a newly emerging expressiveness. When Bach revived it in Leipzig he significantly enlarged the orchestration, adding doubling violins and an oboe.

Cantata 12, the second of Bach's new cantatas for Weimar, was first heard on 22 April 1714, the third Sunday after Easter, and is one of the best known of Bach's earlier cantatas because its famous first chorus was reused as the 'Crucifixus' of the B minor Mass. In contrast to earlier works Bach now sets a poetic text, probably by the Weimar court poet Salomo Franck; even though the liturgical Sunday is called 'Jubilate', the mood is dour as the poet emphasises shared suffering with Christ rather than the joy to which it leads: 'weeping, wailing, grieving, trembling'. A plaintive solo oboe leads the Sinfonia, and the opening chorus (in F minor, later transposed to E minor) is based on a combination of a chromatic descending ground bass (the traditional 'lament', not unlike Purcell's *Dido*) with long-held suspensions in each vocal part, while the steady tread of the music is emphasised with string chords. There is a more upbeat central section which however collapses into the return of the opening. A recitative and complex aria for alto, with oboe again prominent, leads to an aria that takes the text 'I follow after Christ' very literally: two violins in imitation followed by the continuo and then bass solo. A demanding tenor aria with a chorale for trumpet lightens the mood only slightly, and the final chorale has a noble descant, though it is not clear for whom.

Cantata 172 is the third of Bach's surviving Weimar cantatas and was performed on 20 May 1714, Pentecost Sunday. Bach clearly valued the work, for he revised it for Leipzig, probably transposing it from C to D (and maybe back again for later performances). The mood is exuberant: 'Resound, you songs, ring out you strings!'; the slightly four-square opening chorus becomes imitative in the darker central section in A minor. Bach seems intent to show off his trumpeters in the blustery bass aria that follows, praising the Trinity, and after a tenor aria with violin there is a duet movement that looks forward to many such ecstatic duets in later cantatas; the chorale is heard on either oboe or organ obbligato. A descant for violin crowns the chorale, giving a sense of climax sometimes absent from the Leipzig cantatas with their plain final chorales.

Cantata 21 has long been prized by Bach lovers from Brahms onwards, but it is not clear how it originated – perhaps as a duet cantata written to apply for the post in Halle that Bach desired. In its present form it is a substantial eleven-movement work and was performed on 17 June 1714 at Weimar, on the Third Sunday after Trinity, performed again at Cöthen between 1717 and 1723, and then revised for later Leipzig performance. Nicholas Anderson writes that it reveals 'a masterly organisation of musical ideas, a cohesive strength, and a dramatic intensity hardly inferior to (though on a smaller scale) that of the two great Passions'. Even though it still exhibits tendencies to four-squareness that Bach would soon overcome, it is a sturdy and splendid piece. As in the previous cantata the opening Sinfonia features a solo oboe, this time duetting in anguish with violin ('I had sore affliction in my heart, but your consolation revives my soul'), and Bach emphasises the personal nature of his setting with three hammer-stroke chords on 'Ich, ich, ich' before the fugue begins to a familiar baroque tag. The movement stops oddly on the word 'aber', but picks up a brighter tempo for 'your consolations revive my soul'. There is a languorous, concise soprano solo with chromatic oboe solo marked *Molt' Adagio*, followed by a brisk tenor solo with obsessive strings and a motet-style ending to the first part. The second part opens with a dialogue between the soul and Jesus, for soprano and bass, with a cheerful continuo duet that looks forward to Cantata 140, and an elegiac triple-time chorus which eventually reveals a chorale melody. After a tenor aria, the final chorus is a real stunner, setting the same words as Handel in *Messiah*: 'Worthy is the Lamb that was slain.' Trumpets and drums are added: the bass announces a fanfare-like fugue rising up through an arpeggio, and then tumbles down in semiquavers, until swirling Amens and Alleluias take over, ingeniously combined with the fugal material now in the trumpet choir. The end is breathtakingly abrupt.

Cantata 199 is the first of Bach's solo cantatas to have survived, and may have been first heard in August 1713; it was certainly performed on 12 August 1714, and revised for later use in Leipzig. This exceptionally intense work – 'My heart swims in blood, for sin's brood turns me into a monster in God's eyes'– raises all the problems of excessive lugubriousness to which those who take Bach's cantata texts too seriously object, but its music is remarkable for being achieved with such tiny forces. Once again the oboe is prominent: this part may have been written for Gregor Eylenstein, who worked in the Prince's service. There is a virtuosic viola solo, perhaps written by Bach for himself. The fourth movement is a stately, restrained aria of the sort Bach would develop, but is more familiar to us from Handel. The mood is transformed as the soloist speaks of being contented and joyful (with a huge roulade on 'fröhlich'), and the final aria is an unbuttoned dancing gigue: quite an emotional journey.

♩ *Cantatas Vol. 3: 12, 54, 162, 182*
Cantatas Vol. 4: 199, 165, 185, 163
Cantatas Vol. 12: 147, 21
Soloists/Bach Collegium Japan/Suzuki
BIS CD 791, 801, 1031

WEIMAR CANTATAS:
ADVENT 1714–EASTER 1715

Cantata 61 *Nun komm, der Heiden Heiland*
Cantata 63 *Christen, ätzet diesen Tag*
Cantata 152 *Tritt auf die Glaubensbahn*
Cantata 18 *Gleichwie der Regen und Schnee vom Himmel fällt*
Cantata 54 *Widerstehe doch der Sünde*

In his earliest Weimar cantatas, we sense Bach using his full resources to impress his new employers, and occasionally over-extending himself; but now, with these fully achieved master-pieces, problems of scale and length seem to be overcome: they are triumphantly well balanced. Indeed it would be difficult to find a more perfect movement than the one with which Bach opens the liturgical year on the First Sunday of Advent, 2 December 1714: Cantata 61 begins with an 'Ouverture' in the French dotted style, showing Bach's supreme skill at combining a secular form with the chorale-based style that underpinned his liturgical writing, welcoming Christ's coming from highest heaven. The chorale melody is announced by each voice in turn, leading to a triple-time section which is rounded off by a single line of the returning chorale and a dramatic orchestral flourish. In the recitative for tenor and strings, 'Come Jesus, come to your church', the flowing triple time returns, and then the bass with pizzicato strings evokes Christ knocking on the door. A short soprano aria with continuo leads to the exuberant final chorale. Here the text is radically shortened and unusually begins with bell-like Amens, before the chorale melody chimes out in the soprano, decorated with imitative entries and violin parts that rise at the end to an unprecedented high G, as if Christ has arrived back in heaven. This is a perfect, concise cantata, which Bach understandably revived at Leipzig as well as making another later setting that begins with the same text (Cantata 62).

Cantata 63 was probably written for Christmas Day 1714 in Weimar, but there is doubt as to whether it was performed then: it was heard at Bach's first Christmas in Leipzig, 1723, and again in later years. The opening movement slightly returns to the four-square language and antique polychoral layout of Cantata 71, this time with groups of four trumpets and drums, three oboes and bassoons, and strings. The sheer exuberance of the choral writing makes up for lack of harmonic interest, which is however supplied by the central section and the alto recitative that follows. The soprano and bass duet had an oboe obbligato which Bach later replaced by organ (presumably when his Weimar virtuoso was no longer playing), while the bouncy alto and tenor duet has a lightness found in Telemann. The symmetrical structure has its heart in a tiny bass recitative which, as Robin Leaver notes, makes the central word of the cantata 'Gnaden': the grace that comes on Christmas Day. The final chorus returns to the polychoral style with shooting scales and wide-open harmonies: 'Let the thanks we bring you sound agreeable.' Rather than employing his forces throughout, Bach reduces them for motet-like sections in the voices, including a chromatic moment in the central section when Satan's name is mentioned.

Cantata 152 was written for the Sunday after Christmas, 30 December 1714, and is the first of the cantatas to be based on the idea of a relationship between Christ and his church. Only two singers are needed (perhaps the others were on a Christmas break). Like Cantata 199 this has no chorale, but a two-part sinfonia for recorder, oboe, viola d'amore, viola da gamba and continuo. The first aria puts the bass with oboe solo, and then his recitative conjures up the world's fall to hell in a long descent. The symbolism of Christ as the cornerstone of salvation is fully worked out: a beautiful pairing of recorder and viola d'amore expresses the soprano's faith in salvation, and the final duet is a dance-like number with an oddly unison line for the instruments, probably symbolising the unity of Jesus and the soul.

Cantata 18 is for the feast of Sexagesima and has been dated to 24 February 1715 (though some prefer Sexagesima 1713). Once again this is a work that Bach reworked for Leipzig, but the scoring for Weimar is very special: four violas and continuo, which provide an opening Sinfonia like that for Brandenburg Concerto No. 6. Another unusual feature is that there is only one aria, for soprano, but a dramatic central recitative/chorale for the singers. This four-part movement links recitative-based extracts from the Litany, for which the singers all join in: 'Hear us, dear Lord God.' The solo sections have bizarrely exaggerated word-painting of the kind that Bach later integrated much more profoundly, but here stand out: the bass's leaping 'berauben' (rob) and the tenor's hysterical 'verfolgung' (persecution). The final chorale is a simple plea to place our trust in God. For Leipzig in 1724 two recorders were added to the scoring.

Cantata 54 is a beautiful cantata for solo alto and strings. Quite when it originated in 1714–15 must remain unsure, but it would have been suitable for the Third Sunday of Lent, 24 March 1715. Alfred Dürr has drawn attention to the similarity between its startlingly dissonant opening, in which the strings build up an imitative texture over a seventh chord, and a similar chord in Cantata 61, representing a challenge to the temptations of sin. The text was written by the Darmstadt poet Georg Christian Lehms: 'Resist sin or its poison will take hold of you.' There is something sinfully tempting in the onward tread of the first movement, propelled by suspensions on the beat and never coming to rest. The central recitative ends with an arioso, like so many Bach recitatives, and then the strings combine into two lines for the chromatically fugal final aria in which the voice equally balances the other protagonists in dismissing the Devil. This lovely piece has been adapted – recently, for example, to make a concerto for oboe d'amore.

🎧 *Cantatas Vol. 5: 199, 165, 185, 163*
Cantatas Vol. 7: 63, 61, 132, 172
Soloists/Bach Collegium Japan/Suzuki
BIS CD 841, 881

WEIMAR CANTATAS: EASTER–NOVEMBER 1715

Cantata 31 *Der Himmel lacht! Die Erde jubilieret*
Cantata 165 *O heilges Geist- und Wasserbad*
Cantata 185 *Barmherziges Herze der ewigen Liebe*
Cantata 163 *Nur jedem das Seine*

For Easter 1715 Bach, now into his mature stride as a composer of cantatas, turned to a libretto by Salomo Franck and created a huge paean of rejoicing: 'Heaven laughs, the earth rejoices.' Cantata 31 begins with an invigorating Sonata surely adapted from a lost concerto, for groups of three trumpets and drums, three oboes and bassoon and strings with continuo, like the Hosanna of the B minor Mass or Brandenburg Concerto No. 1. The first chorus unusually has five voices, continuing in bright C major and finishing with an instrumental postlude. The arias celebrating the Resurrection are well contrasted: an adagio in dotted rhythm for bass, and a flowing one with strings for tenor. The soprano duets with an oboe (or oboe d'amore), while the chorale melody is heard low on the violins, a magical effect. The same chorale tune returns for the last movement, with a descant that surely goes dangerously high for the trumpet to join in.

Cantata 165 is not preserved in first-hand sources but seems likely to have been performed in Weimar on Trinity Sunday 16 June 1715; it is based on a text by the poet Salomo Franck, based on Jesus's words that a man has to be reborn of water and the Holy Spirit to enter the Kingdom of God. This intimate piece could be performed by just four solo singers, with strings and continuo. In the opening movement the soprano is the equal partner of the strings in exploring a gentle theme: 'O holy washing of the spirit and water.' A simple bass recitative leads to an alto aria with continuo; but then the next recitative, marked *con stromenti*, has a striking portrayal of the Lamb of God and an almost witty conclusion: 'when all strength departs', the voice and instruments fade, and the continuo is left alone. A vigorous G major tenor aria with violins leads to the final chorale.

Cantata 185 is inscribed by Bach '1715', and was heard on 14 July. It was revived both in Weimar and Leipzig. 'Compassionate heart of eternal love, move my heart through you', begins the text, and the first movement is a lilting love duet for soprano and tenor over a running bass, which could easily find a place in an opera were it not for the instrumental chorale melody that hovers over them. The intimate mood is maintained with a recitative in which the strings are marked *pianissimo* and an elaborate aria for alto with oboe and violin in which the words 'auszustreuen' (scatter) and 'Ewigkeit' (eternity) provoke lavish pictures. The bass has a plodding aria with continuo to illustrate the truth of the dedicated Christian way, and the final chorale is the melody heard in the first movement, with a crowning descant.

Cantata 163 is the last of the new cantatas that Bach composed for the liturgical year in 1714–15, and was heard on 24 November 1715. It is once again an intimate setting for four singers and strings, with a text by Salomo Franck, and as innovative as ever. There is an opening *da capo* aria for tenor, unusual in itself, a recitative for bass followed by a unique bass aria with a duet for two cellos (surely the players for whom Brandenburg Concerto No. 3 was written). A duet recitative for soprano and alto in close imitation prays to be emptied of all lusts, so that they turn into true Christians. The duet with chorale that follows is more restrained, and the final chorale is missing except for its basso continuo part, though there is an indication for a 'Chorale in semplice stilo'.

𝄞 *Cantatas Vol. 5: 199, 165, 185, 163*
Cantatas Vol. 6: 31, 21
Soloists/Bach Collegium Japan/Suzuki
BIS CD 841, 851

WEIMAR CANTATAS:
ADVENT 1715–TRINITY 1716

Cantata 132 *Bereitet die Wege, bereitet die Bahn*
Cantata 155 *Mein Gott, wie lang, ach lange*
Cantata 161 *Komm, du süsse Todesstunde*
Cantata 162 *Ach! ich sehe, itzt, da ich zur*
Hochzeit gehe

The small-scale, chamber-like nature of many of Bach's Weimar cantatas continues in Cantata 132, the first new piece for the liturgical year 1715–16, performed on the Fourth Sunday of Advent, 22 December 1715. Just four voices, oboe, bassoon and strings explore this Salomo Franck meditation on the texts of the day, echoing Handel's *Messiah* in the opening: 'Prepare ye the way of the Lord, make straight in the desert a highway for our God.' But Handel never asked his singer to tread a path like this; Bach first writes sixty consecutive semiquavers followed by a long-held note for the single word 'Bahn', then on repeating extends the run to eighty-four notes! The arrival of the Messiah (announced in the central section) must never have been more welcome. A tenor recitative leads to a bass solo with obbligato cello using one of Bach's favourite repeated rhythmic tags to propel the movement. The strings accompany the alto recitative and then the solo violin has a rhapsodic solo that looks forward to the 'Laudamus te' of the B minor Mass. The final chorale is given only in Franck's text.

Cantata 155 is another intimate piece to a text by Franck, this time related to the parable of the Wedding Feast at Cana: it was first performed on 19 January 1716 and repeated later in Leipzig. Strings are joined by a bassoon, which is required to be very agile in the duet that follows the opening soprano recitative. (Who was the bassoonist? One note Bach writes here is too low for the instrument.) The text is built around Christ's statement that his hour is not yet come; the bass, traditionally associated with Christ, brings consolation in the next recitative and the soprano has a chirpy aria casting herself in God's arms, before the final chorale.

Cantata 161 followed, probably on 27 September 1716, to another text by Franck that had been written for the previous year (when public mourning curtailed performances); there are doubts over its Leipzig revival. The text longs for union with Christ, wishing for death to come quickly. The Weimar version turns right back to the two recorders of the *Actus Tragicus* for its opening alto aria, in which the organ plays the chorale (in Leipzig a soprano sings it, to the words familiar from the Passion chorale 'Herzlich tut mich verlangen'). Then follows a dramatic tenor recitative and more restrained aria of longing to embrace the Saviour, in which Bach emphasises 'prangen' in a long melisma. An alto recitative climaxes in the ringing of the bell that marks the end of time: 'then strike, you stroke of the last hour' – the recorder chirruping on high while the alto descends to the depths. The singers join in a simple chorus yearning for the next life, with some elaborate instrumental decorations, and the final chorale has an unusually detailed descant for the recorders (in Leipzig they were replaced by flutes) over the return of the Passion chorale.

Cantata 162 is a small cantata for four singers, strings and continuo, which was first performed on 25 October 1716. The text by Franck refers to the Gospel of the day, the story of the royal wedding feast, and the opening bass aria declaims 'Ah I see now as I go to the wedding, weal and woe', with closely worked string figures against the singer. After a tenor recitative, there is a soprano aria which seems to be missing its obbligato parts (but can be performed with continuo alone), and then a recitative for alto and duet with tenor, rounded off by a final chorale.

(Bach's remaining cantatas for Weimar, all for Advent, have been lost. They include Cantata 70a, performed on the Second Sunday of Advent, 6 December 1716; Cantata 186a, which was performed on the Third Sunday of Advent 1716; and Cantata 147a. All survive as later rewritten for Leipzig, so are better treated there. At Cöthen, Bach's responsibilities were for instrumental music, and concerted vocal works were performed only rarely, and usually for secular purposes. None survives in its original form; they include Cantatas 66a, Anh. 5, 134a, Anh. 6 and Anh. 7, 173a, 194a, 184a and Anh. 8.)

LEIPZIG CANTATAS 1723

Cantata 22 *Jesus nahm zu sich die Zwölfe*
Cantata 23 *Du wahrer Gott und Davids Sohn*
Cantata 59 *Wer mich liebet, der wird mein Wort halten*

When Bach applied for the post of Thomaskantor in Leipzig he had to provide a test-piece cantata, but he followed his rival Graupner and supplied two substantial cantatas, both of which were heard in Leipzig on 7 February 1723. Cantata 22 bears the inscription 'This is the Leipzig trial piece' and was heard first in the service, before the sermon. The anonymous text is a narrative of Christ's journey to Jerusalem before his Passion, with the moral that the soul should follow Christ on his journey. Modestly scored for oboe, strings and four singers, Bach's highly original approach is evident from the start, where a concerto-like texture supports the tenor narrator and bass voice of Christ; the other voices join in with their desire to understand Christ's message. An alto aria with oboe leads to a bass recitative with long melismas for 'laufen' (run) and 'Freuden' (joys), and a lively tenor aria. The best-known movement, familiar from arrangements, is the final chorale, which involves the instrumentalists in a continuously flowing line over a walking bass, against which the singers place an unadorned chorale, surely portraying the world following Christ.

Cantata 23 would have been heard later in the service, either after the sermon or during the Communion (where the Agnus Dei was traditionally sung in the Lutheran liturgy), as the text concludes with the German version 'Christe, du Lamm Gottes'. It was previously thought unlikely that it was included in Bach's trial, and was performed only later in a revised version, but recent discoveries of performing material suggest that the same copyists who copied Graupner's cantatas for Leipzig use also worked on both Cantatas 22 and 23. Together the two works must have made a considerable impact. The first three movements were written in Cöthen and the remainder finished in Leipzig. Bach seems intent on demonstrating the heights of his art: the complex opening movement, a plea for mercy from God, pits canonic imitation between the oboes d'amore against very different imitation between soprano and alto. An angular accompanied recitative for tenor ('Ah! Do not pass by, Saviour of mankind') leads unexpectedly to a chorus in triple time in full motet style, with solo passages indicated in the score: 'The eyes of all wait upon you Lord.' And then, instead of a simple final chorale, for his Agnus Dei Bach writes an expressive Adagio over a detached bass tread and oboe d'amore duet; it moves to Andante for the final lines and a final Amen is worked to a noble climax in stretto. In the later revised version for Leipzig, cornett and trombones supported the vocal lines, and the work was lifted into C minor. (Cantata 59, meanwhile, might have been performed on Whit Sunday 16 May 1723, before Bach embarked on his first full cantata cycle.)

🎧 *Cantatas Vol. 8: 22, 23, 75*
Soloists/Bach Collegium Japan/Suzuki
BIS CD 901

LEIPZIG CANTATAS YEAR ONE: SUNDAYS 1–11 AFTER TRINITY 1723

Cantata 75 *Die Elenden sollen essen, dass sie satt werden*
Cantata 76 *Die Himmel erzählen die Ehre Gottes*
Cantata 24 *Ein ungefärbt Gemüte*
Cantata 167 *Ihr Menschen, rühmet Gottes Liebe*
Cantata 147 *Herz und Mund und Tat und Leben*
Cantata 186 *Ärgre dich, o Seele, nicht*
Cantata 136 *Erforsche mich, Gott, und erfahre mein Herz*
Cantata 105 *Herr, gehe nicht ins Gericht*
Cantata 46 *Schauet doch und sehet, ob irgend ein Schmerz sei*
Cantata 179 *Siehe zu, dass deine Gottesfurcht nicht Heuchelei sei*

The energy with which Bach approaches his new task in Leipzig, providing cantatas for every Sunday and feast day of the year (apart from Lent and Advent), is extraordinary. He produced a dazzling series of works which must have strained all resources to the limits – Bach as a composer, his copyists and assistants, his players and his singers. The weekly pressure must have been relentless, and we have little evidence as to how good the resulting performances were. But what music! As Malcolm Boyd remarks, given that the cantata would usually be expected to start at about 7.30 am, this was 'not the best time of day, one might think, for young choristers and instrumentalists to come to grips with some of the most demanding new music in the whole of Europe!' The cantata was sung by the first choir of the school at the two main churches on alternate Sundays, though at the main festivals of Christmas, Easter and Whitsun both major churches heard the cantatas, as they were repeated.

With Cantata 75, Bach begins a series of major two-part cantatas on a scale that was unprecedented for him. It was performed on 30 May 1723, the First Sunday after Trinity, and was even reported in the local press, which noted it was received 'mit guten applausus' (with great success). These are massive works on a splendid scale, with three recitatives enclosing two arias between the opening and closing chorale movements. The Gospel for the day is the story of Lazarus and the rich man, and the contrast between poverty and riches goes through the anonymous text. Bach designs the opening movement as a choral prelude and fugue, the triple-time opening section leading to a rising climax of great power on the word 'praise'. The scoring is light, for two oboes and strings, and a solo oboe flowers in the first tenor aria, while it is an oboe d'amore that accompanies the more popular-style second aria for soprano. A concerted chorale setting ends the first part, and the second opens with an extended orchestral chorale prelude with the same melody of the hymn 'Was Gott tut, das ist wohlgetan', with trumpet over strings. A simple alto aria with violins leads to a more declamatory bass aria with trumpet solo, and the same chorale setting that ended part one concludes the cantata. (Was Bach perhaps waiting to assess the strength of his singers? There is nothing here for the performers as testing as in some of his Weimar cantatas.)

Cantata 76 is another two-part cantata on the largest scale (these pieces would have lasted some thirty-five to forty minutes) and was heard a week later on 6 June 1723 for the Second Sunday of Trinity. 'The heavens declare the glory of God', sings the opening chorus, and a solo trumpet over oboes and strings begins the celebration, before a bass solo leads into the brilliant entry of all the singers and instruments. The tenor launches the choral fugue and this builds over a long section of counterpoint (which Bach indicates for vocal soloists) until the instruments gradually re-enter with the rest of the voices. The text advises Christians to turn away from idolatry to God. A tenor arioso leads to a soprano aria with violin, and the trumpet is back to accompany a bass aria with long melismas on 'Verehren' (honour). The chorale that ends part one is another elaborate setting with trumpet introducing the melody before the chorus enters, under an oboe and violin descant. Part two starts with oboe d'amore and viola da gamba duetting in a substantial movement, which was later reused in an organ trio sonata. The tenor's aria is angular and insistent, while the alto aria that follows has a relaxed duet for the oboe d'amore and viola da gamba, expressing the patience of the true Christian.

Cantata 24 is a smaller work than 75 or 76, and was presented alongside a revision of Cantata 185 on 20 June 1723, the Fourth Sunday of Trinity. The text is by Neumeister, with distinctly nationalist overtones: 'An unstained mind of German truth and goodness makes us shine before God and man.' The alto's line is accompanied by driving repeated notes in the unison strings; the centrepiece is a chorus in which the instruments answer the voices, leading to a *vivace e allegro* fugue presented with two parts simultaneously: every 'that you wish' (tenors then altos) is already answered by 'you do to them' (basses then sopranos). The tenor aria gives the two oboes d'amore strict imitation to reflect the text's faithfulness to constancy and truth. The final chorale is 'O Gott, du frommer Gott', given a setting in which the instruments punctuate and then accompany the vocal lines, with the melody assigned to clarino (probably here a horn).

Cantata 167 was performed on 24 June 1723, the Feast of St John the Baptist, and perhaps there was not the scope on this feast day for a longer cantata. The soloists would not have needed to be joined by any more singers for the final chorale. The text is about St John's birth and includes the traditional Benedictus. There is an opening aria for tenor with strings, a lilting number praising God's goodness with strings, then a recitative and duet for soprano and alto with the low-pitched oboe da caccia, with a faster middle section. Bach finds room for a final elaborate chorale setting, oboe and violins bustling along over repeated rhythmic figures in the bass, complete with chorale on the clarino (horn), making a gloriously exuberant close: 'Blessing and praise and honour be to God.'

Cantata 147 is one of the best loved of all Bach cantatas because arrangements of the chorale movement that close each part, 'Jesu joy of man's desiring', have immortalised it in so many different forms. It was performed on 2 July 1723, the feast of the Visitation, but some of it originated earlier in Weimar, where the text was written by Salomo Franck for the Advent liturgy. The chorale arrangements that made it famous were new for Leipzig, but the clarity of the opening of the autograph score suggests that Bach was making a fair copy from a previous source. The text refers to the Magnificat, making it suitable for a Marian feast. It begins in triumphal C major, with solo trumpet and choirs of wind and strings recalling the polychoral style of earlier Bach cantatas, with a choral-only central section before the opening returns; unusually the instruments finish the movement. A tenor recitative and a triple-time alto aria in A minor lead to a bass recitative and soprano aria with a very active violin solo in triplets. Then the gently swaying triplets immortalised by Myra Hess in her arrangement for piano are heard: in Bach's original, for oboe and violins, against a very simple chorale setting 'Wohl mir dass ich Jesum habe' (the orchestral theme is derived from the chorale melody). Drama returns at the opening of the second part, where the tenor asks for Jesus's help against a barrage of triplets from the continuo. A bass solo with trumpet and all the instruments is in Bach's most grandiose style, and then the famous chorale setting quietly returns.

Cantata 186 for 11 July 1723 enlarges the lost Weimar cantata 186a, and is an imposing work which has been expanded to two parts with a lavish instrumental scoring, meditating on the miracle of the feeding of the crowds and our gratitude for Jesus's goodness. Especially notable is the extended chorale setting that ends both parts of the cantata, a preparation for the kind of extended chorale fantasia that Bach was to include in his next cantata cycle. Cantata 136 was heard on 18 July 1723, the Eighth Sunday after Trinity. (Dürr believes that the work makes use of older material.) Bach clearly valued the piece, because it was the earliest of his cantatas that he remembered when assembling his Missa Brevis settings in the 1730s. 'Search me O God, and know my heart', the text begins: it's a rich and diverse piece, its hunt-like triple-time theme announced on horn but then taken up immediately by soprano in a wide-ranging fugue, over which the violins rush with glee. The alto sings with oboe d'amore, the tenor and bass duet under unison violins, and there is a final chorale with violin descant.

Cantata 105 was performed on 25 July 1723, the Ninth Sunday of Trinity, when the Gospel tells the parable of the unjust steward. So the text implores God not to enter into judgement on us, and the music is resultantly strict and guilt-laden. The sober motet-like opening must have come as a shock, but this Adagio is broken by cries of 'Herr' (anticipating the bold gesture at the start of the St John Passion), and the tension is gradually increased through the movement. An alto recitative leads to a very striking soprano aria without basso continuo (another anticipation of the St John). Oboe and soprano duet over continuous string semiquavers and a light viola line, an eerie effect representing the 'trembling and waving' of the thoughts of the sinner. The continuo returns (but pizzicato) for a bass arioso, and then there is a bold tenor aria with horn and violin, with lavish figuration around the voice. The final chorale is accompanied by more of the trembling string chords, which gradually reduce in frequency until they lose impetus and collapse in a tiny chromatic cadence after the voices have finished: a unique touch. Dürr feels that this cantata 'might well be numbered among the most sublime descriptions of the soul in baroque and Christian art'.

Cantata 46 takes its cue from the opening biblical quotation, 'Behold and see if there be any sorrow like my sorrow'; it was first performed on 1 August 1723, the Tenth Sunday after Trinity. A pair of recorders set the restrained mood and the choir enters with gently falling lamenting phrases; joined by wind, the movement moves into a faster tempo for an extended fugue in which the recorders add their own voice. (The prelude was later adapted for the 'Qui tollis' of the B minor Mass.) The recorders are again prominent in the tenor's recitative, obsessively repeating a little phrase (like the falling tears of the words); the trumpet takes over as virtuoso soloist for the bass aria, which conjures up the storm of thunder and lightning, colouring the word 'unerträglich' (unbearable) with a *pianissimo* (even in the trumpet's part), and a surely impossible ten-bar phrase of semiquavers for the soloist. The recorders emerge to accompany an alto aria without continuo, but with the oboes da caccia on the lowest line, and then they provide punctuation in the powerful final chorale like an unearthly cadenza between the lines.

Cantata 179 was written for the Eleventh Sunday after Trinity on 8 August 1723, but as it is a short cantata it is possible a second work was heard that day, perhaps Cantata 199. It was returned to by Bach in search of material for the Latin Missas of the 1730s. 'See to it that your fear of God be not hypocrisy': the first movement is an old-style motet with the choral entries built up and supported by instruments, highlighting the word 'falschen'. An elaborate obbligato, oddly for both oboes and first violin, is echoed by the tenor, the oboists moving to the oboe da caccia for the expressive soprano aria 'Dearest God, have mercy'. The final chorale is richly harmonised in its inner parts: 'Strengthen me with your spirit of joy.'

🎧 *Cantatas Vol. 9: 76, 24, 167*
Cantatas Vol. 10: 186, 179, 105
Cantatas Vol. 11: 136, 138, 95, 46
Soloists/Bach Collegium Japan/Suzuki
BIS CD 931, 951, 991

LEIPZIG CANTATAS YEAR ONE:
12TH–26TH SUNDAYS AFTER TRINITY 1723

Cantata 69a *Lobe den Herrn, meine Seele*
Cantata 77 *Du sollst Gott, deinen Herren, lieben*
Cantata 25 *Es ist nichts Gesundes an meinem Leib*
Cantata 119 *Preise, Jerusalem, den Herrn*
Cantata 138 *Warum betrübst du dich, mein Herz?*
Cantata 95 *Christus, der ist mein Leben*
Cantata 148 *Bringet dem Herrn Ehre seines Namens*
Cantata 48 *Ich elender Mensch, wer wird mich erlösen*
Cantata 109 *Ich glaube, lieber Herr, hilf meinem*
  Unglauben
Cantata 89 *Was soll ich aus dir machen, Ephraim?*
Cantata 60 *O Ewigkeit, du Donnerwort*
Cantata 90 *Es reisset euch ein schrecklich Ende*
Cantata 70 *Wachet! betet! betet! wachet!*

Bach's creativity was unflagging in this magnificent sequence of cantatas, though he backed away from continuing the long two-part structure established earlier in the year. Cantata 69a is a substantial piece, however, for the Twelfth Sunday after Trinity, 15 August 1723, with an opening chorus that for the first time puts the trumpet and drum choir into bright D major (many of Bach's Weimar movements were transposed up a tone for Leipzig). The vocal parts are of the highest virtuosity: they would have stretched his singers, and would surely have been sung mainly by soloists. Indeed the opening vocal subjects sound wholly instrumental in nature until a more motet-like fugue takes over and then the original material returns, brilliantly intensified. In contrast with Bach's earlier triumphal movements, this one shows how far he has developed in terms of the expressiveness of the material and the sense of culmination he brings to it. A soprano recitative introduces a flowing tenor aria for recorder and oboe da caccia (probably played by the two oboists from the opening chorus), and an alto recitative then leads to a dotted-rhythm bass aria with oboe d'amore: a striking effect in the middle is obtained for the words 'stand by me in cross-bearing and suffering', with angular phrases leading to an outburst of joy at 'my mouth sings with joy'. The final chorale is a simple version of 'Was Gott tut, das ist wohlgetan'. This cantata was reworked for the council elections in Bach's last decade, as late as 26 August 1748.

Cantata 77 was written for the Thirteenth Sunday after Trinity on 22 August 1723. The parable of the Good Samaritan provides the quotation for the opening chorus, 'You must love God with your whole heart and soul': the voices enter in counterpoint with the strings, and the *tromba da tirarsi* provides the chorale melody ingeniously in canon with the continuo. The melody is that of 'Dies sind die heilgen zehn Gebot' and the relationship to the Ten Commandments is clearly marked by repeated notes in both chorale and singers; the fact that the trumpet enters ten times is no coincidence – finally it repeats the whole melody. The two oboes pair up for the soprano aria, while the tromba has a remarkably melodic obbligato in the alto aria in D minor, where it has been suggested that the imperfection referred to in the text might be justly be reflected in performance. The final chorale lacks its text.

Cantata 25 for the Fourteenth Sunday after Trinity, 29 August 1723, has an unfortunate libretto, dominated by talk of sin as leprosy; lust, pride and greed are characterised as forms of the disease that only Christ can cure. The opening chorus announces the well-known Passion chorale theme first in the bass, and later in the group of cornett and trombones, while the singers have more involved music to demonstrate their distress. A tenor recitative introduces a bass aria propelled by syncopations in the continuo, while the three recorders acquire independent parts in the soprano aria that follows. The last chorale is simply harmonised.

Bach then had to interrupt his liturgical sequence to write a cantata for the very next day for the council elections: this was Cantata 119 for 30 August, whose autograph score bears the date 1723. This fine work with four trumpets (most unusual), two recorders, three oboes, strings and continuo is very lavish, praising the people of God, giving thanks to the city fathers, and singing Martin Luther's *Te Deum* to conclude. Cantata 138 is an extremely dense and ambitious work, using a traditional hymn text and written for the Fifteenth Sunday after Trinity, 5 September 1723, for which the Gospel reading is from the Sermon on the Mount: the text creates a tension between God's goodness and the evanescence of earthly things. Over a familiar detached bass, two violins and viola develop imitative lines while one oboe d'amore plays the chorale melody against a chromatic line in the second oboe d'amore. This is already a complex texture into which the voices then enter, the tenor introducing each line of the chorale sung by all, and the bass harmonising it with a chromatic descent. The alto interrupts in a recitative – 'I am wretched, heavy cares oppress me' – before the chorale returns to offer consolation. Then it is the bass's turn to complain – 'I am despised' – and to be answered again by the chorale. It is not until both soprano and alto have interjected their personal pleas and the chorale has returned that this remarkable three-movement structure ends. There is one more aria which Bach reused in his later G major Missa, then a richly orchestrated optimistic chorale to finish, in which the violins sweep constant figurations between the oboes and voices – a highly vivid and original chorale setting, and a pointer forward to Bach's more extensive use of chorale material in the coming period.

Bach seems to have been stimulated by his experimentation with the use of the chorale in the last cantata to try again a week later in Cantata 95, written for the Sixteenth Sunday,

12 September. The instrumental resources are smaller – horn, two oboes, strings and continuo – and the opening movement strives above all for openness and clarity, with a bouncing offbeat theme that Bach was later to reuse (for example in *Lobet den Herrn*), which makes the appearance of a sudden dissonance on 'Sterben' (to die) the more striking. The tenor interrupts with his willingness to die, and the singers take off again with a quite different chorale setting over a walking bass, bizarrely and not quite successfully harmonised. There is a new chorale as a soprano solo with oboe d'amore interpolations, and the tenor has an aria with a lovely new sonority, oboes together over gentle pizzicato strings imitating the bell-stroke referred to in the text; a bass recitative leads into the final chorale with violin descant.

It cannot be certain that Cantata 148 is part of the first Leipzig cycle, but it seems to fit as the work given on the Seventeenth Sunday after Trinity, 19 September 1723, though its scoring for clarino with strings and probably oboes is quite festive: perhaps it has its origins in a concerto. Its lively D major writing for chorus is clear and open, with little chromaticism. The text is about Christ's healing on the Sabbath, and the tenor aria with violin solo in virtuoso style expresses desire for healing in life; then a G major alto aria with three oboes is in the rather popular style to which Bach was later to aspire, and a recitative leads to the final simple chorale.

The text of Cantata 48 for the Nineteenth Sunday, 3 October 1723, derives from Paul the Apostle's cry: 'O wretched man, who will deliver me!' The music reverts to a motet-style opening movement in triple time, in G minor, with the voices in imitation, chromatically inflected violins and a trumpet or horn on the chorale tune in canon with unison oboes. There is a chorale halfway through the cantata, then an aria with oboe and a remarkable fully scored tenor aria, which creates at the words 'He can raise the dead' what Stephen Crist describes as 'nothing less than a musical representation of resurrection', before the final chorale.

After a revival of Cantata 162, Bach then wrote Cantata 109 for the 21st Sunday after Trinity, 17 October, based on the struggle between belief and disbelief. He added a part for *corno di tirarsi* (horn, not trumpet), but it largely fulfils a doubling role. The opening movement has an unusually lavish amount of material, with different themes for the instrumental introduction and for the vocal statement, in which the soprano's 'hilf' (help) rings out above the textures; each voice in turn takes the lead, until the final entries pile voice on voice in the superb stretto, followed by a long coda. An overlong tenor solo with dotted-rhythm violins like a Passion aria, characterising unbelief, leads to a simpler, open aria for alto with the two oboes, representing the joy of belief. The final chorale is a splendid fully fledged concerto-style movement with rushing oboes and violins, with the chorale *Durch Adams Fall* declaimed by the singers, led by the soprano: why didn't Bach write this sort of conclusion to his sacred cantatas more often?

The sequence of new works continued with Cantata 89 for 24 October 1723, the 22nd Sunday after Trinity. The theme here is the gulf between man's sin and God's grace, and the Old Testament text with which the cantata starts ('How shall I give you up, Ephraim') inspired Bach to a dark-coloured introductory aria in C minor for bass with horn, oboes and strings. The two remaining arias are lighter in scoring and the final one is dance-like in its contentment, expressing optimism for the future. There is a simple final chorale verse.

With Cantata 60 (not to be confused with Cantata 20 of the same title), first performed on the 24th Sunday after Trinity, 7 November 1723, we reach a new style in Bach's output, a pure duet which Bach himself labelled 'dialogus', characterising the characters as Fear (alto) and Hope (tenor), plus the voice of Christ (bass). There are no solo arias. This is the nearest Bach came to a sacred opera, and it reminds us of Handel's characterisations of Truth, Beauty and Deceit in his early Italian works. As ever it is the Lutheran chorale that provides Bach with his inspiration: the alto sings soberly of eternity amid turbulent strings and oboes d'amore, and then hope dramatically interjects: 'Lord, I wait for your salvation.' The central movement is a duet for Fear and Hope matched by oboe d'amore and violin. A dramatic duet recitative, which highlights the familiar text 'Blessed are the dead who die in the Lord', introduces a Christ-like bass alongside the alto. This leads to the final chorale which would have required only one extra singer, the famous 'Es ist genug' which Alban Berg quotes in his Violin Concerto and which Magnus Lindberg has also arranged: the opening line, with rising tones that span a tritone, must have seemed bizarre in its time, but is what attracted later composers – 'a gripping dramatisation of existential angst', says Stephen Crist.

Cantata 90 followed for the 25th Sunday, 14 November. Strangely there are no indications of scoring in the autograph, and there is no opening chorus, but there is clearly a trumpet solo in the hectoring bass aria, depicting the avenging judge at work, with rising arpeggios and swirling scales. These are foreshadowed in the opening virtuosic tenor aria with strings. The final chorale melody is 'Vater unser in Himmelreich'.

The last work of the liturgical year was Cantata 70, for the 26th Sunday after Trinity, 21 November, and this was adapted from a Weimar cantata for Advent. It deals with the Second Coming of Christ at the end of time: to create a two-part structure, a further chorale and recitatives have been added to the Weimar original. The opening chorus is in Bach's grandest style, though there is only one trumpet and one oboe with the strings, contrasting instrumental fanfares with rushing scales in the unidiomatic vocal parts. The juxtaposition of the blocks of sound and the pacing of the final climax are handled with unerring skill. The shuddering accompaniment returns in the next recitative, 'Tremble, you stubborn sinners', and arias for alto (with cello) and soprano (with violins) lead to the central chorale. Part two opens with a tenor aria that might well be a lost concerto, then a vivid recitative, about the drama of the Day of Judgement, followed by the joy of Paradise. An ethereal bass aria, 'Blessed day of refreshment', follows (in almost homely triple time, like the Last Supper from the St Matthew Passion), broken by a vicious Presto section: 'sound, crack, last stroke, world and heaven go to ruins'. With this extraordinary drama, and a richly scored final chorale, Bach's first series of cantatas for the Sundays of Trinity comes to an end.

♩ *Cantatas Vol. 13: 64, 25, 69a*
Cantatas Vol. 14: 148, 48, 89, 109
Cantatas Vol. 15: 40, 60, 70a, 90
Soloists/Bach Collegium Japan/Suzuki
BIS CD 1041, 1081, 1111

LEIPZIG CANTATAS YEAR ONE:
CHRISTMAS 1723–EPIPHANY 1724

Cantata 40 *Darzu ist erschienen der Sohn Gottes*
Cantata 64 *Sehet, welch eine Liebe hat uns der Vater erzeiget*
Cantata 190 *Singet dem Herrn ein neues Lied* [incomplete]
Cantata 153 *Schau, lieber Gott, wie meine Feind*
Cantata 65 *Sie werden aus Saba alle kommen*

Concerted music was heard only on the First Sunday of Advent in Leipzig, and for that day in 1723 Bach revived one of his Weimar successes, Cantata 61, and then for Christmas Day presented Cantata 63. He was not inactive, however, for he also wrote the version of the Magnificat with Christmas interpolations (see p. 157) and the Sanctus BWV 238 (see p. 155). He was soon in action again with more new compositions, Cantata 40 for the Second Day of Christmas and Cantata 64 for the Third Day.

Cantata 40 uses two horns and two oboes with strings; they give the work a pastoral character not unlike parts of the much later Christmas Oratorio. The opening of the work has a concerto-like nature with the chorus in declamatory mode, but this breaks off for a choral fugue on the same text ('The son of God has appeared so he may destroy the works of the Devil') before a new version of the opening, tightened and with extra contrapuntal skill. This movement was reused in the Missa in F BWV 233. Possibly because of the Christmas season, there are extra chorales between the arias, making a more extended piece. A lovely alto recitative rises to Paradise through string arpeggios; the bass has an aria with oboes and violins, and Bach saves his two horns for the Brandenburg Concerto-like energetic tenor aria, in praise of the Christ child.

Cantata 64 for the next day has a similar structure with extra chorales, and is based on a text by Johann Knauer, but its style is strongly contrasted. The opening in E minor is sober, in old-style counterpoint, with the voices doubled by the ancient sonority of cornett and trombones: 'See what love the father has shown us.' There is a chorale, recitative and another chorale (with active bass line, a characteristic also of Cantata 40), and then a soprano aria in dancing tempo with violins depicting 'fading smoke' and a long middle section. An oboe d'amore is brought in for the alto's 6/8 aria, 'From the world I desire nothing', but doesn't play elsewhere; the final resigned chorale is familiar from *Jesu, meine Freude*.

Cantata 190 for New Year's Day, 1 January 1724, has unfortunately survived incomplete, with parts for voices and violins only in the first two numbers. But it has been reconstructed and is well worth performing for the exuberance of the opening chorus alone, with its energetic fugue and Alleluias, based on the text of the German Te Deum: 'All that has breath, praise the Lord.' The chorale is also heard in the following recitative, and an alto aria with strings maintains the spirit of celebration. After a duet for tenor and bass, the final chorale shows off the full instrumentation with fanfaring trumpet choir in between the verses of the chorale.

Cantata 153 is a modest affair for the Sunday after New Year, 2 January 1724, which was doubtless intended not to strain Bach's singers in between the rigours of Christmas and Epiphany. The text is related to the flight of the Holy Family to Egypt. Unusually, there's only a simple chorale at the beginning, middle and end needing no more than four singers; in addition there is a simple bass aria, but a very difficult tenor aria with strings, based on the image of a whirlwind of tribulation. The bass recitative tells the heart to be calm, and the alto has a beautifully calming aria before the last chorale.

Cantata 65 for Epiphany, 6 January 1724, is one of the most splendid creations of Bach's first period in Leipzig, relishing the use of two *corno di caccia* to create a processional opening movement of great richness and variety: 'They will come from Sheba bearing gifts.' In the voices the procession builds up from the basses: first quickly, then with a longer fugue, adding back the instruments with great intensity, but saving the horns for the climax of the movement. After a chorale and recitative the two oboes da caccia duet for the bass aria, and the horns return for a rustic dancing tenor aria, 'Accept me as your own', before the final chorale. Reflecting on this outpouring of music over a two-week period, Alfred Dürr aptly wonders 'whether the people of Leipzig truly appreciated what riches had been unveiled before them'.

🎧 *Cantatas Vol. 17: 153, 154, 73, 144, 181*
Cantatas Vol. 21: 65, 81, 83, 190
Soloists/Bach Collegium Japan/Suzuki
BIS CD 1221, 1311

LEIPZIG CANTATAS YEAR ONE:
EPIPHANY–EASTER 1724

Cantata 154 *Mein liebster Jesus ist verloren*
Cantata 73 *Herr, wie du willt, so schicks mit mir*
Cantata 81 *Jesus schläft, was soll ich hoffen?*
Cantata 83 *Erfreute Zeit im neuen Bunde*
Cantata 144 *Nimm, was dein ist, und gehe hin*
Cantata 181 *Leichtgesinnte Flattergeister*
Cantata 66 *Erfreut euch, ihr Herzen*
Cantata 134 *Ein Herz, das seinen Jesum lebend weiss*

Cantata 154 takes the annual cycle forward into its next phase: it was written for the First Sunday after Epiphany on 9 January

1724, and revived probably in 1737. 'My dearest Jesus is lost' suggests the theme of the young Christ disappearing from his family, but the point of the text is provided by Jesus's words when found in the temple: 'Know you not that I must be about my father's business?' There is a fine arioso for bass in the middle, setting Christ's reproach, which leads to a glorious duet for alto and tenor which shifts tempo as they sing 'I will never leave you again, Lord Jesus'. Cantata 73, 'Lord, if you will, ordain it to me', followed for 23 January 1724, the Third Sunday after Epiphany, highlighting the story of the leper and presenting Christ's healing mercy as the salvation for the soul. There is a complex opening chorale-based movement, a tenor aria, bass aria, and final chorale. Cantata 81 for the Fourth Sunday after Epiphany (which does not occur every year, depending on the date of Easter) fell on 30 January 1724, and Bach wrote music requiring alto, tenor and bass soloists who would have been joined by a soprano for the final simple chorale.

Cantata 83 was written for the Feast of the Purification in 1724 on 2 February. The text highlights the words of the Nunc Dimittis, welcoming death, but the opening solo alto aria reflects on the glad time of the New Covenant. The two horn players from the Epiphany are used again, but it is the principal violin who is more heavily featured in the gracious, sweetly turned opening – which must have been adapted from a violin concerto, especially with the cross-string figuration in the central section. The second movement stands out: it places the Nunc Dimittis text in the bass set to a simple psalm tone, in a strict canon between the violins and the continuo, broken by recitative sections. Then the tenor has a busy skipping aria in triplets with violin solo, hastening towards the throne of mercy, before a recitative and the final chorale.

Cantata 144 takes us back to the church year and the Third Sunday before Lent, called Septuagesima, which fell on 6 February 1724. The text preaches contentment with one's lot: whatever God wills, that will be best. The opening reverts to a strict motet style with only doubling instruments. A quiet alto aria with strings low in their register and a soprano aria with oboe d'amore are enclosed by two simple chorales. This cantata was often cited after Bach's death as a model example of the form, probably more for its old-style writing than for its imaginative elements.

Cantata 181 is for Sexagesima, first performed on 13 February 1724, Dürr believes, alongside a revival of Cantata 18. A transverse flute part survives but this must be from a later revival; strings are adequate to support the bass in the opening Vivace in E minor, as he denounces the 'frivolous fluttering spirits who rob themselves of the Word's power' with clearly marked staccato notes and throwaway pauses. After an alto recitative about the seed that falls on stony ground, the central tenor aria is with continuo only, though it may lack a violin solo. A soprano recitative leads to the last movement, which is a fully worked chorus in D major of the kind we might expect at the start, with solo trumpet, dazzling vocal lines, and a quieter central section which is a duet for soprano and alto, celebrating the word of God that transforms the heart of the believer.

Cantata 66 was written for Easter Monday, 10 April 1724, and is thought to be drawn from a lost secular work from Cöthen of December 1718, Cantata 66a. The words have been skilfully altered, and the original finale brought to the beginning of the work. The use of oboes and bassoon against strings and voices is added to by an optional trumpet whose role is mainly to reinforce the top line; amid the rushing and dashing of the opening celebration, the central section with its chromatic descent for 'you can drive away sorrow, fear, anxiety' is set for bass and alto, representing Fear and Hope (in the secular original they were Fame and Happiness). This section in the secular original is for soloists, but Bach does not indicate that here: he surely presumed it. A dance-like bass aria has clearly secular origins and the accompaniment is wonderfully syncopated. Fear and Hope have a duet arioso and then a duet with virtuoso violin (originally for a Cöthen soloist), against dance-like triple metre. The chorale at the

close sings 'Alleluia, Lord have mercy': 'Christ ist erstanden'
(Christ is risen).

Cantata 134, written for 11 April 1724, Easter Tuesday, is
a parody of another earlier Cöthen work, the secular Cantata
134a for New Year's Day (which untypically survives).
Unusually for a church work (and like Cantatas 173 and 184),
a recitative begins the cantata, which in the secular version
introduced the soloists as Time and Divine Providence,
leading to a tenor aria in B flat with oboes and violins. This
is dance-like, and the very enjoyable alto and tenor duet in
the centre of the work is also quite rustic, with Brandenburg
Concerto-like writing for the strings. There is a long and
exuberantly full worked-out final chorus with a lengthy
middle section bringing back the alto and tenor. Bach was
evidently dissatisfied with the adaptation of the recitatives,
and rewrote these for a later Leipzig revival.

🎧 *Cantatas Vol. 17: 153, 154, 73, 144, 181*
Cantatas Vol. 18: 66, 134, 67
Soloists/Bach Collegium Japan/Suzuki
BIS CD 1221, 1251

LEIPZIG CANTATAS YEAR ONE:
EASTER–TRINITY 1724

Cantata 67 *Halt im Gedächtnis Jesum Christ*
Cantata 104 *Du Hirte Israel, höre*
Cantata 166 *Wo gehest du hin?*
Cantata 86 *Wahrlich, wahrlich, ich sage euch*
Cantata 37 *Wer da gläubet und getauft wird*
Cantata 44 *Sie werden euch in den Bann tun*
Cantata 184 *Erwünschtes Freudenlicht*
Cantata 194 *Höchsterwünschtes Freudenfest*

With Cantata 67, a tight-knit, gloriously memorable cantata,
Bach went up a notch in the sheer brilliance and concision of
his writing, and conceived a work of little over fifteen minutes
which is completely original. It was written for the First Sunday

after Easter, 16 April 1724. One secret is surely in the simplic-
ity of the fanfare-like opening gesture, 'Hold in remembrance
Jesus Christ', with solidly descending bass line, which under-
pins the whole movement. 'Halt' is often declaimed as a chord
or in long notes, and both voices and the *corno di tirasi* (which
here is a trumpet, dancing above the textures) then extend
this endlessly, with increasingly close imitation and a perfectly
paced close. As a piece of liturgical and musical communication this movement could not be surpassed. Without any
break a tenor aria follows in bright E major, and then a chorale
framed by recitatives. The next movement is unprecedented
and extraordinary, alternating vividly active strings with con-
soling wind, the strings conjuring up turbulence and the wind
calming as the bass sings 'peace be with you'. Soprano, alto
and tenor interrupt to sing that 'Jesus helps us fight against the
enemy': three times this happens, the bass involving himself
in the turmoil and returning to close the movement in peace.
This is as vivid and operatic a tableau as Bach ever wrote. (He
adapted it in his Missa in A in the 1730s.) There is nothing
more to do except close with the chorale.

Cantata 104, for the Second Sunday after Easter, 23 April
1724, inspired by the picture of the Shepherd of Israel, is
completely different from anything else around this time: a
masterpiece in pastoral mode, with swinging rhythms and
chiming thirds that could as easily be about nymphs and
shepherds as it is about followers of Christ. Bach resourcefully
mines a vein of complete serenity as opposed to his frequent
self-flagellation: how wonderfully he extends the lines on the
word 'Schafe' to create a feeling of almost hypnotic happiness. The arias are for tenor with two oboes d'amore, warm
and enfolding, and for bass with strings and oboe d'amore –
another lilting pastoral number, with a simple final chorale.

After reviving Cantata 12 for Jubilate Sunday, Bach's next
new work is Cantata 166, for Cantate Sunday, the Fourth after
Easter, 7 May 1724. 'Where are we going?' asks the Christ-
like bass in the opening arioso, and the tenor answers in a
G minor aria with oboe and (reconstructed) violin solo that

he will think only of Christ. The following chorale, with the line 'Hold me to these thoughts', uses a very inflexible phrase in the continuo and violins under which the soprano sings the chorale. The alto aria recalls one in the St John Passion, though the text tells of 'good fortune laughing' and the final chorale is simple.

Cantata 86 was written for the Fifth Sunday after Easter, 14 May 1724, when the Gospel is Jesus's farewell: 'Ask for something in my name and it will be given to you.' The opening in E major is severe, antique, and within a small vocal range, but then the alto aria that follows has the most florid violin solo full of arpeggiation, inspired by the line 'I would gather roses even though the thorns should prick me'. The following chorale uses imitation between the two oboes d'amore to frame the chorale melody, while the tenor's recitative and aria praise God's help as secure, and the finale chorale encourages us to live in hope.

Cantata 37 was written for Ascension Day on 18 May 1724, and is based around Jesus's words that whoever believes and is baptised shall be saved. The opening movement in A major is quite severe, in motet style, and the repeated notes seem to refer to the commandments. The following tenor aria lacks an obbligato player. Then there is an outstandingly beautiful canonic treatment of the chorale for soprano and alto with continuo, a bass aria with violins, and a final chorale. Cantata 44 (not to be confused with 183 of the same title) was written for the Sunday after Ascension on 21 May 1724, and shows Bach once again inventing a different way of presenting his material: here the first movement is a duet for tenor and bass in close imitation with two oboes, leading straight to all the voices joining in the second section (a procedure Dürr says Bach derived from Telemann). There is an alto solo with oboe, and another solo chorale for the tenor. The bass recitative leads to a dancing soprano *da capo* aria in B flat, and the last chorale.

Cantata 59 may have been written for Whit Sunday 1723, though the performing parts are not from until a year later, so it possibly belongs in 1724. It is brightly scored with two trumpets and drums, strings and voices, beginning with a duet for soprano and bass; it has only one aria for bass, preceded by a chorale setting on 'Komm Heiliger Geist'. There may be another chorale missing at the close, as one part indicates 'Chorale segue'.

Some confusion surrounds the end of this cantata cycle, because Cantata 173 has now been redated to 1727. Cantata 184 was adapted, rather hastily, for 30 May 1724, and was also revived in 1727. The 'desired light of joy' is here depicted by two prattling flutes over a tenor recitative and they are also kept busy in the soprano and alto duet that follows. After a tenor aria there is both a simple chorale and then a Gavotte-like final chorus – 'Good Shepherd, comfort your people' – with a middle-section duet for soprano and bass.

However, it is still likely that Cantata 194 was given on Trinity Sunday 1724. This is an extensive two-part work in itself, an adaptation of the organ consecration cantata for the church at Störmthal near Leipzig in November 1723, in turn based on a secular original. It is a grandiose work with a French Overture opening chorus, the instrumental dotted section returning at the end of the middle section, with a clever sudden vocal entry at the very end of the movement. The arias include a pastoral one for bass, a gavotte for soprano, a gigue for tenor, and a minuet with oboes for soprano and bass, all in extrovert style, the dance forms emphasising its secular origins. Even the final chorale dances in triple time.

♫ *Cantatas Vol. 19: 86, 37, 104, 166*
Cantatas Vol. 20: 184, 173, 59, 44
Soloists/Bach Collegium Japan/Suzuki
BIS CD 1261, 1271

LEIPZIG CANTATAS YEAR TWO:
SUNDAYS 1–14 AFTER TRINITY 1724

Cantata 20 *O Ewigkeit, du Donnerwort*
Cantata 2 *Ach Gott, vom Himmel sieh darein*
Cantata 7 *Christ, unser Herr, zum Jordan kam*
Cantata 135 *Ach Herr, mich armen Sünder*
Cantata 10 *Meine Seel' erhebt den Herren*
Cantata 93 *Wer nur den lieben Gott lässt walten*
Cantata 107 *Was willst du dich betrüben*
Cantata 178 *Wo Gott der Herr nicht bei uns hält*
Cantata 94 *Was frag' ich nach der Welt*
Cantata 101 *Nimm von uns Herr, du treuer Gott*
Cantata 113 *Herr Jesu Christ, du höchstes Gut*
Cantata 33 *Allein zu dir, Herr Jesu Christ*

Whereas Bach's first cantata cycle seems to have been an exuberant and diverse response to the opportunities offered by
his new place of employment, the next annual set appears to
have been much more systematically planned. In particular,
Bach uses Lutheran chorales to unify the set in a way that he
had not previously attempted – though he had written one
early work of 'pure' chorale variations in Cantata 4.

Is it a coincidence that the first cantata of the new cycle,
for the First Sunday after Trinity on 11 June 1724, opens
with a French Overture? Bach had also done this in the first
cantata of the liturgical year in Weimar (Cantata 61). Dürr
has noted a conscious planning, too, in the way that in the
first four cantatas of the cycle the great opening movements
are in different styles, the Overture followed by a motet-style
opening to Cantata 2, a concerto-like opening to Cantata 7,
and a chorale fantasia in Cantata 135; and in each the chorale
is given to a different voice: soprano, alto, tenor and bass in
turn. Usually chorale cantatas use the first and last verses
of the chorale unchanged, and then modify freely the inner
verses so that they are suitable for recitative and arias; we do
not know who collaborated with Bach on this task, but it must
have been someone local, perhaps Andreas Stübel, the former

co-rector of the Thomasschule, whose early death in 1725 might account for the sudden end of the sequence.

Cantata 20 immediately shows Bach relishing a new freedom in the formulation of his material, for though the opening is related to the chorale melody, the fugal material is very free and seems more prompted by the sentiments of the text, about the terror suggested by the thought of Eternity. The chorale text recurs literally in the tenor recitative and aria, and there is a lovely, flowing bass aria with three burbling oboes: 'God is just in all his deeds'. The alto aria that follows is much more chromatic, and leads to a simple chorale at the end of part one. Part two uses a solo trumpet in a bass aria to arouse man from his sleep, and an alto recitative leads to an alto and bass duet before the final chorale. Cantata 2 followed on the Second Sunday, 18 June 1724: the opening movement could not have been more of a contrast, in a severe D minor with the alto's chorale line prepared by old-fashioned imitation in the other voices: 'Ah God, look down from heaven and take pity on us!' There is a much more modern aria for alto with violin, with some symbolism in the crossing lines of the tenor aria about the purification offered by the Cross.

Cantata 7 was written for the Feast of St John the Baptist on 24 June 1724, and therefore makes use of Martin Luther's hymn for baptism. The fine opening E minor movement dominates the work, with the tenor taking the *cantus firmus* and the oboes d'amore and strings both evoking the waters of the Jordan (the tutti dotted rhythm has been associated with the rocks through which the river flows, which may be going a little far). The baptismal imagery continues in the following recitatives and arias, of which the most unusual is the last for alto, in which the instruments gradually join and eventually conclude together. Cantata 135 was performed on the Third Sunday after Trinity on 25 June 1724, and the marvellous opening E minor fantasia, starting with the high instruments, brings in the bass as the bearer of the chorale melody, 'Ah Lord do not rebuke me a sinner in your anger.' The sequence of recitatives and arias includes a finely scored tenor aria with two oboes and a passionate bass aria with strings. Cantata 10 for the Visitation on 2 July 1724 is another remarkable work, using a Gregorian theme for the Magnificat as its melody. Its lively opening movement thus acquires an antique air, but Bach's writing is purposefully modern, with a full-scale concerto texture and an increasingly exciting contrapuntal texture which reaches a unanimous climax. The arias are all busy: the soprano is surrounded by strings and oboes, the bass with only a solidly repeated continuo figure. Then a chromatic-based duet for alto and tenor, 'He, remembering his mercy', lets the chorale be heard instrumentally and the final tenor recitative moves towards arioso. The final chorale is a simple version of the Gregorian theme.

Cantata 93, for the Fifth Sunday on 9 July 1724, maintains the freedom of contrast between the instrumental and vocal lines with a superb opening fantasia in C minor in which the soprano and alto, and then the tenor and bass, elaborate on the theme before it enters, while the instruments develop different material. The chorale melody is heard again in the instruments in the duet for soprano and alto (as in the previous cantata), and even the free arias manage to make some reference to the chorale melody. Cantata 107 is entirely based on a 1630 hymn by Johann Heermann, and was written for 23 July 1724, the Seventh Sunday after Trinity; unusually, the text is not rewritten for the arias or for the single recitative. Two flutes appear alongside the more familiar oboes d'amore and strings, and the chorale melody is heard on a corno da caccia – there is no choral elaboration, and the soprano leads off each line. There is a sequence of four arias, a lively one for bass with strings, with melismas on 'erjagen' (hunt) and 'Rat' (counsel), followed by arias for tenor and continuo, and for soprano with oboes d'amore. The final tenor aria is scored with flutes and violin playing together against a pizzicato bass line. The last chorale is a lilting chorale like the pastoral symphony from the Christmas Oratorio.

Cantata 178 was written a week later for 30 July 1724, the Eighth Sunday. This is another masterpiece, based on Psalm 124 and the idea of God's support in times of conflict. The independence of singers and instruments is more marked than ever in the opening fantasia, with different ways in which the voices support the chorale melody, now in block chords, now in imitative fragments, and the instrumentalists fly with their own free concerto for the oboes and violins. The alto takes up the chorale, alternating presto lines (accompanied by a rapid version of the chorale tune in the continuo) with more meditative recitative. After a bass aria based on the idea of rolling waves, the tenor has a delightful setting of the chorale within a trio sonata for two oboes and continuo, and the other chorale movement is also highly original, choir alternating with recitative but over an unchanging continuo pattern. The tenor sings an aria about 'tottering reason' before the simple final chorale.

Cantata 94 for the Ninth Sunday, 6 August 1724, marks the emancipation of the transverse flute which launches this cantata and from here on receives special attention: the chorale is very concisely stated by the choir, and the attention is more on the flute's solo. A bass aria with offbeat continuo leads to a tenor arioso with two oboes, broken by recitatives. The alto aria thrusts the flute into great prominence in an extravagant denunciation of the deluded world, but the tenor's view of the world is more relaxed in the swinging aria that follows. The soprano is accompanied by oboe d'amore, dismissing the world in a carefree spirit, and the chorale returns in the final simple setting.

Cantata 101 is permeated by the chorale text 'Take from us Lord, you faithful God, severe punishment and great distress', to the famous melody 'Vater unser in Himmelreich': even the recitatives quote the hymn directly, broken up by commentary. The cantata was written for the Tenth Sunday on 13 August 1724; the noble opening movement is in strict motet style, in modal D minor, but instrumentally rich, with wind and strings complemented by cornetto and trombones doubling the voices. Between the lines of the chorale the orchestra's drooping figures are reminiscent of the 'Et incarnatus' from the B minor Mass. There is a much lighter tone in the first aria for tenor with flute (later replaced by violin). In the third, elaborate fourth and simpler fifth movements, the chorale is juxtaposed with recitatives (the bass aria has the strongest contrasts between the calm of the chorale and the dancing oboe-dominated energy of the surrounding material) and the beautiful 12/8 duet for soprano and alto in the sixth is accompanied by flute and oboe da caccia.

Cantata 113 for the Eleventh Sunday after Trinity was performed on 20 August 1724. The text pleads with God to be merciful to us sinners, in a 1588 hymn by Ringwald. In the opening movement, while the two oboes d'amore weave an imitative line, the violins are continually active and the chorale is declaimed without counterpoint. That is saved for the second movement, where violin and continuo surround the alto's chorale melody, and for the duetting of the two oboes d'amore in the beautiful bass aria that follows (like the 'Et in spiritum' from the B minor Mass). He then has a chorale movement over a busy bass line, and the brilliant flute obbligato in the tenor aria once again suggests the presence of a new virtuoso. The soprano and alto extend the chorale melody with endless roulades, and the cantata ends simply. Cantata 33 is for the Thirteenth Sunday after Trinity and was first heard on 3 September 1724. The hymn is by Konrad Hubert and text is included not only in the opening and closing movements: 'In you alone, Lord Jesus Christ, my hope is placed on earth'. The singers once again declaim the chorale simply and the emphasis is placed on the surrounding instrumental texture in A minor, launched with rushing scales by two oboes and then two violins. There's a vivid portrayal of the fearful, wandering soul in an aria for alto with muted violins and pizzicato strings. Then there is an unusual duet for tenor and bass with two oboes, sounding like a trio sonata, and a final chorale.

Cantatas Vol. 21: 65, 81, 83, 190
Cantatas Vol. 22: 20, 7, 94
Cantatas Vol. 23: 10, 93, 178, 107
Soloists/Bach Collegium Japan/Suzuki
BIS CD 1311, 1321, 1331

LEIPZIG CANTATAS YEAR TWO:
SUNDAYS 15–25 AFTER TRINITY 1724

Cantata 78 *Jesu, der du meine Seele*
Cantata 99 *Was Gott tut, das ist wohlgetan*
Cantata 8 *Liebster Gott, wenn werd ich sterben?*
Cantata 130 *Herr Gott, dich loben alle wir*
Cantata 114 *Ach, lieben Christen, seid getrost*
Cantata 96 *Herr Christ, der ein'ge Gottessohn*
Cantata 5 *Wo soll ich fliehen hin?*
Cantata 180 *Schmücke dich, o liebe Seele*
Cantata 38 *Aus tiefer Not schrei ich zu dir*
Cantata 115 *Mache dich, mein Geist, bereit*
Cantata 139 *Wohl dem, der sich auf seinen Gott*
Cantata 26 *Ach wie flüchtig, ach wie nichtig*
Cantata 116 *Du Friedefürst, Herr Jesu Christ*

Cantata 78 is one of the absolute high points of Bach's cantatas, a concentrated masterpiece which unites all his concerns with musical form, liturgical meaning, and intense expressivity. Written for the Fourteenth Sunday after Trinity on 10 September 1724 but subsequently reused, it was based on a hymn by Johann Rist: 'Jesus, you who have rent my soul'. The genius of the opening movement (which has been penetratingly analysed by Laurence Dreyfus) is to combine an old form, the descending chromatic passacaglia, with both imitative choral writing and the chorale melody (in this first version doubled by *corno di tirarsi*), moulding both to the text to create an effect of unsurpassed power. Though the movement is basically in G minor, there is a contrasted section in the major, as the chorus reflects on God as Saviour. The second movement is unique in Bach's output: a dancing, exuberant duet for soprano and alto with continuo that is indeed continuous, inspired by the idea of following God, racing exuberantly onwards. This extrovert piece has become well known as a separate item, but gains in power from following the initial chorus. There is a tenor aria with flute, a dramatic Passion-like recitative for bass which ends with an expressive arioso, and then a solid bass aria with oboe, of great originality. The chorale returns to conclude the work, with the flute high above the texture. A perfect cantata, taut and moving.

Alfred Dürr's redating of the cantatas was based on close analysis of paper watermarks, handwriting and liturgical usage; it has been strikingly confirmed by Tatiana Shabalina's new discovery of a cantata libretto booklet for this period of the Thirteenth to the Sixteenth Trinity Sundays in 1724, and Michaelmas, giving the texts of Cantatas 33, 78, 99, 8 and 130, showing that Dürr's deductions were correct. Cantata 99, for the Fifteenth Sunday on 17 September 1724, opens with a full-scale concerto in G major to which the chorale seems almost incidental: flute, oboe d'amore and violins in their lowest register create a concertino group of wonderful sonorities. Each line is begun by the sopranos and soon supported by the others, but there is no contrapuntal elaboration here. The flute has a brilliant obbligato for the tenor aria, and returns for the soprano and alto duet, this time duetting with the oboe d'amore.

Cantata 8 for the Sixteenth Sunday on 24 September 1724 is one of the most famous of the set because of the unique sonorities of the opening movement in the unusual key of E major, which reflects the chorale text by Caspar Neumann. The flute is again prominent, with a part so high that Bach had to transpose the whole cantata down when he revived it in the 1740s. Over the oboes d'amore and muted strings the high flute chimes the funeral bell which will take the soul to Christ, while the chorus sings the hymn by Daniel Vetter, set as a lilting pastoral melody, an exquisite multi-layered effect. The second movement has a pizzicato bass, for a tenor aria with oboe d'amore, keeping the lightness of touch, though the text is about man's agitation in the face of death; and the bass has a triple-time aria with flute or flauto piccolo in the stratosphere. The final chorale unusually keeps a touch of imitation in the entries of the voices.

Cantata 130 is a dramatic cantata written for St Michael's Day, 29 September 1724, and conjuring up in its first movement the bustle of the angels in war-like mode, with trumpets, wind and strings vying for attention in bright C major. The chorale in the soprano is supported by counterpoint in the lower voices, which enter under rather than before the melody. The battle mode continues in the first aria for bass, which retains all three trumpets in a picture of the angels battling the dragon. (For a later revival Bach had to replace these parts with strings.) A duet recitative restores calm, and the tenor solo with flute is a formal gavotte with a vivid picture of the soul being carried up to heaven. The trumpets seal each line of the final chorale. Cantata 114 is for the Seventeenth Sunday after Trinity on 1 October 1724. The chorale from the hymn by Johannes Gigas is heard not just in the first and last movements but also in the central movement, a solo for soprano with short-breathed, biting phrases in the continuo. The instrumental textures of the splendid first movement are also derived from the chorale, with the singers reinforcing the contrast between courage and despair. There is an aria for tenor with virtuoso flute (who is however told not to play in the opening movement, an unusual marking), and one for alto with oboe and strings.

Cantata 96 was written for the Eighteenth Sunday after Trinity, 8 October 1724, and is based on a hymn by Elisabeth Creutziger of 1524. In the opening movement Bach depicts the shining of Christ as the Morning Star in the bright notes of a flauto piccolo (a high recorder rather than a piccolo), while putting the chorale melody in the alto part rather than as usual in the soprano part. The tenor aria once more uses the virtuoso flute player, while the bass aria charts the course of the soul as it walks with Christ. Some revisions of scoring were made when Bach revived this cantata and no longer had a piccolo flute available. Cantata 5 is for the Nineteenth Sunday after Trinity on 15 October 1724, based on a hymn by Johann Hermann of 1630: the autograph score is in the British Library, having belonged to Stefan Zweig. The G minor opening uses material from the chorale melody to build up the opening fantasia in which the soprano with *tromba di tirarsi* announces the theme: 'Where shall I flee? For I am burdened with many sins.' In the middle of the vividly drawn arias depicting the rushing of Christ's blood (tenor with an unusual viola solo) and the taming of the forces of hell (bass with trumpet), there is a central recitative for alto in which the oboe pays the chorale melody.

Cantata 180 for the Twentieth Sunday after Trinity, 22 October 1724, has the title of one of Bach's most famous chorale preludes, but this cantata by contrast is cheerfully upbeat, with the text encouraging the soul to emerge into the light of God's love, and the music flowing in F, in 12/8 rhythm with the chorale in the top line with supporting counterpoint. Two recorders in the opening movement are joined by oboe and oboe da caccia, and it seems that one recorder player would then have played the flute in the equally cheerful tenor aria that follows. The soloist in the recitative is a 'cello piccolo' with an extra high string, which features in several cantatas over the next few months. The recorder and strings return for the soprano aria, a perhaps deliberately undemanding number, and a bass recitative leads to the finale chorale.

Cantata 38 for the 21st Sunday, 29 October 1724, is a penitential cantata on the famous hymn by Martin Luther of 1524, which Bach also set as an organ chorale prelude; as befits its sombre character the first movement is an old-style motet with voices doubled by trombones. Two oboes duet happily with the tenor portraying God's words of comfort, and after a soprano recitative with chorale there is something very unexpected: a trio, or Aria Terzetto as it is called here (looking forward to the Christmas Oratorio which also has a trio), for soprano, alto and bass in close imitation with continuo, contrasting the trials and tribulations of life with the comfort God brings. A simple chorale ends this rather stern cantata. Cantata 115 for the 22nd Sunday after Trinity was first performed on 5 November 1724, and is based on Johann Freystein's hymn of 1695. The outstanding opening setting in G, for horn, flute, oboe d'amore, strings and voices derives its energy from octave leaps in both instruments and voices; the superb pacing of the material accumulates huge power during the movement. There is a slow alto aria with oboe d'amore in sustained triple time, depicting the slumbering soul, with a racing central section as the soul awakes. The cello piccolo returns with flute to provide an elaborate duet accompaniment to the soprano's sublime aria, and the tenor recitative leads to the final chorale over a steady tread of bass notes.

Cantata 139 uses the hymn by Johann Rube of 1692 and was first performed on the 23rd Sunday after Trinity, 12 November 1724. This is an example of an opening fantasia in which Bach's instrumental ideas stem from the opening of the chorale melody, providing an inexorable logic when it appears in the sopranos. In order to highlight the chorale, the lower voices are kept to imitative textures mostly under the melody. There seems to be an instrument missing from the second aria; the extended bass aria depicts misfortune on all sides, contrasted with the comfort of God's light. Cantata 26 was first performed on 19 November 1724, the 24th Sunday after Trinity, and uses the hymn by Michael Franck of 1652 which reflects on the emptiness of earthly things. The evanescence of life is superbly evoked in the opening A minor movement with shooting scales for oboes, strings and continuo (Dürr calls them 'spectral showers'), while the voices are mainly kept to solid interjections under the chorale line. This taut, tense movement leads to a complex tenor aria, and an alto recitative with the longest melisma at the very start on 'Freude' (joy). The dance-like bass aria is in bourrée form, with the shooting scales appearing again in its central section. This is surely one of the best unified and condensed of all Bach's chorale cantatas.

Cantata 116 has a most lovely opening movement using Bach's increasing liking for offbeat accents: this one derives its energy from a suspension over the middle beat of the bar. It was written for the 25th Sunday after Trinity, 26 November 1724, to the hymn by Jakob Ebert of 1601. The first two lines and the last two lines of the chorale are plainly sung, but the middle lines are more elaborated by the lower voices. An expressive oboe d'amore solo with alto leads from a recitative to another rare terzett (as in Cantata 38) for soprano, tenor and bass, also using suspensions across the bar lines (mirrored in the silent downbeat of the continuo part).

🎧 *Cantatas Vol. 25: 78, 99, 114*
Cantatas Vol. 26: 180, 122, 96
Cantatas Vol. 27: 80, 5, 115
Soloists/Bach Collegium Japan/Suzuki
BIS CD 1361, 1401, 1421

LEIPZIG CANTATAS YEAR TWO:
ADVENT–CHRISTMAS 1724

Cantata 62 *Nun komm, der Heiden Heiland*
Cantata 91 *Gelobet seist du, Jesu Christ*
Cantata 121 *Christum wir sollen loben schon*
Cantata 133 *Ich freue mich in dir*
Cantata 122 *Das neugeborene Kindelein*

One would think that Bach might have rested after his extraordinary sequence of chorale cantatas. But he pressed onwards with the series into the new liturgical year, creating some of his greatest masterpieces within a short space of time, and also writing the Sanctus in D for Christmas 1724 that later found a place in the B minor Mass. Cantata 62 is an outstanding example: using the same chorale by Martin Luther as Cantata 61, Bach creates a very different mood for the first Sunday of Advent, 3 December 1724. The masterstroke here is the creation of a busy, celebratory orchestral texture under which the continuo surprises us with the first statement of the chorale tune. The voices then prepare the way for the full statement in the soprano, 'Now the Lord comes from highest heaven.' The effect is brilliantly integrated, and perfectly paced. There is a tenor aria celebrating the coming of Christ, a bass aria where the strings join with continuo to provide a unison accompaniment, and then a rhapsodic duet for soprano and alto, before the final chorale.

Cantata 91 was written for Christmas Day 1724: Bach must already have been working on cantatas for the two following days as well as for the next week: four extensive vocal works in seven days. Once again the hymn is by Luther from 1524, and Bach allows himself a full four bars in G major to establish the celebration with energetically burbling horns in thirds, before the chorale tune is announced. The chorale is heard again in the second movement, a recitative for soprano, and the tenor has three oboes gracefully supporting him in his aria. As the bass depicts the 'vale of tears' that is life, he sings chromatically, and the first violin rises in an ethereal postlude. Jagged violins in unison drive the soprano and alto duet; horns and drums add reinforcement to the final chorale. Cantata 121 for the Second Day of Christmas, 26 December 1724, features yet another Luther chorale: 'A solis ortus cardine', one of those derived from plainsong. Perhaps to acknowledge this ancient root, he makes his first movement an old-style motet in E minor with instruments doubling the voices and the chorale in the top line. There's a tenor aria with oboe d'amore and a lively bass aria with strings in C. The final chorale harmonisation at the close extends the final work to 'eternity' ('Ewigkeit').

A day later, the Third Day of Christmas, for Cantata 133, Bach found an unfamiliar chorale tune for the hymn 'Ich freue mich in dir' of 1697 by Caspar Ziegler, and jotted it down on the manuscript of his Sanctus for Christmas Day. Initially this exuberant work sounds like a lively concerto (could it have been one?), into which the simply harmonised chorale melody is ingeniously slotted – the last line is extended, but the instruments rather than the voices then complete the movement. The two oboes d'amore duet with the alto, and then the strings with the soprano, whose aria has a beautifully contrasted central section without continuo support. Cantata 122 was Bach's last cantata of 1724, for the Sunday after Christmas, performed on 31 December; this is a small, intimate work with oboe and violins doubling in the opening movement, which it is hard to imagine sung other than by a group of soloists. The bass sings over the continuo, and three recorders strangely appear for a single soprano recitative; there is a terzett, a bass recitative, and then 'the true year of jubilation arrives' in the final chorale, ushering in 1725. Bach must have looked back with some satisfaction at the achievements of the completed year and the sequence of cantatas he had created.

🎧 *Cantatas Vol. 28: 62, 139, 26, 116*
Cantatas Vol. 31: 91, 101, 121, 133
Soloists/Bach Collegium Japan/Suzuki
BIS CD 1451, 1481

LEIPZIG CANTATAS YEAR TWO:
NEW YEAR'S DAY–LENT 1725

Cantata 41 *Jesu, nun sei gepreiset*
Cantata 123 *Liebster Immanuel, Herzog der Frommen*
Cantata 124 *Meinen Jesum lass ich nicht*
Cantata 3 *Ach Gott, wie manches Herzeleid*
Cantata 111 *Was mein Gott will, das g'scheh allzeit*
Cantata 92 *Ich hab in Gottes Herz und Sinn*
Cantata 125 *Mit Fried und Freud ich fahr dahin*
Cantata 126 *Erhalt uns Herr, bei deinem Wort*
Cantata 127 *Herr Jesu Christ, wahr' Mensch und Gott*
Cantata 1 *Wie schön leuchtet der Morgenstern*

Bach did not rest as 1725 arrived, but pressed on with his sequence of chorale cantatas. Cantata 41 for New Year's Day uses the chorale by Johann Hermann of 1591. The opening movement has a very long verse to set, praising God at the New Year and hoping for future blessings. Bach puts between the opening and closing lines of the chorale a contrasted adagio and presto (fugal) central section. The grandeur is reinforced by groups of three trumpets and drums, three oboes and strings. The soprano aria has three oboes and a gentle pastoral nature, while the cello piccolo appears again in the next aria with tenor. After the bass recitative, in which all the singers deliver a line of the chorale, the final arrangement uses the trumpets to intersperse the chorale lines, and there is because of the length a central section in triple time.

Cantata 123 was written for the Epiphany, on 6 January 1725. The hymn is by Fritsch from 1679, and the opening movement in 9/8 time in B minor perhaps depicts the 'devout' referred to in the opening stanza. There are two recitatives and arias, one of which is intensely chromatic, to depict the 'hard journey of the cross', and the other for bass with flute, depicting loneliness as the instruments fall away to leave the voice alone; the final chorale is indicated to end quietly. Cantata 124, for the Sunday after Epiphany, 7 January 1725, makes use of the hymn by Christian Keymann (1658), with a text that is an outstanding example of the longing for escape from the world and death which will lead to heaven. The opening movement features the oboe d'amore in a minuet-like concerto which integrates the chorale melody simply into the textures. Then after the recitative the oboe d'amore is heard again in the tenor's aria, conjuring up the moment of death with repeated string figures; a soprano and alto duet with continuo alone leads to the final chorale.

Cantata 3 takes us to the Second Sunday after Epiphany, 14 January 1725, and to the hymn by Martin Moller of 1587, in its turn based on 'Jesu dulcis memoria': 'It is hard for the soul to travel through life and turn to Jesus in heaven.' The opening movement is marked Adagio and the chorale melody is anticipated by the pair of oboes d'amore. The vocal chorale is unusually in the bass supported by trombone. The chorale recurs in the following recitative, and the bass has an impassioned aria with continuo about 'Hell's anguish and pain'. A lovely, swinging duet for soprano and alto is accompanied by the oboes and violins.

Curiously, Cantata 111 is based on a hymn by Duke Albrecht, Margrave of Brandenburg, and so an ancestor of the man to whom Bach fruitlessly sent his concertos. It is a chorale cantata for the Third Sunday of Epiphany, 21 January 1725. Oboes and violins create the relatively simple instrumental Vivaldi-like texture into which the chorale is sung in long notes by the soprano line. The aria is for bass and continuo, followed by a duet for alto and tenor with strings, depicting 'resolute footsteps'. The final recitative turns to arioso to introduce the chorale. Cantata 92, for Septuagesima on 28 January 1725, is an extended work in nine movements, using much of the twelve-verse hymn by Paul Gerhardt (1647). The chorale melody, set in B minor, is independent of the surrounding lines for oboes and violins. The following bass number is dramatic, depicting the falling of mountains and hills in tumbling continuo lines, and continually interrupting the meditation with lines from the chorale. There is more 'breaking and falling' in the violin obbligato to the tenor aria, but a calmer mood prevails in the lovely oboe d'amore duet for the alto's chorale melody, and the bass has another furiously energetic, 'blustering' ('Brausen') aria with continuo. The chorale returns in the next recitative for four voices, and then there is a lightly scored soprano aria for oboe d'amore and pizzicato strings.

Cantata 125 sets the Nunc Dimittis, in the version by Martin Luther (1524), which is associated with the Purification on 2 February. The aching, rising figures of the first movement, in 12/8 E minor, like the opening of the St Matthew Passion, creates a flowing texture and the changing surroundings are able to reflect the text ('death' and 'sleep' are treated quietly). The alto is accompanied by flute and oboe d'amore in an elaborate aria, and the opera buffa-like duet for tenor and bass brings two violins and continuo to create a five-part texture. Cantata 126 for Sexagesima (4 February 1725) draws on several hymns and needs a good trumpeter to announce the A minor opening with a fanfare figure recalling Cantata 67. The chorale line is simple, but the contrapuntal imitation underneath reflects the changing text. The tenor has a lively aria with two oboes and hair-raising melismas on 'erfreuen' (delight) and 'zerstreuen' (dispel). An alto and tenor recitative includes the chorale again, and racing scales for the continuo depict the bass's 'cast to the ground bombastic pride'. The final chorale ends with a rich Amen.

Cantata 127 for Quinquagesima Sunday, 11 February, returns to an old-style format with its pairs of recorders and oboes, with an elegiac mood and gently dotted pastoral rhythms (as if for Handel's Galatea). Wonderfully, Bach combines two different chorales, Herr Jesu Christ in the voices and the German Agnus Dei Christe, du Lamm Gottes in the instruments (and there is even an echo of the Passion chorale in the continuo as well); there is a surprise in a final entry of all the voices without chorale at the end of the movement. A tenor recitative leads to an aria for soprano with two recorders and oboe, who constantly chime the death-bells of the text, with pizzicato violins in the central section – exquisite. A solo trumpet arrives to conjure up the Day of Judgement in a very exciting movement for bass, interleaving recitative and aria. This is the last chorale cantata Bach completed before the second version of the St John Passion a few weeks later: Nicholas Anderson remarks on its 'great expressive intensity'.

Cantata 1 is based on a favourite hymn-tune and was heard on the Annunciation, 25 March 1725; music was rarely performed on this feast day as it fell during Lent. Unusually, however, this year it actually fell on Palm Sunday and so was celebrated then. The full richness of Bach's treatment is evident in the opening movement, which uses pairs of horns, oboes da caccia and two violins alongside strings and voices to create a resplendent texture. The material of each group is strongly contrasted (the horns fanfaring, the violins running, the oboes dancing) and under it all the famous chorale tune unfolds in the soprano line with expressive touches such as the static chord for 'lieblich', extended slightly for 'freudlich'; the instruments continue to develop the material long after the chorale has finished, as if they cannot bear to leave it. The soprano has an aria with the oboe da caccia, and the tenor one with the violins, while the final chorale has a running part for second horn while the first doubles the melody. (On Easter Sunday Bach performed both the old-style Cantata 4 and the new-style Cantata 249, which later became the Easter Oratorio and is discussed there.) Possibly because of the death of his librettist, Bach reverted to more standard texts from here until Trinity Sunday.

♫ *Cantatas Vol. 32: 111, 123, 124, 125*
Cantatas Vol. 33: 41, 92, 130
Cantatas Vol. 34: 1, 126, 127
Soloists/Bach Collegium Japan/Suzuki
BIS CD 1501, 1541, 1551

LEIPZIG CANTATAS YEAR TWO:
   EASTER—TRINITY 1725

Cantata 6 *Bleib bei uns, denn es will Abend werden*
Cantata 42 *Am Abend aber desselbigen Sabbats*
Cantata 85 *Ich bin ein guter Hirt*
Cantata 103 *Ihr werdet weinen und heulen*
Cantata 108 *Es ist euch gut, daß ich hingehe*
Cantata 87 *Bisher habt ihr nichts gebeten in
   meinem Namen*
Cantata 128 *Auf Christi Himmelfahrt allein*
Cantata 183 *Sie werden euch in den Bann tun*
Cantata 74 *Wer mich liebet, der wird mein Wort halten*
Cantata 68 *Also hat Gott die Welt geliebt*
Cantata 175 *Er rufet seinen Schafen mit Namen*
Cantata 176 *Er ist ein trotzig und verzagt Ding*

There is no lessening of Bach's creative effort as he moves
beyond the chorale cantata format. Cantata 6 is based on the
moving story of the disciples meeting the risen Christ on the
road to Emmaus and their invitation to 'stay with us, for it is
towards evening'; the setting was written for 2 April 1725,
the Second Day of Easter. Schweitzer described the opening
movement as 'a masterpiece of poetry in music'; freed from
the restriction of the chorale melody, there is more than a
reminiscence here of the closing pages of the St John Passion
in the C minor triple-time metre, contrasted with a fugal
central section. The first aria for alto is scored for oboe da
caccia (later changed to viola), while the next movement is
a brilliant chorale setting for soprano with cello piccolo in
active mode, an arrangement also heard in the Schübler
chorales for organ. A tenor aria with awkward vocal leaps
leads to the final chorale.

   Cantata 42 was written for 8 April 1725, the First Sunday after Easter, with a text related to the Gospel reading
of the day, and begins with a fine instrumental sinfonia for
two oboes and bassoon with strings, probably derived from
the secular Cantata 66a written in Cöthen. This attractive

movement, with its central section marked *cantabile*, is often played separately, as it does not appear in any extant concerto. The chorale occurs in the fourth movement as a duet between soprano and tenor, and a bass aria (with a representation of the cross in the vocal line) leads into the final chorale. Cantata 85 was written for the following week, 15 April 1725: freed from the model of the chorale cantata, Bach writes a bass solo with florid oboe to begin and introduces the chorale in the third movement for soprano with two oboes. 'I am the Good Shepherd,' says the text, and the result is correspondingly pastoral. The alto is accompanied by another cello piccolo solo. The tenor sings with all the strings in a lilting pastoral number before the final chorale.

The nine cantatas to texts by Mariane von Ziegler, which took Bach from Jubilate through to Trinity Sunday in 1725, may be more briefly summarised. He seems to have altered the texts a good deal and not to have returned to her work. But they are all formally interesting. Cantata 103 (22 April 1725) has an extensive opening movement which brings together fugal development in the voices with instrumental writing for high flauto piccolo and oboe d'amore: the first section reaches a climax and the bass has an accompanied recitative (not indicated as a solo, so presuming solo performance of the whole), and then a further fugue. Cantata 108 (29 April 1725) begins with a bass solo: the chorus occurs in the centre of the work in three fugal sections in which the last develops the first. Cantata 87 (6 May 1725) has a glorious tenor solo with strings in siciliano form, and the opening movement is again a bass solo, but there is no movement for all the singers except the final chorale. Cantata 128 (10 May 1725) opens with a chorale-based movement and so Bach later collected this with his chorale cantatas; its exuberant G major spirit recalls the great chorale cantatas with a concerto-like structure into which the melody is placed. There is bass aria with trumpet, and the following duet provided the theme for Reger's *Bach Variations* Op. 81. Cantata 183 (13 May 1725, the Sunday after Ascension) is the second cantata to have this title; here Bach uses two oboes d'amore and two oboes da caccia and also a cello piccolo part. Each of the four singers has a solo number, and they join in the final chorale. Cantata 74 (20 May 1725, for Whit Sunday) reused some movements from Cantata 59 but the text was not perfectly suited to the changes. The opening chorus expands an earlier duet, 'Whoever loves me will keep my word', and three trumpets and drums are juxtaposed with oboes and oboe da caccia. The arias are one each for alto, soprano, bass, and tenor.

Cantata 68 for the next day (Whit Monday, 21 May 1725) is the real gem of this set, with a stirring opening chorus; like Cantata 128, it opens with a chorale-based chorus, so Bach later included it among his chorale cantatas. 'God so loved the world that he gave us his Son,' the text begins, and the siciliano of the opening movement is rich and free. The second movement is the eternally popular aria, 'My heart ever faithful', adapted from Cantata 208. Its soprano part here becomes much more elaborate (an object lesson in Bach's ability to find a fresh new idea from old material), and the bass part is given to a cello piccolo, which then takes the bass line, as an exquisite little trio sonata emerges on violin and oboe when the soprano finishes: a delightful surprise omitted in most arrangements of the aria. For once, the final movement is arranged as a choral fugue, giving an apt sense of conclusion. Cantata 175 for the following day (22 May 1725) has the text 'He calls his sheep by name', and the brief opening movement uses three recorders followed by a pastoral aria with the same scoring. The energetic cello piccolo player is rewarded with another solo with tenor, and then two trumpets unusually join the bass in an aria (doubtless suggested by the injunction to 'open up, you two ears'), and the final chorale allows the recorders to float high above the texture. Finally, for Trinity Sunday (27 May 1725), Cantata 176: a cantata with the words 'there is something perverse and desperate about all human hearts', for which Bach devises a solidly impressive fugal texture in C minor without chorale; a gavotte aria for high soprano, a bass arioso and an alto aria lead to the final chorale.

🎧 *Cantatas Vol. 35: 128, 176, 87, 74*
Cantatas Vol. 36: 42, 103, 108, 6
Cantatas Vol. 39: 68, 175, 28, 183, 85
Soloists/Bach Collegium Japan/Suzuki
BIS CD 1571, 1611, 1641

LEIPZIG CANTATAS YEAR THREE: TRINITY SUNDAYS 1725–NEW YEAR'S DAY 1726

Cantata 168 *Tue Rechnung! Donnerwort*
Cantata 137 *Lobe den Herren, den mächtigen König der Ehren*
Cantata 164 *Ihr, die ihr euch von Christo nennet*
Cantata 79 *Gott, der Herr, ist Sonn und Schild*
Cantata 110 *Unser Mund sei voll Lachens*
Cantata 57 *Selig ist der Mann*
Cantata 151 *Süsser Trost, mein Jesus kömmt*
Cantata 28 *Gottlob! nun geht das Jahr zu Ende*
Cantata 16 *Herr Gott, dich loben wir*

As Bach enters on his third annual series of Trinity Sundays, the survivals among his cantatas become more patchy, and we cannot be sure that we have a complete record of what was intended, let alone what was performed. A text-book for the Third to the Sixth Sundays after Trinity was discovered in 1971, but no Bach settings of these texts survive. The situation is further complicated because Bach was still writing new cantatas to fill in the gaps in the previous cycles. Cantata 168 was probably first performed on the Ninth Sunday after Trinity, 29 July 1725, and its text is by Franck. It has a small-scale scoring with two oboes d'amore, and tells of the terrified soul giving an account of itself to God – the thundering triplets and dotted rhythms of the opening aria are disturbing, echoed in the rushing figuration of the final duet.

The exhilarating Cantata 137, with its rousing, brilliantly organised opening chorus using the famous chorale tune, was for the Twelfth Sunday, 19 August 1725, and uses all the verses of the chorale unmodified, each verse praising a different aspect of God: the alto aria later became one of the Schübler organ chorales. The final chorale creates a magnificent seven-part texture with trumpet parts. Cantata 164 for the following Sunday 26 August is another setting of Franck; Dürr says that the composition score looks new. The work opens with a tenor and then an alto aria, but the outstanding movement is the long duet for soprano and bass with its complex imitations and canons, followed by an instrumental conclusion.

There is a gap of new works until Cantata 79 for the Reformation Festival on 31 October 1725. If Bach had been saving himself for this exercise, the result is one of his very finest, most thrilling cantatas (which Bach both revived in 1730 and then reused in his G major and A major Missas). The dense opening movement contrasts ringing horn calls with a tense string figure, which allows all manner of close imitation and dissonance between the voices, as the singers praise 'God the Lord as sun and shield'. For me this is among the miracles of Bach's output, where intensity of counterpoint leads inevitably to intensity of expression, raising the text into an eschatological vision. Both chorale settings that follow use the horns to enhance the texture; the alto aria and duet for soprano and bass are rather overshadowed by all this splendour. Cantata 110 was written for Christmas Day 1725, and its opening chorus will be recognisable as the Overture of the Orchestral Suite No. 4, transformed in one of Bach's masterstrokes into this brilliant choral fantasia. The biblical sentiments of Georg Christian Lehms's libretto, 'May our mouth be full of laughter and our tongue full of praise,' are aptly reflected in the swinging triplets of the opening movement. There's a little recitative for bass, a duet adapted from one of the Christmas Magnificat interpolations, 'Virga Jesse', and a tremendous bass aria: 'Wake up, veins and limbs, and sing such joyful songs as are pleasing to our God.'

Cantata 57 for the Second Day of Christmas, 26 December 1725, is about martyrdom, as Dürr points out, rather than Christ's birth, and is therefore a true St Stephen's Day cantata. It's a dialogue between Jesus and the Soul, to a libretto by

Lehms. The orchestral writing is pictorial in the extreme, with leaps downward to represent death and casting oneself into the arms of Jesus – as operatic as Bach's writing ever became. Finally the alto asks 'What will you grant me?' and a simple chorale says that Christ will lift the soul to heaven from its tortured body. Cantata 151, for the Third Day of Christmas, 27 December 1725, has a lovely opening soprano aria inspired by the birth of Christ, 'Sweet comfort, my Jesus comes,' which Nicholas Anderson calls 'one of Bach's most sublime creations for the solo voice, lightly and translucently scored' with flute, violins (one doubled by oboe d'amore) and continuo.

Cantata 28 for 30 December 1725 is another masterpiece (you could well perform this set of late 1725 cantatas as a second Christmas Oratorio). 'Praise to God, the year is drawing to its close; the new one already draws near' is the reflective sentiment of Neumeister's text. The soprano sings with strings and three oboes, and then a strict motet-style chorale movement with added trombones and cornetto seems to invoke the past, while a duet for alto and tenor points towards the progressive future before the closing chorale. Cantata 16 completes this series, written for New Year's Day 1726 to a libretto of praise and thanksgiving by Lehms. It was clearly a favourite, revived several times: in 1731, after 1745, and perhaps as late as 1749. The strong opening uses the Te Deum in Luther's German setting. The most original movement is the third, juxtaposing bass soloist and choir in a series of fugues, solos, and orchestral interpolations of great originality, all stimulated by the opening 'Let us exult, let us rejoice'.

♩ *Cantatas Vol. 39: 68, 175, 28, 183, 85*
Cantatas Vol. 40: 137, 168, 79, 164
Cantatas Vol. 43: 110, 57, 151
Soloists/Bach Collegium Japan/Suzuki
BIS CD 1631, 1671, 1761

LEIPZIG CANTATAS YEAR THREE: EPIPHANY—TRINITY SUNDAY 1726

Cantata 32 *Liebster Jesu, mein Verlangen*
Cantata 13 *Meine Seufzer, meine Tränen*
Cantata 72 *Alles nur nach Gottes Willen*
Cantata 146 *Wir müssen durch viel Trübsal*
Cantata 43 *Gott fähret auf mit Jauchzen!*

In January 1726 Bach writes a series of three cantatas for the Sundays after Epiphany but then, for unknown reasons (though compositional exhaustion would be a perfectly reasonable excuse), breaks off original composition altogether and performs eighteen cantatas by his ancestor, Johann Ludwig Bach.

Cantata 32 for 13 January 1726, with a libretto by Lehms, is a famous 'Concerto in Dialogo' depicting Jesus and his bride, opening with a long and expressive oboe solo over quiet and detached strings, matched by the soprano soloist. A virtuoso violin solo matches the bass in his aria, and the two come together in the recitative and duet which express the union of Christ and the Soul. Cantata 13 is for the Second Sunday after Epiphany, 20 January 1726, and has an unusual scoring of deep-voiced oboe da caccia and two lighter recorders, who combine to express the sighs and tears of the opening movement with the tenor soloist. Grief and sorrow dominate the cantata, though the F major chorale for alto brings a moment of hope before the weeping and mourning of the final bass aria, full of sevenths and seconds. Even the chorale that ends the cantata conjures up to us its setting in the St Matthew Passion. Cantata 72 for the Third Sunday, 27 January 1726, 'All only according to God's will', has a text by Franck, closely based on the Gospel. For this cantata the opening ensemble returns in a splendid movement that was later reworked as the Gloria of the G minor Missa BWV 235; here the word 'alles' is prominent in the setting, with a fine central canonic section, 'God's will calms me.' The following recitative has a litany-like quality; the alto aria unusually begins without the instruments – when they enter, it is as a fugue for two violins. The cantata works towards release in a dance-like soprano aria, almost a polonaise.

Then follows the break when Bach used other cantatas until May 1726. Cantata 146 could have marked his return to cantata composition, though Dürr says the following two years are also possible origins for this cantata. This work has been doubted as authentic because the copies are from later, but the opening movements are immediately recognisable as the first two of the concerto which later became the famous Concerto in D minor BWV 1052, probably derived from an earlier violin concerto. Here the opening becomes a huge organ concerto (the first of several cantatas featuring the organ in this period), and the opening vocal movement is beautifully woven around the concerto's central slow movement. The next alto aria uses the organ (or a violin), and there is an active soprano aria with flute and two oboes d'amore, and a duet for tenor and bass, perhaps from a secular source. No one seems quite sure of the text of the final chorale, for which only the music survives. Cantata 43 is an especially lavish two-part work with trumpets and drums for Ascension Day, 30 May 1726; William Scheide showed that the libretto is one of the Meiningen texts that Johann Ludwig Bach set in the cantatas Bach had been performing during 1726: 'God is gone up with jubilation and the Lord with ringing trumpets.' A slow introduction and chorale fugue make the opening movement sound almost symphonic, and the arias include a busy one for soprano with strings and oboes, and a bass aria with a virtuosic part for trumpet (later replaced by violin). Most striking is the bass recitative that opens part two after the sermon, 'The hero of heroes comes', with the strings in operatic mode.

♫ *Cantatas Vol. 42: 72, 32, 13, 16*
Cantatas Vol. 44: 146, 88, 43
Soloists/Bach Collegium Japan/Suzuki
BIS CD 1711, 1761

LEIPZIG CANTATAS YEAR THREE: SUNDAYS AFTER TRINITY 1726

Cantata 39 *Brich dem Hungrigen dein Brot*
Cantata 88 *Siehe, ich will viel Fischer aussenden*
Cantata 170 *Vergnügte Ruh', beliebte Seelenlust*
Cantata 187 *Es wartet alles auf dich*
Cantata 45 *Es ist dir gesagt, Mensch, was gut ist*
Cantata 102 *Herr, deine Augen sehen nach dem Glauben!*
Cantata 35 *Geist und Seele wird verwirret*
Cantata 17 *Wer Dank opfert, der preiset mich*
Cantata 19 *Es erhub sich ein Streit*

Bach returned to full productivity during the Sundays after Trinity in 1726, with cantatas of a range and ambition that place them among his finest works; there is, however, no strict unifying design, and Bach is striving for maximum variety. Organ solos now appear, as do solo and dialogue cantatas which would seem to show Bach relying on his more experienced singers.

Cantata 39 was once known as the Refugee Cantata because it was believed it was written in 1732 for the Protestants who had been banished from Salzburg. This 'agreeable legend' (Dürr) masks its origin on 23 June 1726 as part of his use of Meiningen texts, with their alternation of Old and New Testament sentiments. You can only be overwhelmed by the opening movement, with its huge structure in three blocks presenting a wealth of different contrapuntal techniques: 'Break your bread with the hungry, and bring those who are in distress into your house.' The arias enhance this opening, but never reach its power. Cantata 88, for the Fifth Sunday after Trinity, 21 July 1726, is another two-part cantata on the Meiningen model based on the calling of Peter and the Apostles to be fishers of men. The unusual opening movement uses the bass to declaim Jeremiah's words in a motet-like setting, conjuring up both a pastoral fishing scene and a central hunt scene with horns. At the start of the second part there is a tiny Evangelist–Christ scene for tenor and bass, and soprano and alto duet fugally with the delightful text 'the pound that he has given us he would have back with interest'.

Cantata 170 for the Sixth Sunday on 28 July 1726 is one of Bach's loveliest solo cantatas, for alto with solo organ, without even a final chorale. (Its brevity may be explained by Bach's including another cantata by Johann Ludwig during the same service.) The hypnotic swing of the first movement, shared between alto and oboe d'amore, conjures up perfectly 'contented rest, beloved pleasure of the soul'. The central aria, without continuo but with two independent organ lines, is a tour de force, its dissonance depicting the singer's distance from God. Harmony is restored in a dancing aria (unusually, using an augmented fourth or tritone at the start of the vocal line), which looks forward to a later galant style.

Bach must have been happy with Cantata 187, as he drew no fewer than four movements from it for his Missa in G minor BWV 235. It is based on the miracle of the feeding of the five thousand, and Christ's reassurance in the Sermon on the Mount that God will provide: 'Out of the earth, wine and bread he makes and gives us plenty,' sings the final chorale. It was written for 4 August 1726 to a Meiningen text. The arias for soprano and alto add variety and the second part opens with a bass solo, but once again the opening movement is the highlight: a giant fresco introduced by the instruments, presenting the voices but then leading to a full-scale choral fugue from which the instruments emerge with their own parts: magnificent!

If I had to pick a Bach cantata whose every movement was top-notch and added up to an overall shape that was perfect, then Cantata 45 would be on the list. Written for 11 August 1726, the Eighth Sunday after Trinity, its first movement, in the unusually bright key of E major, is based on a swirling, not altogether vocal, but highly expressive theme which Bach works through a dazzling variety of complicated contrapuntal devices, contrasting fugal entries with the block chords of 'nämlich: Gottes Wort' (namely, God's words). After a strong triple-time tenor aria, there is a superb bass arioso, almost a mini-opera, in which Christ tells evil-doers to depart, and an exquisite alto aria in F sharp minor with flute (which attracted me to this cantata when I first heard it sung in the Telefunken recording by René Jacobs with Frans Brüggen on flute). The final chorale is simple and clear in its harmonies.

Cantata 102 for the Tenth Sunday, 25 August 1726, is a further work on which Bach drew for his short masses; the opening chorus, which became the Kyrie of the Missa in G minor, has been described as 'one of the great achievements of the mature Bach'. It is indeed a panoramic, almost cinematic picture of faith in God, with three fugal sections (hence suitable for the tripartite structure of the Kyrie) exploring every note of their eloquent themes. The arias contrast the lostness of the soul with the clear guidance God brings (the tenor aria that starts part two has different material for voice and flute), and the final chorale looks forward to the soul's homeward journey to Christ. The organ assumes its solo role again in Cantata 35 for the Twelfth Sunday, 8 September 1726, a solo cantata for alto to a text by Lehms. Probably a solo concerto for oboe (or violin) lies behind the movements featuring the organ; Bach began to arrange it later for harpsichord, oboe and strings (BWV 1059), but broke off. The opening Concerto movement is slow, and then the first richly scored aria leads to the end of part one, an aria with organ obbligato. Another concerto movement opens part two, with a final aria expressing the wish to live only with God.

Another cantata that Bach reused for his short Missas and thus surely rated highly is Cantata 17 for the Fourteenth Sunday, 22 September 1726. This is the last of the Meiningen-influenced cantatas and has a rich biblical text praising God's goodness and majesty. The energy of the opening movement, in A major, is invigorating: it starts with a full concerto-like introduction, and then with vocal entries which derive their strength from suspensions over the bar lines of a walking bass. Thanks and praise are prominent in the elaboration of the word-setting in the tenor aria, and the final chorale is beautifully suited to its pictorial words of grass, flowers, and falling leaves.

Bach's strong ties with his family tradition are evident in Cantata 19 for St Michael's Day, a vivid story about the struggle between St Michael and Satan which had already been used by his relative Johann Christoph Bach (in a composition later described by C. P. E. Bach as a masterpiece, which Bach performed in Leipzig during the 1740s). This new work for 29 September 1726 sets text adapted from Picander, and gives Bach the opportunity for an opening movement of the greatest impact, with choirs of voices, trumpets, oboes and strings all vying for supremacy – but nothing could better illustrate the development and maturity of Bach's style than the subtlety with which these forces are now integrated to produce a turbulent, visionary movement in C major. After a sequence of arias including the ravishing tenor aria, 'Bleibt, ihr Engel', and a siciliano in which a solo trumpet plays a chorale, all the trumpets return to clothe the final chorale.

♫ *Cantatas Vol. 45: 129, 187, 39*
Cantatas Vol. 46: 102, 19, 45, 17
Soloists/Bach Collegium Japan/Suzuki
BIS CD 1801, 1851

LEIPZIG CANTATAS YEAR THREE: 16TH–23RD SUNDAYS AFTER TRINITY 1726

Cantata 27 *Wer weiss, wie nahe mir mein Ende?*
Cantata 47 *Wer sich selbst erhöhet, der soll erniedriget werden*
Cantata 169 *Gott soll allein mein Herze haben*
Cantata 56 *Ich will den Kreuzstab gerne tragen*
Cantata 49 *Ich geh und suche mit Verlangen*
Cantata 98 *Was Gott tut, das ist wohlgetan*
Cantata 55 *Ich armer Mensch, ich Sündenknecht*
Cantata 52 *Falsche Welt, dir trau ich nicht!*

The sequence of rich and varied cantatas for the Sundays after Trinity in 1726 continues with Cantata 27, for the Sixteenth Sunday, 6 October. A reflection on death by an unknown librettist, 'who knows how near my end is', it presents another original opening movement in C minor: not content with his usual working of complex contrapuntal wonders, Bach interrupts the flow three times for interpolations in recitative, commenting on the text but maintaining the impetus by keeping them in triple time. There is an aria for alto which has an oboe da caccia and independent keyboard part, seemingly for harpsichord though organ would be more logical in this period (and was certainly used in a later revival), and then an bass aria of strong contrasts between the peacefulness of 'Gute Nacht' and the busy world. Bach took the final chorale and its five–part antiphonal harmonisation from the earlier Leipzig composer Johann Rosenmüller. Cantata 47 was for 13 October 1726, the Seventeenth Sunday after Trinity, and uniquely for Bach uses a text by the Eisenach official Helbig, which Telemann also set. It's a pretty ordinary text of which Bach inevitably made something quite remarkable, announcing a sober instrumental concerto with contrasting strings and wind and then introducing the singers in a huge fugal structure which then develops the instrumental section with breathtaking results. The organ may be intended for the florid obbligato of the soprano aria, which Bach later arranged for violin. Then there is a recitative and aria for bass, full of dissonances and well suited to the over-the-top denunciation of man as 'Kot, Stank, Asch und Erde' (excrement, stench, ashes and earth). The cantata pleads with Jesus to raise up the sinner and 'curse arrogance'.

The genre of solo cantatas with obbligato organ produces a fine work in Cantata 169, for the Eighteenth Sunday, 20 October 1726, but there are more instruments, including two oboes d'amore and the lower-pitched taille. Bach later reused the material from the opening Sinfonia and the second aria in his E major Concerto for harpsichord, but it doubtless also had an earlier life as an oboe or violin concerto. The alto has an arioso of considerable drama with aria-like interruptions, leading to the first aria with busy organ whose origin is less certain. Another recitative leads to the concerto's siciliano slow movement, 'Stirb in mir' (die in me).

Cantata 56, called by Bach 'Cantata a Voce Sola e Stromenti', for the Nineteenth Sunday, 27 October 1726, is one of Bach's most familiar solo cantatas, a rare work for bass soloist which has been taken up by many soloists: in the recording he directed, Joshua Rifkin suggests that Johann Christoph Samuel Lipsius was the original singer (and it is an interesting contribution to the one-to-a-part vocal debate that the final chorale is indicated to be sung by soprano, alto, tenor and the bass soloist). The image of the cross-beam is apparently a nautical reference to a sextant, and the operatic text suggests that 'my life in the world is like a voyage', depicted by the cello in arpeggios, and followed by a more upbeat movement for oboe and bass soloist. The final chorale has an expressive response to the text as the soul reaches harbour.

Cantata 49, for the Twentieth Sunday, 3 November 1726, is a further example of the dialogue cantata, the Gospel's parable of the royal wedding feast suggesting a duet between Christ and his bride, the Soul. Once again, Bach turns to the concerto which was to form the basis of his Concerto in E major, and uses the finale as a Sinfonia to this cantata. The obbligato organ features strongly in the following movements: the next aria is in C sharp minor, followed by a dramatic duet recitative. The soprano aria, 'I am glorious, I am fair', brings together oboe d'amore and cello piccolo: 'we see the spinning and turning of the bride adorned by her hoop-skirt, taking pleasure in her own beauty' (Dürr). The final duet for soprano and bass features an elaborate organ solo and leaping figuration for the bass, with the shining chorale woven into the soprano line – all beautifully linked and blended.

Cantata 98 is a rare example of Bach using the same hymn text three times, written by Samuel Rodigast in 1676. But this one is not a chorale cantata and does not even include a final chorale, though it has an opening chorale fantasia as the first movement. It was first performed on 10 November, the 21st Sunday after Trinity. There are two recitative and aria pairs, and the final bass aria echoes the chorale melody. Cantata 55 for 17 November 1726, the 22nd Sunday after Trinity, is a solo cantata, this time for tenor – the only one in Bach's output. It features obbligato woodwind, flute and oboe d'amore in the opening aria, and the second aria is for flute. It looks as if only the first movements are new, with the others adapted from an earlier work, perhaps a Passion (that might explain the use of diminished sevenths and expressive intervals), leading to the final chorale which also appears in the St Matthew Passion. Cantata 52 for the 23rd Sunday, 24 November 1726, is the last of this Trinity series, for the end of the liturgical year, and uses a solo soprano with final four-part chorale. Bach looks back, as he has done in several others of this series, to earlier music: the Sinfonia is a version of the first movement of Branden-burg Concerto No. 1 (in this version without violino piccolo), featuring two horns and three oboes. The text, 'False world, I trust you not', stresses the virtues of the soul's faithfulness to God. Among the attractive features of this concise cantata is a dance-like aria for the soprano with the three oboes, and a final chorale with the two horns.

𝄞 *Cantatas Vol. 37: 169, 170, 35, 200*
Cantatas Vol. 38: 52, 82, 55, 58
Soloists/Bach Collegium Japan/Suzuki
BIS CD 1621, 1631

LEIPZIG CANTATAS YEAR FOUR: JANUARY–TRINITY 1727

Cantata 58 *Ach Gott, wie manches Herzeleid*
Cantata 82 *Ich habe genug* [solo bass version]
Cantata 157 *Ich lasse dich nicht, du segnest mich denn*
Cantata 84 *Ich bin vergnügt mit meinem Glücke*
Cantata 173 *Erhöhtes Fleisch und Blut*
Cantata 129 *Gelobet sei der Herr, mein Gott*
Cantata 34 *O ewiges Feuer, o Ursprung der Liebe*

Are the three new cantatas of early 1727 (including his much loved solo cantata *Ich habe genug*) the end of Bach's third cycle, or the fragmentary survival of the start of a fourth cycle? The latter view has been supported by the discovery of a cantata libretto book indicating that more new cantatas were written around Whitsun and Trinity 1727. Cantata 58 for the Sunday after New Year's Day 1727 survives only in the version revised for 1733 or 1734, but this early version is for strings only, with soprano and bass soloists. The first movement is in dotted rhythms over a chromatically falling bass, and in the aria that follows the soprano's singing line contrasts with the violin's activity. The combination of chorale and aria in both the first and the final movement shows Bach still experimenting: it sounds like a concerto (helped by a similarity to the E major Violin Concerto's initial theme).

Cantata 82 has become the best known of Bach's solo cantatas, existing in several versions and with a special character that has enabled its performance by all sorts of different singers from Dietrich Fischer-Dieskau to Emma Kirkby. It was written for the Feast of the Purification, 2 February 1727, and must have been as beloved in Bach's day as it is in ours, since its central aria appears in Anna Magdalena's *Clavierbüchlein*. It was originally in C minor, and Bach revised it as a cantata for soprano in E minor, then for alto in C minor; more recently sopranos and tenors have adopted it in G minor. The opening aria with oboe has a strongly profiled phrase which Bach varies infinitely. A recitative echoes the opening phrase and leads to the famous central aria, 'Schlummert ein, ihr matten Augen', a sublimely reposeful aria which flows with effortless peace, moved on by syncopation and interrupted by long pauses. Some have felt that the final aria of rejoicing does not match the weight of the preceding movements, but it is an ethereal dance of resignation which accepts death and the world to come.

Cantata 157 was first a funeral cantata for 6 February 1727 with a text by Picander: it was not published in his 1728 collection. Then it was revived after 1727 for the Feast of the Purification. The longing for God in death is outlined in the beautiful opening duet in B minor by flowing lines for flute and oboe d'amore solo with violin, a chamber-music combination that harks back to earlier Weimar cantatas. The two soloists then have arias in what Dürr describes as 'a happy combination of aural charm and compositional mastery', and there is a final four-part chorale.

Cantata 84 is likely to have been written for 9 February 1727, Septuagesima Sunday, where the Bible reading is about the labourers in the vineyard and the text stresses that 'I am content with the fortune which our dear God has allotted to me'. The scoring is for solo soprano with final chorale (but makes it explicit that this chorale requires only three extra singers alongside the soloist). The very fine opening aria allows the oboist elaborate roulades and decorations, and the recitative leads to the second aria in which the oboe duets with the first violin. The text is from a Picander collection mentioned just below.

Cantata 173 has recently been reassigned from Whit Monday 1724 to 1727, on the basis of a cantata libretto booklet newly discovered in Russia. It is adapted from a Cöthen secular cantata BWV 173a, and the version that survives is of a later revision for Leipzig in 1731. We now know that Cantata 184 was also revived for Whitsun 1727, and Cantata 129 which was thought to have been written for Trinity Sunday 1726 was actually written for Trinity Sunday a year later. Together with the first sacred version of Cantata 34, this creates quite a compelling sequence of new works that had not previously been suspected in 1727.

The text of Cantata 129 was designed to fill a gap in the earlier chorale cantata sequence and is entirely in chorale verses: its structure praises Father, Son, Holy Spirit and then the entire Trinity. The scoring is splendid: three trumpets interject their cries in the opening chorus, the flute and violin accompany one aria, the oboe d'amore another. The unusually elaborate finale, in which trumpet fanfares and orchestral figuration surround the chorale, was arranged by Walton in his ballet *The Wise Virgins*.

Cantata 34 is based on a wedding cantata from 1726, and is now known to have been performed at Trinity 1727; in its final form it is one of the most perfect and powerful of all Bach's cantatas, which encapsulates his involvement with cantata composition. This cantata lasts only twenty minutes, but concentrates everything that is most theologically penetrating and musically inventive in Bach's response to his texts. 'O eternal fire, a source of love' is led off by the solo trumpet in a concerto-like structure and then joined by all the voices with the bass leading. The A major aria for alto with muted violins and flutes at the octave is a delicate pastoral vision, while the masterstroke is reserved for the end. A bass recitative, 'The Lord calls out over his consecrated house these words of blessing,' is followed by massive block chords from the chorus 'Friede über Israel' (peace upon Israel); the instruments race away with a rising scale that the sopranos then follow: 'Thank the wondrous hands of the highest.' This cantata was revived right at the end of Bach's involvement with cantata performance, around 1747.

(There is also Cantata 193, for the Leipzig council elections, probably on 25 August 1727, which only survives incomplete and was partly based on a secular Cantata 193a from earlier in that month, whose music is also lost.)

🎧 *Cantatas Vol. 38*: 52, 82, 55, 58
Cantatas Vol. 41: 56, 82a, 158, 84
Soloists/Bach Collegium Japan/Suzuki
BIS CD 1631, 1691

LEIPZIG CANTATAS YEAR FIVE: 'PICANDER' SERIES 1728–9

Cantata 149 *Man singet mit Freuden vom Sieg in den Hütten der Gerechten*

Cantata 188 *Ich habe meine Zuversicht*

Cantata 117 *Sei Lob und Ehr dem höchsten Gut*

Cantata 171 *Gott, wie dein Name, so ist auch dein Ruhm*

Cantata 156 *Ich steh' mit einem Fuss in Grabe*

Cantata 159 *Sehet, wir gehn hinauf gen Jerusalem*

Cantata 145 *Ich lebe, mein Herze, zu deinem Ergötzen*

Cantata 174 *Ich liebe den Höchsten von ganzem Gemüte*

We now enter the period where Bach's cantata composition becomes more intermittent and less well recorded, and we have to presume many cantatas lost. But one source is the 1728 publication by the poet Picander of cantata libretti, nine of which Bach definitely set. Picander wrote in his preface that 'encouraged by the requests of many good friends, and by much devotion on my part, I resolved to compose the present cantatas. I undertook the design more readily because I flatter myself that the lack of poetic charm may be compensated for by the loveliness of the music of our incomparable Kapellmeister Bach, and that these songs may be sung in the main churches of our pious Leipzig.' Beside these nine, possible echoes of other lost cantatas may be found in the collected chorale harmonisations of Bach that were published later. (Cantata 84 in the group discussed above is the earliest of these Picander settings; the others begin with Cantata 197a *Ehre sei Gott in der Höhe* for Christmas Day, perhaps in 1728 or later. But this is incomplete, and in spite of the fact that some music was transferred into Cantata 197, for a wedding, it's impossible to reconstruct.)

Cantata 149 is for St Michael's Day – whether 1728 or 1729 is difficult to say (only the first fourteen bars exist as an autograph sketch). The first chorus is drawn from Cantata 208, the 'Hunting Cantata', with fanfares and rising fugal figures.

The bass sings of 'power and strength' with wide leaps over an octave and more, the soprano has a gentle triple-time aria about the constant presence of God's angels, and then there's a duet with an extremely unusual solo bassoon, in a rather jovial popular style. The simple final chorale is suddenly crowned by the trumpets. Cantata 188 is for the 21st Sunday after Trinity, probably 17 October 1728: its simple, almost galant style in the first aria has caused Bach's authorship to be doubted, but Dürr points out that the manuscript is a composing draft. It originally started with a big Sinfonia arranged from the concerto that we know as the D minor Harpsichord Concerto BWV 1052, and the alto solo with organ obbligato sits well with Bach's practice: inspired by the text 'unsearchable is the way in which the Lord leads his people', there is a rhythmic maze of invention for the organ. The autograph of this cantata was cut up and sold in bits around the world.

Cantata 117 is not a Picander text but sets a hymn by Johann Jakob Schütz in the manner of a chorale cantata; it was written between 1728 and 1731 and may have been for a wedding. The lilting opening chorus feels like a choral version of the Christmas Oratorio Sinfonia – unusually it is repeated as the last movement – and the mood of the whole cantata is serene. The chorale is heard once more in the centre of the piece, but the other verses of the chorale are treated as recitatives and arias. Cantata 171 is a Picander text for New Year and so probably dates from 1 January 1729, though a later date in the 1730s cannot be ruled out. The magnificent, old-style chorus in D major that begins the cantata is recognisable from its later version as the 'Patrem omnipotentem' of the B minor Mass, though both probably had an even earlier original. The text is from the psalms: 'God, as your name is, so is your renown to the end of the world'; Bach brilliantly gives the first trumpet an independent version of the fugue subject. There is an A major tenor aria, a soprano aria with a leaping violin solo, a most inventive bass recitative with interpolations for the two oboes, and a final chorale from another New Year Cantata 41, with blazing trumpets.

Cantata 156 is probably for 23 January 1729, the Third Sunday of Epiphany, based on Jesus's healing of the sick. 'Lord, if you will, make me clean,' the leper cries, and Picander's text reflects this in a short sequence of recitatives and arias prefaced by a Sinfonia, here for oboe solo, known to us as the Adagio of the F minor Harpsichord Concerto. Cantata 159 is dated by Dürr to 27 February 1729 because of its Picander text: Quinquagesima Sunday, though before Lent, was treated as a Passion Sunday, so the text is about our links to Jesus's suffering. The opening movement is a dialogue between Jesus and the Soul; the long melisma with which the bass arioso starts on the word 'see' is striking, and the following duet for soprano and alto (with the famous Passion chorale) is in the long tradition of a call to follow Christ. The tenor recitative and the bass aria with the words 'Es is vollbracht' (it is finished), with oboe solo, eloquently strengthen the resemblance to a Passion, and the final chorale is beautifully harmonised with inner-part suspensions. Cantata 145 has come down to us in an odd form, with a simple opening chorale, and then a chorus by Telemann. It is a short cantata for Easter Tuesday, of which only part of the text is by Picander, developing the theme of the union of Christ and the soul in a setting that could be completely secular. The most striking aria is for bass with trumpet and flute, combining fanfares with expressive arpeggios, but it has an oddly mixed feel.

Cantata 174 was written to Picander's text for 6 June 1729, Whit Monday. It opens with a big flourish, the first movement of Brandenburg No. 3, wonderfully enlarged with oboes and horns as well as strings. In adding new string parts Bach let the original string players become a group of soloists against what sounds like a full orchestral background – a fascinating development in his style, surely inspired by his new direction from 1729 of the larger forces in the Leipzig Collegium Musicum. There are arias for the alto and bass (in popular style) and a central recitative for the tenor which uses the three violins and three violas from the concerto.

LATER LEIPZIG CANTATAS:
BEGINNING OF THE 1730S

Cantata 51 *Jauchzet Gott in allen Landen!*
Cantata 192 *Nun danket alle Gott*
Cantata 112 *Der Herr ist mein getreuer Hirt*
Cantata 29 *Wir danken dir, Gott, wir danken dir*
Cantata 140 *Wachet auf, ruft uns die Stimme*
Cantata 36 *Schwingt freudig euch empor*
Cantata 177 *Ich ruf zu dir, Herr Jesu Christ*
Cantata 9 *Es ist das Heil uns kommen her*

Bach's cantata composition becomes infrequent after 1730, when he was occupied with work on the Collegium Musicum; however, it is important to remember, in contrast to some modern rewritings of his biography, that his commitment to church music did not just disappear. Instead, its emphasis went towards collections and reworkings, the creation of an oratorio cycle for Christmas, Easter and Ascension (see above), and more occasional cantata compositions for special occasions. And among these are some of his very greatest and most mature works in the form.

When and why did the brilliant and unique Cantata 51 for solo soprano with trumpet originate? Bach did originally write *in ogni tempo* (for any time), on the score, so let's perform it any time: the music is unmatched. It's far more difficult than any other soprano work in the cantatas, and its virtuoso trumpet solo adds to the challenge; the models are Italian rather than German. It was probably written for a woman rather than a boy, and it's been guessed that it might have originated for a wedding at the court of Weissenfels in 1729 and then been adapted for the Fifteenth Sunday after Trinity, 17 September 1730. Fanfares dominate the opening movement, 'Shout for joy to God in all lands'; the recitative and aria that follow are contrastingly relaxed, 'make your goodness new every morning', and then a delicious chorale-prelude setting has the soprano sing against a dancing texture for violins and continuo. Bach saves his most masterly addition for the

end: a fugal movement of lavish virtuosity to the single word
'Alleluia', in which the trumpet matches the soprano and the
singer (she or he) climbs to a top C – exhilarating.

Linked to that cantata by its date and performing material,
Cantata 192 is incomplete, lacking its tenor part, and rarely
performed. But its three movements are very fine, and it
treats one of the most famous chorale melodies: the darting
opening movement (reminiscent of Cantata 62) and the
gigue-like final movement are especially impressive, with the
chorale ringing out across the dancing textures. Cantata 112
was definitely written for the Second Sunday of Easter on
8 April 1731, and it's one of the chorale cantatas written to
fill gaps in Bach's earlier cycle. The text is from the familiar
Psalm 23, 'The Lord is my shepherd', and there is a hunting,
pastoral emphasis in the horns and the use of G major, with
each chorale line prepared by an imitative texture. The alto
sings with oboe d'amore, the bass has a most inventive arioso
wandering through the dark valley of the continuo, and there
is a duet for soprano and tenor ('You prepare a table for
me in the heart of my foes') in the most up-to-date style of
the secular cantata, before the final chorale: 'Goodness and
kindness shall follow me all the days of my life.'

One of Bach's most spectacular creations, on which he
seems to have lavished special care, is Cantata 29 for the town
council elections of 1731. (What a pity we have lost the one
for the previous year, whose text is BWV Anh. 3.) Every movement is superb, and the cantata was revived in 1739 and 1749,
as well as its music being used elsewhere. The most amazing
experiment is the opening Sinfonia, expanding the Prelude for
solo violin in E major into a full-scale organ concerto movement with trumpets and wind (Bach had already tried a simpler
version of this in Cantata 120a): here you sense Bach experimenting, in the light of his new Collegium Musicum activity,
with what the sound of an 'orchestra' could be. The opening
chorus, rising gravely and ceremoniously, became the 'Gratias'
and the 'Dona nobis pacem' of the B minor Mass: Bach must
have recognised it as especially successful, with two of the

three trumpets rising above the texture to add their own counterpoint. The unusual tautness of the cantata partly derives
from the music of the lively tenor aria with violin returning for
alto, after a soprano siciliano: 'Hallelujah, strength and might'.

Equally mature and impressive, another peak of his cantata
output, is the famous Cantata 140, for the rare 27th Sunday
after Trinity. The number of Trinity Sundays is determined
by the date of Easter, so because of the calendar this Sunday
occurred during Bach's Leipzig years only twice: in 1731 on
25 November, and again in 1742. Though this is a chorale
cantata of great splendour, its unique appeal surely comes
from the rich combination of this element in the first, fourth
and seventh movements (the middle of which became a
published organ chorale) with the spiritual love duets of the
other movements. Here Christ and the Soul come together
in frankly sensuous music of great beauty, drawing texts from
the Song of Songs. The first duet has a violin piccolo ('among
the most beautiful love duets in the musical literature of the
world', says Dürr) while the second has a dancing oboe. The
noble opening movement, bouncing dotted rhythms between
the choirs of strings and wind, as the chorale melody ascends
over a detached descending bass line, is equally among the
greatest choral creations of the literature, and the final
chorale, though unelaborated, is magnificently harmonised.

One feels that Bach could achieve no more in the cantata
form, but he continued to experiment and to rework earlier
music. Cantata 36 had already gone through many versions
before he revised it again for the First Sunday of Advent 1731.
It has a unique plan: alternating chorales (in place of recitatives) and arias, giving a specially balanced form. The opening
chorus goes back to a 1725 secular cantata, 36a, thoroughly
revised. The second movement sets 'Nun komm, der Heiden
Heiland' as a duet for soprano and alto; the opening of the
second part is a blustering bass aria, 'Welcome dear treasure';
the next chorale is for tenor against racing oboes d'amore; and
then there is a ravishing aria for soprano with violin marked
to be muted, a gorgeous effect. Cantata 177 was written for

6 July 1732, again to fill a gap in Bach's previous chorale cantata cycle: all five movements set Agricola's chorale text. The
G minor opening movement contrasts florid violin lines with
long-held oboe notes. There are arias for alto (with plain continuo), soprano (with oboe da caccia) and tenor (with the rare
combination of bassoon and violin soloists), each coloured by
some chromaticisms that reflect the text. The final chorale
'I lie amid strife and resist, help me!' is harmonised with
expressive care, ornamenting the melody line.

Cantata 9 for the Sixth Sunday after Trinity, probably completed in 1732–5, is yet another late addition to the chorale
cantata cycle (Bach missed that Sunday, as he had been absent
from Leipzig revisiting Cöthen). It is in the bright key of E
major, and the chorale is sung only in the first and last movements; the first a large-scale fresco contrasting flute with oboe
d'amore and strings, and the melody in the soprano (and so
not requiring too much preparation and rehearsal with the
boys?). The soprano reappears only in a duet with the alto,
which builds up a lovely five-part texture with the solo instruments. The bass has two recitatives, and the tenor has an aria
with a fine depiction of being sunk into the 'abyss which has
swallowed us up' with plunging violin lines (originally *tutti*,
but later marked by Bach for solo violin, perhaps because of
their difficulty).

LATE LEIPZIG CANTATAS: 1734–7

Cantata 100 *Was Gott tut, das ist wohlgetan*
Cantata 97 *In allen meinen Taten*
Cantata 14 *Wär Gott nicht mit uns diese Zeit*
Cantata 80 *Ein feste Burg is unser Gott*
Cantata 195 *Dem Gerechten muss das Licht*
Cantata 197 *Gott ist unsre Zuversicht*
Cantata 30 *Freue dich, erlöste Schar*

As the 1730s progress, contrary to what was assumed by Spitta,
Schmieder and earlier scholars who dated various mature
cantatas to this period, Bach's original cantata composition

becomes rarer and almost dries up, while he works on secular music and the religious oratorios. Cantata 100 from about 1734 is an exception: it is unusual in that it survives with copious sources (it was clearly valued as it was revived in 1737 and 1742), and also in that Bach had already used this text earlier in a different form. So he borrows the opening chorus from Cantata 99 of the same title, but wonderfully clothes it with two horns and drums (again in the light of his experience with the Collegium he seems to be experimenting with orchestral sonorities). The other chorale verses then unfold: the second a duet for alto and tenor, the third an aria for soprano and flute, the fourth for bass, the fifth for alto with oboe d'amore – both these two lively dancing movements. The final chorale setting is an elaborate one adapted from an earlier model, this time Cantata 75, with only a different note in the chorale melody revealing its source.

Bach wrote 1734 on his score of Cantata 97 (which is kept in the New York Public Library at Lincoln Center), and Richard Jones, following Stiller, suggests it is a wedding cantata. It is a strict chorale cantata, so could surely have been for a missing Sunday in that cycle, and the Fifth Sunday after Trinity on 25 July 1734 has been suggested on the basis of a later copy. The opening is a French Overture in grand style, and the chorale melody is perfectly interwoven into an increasingly complex and exciting texture: 'In all my deeds I let the most high counsel me.' The arias move upwards from bass to soprano, the bass aria has winding chromaticisms and the tenor a most elaborate violin obbligato, but the soprano aria with two oboes is much simpler and clearer.

During the later part of 1734 Bach would have been pre-occupied with the preparation of the Christmas Oratorio, performed at the end of 1734 and the beginning of 1735. One of his few new cantatas was Cantata 14 for the Fourth Sunday after Epiphany, 30 January 1735, which filled a gap in his previous chorale cantata cycle. There is something innovative in every movement, from the inversion of the severe opening themes in the motet-like first chorus, to the high-lying corno da caccia part in the soprano aria, the sweeping bass figures in the tenor's recitative, and the duetting oboes of the G minor bass aria. Hearing a work like this, written after so many other cantatas, you feel Bach's creativity is endless.

At around the same time as Cantata 14 Bach may have revived his earlier but lost Cantata 80a, already reworked as a chorale cantata in BWV 80b of 1728–31, creating the famous Cantata 80 for the Reformation Festival. As Robin Leaver points out, this is one of the most theologically dense and musically impressive of all Bach's Leipzig cantatas; in the massive opening movement of 228 bars the chorale melody is heard as an instrumental canon framing the five-part counterpoint of voices and continuo, making a seven-part texture, which Bach reinforced by giving the canon a separate lower octave part. Then follow adapted movements: the bass sweeps up the scale – 'All, who are born of God' – with an interpolated chorale. After the soprano aria the central chorale, new for Leipzig, has the voices unusually singing in unison around a full orchestral panoply of sound. There is a duet for alto and tenor before the final chorale. (It was later adapted by W. F. Bach, who added trumpets and timpani to the first and fifth movements; they do not belong, even though the old Bach edition retained them.)

Cantata 195 has been problematical in origin, but Peter Wollny recently discovered a libretto which proves it was performed – not by Bach but by other family members – in Ohrdruf on 3 January 1736 for a wedding celebration; it may then have been performed on 11 September 1741 for another wedding (of a distant descendant of Schütz!) and revised in the late 1740s. It is worth struggling with the uncertainty, for there is fine music here with lavish instrumentation including three trumpets and drums: the concerto-like D major opening chorus, and the rising scales of the chorus at the end of part one: 'We come to praise your holiness.' The bass aria is an example noted by Gerhard Herz of Bach's using Lombard or snapped dotted rhythms, which recur in the B minor Mass.

A new highlight occurs with the marvellously extrovert Cantata 197: also a wedding cantata, dated around 1736, and also making some use of earlier material from the Christmas cantata BWV 197a of *c.*1728, which the librettist consciously rewrote to accommodate. But as in the B minor Mass, these adaptations are so triumphantly successful in their new form that it sounds like a freshly minted masterwork. Did Bach ever write a more exuberant and unbuttoned opening chorus than this, which is at the same time so contrapuntally sophisticated? The opening vocal theme is simple, with just one rising note among the unisons, but it then swings into syncopations across the bar line which provide the music's energy. The central section is more homophonic, and then the beginning returns in *da capo* format, unlike in the movements based on chorales. The alto aria with oboe d'amore in A major is a 'sleep' aria, while the bass aria over lilting bassoon figures is equally pastoral. The last aria, for soprano with solo violin and two accompanying oboes d'amore is a classic which has become justifiably famous on its own: a totally memorable, indelible melody in flowing 6/8, G major, based on sequences, which lifts us towards eternity – 'pleasure and delight, prosperity and salvation will grow'. (No performance by a great soprano is quite as lovely as that of the boy who sings on Harnoncourt's recording.) At the very end of Bach's work in this form, this is a master cantata.

Cantata 30 derives from a secular cantata performed on 28 September 1737 and reworked for the Feast of John the Baptist, probably between 1738 and 1742. Unusually Bach reduced the forces for the sacred version, omitting trumpets and drums, but the new version still has a festive air, and the opening movement in D major swings along powerfully, and is satisfyingly repeated at the close, giving the balance that so many of Bach's cantatas lack because of their emphasis on big first movements. Among the arias a skipping one for flute and alto is memorable; the bass has two arias, the first in popular-style G major, while the tenor has only a recitative.

LAST LEIPZIG CANTATAS: 1740S

Cantata 120 *Gott, man lobet dich in der Stille*
Cantata 69 *Lobe den Herrn, meine Seele*
?Cantata 50 *Nun ist das Heil und die Kraft*
Cantata 191 *Gloria in excelsis Deo*

The cantatas of the 1740s include no completely original new works, but several adaptations which show Bach working at the height of his powers to refine and improve his earlier work. Survival is patchy: for example the cantata for the council elections of 1740, *Herrscher des Himmels*, listed as Anh. I 193, survives only as a text, though the last movement adapted that of Cantata 208. Another cantata Anh. I 4, *Wünschet Jerusalem Glück*, was revived on 28 August 1741, and we now know it originated on 27 August 1725; the text was included in Picander's 1729 collection.

Cantata 120, for the city council elections, has an autograph score of 1742 and was undoubtedly adapted from earlier material (including the earlier model of a violin sonata as well as vocal works). Its reference to stillness leads to an opening for solo voice, with however one of the most elaborate melismas in all Bach's writing on the word 'lobet', (praise), followed by a triumphal chorus, which was freely adapted as the 'Et exspecto' of the B minor Mass, and two recitatives framing a soprano aria. Cantata 69 was for a later city council election, perhaps as late as 1748 (Dürr suggests 26 August 1748), and was drawn from Cantata 69a (see 15 August 1723); only the recitatives have been changed and freshly recomposed.

Another fragment can be included here: much better known, but we have really no idea when it was written or whether it is actually by Bach. Cantata 50 is a fragment for double choir, perhaps based on an existing four- or five-part choral movement. It is not preserved in its original form, and Daniel Melamed following Joshua Rifkin questions whether it is necessarily by Bach. Is it an opening chorus of a lost cantata, or a stand-alone piece? It is contrapuntally exhaustive in its treatment, and impressive in its effect, and quite frequently performed as a result. If it is not by Bach, then who else could have written it?

From the mid-1740s there is a most unusual survival: a cantata in Latin. Cantata 191 is an ingenious adaptation of three movements from the Missa (the Kyrie and Gloria) of the B minor Mass which had been written in the early 1730s, and is well worth hearing in this form. The 'Gloria in excelsis' sequence is not surprisingly reused, and the other two movements are the Doxology (which also occurs at the end of the Magnificat text that Bach set): 'Gloria Patri' set to the music of the 'Domine Deus' from the Mass, and the final 'Sicut erat in principio', adapted to the 'Cum sancto spiritu' from the Mass. This makes a taut and exciting structure, but for what occasion what was it written? Gregory Butler suggested the celebration of the signing of a peace treaty on Christmas Day 1745. If so it would coincide with Bach's continuing involvement with the music of his Missa, revising it and expanding it to create the B minor Mass.

Bach continued to work creatively with his cantatas, reworking Cantata 8 and transposing it from E major to D major in around 1746–7 (a soprano part from this version was in the initial exhibition at the Bach Museum Leipzig), as well as adjusting Cantata 69 for the council elections. Bach recreated the superb Cantata 34 (now known to have originated in 1727) for a late performance in 1746–7, a work of breathless brilliance. At this point, with touching devotion, he is also increasingly engaging with old material from his family archive, helping to prepare works by his ancestors for performance. Probably the final documented performance of one of his own works is the revival of the splendid Cantata 29 *Wir danken dir* on 25 August 1749. Thus comes to an end one of the most remarkable and profound series of works in all Western music, an extraordinary demonstration of Bach's dedication to musical art and the service of God.

COMPLETE CANTATA CYCLES

♩ *Complete Sacred Cantatas BWV 1–200* Concentus Musicus
Wien, Leonhardt Consort/Harnoncourt, Leonhardt
Warner Classics 2564699437 (60 CDs) recorded 1971–1989
♩ *Complete Cantatas Vols. 1–22: BWV 1–200, 201–215, Missas
BWV 233–236, Quodlibet BWV 524* Amsterdam Baroque
Orchestra and Choir/Koopman
Challenge Classics CC72350 (67 CDs) recorded 1999–2006
♩ *Complete Cantatas Vols. 1–60, BWV 1–200; Vols. 61–68,
BWV 201–215* Bach-Collegium Stuttgart and Gächinger
Kantorei/Rilling
Hänssler Bachakademie 92.001–92.068 (68 CDs) recorded
1969–1985
♩ *Sacred Cantatas Vols. 1–27 (170 cantatas)* Monteverdi Choir
and English Baroque Soloists/Gardiner
Soli Dei Gloria SDG 101–174 (recorded 2000)

CYCLES IN PROGRESS

♩ *Sacred Cantatas Vols. 1–54; Secular Cantatas Vols. I–III* Bach
Collegium Japan/Suzuki
BIS (recording started 1995)
♩ *Sacred Cantatas Vols. 1–11 (38 cantatas)* La Petite Bande/
Kuijken
Accent (recording started 2001)

CANTATA COLLECTIONS

♩ *Famous Cantatas, Vol. 1: BWV 12, 38, 75, 21, 27, 84, 95,
161, 4* Collegium Vocale/Herreweghe
Harmonia Mundi 5908357 (3 CDs)
♩ *Famous Cantatas, Vol. 2: BWV 29, 119, 120, 198, 214, 207*
Collegium Vocale/Herreweghe
Harmonia Mundi 5908363 (3 CDs)
♩ *Cantatas BWV 2, 20, 176, 43, 44; Easter Oratorio, Ascension
Oratorio* Collegium Vocale/Herreweghe
Harmonia Mundi 5908354 (3 CDs)

🎧 *Early Cantatas: Vol. I BWV 4, 106, 131, 196; Vol. 2 BWV 12, 18, 61, 161; Vol. 3 BWV 21, 172, 182* Kirkby, Chance, Daniels, Harvey/Purcell Quartet
Chandos 715, 742, 742

🎧 *Historic recordings from 1931: BWV 67, 76, 75, 70* Soloists, Thomanerchor, Stadt- und Gewandhaus-Orchester Leipzig/ Karl Straube
Bach Archiv Leipzig

🎧 *Cantatas BWV 36, 57, 65, 41, 73, 111, 72, 144, 92, 67, 42, 103, 12, 128, 43, 117, 177, 24, 179, 137, 138, 51, 95, 79, 131, 106, 119, St John Passion BWV 245* Soloists/Leipzig Gewandhaus Orchestra, Leipzig St Thomas Choir/Günther Ramin
Berlin Classics 32912 (8 CDs)

🎧 *Cantatas: Vol. 1 (27 cantatas), Easter Oratorio, Ascension Oratorio* Soloists/Schütz-Chor Heilbronn, Pforzheimer Chamber Orchestra/Fritz Werner
Warner Classics 2564 61401 (10 CDs)

🎧 *Cantatas: Vol. 2 (33 cantatas)*
Soloists/Schütz-Chor Heilbronn, Pforzheimer Chamber Orchestra/Fritz Werner
Warner Classics 2564 61402 (10 CDs)

SOLO CANTATAS

Soprano
🎧 *BWV 82a, 199* Hunt Lieberson/Emmanuel Music/Smith
Nonesuch 79692
🎧 *BWV 82a, 199* Kirkby/Freiburg Baroque Orchestra/ Von der Goltz
Carus 83302
🎧 *BWV 199, 179, 113* Kozená/English Baroque Soloists/ Gardiner
DG Archiv 463 591

Alto

🎧 *BWV 169, 170, 35* Fink/Freiburg Baroque Orchestra/
Müllejans
Harmonia Mundi HMC 902016

🎧 *BWV 169, 170, 35* Bowman/The King's Consort/King
Helios 55312

🎧 *BWV 170, 35, 54* Scholl/Collegium Vocale Gent/
Herreweghe
Harmonia Mundi HMC 901644

Bass

🎧 *BWV 82, 56* Fischer-Dieskau/Karl Ristenpart Chamber
Orchestra/Ristenpart
DG The Originals 449756

🎧 *BWV 82, 56, 158* Quasthoff/Berlin Baroque Soloists/
Kussmaul
DG 000345802

Organ music

What would one give to have heard Bach improvise on the organ? Even those who had reservations about his compositions acknowledged his pre-eminence as an organist. Forkel reported of his recitals:

> When Bach seated himself at the organ when there was no divine service, which he was often requested to do by strangers, he used to choose some subject and to execute it in all the various forms of organ composition so that the subject constantly remained his material, even if he had played without intermission for two hours or more . . . First he used this theme for a prelude and a fugue, with the full organ. Then he showed his art of using the stops for a trio, a quartet etc. always upon the same subject. Afterwards followed a chorale, the melody of which was playfully surrounded in the most diversified manner by the original subject, in three or four parts. Finally conclusion was made by a fugue with the full organ in which either another treatment only of the first subject predominated, or one or, according to its nature, two others were mixed with it.

It is perhaps misleading to separate completely the genres of (sacred) organ music and other keyboard music (gathered below under the heading 'secular'), since the two doubtless overlapped at many points. But it has been a tradition of Bach cataloguing and of Bach recording to do so, and it provides a useful distinction, for there is certainly a developing Bach organ style. What is perfectly possible is that much of the smaller-scale organ music treated below was also heard in a domestic setting on a house organ of chamber size, or a pedal harpsichord, and that pieces were interchangeable between organ, harpsichord and clavichord.

The *Neue Bach Ausgabe* gathers all the organ works together irrespective of chronology; until Richard Jones's

2007 discussion, every listing, whether in Peter Williams's magisterial survey, *The New Grove* or elsewhere followed the old BWV numbers rather than an emerging chronology. Peter Williams's revised volume (2003) 'still resists dating this music . . . there may be a misleading, old-fashioned positivism in the whole notion of trying to pinpoint a particular moment.' The problem is that many of these pieces were continually refined and – especially when used for teaching – revised over the years. This survey is therefore a compromise, grouping works loosely together within an evolving (but not rigorous) chronological framework, to make sense of Bach's development. Interestingly, the quest of the *NBA* for a single version of the pieces has been given up in the latest volumes, where variants are included, and the net has been cast ever wider in a 2008 volume of organ chorales, where a whole range of pieces from various sources has been included, seemingly on the off-chance that some might be by Bach. As the editor Reinmar Emans puts it:

> Given our present state of knowledge, a critical evalua-
> tion of the sources did not produce sufficient evidence
> to preclude the possibility of Bach's authorship for the
> chorale preludes presented in our volume . . . the editor
> feels it incumbent on himself to provide maximum breadth
> of material for future debates on the authenticity of the
> pieces concerned.

This is perhaps taking inclusiveness a little far . . .

We are learning more all the time. The valuable identi-
fication by the leading Bach scholar Hans-Joachim Schulze of two important sources of early music, called the Möller Manuscript and the Andreas Bach Book, as being in the hand of Johann Christoph Bach immediately led their attributions to Bach to be taken more seriously, and some pieces were restored to the canon. A key link in our understanding of Bach's organ music has turned up with the discovery of his own transcriptions in tablature of music by Buxtehude and Reincken, inscribed as having been made in the house of

Georg Böhm in Lüneburg in 1700. The Buxtehude transcription may even be a little earlier, from 1698/9. So these are thrilling documents of Bach's musical learning and development between the ages of thirteen and fifteen, which may lead on to other discoveries.

Free works

Prelude and Fugue in C BWV 531
Prelude and Fugue in E minor BWV 533
Prelude and Fugue in C/D minor BWV 549/549a
Prelude and Fugue in G minor BWV 535a
Fantasia in B minor BWV 563
Fantasia in C BWV 570
Fantasia in C minor BWV 1121/Anh. 205
?Fantasia in G BWV 571
Canzona in D minor BWV 588
Prelude in A minor BWV 569

These are early works, all probably from before 1708 (several appearing in the authentic Möller manuscript), as can be seen in the Prelude and Fugue in C from the rather basic harmonic language in the prelude, and awkwardly repeated notes in the fugue subject. Yet they have enough Bachian energy and drive to command interest. The E minor, in Buxtehude style, must also be early, and has an oddly static fugue subject, as if stuck in a rut, but Spitta admired its melancholy, linking it to the E minor keyboard Toccata and later Partita in the same key. The D minor Prelude and Fugue was later transposed down to C minor and improved: its fugue has a four-square but very cheerful swinging theme which really gets going when it enters in the pedals, an early sign of Bach's later pedal style in BWV 546. The fugue subject of BWV 535a (later revised with a better version of the Prelude) also uses repeated notes but with more sense of direction.

The old-fashioned Fantasia in B minor from the Andreas Bach Book has an opening section and then one marked

'Imitatio' (copied by the same hand as the later Passacaglia). The Fantasia in C, an essay in sustained harmonies, has logic and a good sense of harmonic movement, pointing forward to the more famous Fantasia in G; this is authentic as it appears in the Andreas Bach Book. So does (in autograph tablature) the stern Fantasia in C minor, previously doubted. A little Fantasia in G BWV 571, not to be confused with the great Fantasia BWV 572 below, has been excluded from the *NBA* but is in *Grove*. Peter Williams says 'composed by whom?' The attractive D minor Canzona is in the Möller Manuscript and its logical progress surely qualifies it as Bach's. The A minor Prelude is perhaps an early essay showing Bach trying out a few recurrent ideas, but it struggles to sustain its length.

Toccata and Fugue in D minor BWV 565
Allabreve in D BWV 589
Prelude and Fugue in E/C BWV 566
?Prelude in G BWV 568
Fugue in G minor BWV 578
Prelude and Fugue in A minor BWV 551
Prelude and Fugue in G BWV 550
Fugue in C minor after Legrenzi BWV 574
Fugue in B minor after Corelli BWV 579
?Fugue in C minor BWV 575
Pièce d'orgue in G (Fantasia) BWV 572

These pieces might be among the second wave of Bach's early experiments before 1708, as some appear in the Andreas Bach Book. But here is a shock: the Toccata and Fugue in D minor BWV 565 is the most famous of all Bach's works, thanks to the Stokowski orchestration heard in Walt Disney's *Fantasia* and countless other uses, yet to judge from the scholars it may not be by him at all, and even more likely may not be an organ work. Who is to say? Peter Williams thought it an arrangement of a solo violin work, and David Humphreys took the opportunity to wonder why it had ever been accepted as Bach's. But in Wolff's biography and

Grove it is accepted. Arguments derived from the violinistic nature of the piece scarcely stand up, because there are many other Bach works which adopt this cross-string style, like the opening of both Prelude and Fugue in A minor BWV 543. Much more significant is that although the Toccata section is entirely gestural, and much of it is in unison, it is well paced, and flows seamlessly into the violin-style fugue. This builds a head of steam, but then finishes in North German style with a recitative, block chords, and then a set of violent contrasts, marked *adagissimo* and *presto*, *adagio*, *molto vivace*, and finally *molto adagio* for the grand last few chords. Whoever wrote it, is it any wonder Stokowski loved it? Henry Wood's 1929 orchestration, originally announced as by Paul Klenovsky, was hugely popular. For us, whether it is authentic or not, it is part of 'Bach' today.

Though not well sourced, the Allabreve in D is well established as Bach's, and is a piece of taut counterpoint. The E major Prelude and Fugue with its repeated-note fugue is not very interesting, until the fugue is followed by another recitative and a triple-time fugue – which however sounds even less like Bach and more like Bruhns or his contemporaries. (There is another version of the piece in C.) The G major Prelude is doubted by Williams and Stauffer; Krebs has been suggested as the composer, but it could show Bach warming up for the much more idiomatic G major Prelude and Fugue below. It is good to find, however, that the popular little Fugue in G minor BWV 578 is in the Andreas Bach Book, because this feels like the real thing, with a subject that is melodic. The A minor Prelude and Fugue is a chirpy little work with a theme in semitones that Bach would surely later have varied more: it shows him beginning to master the Buxtehude style, and it creates a good sense of climax. The Prelude and Fugue in G has links to the *Orgelbüchlein* prelude in the same key on 'In dir ist Freude' but is less well shaped; it must be relatively early because the sense of harmonic direction is still not clear and the sequential fugue subject makes the working-out relentlessly clumsy.

The Legrenzi fugue uses an adapted Italian theme – not great, as the subject repeats itself (though the answer does not) – in order to work on the pacing and study of contrapuntal development; the final section explodes into a breathless and bold toccata-like passage. The Corelli fugue is more successful; it is a much longer extension of Corelli's original, from his Trio Sonata Op. 3 No. 4. The Fugue in C minor has a disjointed theme of a kind that Bach was to handle much better in the future: the answer fills in the subject's pauses as if creating one continuous line. As the climax to this group, the G major Fantasia is a unique three-section work of great appeal, with French markings: 'Très vitement', opening flourishes which could be violin figuration, 'Gravement', a massive, magnificent central section of sustained chordal writing full of aching suspensions, and then 'Lentement', another flurry of soloistic figuration. This is surely the kind of music Bach must have regularly improvised, gloriously captured for posterity.

Prelude and Fugue in D BWV 532
Prelude and Fugue in G minor BWV 535
?Prelude and Fugue in A BWV 536
Toccata, Adagio and Fugue in C BWV 564
Passacaglia and Fugue in C minor BWV 582

After about 1708 and up to 1712 Bach's organ writing advances by leaps and bounds. An immediate step forward can be heard in the brilliant Prelude and Fugue in D, one of Bach's most effective and exciting early works. Although the harmonic language is simple in the Prelude, there is an *alla breve* central section and the fugue takes off, based on repeated sequences: the gestures are dramatic and the pacing is excellent, with the chugging engine and revolving wheels of the fugue subject driving an exhilarating momentum and energy. (This must date from around the same time as the keyboard Toccata in D.) The Prelude and Fugue in G minor has a simple arpeggiated prelude and a fugue with distinctively early-style repeated notes in sequence.

The Prelude and Fugue in A, with its arpeggiated prelude and odd triple-time fugue subject, feels suspect, and David Humphreys has suggested it is a polyglot work; the fugue could be by any one of a dozen minor composers: missable. The Toccata, Adagio and Fugue in C belongs here, though some have dated it later, showing the range of opinion: Stauffer and *Grove* say around 1712, Williams is non-committal ('composed for testing an organ?'); the origin reflects its relatively unabsorbed North German style, with solos for treble and pedal but then a propulsive first section. There is an adagio over an octave bass line, rather like that of the famous Air from the Orchestral Suite No. 3, and a fugue subject full of rests which creates an amusingly jerky effect. One senses Bach striving towards a more harmonically varied palette, but the material just doesn't allow it; he does however create a great final climax over a tonic pedal.

If the Passacaglia in C minor is really as early as it is supposed – and maybe it marks the culmination of the period gathered in the Andreas Bach Book and so is from about 1712 – it surely represents the single most decisive breakthrough in Bach's compositional career, a fantastic achievement. (The version in the collection is an early one, so it was refined later.) Buxtehude had written passacaglias before, and had also concluded a fantasia with a chaconne. But no one had done what Bach does here, which is to make the culmination of a passacaglia a fugue on the same subject. Here he is taking an existing form and raising it to the highest level, a springboard for future originality. The sequence and grouping of the variations in the Passacaglia have been variously analysed, showing how subtle Bach's approach to this old form was. If this is indeed an early work, it is the crowning work of that period which shows Bach as having achieved early maturity. Brahms, Reger, Britten, Rubbra and others have followed this form of variations culminating in a fugue.

Concerto in D minor BWV 596 after Vivaldi
  Op. 3 No. 11
Concerto in A minor BWV 593 after Vivaldi
  Op. 3 No. 8
Concerto in C BWV 594 after Vivaldi Concerto in D
  RV 208
Concerto in G BWV 592 after Johann Ernst von
  Sachsen-Weimar
Concerto in C BWV 595 after Johann Ernst von
  Sachsen-Weimar

Bach arranged several concertos by Vivaldi and his patron
Prince Johann Ernst for organ and harpsichord (see below
p. 392) in around 1713–14, following Johann Ernst's return
from studies in Holland where he may have heard such transcriptions performed. The Vivaldi Concerto in D minor is a
straightforward but skilful transcription, with the pulsing bass
Ds of the opening sounding relentless, then a fugue, then the
Largo e spiccato with its eloquent melody without bass line, and
a final brilliant movement for two manuals.

The Vivaldi Concerto in A minor is a two-violin concerto
realised with great flair and carefully indicated manual shifts.
The central movement rises over a unison fragment, and the
finale has pounding descending scales – but in the middle
a glorious melody takes wing at the top of the organ. The
Vivaldi C major Concerto is based on ascending scales and
simple harmonies, sustained with energy (but you wonder if
Bach felt he could do better). The central Adagio is a recitative, and the last movement is once again based around the
common chord of C, but with a chromatic cadenza that might
have led Bach to think of the cadenza in the first movement of
Brandenburg Concerto No. 5.

The Prince's concertos are more modest but still
accomplished, a little four-square in harmony: the first in G
has a first movement which uses double pedal, a nice dotted E
minor Grave at its heart, and a brilliant finale; the second in C
is incomplete, just the extensive first movement of a Concerto

in C with lots of rattling sequences. (For really eager organists, there is also the transcription of two movements of a Trio Sonata by Fasch BWV 585, a canonic trio of unknown origin BWV 586, and an Aria by François Couperin BWV 587 transcribed from a trio sonata.)

?Prelude and Fugue in F minor BWV 534
Prelude and Fugue in C BWV 545
Prelude and Fugue in C BWV 547
Fantasia and Fugue in G minor BWV 542
Toccata and Fugue in D minor BWV 538 'Dorian'
Toccata and Fugue in F BWV 540
Prelude and Fugue in G BWV 541

After 1712 and up to 1717 Bach's organ writing begins to achieve deep expressiveness as well as technical maturity. The Prelude and Fugue in F minor was grouped by Spitta along with others from around this period, as pushing forward Bach's command of form, and there is indeed a new feeling of confident command from the high opening, working its way downwards over a repeated pedal figure, to not over-extended sequences and the final flourish. The fugue is one of the first to explore the diminished seventh interval that would be so important to Bach, for example in the theme of *The Musical Offering*; David Humphreys has strongly questioned its authenticity but Williams says 'it is hard to believe Bach had no hand in the piece'. The Prelude and Fugue in C (BWV 545) went through very many stages: although the fugue may have originated around this period it has a movement that reappears in the trio sonatas. It feels strong and mature. The Prelude and Fugue in C (BWV 547) is surely more likely to be from this period, and the prelude has a light touch, but the fugue is mature and Boyd dates it around 1740.

With the tremendous Fantasia and Fugue in G minor BWV 542, one of Bach's best-loved organ works, we enter a period of total confidence in the creation of large-scale structures.

It is by no means certain that the two pieces always belonged together (and this may apply to other pairs of preludes and fugues), but there seems to be a connection with Hamburg, and the use of a similar theme by Mattheson for a competition in 1725. The perky Fugue, perhaps based on a Dutch tune in homage to Bach's mentor Reincken, is the perfect foil for the tragic grandeur of the Fantasia (which has a good deal in common with the Chromatic Fantasy of around this period). Bach's genius here is to contrast the rhapsodic flourishes with more carefully worked sections, including daring chromatic lunges (such as one up to a remote C flat against B flat in the bass) that are way ahead of their time. The fugue subject has two halves, each a repeated sequence, and they mesh perfectly to provide a constant flow of action with long manuals-only passages, before the single final entry in the pedals clinches things in breathless triumph.

The 'Dorian' Toccata and Fugue, perhaps from the mid-Weimar years, is a virtuoso *moto perpetuo* full of echo effects and alternating manuals – one can hear Bach using this piece to demonstrate his skills, or that of an organ he was examining. It is the only organ work that has authentic manual changes crucial to the structure of the work. In spite of its dark minor-mode colour, this is a thrillingly paced prelude followed by a stern, almost stolid, fugue which builds to a climax and then suddenly reverts to the material of the Toccata. Schweitzer described the fugue with its four strettos as 'a miracle of juxtaposed and superimposed vaulted arches'.

The Toccata in F is another brilliant exercise in musical excitement, building up from its opening page over a tonic pedal to a terrific pedal solo; then the whole thing is reworked over a dominant pedal and takes the two cadential chords and extends them to launch a tug of war between pedals and manuals, tossing material around in the most exhilarating manner. A slightly unpromising angular fugue subject is then combined with another more diatonic one to make a great double-fugue climax – as Peter Williams notes, it is the only thoroughgoing double fugue in the organ works. The Prelude and Fugue in G (BWV 541) exists in a later autograph and is surely a perfectly polished example of an early work that has been revised with every detail in place. There are no harmonic surprises, but a crystal-clear formal framework with racing scales and block chords, and then a fugue subject that is simple but energetic, balanced and logical, enabling some nifty pedal work. This piece raises the spirits infallibly, and must have been a great display piece for Bach and his pupils.

Prelude and Fugue in A minor BWV 543
?Prelude and Fugue in D minor BWV 539
Prelude and Fugue in C minor BWV 546
Fantasia and Fugue in C minor BWV 537
Prelude and Fugue in E minor BWV 548 'Wedge'
Prelude and Fugue in B minor BWV 544
Fantasia and Fugue in C minor BWV 562

The magnificent A minor Prelude and Fugue is thought to be a relatively late organ work, some say as late as 1730; if much of the material seems earlier, it has been superbly revised. The Prelude in violinistic style transfigures the clichés of the North German school into a piece of accumulating power, and the Fugue, with its similarly violinistic cross-string writing, creates one of Bach's most successful sequential subjects, with the suspensions created on the first beat of many bars, propelling the textures along. Another sign of its early origins is that after a powerful sequence of sequential seventh chords, yearningly built up, the final page is a flurry of pedal and toccata-like solos ended decisively by three crashing chords. (Links have been found between this and the early A minor Fugue BWV 944, and there is an early, or varied, version of the prelude BWV 543a.) Liszt made a fine, quite faithful, piano transcription of this work.

The Prelude and Fugue in D minor is recognisable because the Fugue is a straight transcription of the long fugue from the unaccompanied Violin Sonata BWV 1001. But did Bach make the arrangement? And does the sustained Prelude belong with it? It has no pedal marks and is an attractive piece for manuals on its own. The monumental Prelude and Fugue in C minor from after 1722 announces itself in block chords over a low tonic pedal and then strenuously rises through its powerful course, driven by a tension between triplets and slurred quavers with the occasional chromatic flourish in quicker notes. Whether or not the sober fugue was written at the same time or earlier, it is a fine complement. Equally compelling over its opening pedal is the Fantasia and Fugue in C minor, whose fugue develops the standard framework of rising fifth and diminished seventh, adding a chromatically rising pedal line halfway through. This is the piece that Elgar orchestrated to great (if occasionally comic) effect. The E minor 'Wedge' Prelude and Fugue is named after its remarkable fugue subject which unfolds like a huge shark's jaw to engorge its counter-subject. It is developed in relatively old-fashioned sections and flourishes; the Prelude, launched over crashing detached chords, is equally powerful.

The B minor Prelude and Fugue, one of Bach's very greatest, is also one of the most mature, as the autograph (a very rare survival in this genre) dates from 1727–31. Williams suggests that these three big works BWV 544, 546, and 548 'should be roughly contemporary, while the mature pedal-point harmonies might also be thought to belong to the Leipzig years'. Mattheson called the key of B minor 'listless and melancholy', and that is a mood that Bach caught in the middle movement of Brandenburg No. 5 and the aria 'Erbarme dich' from the St Matthew Passion. Something more turbulent is going on in this Prelude, however, with the swirling notes underpinned by pedal octaves expressing an indefinable longing; the working-out is dense and compelling. Then there is a winding Fugue in stepwise motion, no leaps, which accumulates intensity and power. Opening over a low C pedal is the wholly mature Fantasia and Fugue in C minor BWV 562, which could be a really late work: the Prelude is a visionary masterpiece which gazes upwards to the stars and conjures up a distant world over the rumbling bass of inner earth, as if uniting God and man. Its five-part Fugue is in triple time, like the 'St Anne'; this pair might post-date *Clavierübung III*, perhaps 1743/45, and the Fugue could be even later, suggests the handwriting expert Kobayashi.

Trio in D minor BWV 583
Pastorale/Pastorella in F BWV 590
?Eight short preludes and fugues BWV 553–560
?Fugue in G 'Jig' BWV 577
?Kleines harmonisches Labyrinth BWV 591

The lovely Trio in D minor has always been one of my very favourite Bach miniatures, and I hope no one comes along to disprove that it is his. It could be an ignored movement from a trio sonata, as it is perfectly crafted and expressive in a way only Bach managed, with a section of lilting overlapping sequences over a gently falling pedal that is very touching. It must be as mature as the trio sonatas, maybe just pre-1730. The unique Pastorale or Pastorella in F is a curious little sequence of musette-type movements, of which three don't require pedals so can stand on their own, the second especially. It has been questioned whether it is by Bach, but Stauffer defends it and argues, by analogy with other pastoral movements in the cantatas, that this is a Leipzig work of the 1720s. The eight short preludes and fugues are used as teaching pieces but are not as good as the keyboard 'little preludes' BWV 933–938: slight and not reliably Bach's, excluded by Boyd.

One piece I would be sorry to lose from the canon is the exuberant little 'Jig' Fugue, a well-known *moto perpetuo* creation in skipping 12/8 time. Perhaps there is no special reason to connect it with Bach; it is witty and effective none the less, but the scholarly consensus is currently against it. Almost certainly not by Bach (though still his in *New Grove* and in a recent *NBA* volume), and a most curious survival, is the 'Little Harmonic Labyrinth', with its three movements, 'Introitus', 'Centrum' and 'Exitus', surveying the chromatic keys and modulations in a rigorous manner but creating very odd music – surely the work of a theorist rather than of Bach, who was always said to dislike the purely theoretical.

Trio sonata No. 1 in E flat BWV 525
Trio sonata No. 2 in C minor BWV 526
Trio sonata No. 3 in D minor BWV 527
Trio sonata No. 4 in E minor BWV 528
Trio sonata No. 5 in C BWV 529
Trio sonata No. 6 in G BWV 530

These perfect pieces stand apart both from the sequence of preludes and fugues and from the chorale-based settings, as the only organ works before *Clavierübung III* that Bach collected for performance: six three-movement sonatas of the utmost precision and grace. They would sound well on any keyboard instrument – and their intimacy means that many recordings on big baroque organs sound completely wrong. (They have been effectively transcribed for various ensembles, including Julian Bream and George Malcolm's version for lute and harpsichord.) They require absolute equality and independence between two manuals and pedals and must have been very important teaching aids. Forkel says that 'Bach composed them for his eldest son, Wilhelm Friedemann, who, by practising them, had to prepare himself to become the great performer on the organ that he afterwards was. It is impossible to say enough of their beauty. They were composed when the author was in his most mature age and maybe considered as his chief work of this description.' We have Bach's autograph manuscript, and also a copy half in Wilhelm Friedemann's hand and half in the hand of Anna Magdalena; so they must pre-date Friedemann's departure for Dresden in 1733. (Peter Dirksen has recently suggested that Bach might have performed them in Dresden in September 1731, but one wonders whether they were really intended for performance complete, or rather for practice and selective performance.)

Early commentators singled these pieces out for wonder and admiration. What the composer is doing here is to take the familiar texture of the baroque trio sonata and work it into a solo exercise. Each of the six is consciously different in style and content – perhaps they draw on lost Weimar or Cöthen repertory for their material, but as usual with Bach it is scrupulously reworked. The non-organists among us can only listen to these pieces, which demand such perfect co-ordination between two hands and feet, breathless with admiration. (It is worth trying these pieces with two players at one piano, just to marvel at their skill.) The opening bars of the first E flat sonata are an object lesson in how to shape a theme and its extension, so that it rises and falls, acquiring an ideal shape and balance; then the answer takes the lead and is answered in turn by the subject. Bach's now-perfect way of signalling the peak of the movement heralds the return of the subject, first as a false entry in the pedals and then as the cadence. There is a C minor Siciliano and then an Allegro leaping upwards in the first half, downwards in the second. Sonata No. 2 in C minor has a twisting subject, an eloquent central Largo in E flat, and a strict finale over a walking bass which makes room for a quirky little repeated figure as second subject. There almost seems an anticipation of early sonata form in the reprise of the material in these outer movements. The opening of Sonata No. 3 in D minor could well have been taken from a lost chamber work; the Adagio was taken into the Triple Concerto BWV 1044. The final Vivace is in triple time with scampering triplets, presenting a touch of the new galant style for Dresden.

Sonata No. 4 in E minor, with its short solemn opening, begins with a movement we can recognise as the Sinfonia to part two of Cantata 76, written in 1723 but perhaps also drawing on earlier material that Bach liked. The very elaborate Andante intensifies gradually, and the final E minor Allegro is another delicately dazzling display. Sonata No. 5 in C plays to Bach's concept of this key as open and transparent, with a gently bouncing theme worked out in every possible combination including some long pedal passages; the syncopations provide tension. The A minor Largo becomes a stream of intricate demisemiquavers, while the final Allegro returns to the total exuberant clarity of the start. The final sonata of the group sounds like one of the Italian concertos that Bach transcribed a decade and more before, with a striding G major Vivace, lilting E minor Lento, and boisterous final G major Allegro. The tempo markings and detailed articulations in the sources show how carefully Bach prepared these works, doubtless for his son.

Chorale settings

The chorale prelude was a central feature of North German organ music in the period leading up to Bach: these extremely strict and brief settings of Lutheran chorale melodies, widely cultivated around the region, showed how the chorale underpinned the liturgy and was essential for the congregation's understanding of the sentiments of the hymns. The simplest types of chorale preludes take the form of a chorale melody in the soprano, with patterned imitative entries in the lower parts – usually set up before the melody enters, and often based on a melodic tag from the chorale. Sometimes the chorale is elaborated, or turned into a full-scale chorale fughetta. The chorale partita combines treatment of a chorale tune with a set of variations, like Buxtehude's *Auf meinen lieben Gott* with double and Sarabande. From the period of Praetorius, Scheidemann and Scheidt, these preludes became increasingly important to composers; in the second half of the seventeenth century composers with whom the Bach family had close connections, such as Pachelbel, Ahle, and Zachau, cultivated the form. Further north, in more flamboyant and extended manner, so did Reincken, Buxtehude, Bruhns and Böhm, from whom we know Bach learned much, and his direct contemporaries J. G. Walther and Telemann. Walther wrote very Bach-like preludes with, for example, the *cantus firmus* in canon under an imitative texture. Pachelbel's are clear, open and less imaginative, but surely gave Bach a feeling for balance and logic in his music.

Neumeister Chorales BWV 1090–1095, 1097–1120

These chorale settings were the great discovery of the Bach tercentenary year 1985, when there was a rush by two different scholars to publicise the discovery in time for the anniversary. The manuscript called LM 4708 at Yale had been under scholars' noses for years, but its importance was not appreciated; it was compiled by Johann Neumeister some time after 1790, and in it are thirty-eight organ chorale preludes clearly attributed to Bach. It is of interest that of the few of them previously known to scholars, two (BWV 719 and 742) had been excluded from the *Neue Bach Ausgabe* as spurious, but the manuscript forces a rethink on this and indeed on much of Bach's early output.

Dating from probably before 1705 and certainly before 1710, these are quite primitive and sometimes derivative organ chorale settings which undoubtedly represent a very early stage of the young Bach's engagement with this form, and thus provide an invaluable measure of his later progress. Some show a multi-sectional treatment like the models from which Bach learnt; almost all have points of originality and interest but few escape awkwardnesses of phrasing or harmony. Only to compare the generalised settings of the chorales like *Wir glauben all einen Gott* BWV 1098 or *Aus tiefer Not* BWV 1099 with the precisely focused ones Bach achieved less than a decade later in the *Orgelbüchlein* is to hear how far he came in such a short space of time. His debt to Pachelbel is evident, but there are certainly touches of originality here: in *Jesu, meine Freude* BWV 1105 the chorale tune moves around between the parts.

Wolff observes that the sequence of eighty-two chorales in the collection corresponds precisely to that of the *Orgelbüchlein*, and most of the thirty-eight pieces Bach set here are those he intended to set in the *Orgelbüchlein* – which raises the question of whether his natural tendency would have been to revise these early settings for that collection, had he really thought them worthy. The debate about these works seems to have been resolved in favour of authenticity, though Peter

Williams remains sceptical. His reservation is that if they are the work of Bach, 'so must many another piece be, and Bach's work must at first have been indistinguishable from that of his local predecessors'. They thus set the bar somewhat lower than we had previously thought in terms of what Bach achieved during his early years, which in itself is revealing.

Chorale preludes BWV 714–765
Kirnberger/Breitkopf chorales BWV 690–713

?Herr Jesu Christ, dich zu uns wend BWV 749
?Herr Jesu Christ, meins Lebens Licht BWV 750
?Nun ruhen alle Wälder BWV 756
Wie schön leuchtet der Morgenstern BWV 739 and 764
  (fragment)
Gott, durch deine Güthe BWV 724

What were Bach's earliest essays in the chorale prelude form? Here we are into the realms of speculation: Christoph Wolff, who revealed the Neumeister Chorales, felt that those settings could not represent Bach's very earliest chorale works. Instead these first three chorales here, BWV 749, 750, 756, are suggested by him as representing Bach's earliest extant compositions from before 1700: 'modest and perfectly fine', simple chorale fughettas following the models of Johann Christoph Bach and Pachelbel, without special originality. (However, both Malcolm Boyd and Richard Jones exclude them from Bach's works, and Peter Williams says their authenticity is unproven.)

We are on certain ground when we come to BWV 739 and 764, for they are the earliest Bach works preserved in autograph sources, dating from 1702/3, certainly before 1705; the first is in the Möller Manuscript and the second is a fragment. (They were not included in the *Neue Bach Ausgabe* until very recently.) They are well worked out, though not without awkwardness, uniting aspects of the North German and the Central German schools. BWV 724 is the only chorale setting in the Andreas Bach Book, written out in tablature.

Vom Himmel hoch, da komm ich her BWV 700
?Gelobet seist du, Jesu Christ BWV 723
Ach Gott, vom Himmel sieh darein BWV 741

Ernest May's chronology of the early organ works suggests
the first group of BWV 700, 723 and 741 as very early, from
1700–5 (Malcolm Boyd's listing, following Klotz, says the first
and last of the group were revised in the 1740s, for which
there is no real evidence). The first is clear and open, experimenting with fugal treatment of the chorale lines, though not
totally successfully, with a little pedal at the end. The last is a
remarkably ambitious piece with the chorale in the bass and
requiring double pedal, with considerable intensity of feeling:
'undoubtedly the most harshly dissonant of all Bach's early
works', says Richard Jones. The second may be by Krebs or
J. M. Bach.

We can now begin tentatively to distinguish between some
of the chorale preludes rather randomly grouped together in
Schmieder and the Breitkopf collection. For example, BWV
712, 716, 718, 720, 721 and 733 are now mainly datable before
1708/9, with some works such as BWV 702 that were previously doubted, but which the latest *Neue Bach Ausgabe* editor thinks should be firmly admitted as Bach's work. Richard
Jones argues for Bach's authorship of BWV 707 by linking it to
BWV 741. *Erbarm dich* BWV 721 is a most unusual essay over
totally regular pulsing chords with the chorale in the treble: is
this really an organ piece? *Ein feste Burg* BWV 720 is clearly
designed to demonstrate an organ (at Mühlhausen?). Slightly
later but still pre-Weimar are BWV 694, 695, 710, 715, 722,
726, 729, 732, 734 and 738. The beautiful *Jesu meine Zuversicht*
BWV 728 is found in autograph in the Anna Magdalena notebook, and could sound as well on the clavichord. Peter Williams suggests that the group of fughettas BWV 696–699 and
701–4, copied as a set around 1760, could actually be quite late
Leipzig works from around the period of *Clavierübung III*; this
is accepted in *Grove* but not yet by BWV. Several others in this
group are spurious, by Walther, Fischer, Homilius or Böhm.

O Lamm Gottes, unschuldig (not in BWV)
O Lamm Gottes, unschuldig BWV 1085

Scholars debate endlessly whether some of the early chorale preludes are by Bach or not. It seems perverse of BWV to ignore the first of these good settings of 'O Lamm Gottes, unschuldig' when it has two attributions to Bach in reliable sources. It was finally published by Hans Klotz in series IV volume 3 of the *Neue Bach Ausgabe*. The second setting was only recently admitted to BWV as its late number shows; unusually, one source has a second movement, marked 'Choral', which is an ornamentation of the melody.

Allein Gott in der Höh' sei Ehr BWV 715
Gelobet seist du, Jesu Christ BWV 722
Herr Gott, dich loben wir BWV 725
Herr Jesu Christ, Dich zu uns wend BWV 726
Lobt Gott ihr Christen, allzugleich BWV 732
In dulci jubilo BWV 729

This is a distinctive group of chorale settings among those mentioned above, which are not fugal treatments or fantasias but just elaborations of the chorale itself, with the sort of dramatic interpolations and punctuations between the lines that must have driven congregations to distraction in Arnstadt; they probably date from around that period. The best known and most mature is *In dulci jubilo*, a joyous statement of the Christmas hymn with added flourishes.

The Breitkopf Collection, also known as the Kirnberger Collection, BWV 690–713, includes many of those mentioned above, and was gathered together from various manuscripts and assembled only after Bach's death, reflecting those earlier settings which his pupils perhaps preserved and used, including BWV 711 *Allein Gott*, a delightful little Bicinium which was later revised, and BWV 691, a lovely setting from W. F. Bach's book, showing how chorale settings were an important part of home music-making.

Partite diverse sopra: *Christ, der du bist der helle Tag*
  BWV 766
Partite diverse sopra: *O Gott, du frommer Gott*
  BWV 767
Partite diverse sopra: *Sei gegrüsset, Jesu gütig*
  BWV 768
?**Partite diverse sopra:** *Ach, was soll ich Sünder machen*
  BWV 770
?**Partita:** *Herr Christ, der einig Gottes Sohn*
  BWV Anh. 77
?**Partita:** *Wenn wir in höchsten Nöten sein*
  BWV Anh. 78

'Bach began already when he was at Arnstadt to compose
pieces with variations under the title Partite diverse,' wrote
Forkel. This is a group of variations on chorale melodies in
the style that Pachelbel and others made popular, indebted
to Georg Böhm and probably dating from the years of his
influence on Bach, from around 1700 onwards; perhaps they
date from Arnstadt. They are certainly early works, but offer
a tightly disciplined form for Bach to work within, bringing
together the sacred form of the chorale with the secular form
of the suite or sonata. Possibly these were also for domestic
use, the sort of pieces requiring a house organ that we see
illustrated on the title pages of Kuhnau's works, whose form
they also seem to echo, especially as they freely combine
variations with and without pedal.

  Christ, der du bist der helle Tag is in F minor, based on the
German melody of the Latin hymn 'Christe qui lux es et dies',
and providing seven variations in an expressive key which
Bach exploits to the full, with a Largo Partita II echoing 'Ich
ruf zu dir', and a final one with optional pedals. The surviving
source refers to Bach by a French name, Giov. Bast. Bach.
O Gott du frommer Gott is in C minor, with nine variations
that look more suited to harpsichord than organ, some of
the material anticipating the Second Partita in C minor, and
probably used for teaching in Weimar since Krebs produced

a copy. *Sei gegrüsset, Jesu gütig* is in G minor, with eleven variations, several with pedal: this is the most interesting of the group. There is a miscellaneous collection of variations in most sources, so it may have found this form a little later (1708–17). Particularly impressive is the opening chorale harmonisation; the ninth variation is long (105 bars, the longest in these sets) and expressive, while the last movement, which brings together chorale aria with a chorale-based setting, is very striking.

Ach, was soll ich Sünder machen is a Partita in E minor, linked by BWV to the others but left more open in Boyd and *Grove*. Jones thinks it came first of the group, with its adventurous final movement for changing manuals and echoes, but some of it looks equally suitable for the domestic keyboard. Perhaps these were really 'mix and match' works from which one took whatever was suitable on whatever occasion. Finally Peter Wollny in a recent *NBA* volume restores two partitas from the Anhang for our consideration, the first in F with seven verses, and the second using the famous 'deathbed chorale' melody, with seven florid but rather empty variations.

Orgelbüchlein *BWV 599–644*

This unfinished collection of chorale preludes for the liturgical year marks out Bach's decisive achievement of maturity as a composer. They are on a spectacular level of perfection, and although Bach never came near to completing the 164 chorale settings that were planned for the liturgical year, no one coming to these pieces can doubt the finished nature of the compositions, and the advances over earlier models that Bach here achieves. Jones puts it well when he writes that 'the gulf in style and quality between Bach's early chorales and the *Orgelbüchlein* . . . is so immense that it is difficult to account for it in terms of a continuous process of development.' There is a direct link to earlier collections because the last two preludes by Bach to have been copied into the Neumeister collection are the first two he wrote into the *Orgelbüchlein*, but as Neumeister's manuscript dates from after Bach's death this is inconclusive. The greatest proof that Bach had moved decisively on is that although his liturgical plan for the *Orgelbüchlein* contained many chorales he treated in Neumeister, he did not include or revise them, but left the titles blank. By then he was surely, as we say, in a different place. He probably planned the collection in Weimar around 1710, entered some chorales before 1712, and others between 1713 and 1716. He then returned to the planned collection later, writing the title at a later stage in 1722 and adding a couple more chorales in Leipzig after 1726.

The sequence begins at the beginning of the liturgical year in Advent, and the collection's distinctive feel is given by the absolutely sharp characterisation of each chorale's figuration, whether or not the chorale line itself is elaborated: what Jones calls the 'motivicity of the texture'. So in *Nun komm, der Heiden Heiland*, there is offbeat imitation through the parts; in *Gottes Sohn ist kommen*, constant flowing figuration with the chorale in canon between soprano and bass; in *Herr Gott, nun sei gepreiset*, articulated figures in constant rising thirds. *Der Tag, der ist so freudenreich* has buzzing, trilling activity under the simple chorale melody, while *Vom Himmel kam der Engel Schar* has scales of semiquavers flowing between the parts. *In dulci jubilo* dances in triplets, sustaining a treble–bass canon on the theme; although the second canonic voice is played on the pedals, it is not the bass line in the texture. *Lobt Gott, ihr Christen, allzugleich* in G is totally condensed, while *Jesu, meine Freude* (compare the Neumeister setting) again is dominated by one characteristic figuration, a gentle rocking pattern achieved on almost every note of the scale in the course of its few bars. *Christum wir sollen loben schon* is marked Adagio, and unusually puts the chorale in the middle of the texture in the alto, while the other voices begin almost four octaves apart and gradually converge. *Wir Christenleut* is a gigue-like flowing figure of quaver and four semiquavers. The old year ends with *Das alte Jahr vergangen ist* as a highly elaborated tune over a dark chromatic lament: very eloquent.

If you had to pick a single example of Bach's exuberant genius in this short form it would have to be *In dir ist Freude* in G, where the striding chorale tune is intoned in imitation over a bounding cadential pedal figure that returns repeatedly under bell-like scales and chimes, rising to a height of excitement. Where are the precedents for this thrilling, tautly structured writing? There's another example of consistently worked writing in *Herr Gott, nun schleuss den Himmel auf* in A minor, with a haunting running line in 24/16 under the chorale melody; *O Lamm Gottes* is a canon at the fifth which looks forward to the Passion choruses with its slurred pairs of lamenting notes. There is a canon at the twelfth in *Christe, du Lamm Gottes*, and one at the octave for *Christus, der uns selig macht*. One of the most eloquent preludes is *O Mensch, bewein dein Sünde gross*, marked Adagio assai and elaborating the Passion chorale with an ornamented melody, which seems to have been written straight into the manuscript.

It's intriguing why Bach left out some chorales and added others: at the end of the Passion period there are a couple of bars for *O Traurigkeit, o Herzeleid* never completed. As we reach Easter, the mood is stern rather than celebratory: *Christ lag in Todesbanden* is structured around several iterations of a mighty pedal theme, and this concept of repeated articulation under a chorale melody is central to the collection: *Erstanden ist der heil'ge Christ* has isolated pedal cadences to articulate every bar, while *Erschienen ist der herrliche Tag* has the melody in canon while the middle of the texture is in thirds and sixths, and *Heut' triumphieret Gottes Sohn* has an equally decisive four-note pedal theme. The greatest example of this method is *Durch Adams Fall*, where the pedal motif is a descending diminished seventh that represents man's fall into sin; the combination of this with the chorale melody is quite astonishing. There must also be symbolism in the ten repeated notes of the ten commandments in *Dies sind die heilgen zehn Gebot*.

Alongside this are simpler chorale elaborations such as *Liebster Jesu, wir sind heir*, which exists in two versions.

If *In dir ist Freude* represents the optimistic peak of the *Orgelbüchlein*, then the other extreme is the famous *Ich ruf zu dir, Herr Jesu Christ* which Busoni memorably transcribed for piano. It is the only three-part setting in the collection, and it is the unearthly expressiveness of the inner line that Bach weaves between chorale and pulsating regular bass line that is so infinitely touching: it ranges through more than an octave, touching flattened sevenths, and in the penultimate cadence reaches up to touch the chorale and then subside in chromatic grief. (We should not assume from its inclusion in the Neumeister collection that this was an early work, but maybe it soon became a favourite one.) After this, gaps are greater; there is a highly elaborated melody in the setting of *Wenn wir in höchsten Nöten sein*, the chorale to which Bach returned at the very end of his life, simplifying and clarifying it; and the last chorale setting entered is *Ach wie nichtig, ach wie flüchtig*, which like the cantata of that title has running semiquavers around the chorale and, as is characteristic of this collection, has a repeated cadential figure in the pedals.

Clavierübung III *BWV 669–689*

This imposing sequence is one of the most elaborate and important of Bach's collected editions, and the only one devoted to the organ. (*Clavierübung I* consists of the six keyboard Partitas and *Clavierübung II* is a further collection of keyboard music, for which see below. To what extent the Goldberg Variations, also published as *Clavierübung*, belong to this sequence is a matter for debate.) This organ collection was published in September 1739 and represents Bach's Lutheran faith and his musical skill combined at their very highest level. It deliberately covers all the prevailing styles and represents the culmination of a whole period of work with music for the organ. There is a clear relationship to Frescobaldi's *Fiori musicali*, a collection of pieces for the Mass, which Bach copied in 1714. However this is not just an 'Organ Mass' as it is sometimes referred to, but a more complex collection of intersecting groups of pieces.

The description on the publication rather undersells it, perhaps so as not to put purchasers off, as merely 'various preludes on the catechism and other hymns for the organ'. There is symbolism in the grouping of the movements. Enclosed within a huge Prelude and Fugue (known to us as the 'St Anne', because of the fugue subject opening's similarity to that famous hymn melody) are the chorale preludes: the Kyrie and Gloria are contained in Luther's reformed liturgy, and the catechism chorales in his reformed doctrinal teaching. The Trinitarian emphasis is evident from the grouping of tripartite settings of the Kyrie and Gloria from the Mass, the central role of the key of E flat with its three flats, and the three sections of the Fugue. Even the first Prelude is structured in three parts, and there are pairs of settings of Luther's six catechism chorales. These are common chorales for all parts of the liturgical year and not seasonally organised as most chorale preludes (for instance in the *Orgelbüchlein*, see above) would have been. There are twenty-seven pieces in all: a Trinitarian statement of three times three times three. The central piece is thus No. 14, a particularly personal one for Bach. Gregory Butler has cited works by Hurelsbusch and Walther as possible influences, as well as Bach's visit to Dresden, his work on the Schemelli Hymnal and the need to answer the stinging criticisms of Scheibe in 1737. Butler's contention is that behind the sophisticated outline of the collection there was an earlier plan, probably for the pedal chorale preludes alone, to which the manuals-only preludes and finally the framing Prelude and Fugue have been added. In his first review of the publication Mizler wrote, 'The author has given here new proof that in this kind of composition he excels many others in experience and skill. No one can surpass him in this sphere, and very few indeed will be able to imitate him.

This work is a powerful argument against those who have ventured to criticise the music of the Court Composer' – a clear reference to the criticisms of Scheibe.

This magisterial collection contains some of Bach's most satisfying and sheerly powerful writing, even if it requires an effort to unlock some of its stricter riches. 'The very mastery has a forbidding air,' writes Peter Williams, 'and the several organ styles were almost unsympathetically old-fashioned.' There certainly is a flavour of ancient tradition, given by the fact that half the hymn melodies are Gregorian in origin, reflecting Leipzig's conservative Lutheranism in which Latin settings were included in the liturgy – but what a sense of history this provides.

Prelude in E flat BWV 552/1

The opening Prelude is overwhelming in its strength of purpose: the powerful dotted-rhythm opening functions not as you might expect like a French overture introduction, but as the framing device of the movement, repeatedly interrupting it. Within this there is then a jaunty echo 'B' section, and a rushing fugal 'C' section driven by syncopation: these three groups of material are organised in the sequence ABACAB[touch of A]CA. Even though one distinguished organist said the passage before the final reprise is 'one of the worst transitions Bach ever wrote', the impetus of the whole thing is irresistible.

Kyrie, Gott Vater in Ewigkeit BWV 669
Christe, aller Welt Trost BWV 670
Kyrie, Gott heiliger Geist BWV 671

Three stern Kyrie preludes, starting with a three-part fugue on the rising Gregorian theme which introduces the *cantus firmus* in the soprano. Next the Christe, where the treatment is similar but the *cantus firmus* appears in the tenor. Then the final Kyrie where the introductory lines answer each other, rising and falling; this time the *cantus firmus* is in the bass, and Bach instructs *con Organo pleno*. But what happens then is extraordinary: Bach keeps to the principle of the plain *cantus firmus*, but opens out a huge range of expressive possibilities, and this culminates on the last entry of the theme in the pedals, where the running counterpoint evaporates upwards on a top B flat. At that point the musical language changes completely, an implacable pedal line enters, and the world collapses beneath our feet in angular, slow chromaticisms that take us to the heart of some titanic spiritual conflict. They resolve only painfully: this is surely one of the most remarkable moments in Bach's entire output.

Kyrie, Gott Vater in Ewigkeit BWV 672
Christe, aller Welt trost BWV 673
Kyrie, Gott heliger Geist BWV 674

Designed as three lighter, manuals-only reflections on the same chorales, each is in triple time, gently harmonious, and the final Kyrie has a skipping motion in total contrast to the previous setting; the time signatures advance symbolically: 3/4, 6/8, 9/8.

Allein Gott in der Höh' (three settings) BWV 675, 676, 677

The Gloria receives three settings. The first is for manuals only in F with the chorale in the alto, then there is a well-known extended setting in Bach's favourite open G-major style, like a concerto; and finally a little A major Fughetta with marked staccato notes. (The three ascending keys span a third – yet another three!)

Dies sind die heiligen zehn Gebot' BWV 678 and 679

From the three times three settings of the Kyrie and Gloria we move to pairs of settings for the Catechism. This first presents the *cantus firmus* for the first time in the collection in canon in the left hand within a trio-sonata texture that starts over a tonic pedal. The companion is a gigue-like fughetta for manuals only, with far more static repeated notes than Bach would usually employ at this period, indicating an earlier origin.

Wir glauben all' an einen Gott BWV 680 and 681

All Bach's skills converge in this first D minor setting to make it a peerless example of his elemental appeal. The formal articulation of the structure is a recurrent pedal line, here stamping up an octave in thirds and then bounding stepwise downwards – this utterly memorable shape recurs six times, plus a wonderful final intensification. Above this the main imitative texture starts offbeat, creating total rhythmic uncertainty which the syncopation maintains throughout. The companion setting for manuals is a curious little fughetta in dotted French overture style – this may have been deliberate for the middle of the collection, as there is a similar movement in *Clavierübung I* and *II*, as there would be too in the Goldberg Variations. Though the E minor tonality of this fourteenth piece allows no opportunity for a B flat (B in German), the final cadence does contains the notes . . . A–C–H.

Vater unser im Himmelreich BWV 682 and 683

One of the most elaborate (and some would say dry) of all Bach's chorale preludes, with a wealth of rhythmic difficulty because of the many different articulations in the voices; with the *cantus firmus* in canon between the fourth and fifth voices, added to the surrounding chromaticism, this is a very difficult piece to communicate. As if to compensate, the simple, flowing manuals-only setting that follows is absolutely clear and perfectly shaped, the semiquavers running down from the chorale's opening note in scalic motives sustained throughout.

Christ, unser Herr, zum Jordan kam BWV 684 and 685

A joyous trio sonata in C minor over a running bass unfolds

for six bars before the *cantus firmus* enters in the bass, in the pedals at high pitch, and the imitative material in the accompaniment seems to echo and develop the chorale line in an especially integrated way, leading to a long final flourish over the last pedal note. The companion setting for manuals is again in triple time.

Aus tiefer Not schrei ich zu dir BWV 686 and 687

Now a further complexity is added to the texture in Bach's only six-part organ setting, with the use of double pedal: the chorale is in the top pedal part but the bottom pedal part participates in the five-part counterpoint that surrounds the chorale. There is a gradual increase in rhythmic activity as the setting reaches its climax. The manuals setting is unusually in F sharp minor with the imitation based on the same rising and falling fifth; the chorale is at the top.

Jesus Christus, unser Heiland BWV 688 and 689

Another dazzling display of contrapuntal combinations, this time based on a D minor toccata-like subject, a leaping figure that contracts (the opposite of the 'Wedge' fugue subject, which expands). Some have seen here a cross-like motif, and the number of bars, seventy-two, may also be significant: $72 = 8 \times 9$, which is $2 \times 3 \times 3$ squared, bringing together the Trinitarian aspects with the paired aspects of the collection. The manuals-only fugue that follows is one of the tightest in the collection with strettos of six different kinds, after (in order) six, one, two, four, five and six beats, an extreme feat of contrapuntal compression.

Four Duettos BWV 802–805

These four mysterious pieces have long been argued over: they are ultra-strict and honestly unattractive two-part inventions, in what look more a harpsichord than an organ idiom, of no discernible liturgical relevance to this collection (though scholars have tried hard to link them, for instance, to Luther's four teaching precepts). They do, however, carry forward Bach's ideal of exploring every contrapuntal combination, and bring the total number of pieces to twenty-seven.

Fugue in E flat BWV 552/2

Finally, to crown the volume, this great Fugue which has become known to the English-speaking world as the 'St Anne', because the theme with which it starts is identical to that hymn tune. The Trinitarian associations of the three-part structure have been the source of much speculation (can they, or the three sections of the Prelude, really be meant to represent in turn Father, Son, and Holy Ghost?), but there are clear antecedents for this structure in Frescobaldi, Böhm and others; Bach is surely here trying to integrate past and present in a typically humane way. The harmonious, melodic nature of the theme is matched with a rather ancient mode of working-out, but with the addition of a distinctively modern sense of climax. The three sections build gradually, from the old-style first section, to the 6/4 second section using the original theme in triple time over a running sequence, and then the 12/8 section which again brings back the original subject and then builds up brilliantly. The last few bars are among the most overwhelming in Bach's music, as the music cascades steadily downwards from a top B flat, adding voices in culminating harmony as if drawing the world together, until the terrific offbeat final pedal entry seals the triumph of the moment. As Peter Williams writes, 'It is scarcely an exaggeration to see the prelude and fugue as together summing up many, even most, of the resources of organ praeludia which were superseded, current or anticipated during the lifetime of J. S. Bach.'

The 'Eighteen' (or 17) Chorales BWV 651–668

These superb chorale settings show Bach as the constant reviser of his own work. They were probably all begun before 1723, and all but one also have earlier versions. Then BWV 651–655 were assembled as an autograph collection around 1739–45, probably in the hope that they might be published. The printing of *Clavierübung III* had not been a huge financial success, especially as it was so big, so perhaps these chorale collections were an attempt at something more market-friendly.

These are however large-scale works, perhaps designed as a deliberate contrast to the short settings in the *Orgelbüchlein*. They are extrovert, confident pieces with extensive, extended contrapuntal working between the chorale entries (you sometimes forget you are in the middle of a chorale fantasia). The tone is set immediately by the ringing clarity of *Komm, heiliger Geist* which sets off with extended imitation over a tonic pedal – then the pedal becomes the chorale theme, a superbly worked exercise. The companion setting is a quiet triple-time setting with the chorale ornamented in the soprano. *An Wasserflüssen Babylon* was modernised and simplified in its revision; *Schmücke dich, o liebe Seele* has one of Bach's most beautiful triple-time inventions – a gentle trio-sonata movement complete in itself before the chorale enters in the treble. It was this prelude that Schumann heard Mendelssohn play (see p. 17). *Herr Jesu Christ, dich zu uns wend* is a bustling G major trio, with the chorale appearing in the pedals before the end; *O Lamm Gottes* a severely worked setting in three verses. In *Nun danket alle Gott*, a closely argued texture places the *cantus firmus* in the soprano; then *Von Gott will ich nicht lassen* leads to the famous trio of settings of *Nun komm, der Heiden Heiland*. The first of these has an elaborated chorale line over a treading bass line, built up from the bottom; the second is strictly imitative, and the third a flamboyant toccata (reminiscent of the setting of this hymn in Cantata 62) where again the textures are so complete that the chorale tune comes as an added bonus.

Allein Gott in der Höh sei Ehr also receives three contrasted settings, the first with soprano chorale, the second with tenor, and the last a tour de force which is a delightful trio. *Jesus Christus, unser Heiland* (marked 'sub Communione') has two settings, while *Komm, Gott, Schöpfer* is a bouncy setting expanded from the *Orgelbüchlein*, with a hiccupy offbeat pedal phrase that leads to the chorale. The last chorale is called *Vor Deinen Thron tret' ich*, and is a revision of an *Orgelbüchlein* prelude, *Wenn wir in höchsten Nöthen sein*, which Bach then himself revised again at the very end of his life, using it as a musical signature to the incomplete *Art of Fugue*; clearly the change to the text 'Before your throne O Lord I come' had a special personal significance for Bach, as he reached his end but continued to revise and perfect his music.

Schübler Chorales BWV 645–650

This collection dates from very late in Bach's life during the 1740s, when he was working with the engraver Johann Georg Schübler on *The Art of Fugue*. Five of the six chorale arrangements are of successful movements from Bach's cantatas, perhaps drawing especially on pieces with wide appeal: *Wachet auf, ruft uns die Stimme* is one of his few original cantatas from the 1730s, and this setting has become justly famous, its melodic invention chiming perfectly with the chorale tune heard in the tenor; though there are some small problems in the counterpoint, the tunefulness overcomes any difficulty. *Wo soll ich fliehen hin* is the one prelude whose source is not known, though it is presumably from a lost cantata: the piece is in E minor and has a trio texture with the chorale in the bass. *Wer nur den lieben Gott lässt walten* is from a duet in Cantata 93 of 1724, with the *cantus firmus* in the bass. *Meine Seele erhebet den Herren*, from a duet in Cantata 10, is a rather awkward piece to play, with chromatic lines, two parts for the left hand, pedals, and the chorale in the right hand. *Ach bleib bei uns* is another arrangement, from the chorale aria in

Cantata 6 of 1725, where the activity is in the left hand under a simple chorale. Finally *Kommst du nun, Jesu, vom Himmel herunter* from Cantata 137 of 1725, an appealingly light and airy setting in G with the melody given to the pedals at high pitch. Bach continued to refine these settings even after they had been published, marking up his personal copy.

Canonic Variations on 'Vom Himmel hoch' BWV 769

From the end of Bach's life, these dense variations are a culmination of his intense examination of different canonic forms, evident elsewhere but rarely in so concentrated a form. (They are oddly placed by *New Grove* with other more abstract canonic works, but these are clearly pieces for organ.) After the publication of the Goldberg Variations, Bach added to his own copy of the work a set of fourteen canons on a version of the bass line of the aria. Clearly Bach was already preoccupied around this time with both canon and fugue, and was working towards the planned publication of *The Art of Fugue*. What seems to have spurred him into action here was being finally persuaded to join the Society of Musical Sciences of Lorenz Mizler, having delayed a long time (perhaps so that he could become the fourteenth member). Mizler visited Leipzig in June 1747; the first piece Bach sent to the Society members was the canon BWV 1076 from the post-Goldberg set, which also appears on his famous portrait. He could have sent the full set of Goldberg canons, but perhaps felt them too slight for this purpose. Instead, he proceeded with the composition and engraving of these Canonic Variations, and Bach later presented the work to the Society members. There are five variations on the theme, and the order of the published edition (1, 2, 3, 4, 5) is slightly different from that of the autograph (1, 2, 5, 3, 4). It seems clear that the autograph's order is to be preferred, and that there were practical considerations which prevented it being followed in the publication. Any performance should surely conclude with the variation where Bach signs his musical name B–A–C–H in the final bars.

The first variation is a canon at the octave, with the *cantus firmus* in the pedal. The second is a canon at the fifth, with the *cantus firmus* again in the pedal. In variation five, to be played in the middle, there are two distinct sections with canons at the sixth and the third, followed by two at the trickier intervals of the second and the ninth, contrapuntally inverted. Though published as the last movement, this feels like the complex heart of the work. Then follows variation three, a more lyrical treatment of the canon at the seventh, with chromatic inflections dominating. The fourth and last variation in the autograph returns to the interval of the octave with a canon by augmentation, but is elaborated with long passages between the *cantus firmus*. All four lines of the chorale melody are heard together in a combination as skilful as that in Mozart's 'Jupiter' Symphony, before the final B–A–C–H signature.

Though this is by no means among the most attractive of Bach's works, the variations have a strongly intellectual appeal, and Igor Stravinsky orchestrated them for ensemble, giving the chorale melody to men's voices.

𝛺 *Complete Organ Works* Peter Hurford
Decca 444 102 (17 CDs)
𝛺 *Organ Works* Ton Koopman
Teldec 4692817 (some originally on Novalis and Brilliant)
𝛺 *The Organ Works* Simon Preston
DG 469 420-2 (14 CDs)
𝛺 *Complete Organ Works* Gerhard Weinberger
Cpo 777363-2 (22 CDs)
𝛺 *Complete Organ Works* Kevin Bowyer
Nimbus N1721 (8 discs, in MP3 format)
𝛺 *BWV 913, 731, 718, 736, 732, 669–689 etc.* Gustav Leonhardt
DHM RD77868

SECULAR MUSIC

One of the aspects of Bach's music that seems continually to worry writers and listeners is his use of different music for different texts, and especially his transfer of sentiments from secular to sacred contexts. It is evident in everything from his smallest to his most important projects that Bach continually reused music and transferred it between different forms; much of what he conceived was not original for that purpose. These aspects, in a romantic view of composition, are flaws that contradict the essential notion of the inspired originality of the artist. How could Bach transfer a musical setting for the words 'Tönet ihr pauken' (Resound, ye drums) – secular praise, admirably illustrated by an almost unique use of unaccompanied timpani – to the words 'Jauchzet frohlocket' (Rejoice, exult) in the Christmas Oratorio? Even within a sacred context, how could he take a cantata chorus 'Gott, der Herr, ist Sonn und Schild' (The Lord God is a sun and shield) and turn it into the 'Gloria in excelsis' of a Mass without compromising the word-setting? How could a setting of the Passion be plundered for a secular funeral Ode (or worse, vice versa!) How at the very end of his life could he conclude the B minor Mass with the words 'Dona nobis pacem' by simply repeating the setting of the 'Gratias agimus' from earlier in the work?

These were perfectly understandable problems in their time, during the overhang of the romantic period, when the virtue of originality in a composer was prized above all else. But for Bach, sacred and secular were part of the same worldview, and there was no conflict between them: there was no contradiction between praising the Elector and hymning the Almighty. It is also perhaps a misunderstanding of baroque music to think that all music 'expresses' the text in a direct way. Of course there are very vivid examples of particular word-setting and visual devices in Bach's music that express individual words and phrases. But you sense that whatever the text, the music has itself a greater logic and a greater power which overarches the words. What is necessary for successful parody is what *New Grove* calls an 'expressive affinity', but not total similarity. There is always a counterpoint – sometimes a tension, sometimes a complementarity – between the meaning of a text and the meaning of the music. Parody is the sincerest form of flattery. When you look at the range of music Bach adapted and revised, he clearly chose to draw on those pieces that he knew had real value, adapting some of his greatest cantata movements for his short Missas and for the B minor Mass.

Secular cantatas

As well as his huge body of church cantatas, Bach wrote secular cantatas at various stages of his life for special entertainments. These ranged from the visits of dignitaries, their name-days, and other celebrations; they were not very frequent until he went to Cöthen in 1717, though many of these examples have been lost. In Leipzig he wrote major works whose material often overlaps with sacred cantatas: those whose principal existence is as a secular cantata, or feature as such in recordings and broadcasts, are mentioned here. Through the 1730s Bach was especially active in this field, as it enabled him to find favour with the Elector, who sometimes visited Leipzig himself. There is one account of the magnificence with which some of these works were given, captured in an account of the performance of Cantata 215 in Leipzig for the first anniversary of the accession of Frederick Augustus II as King of Poland, on 5 October 1734:

> At about nine o'clock in the evening the students here presented their Majesties with a most submissive evening serenade with trumpets and drums which the Hon. Capellmeister, Johann Sebastian Bach, has composed. For this, six hundred students carried wax tapers, and four Counts acted as marshals in presenting the music. When the musicians had reached the weigh-house the trumpets and drums went up on it, while the others took their places in another choir at the Rathaus . . . afterwards . . . his Royal Majesty together with his Royal Consort and the Royal Princes did not leave the windows until the music was over, and listened most graciously and liked it well.

These secular cantatas, often called a *dramma per musica*, could be seen as mini-operas. Leipzig had been without an opera house since 1720 and the appetite for opera among the public was large. Wolff suggests that 'Bach's pieces were by no means poor or makeshift substitutes for real operas. His compositions demonstrate at every step full mastery of the dramatic genre and the proper pacing of the dialogues.' However, they scarcely have the plot development or characterisation to hold an audience as operas do. They are effective occasional pieces, and in one respect they are better balanced than the sacred cantatas: Bach more often creates elaborate choruses at the end as well as the beginning of the works. But they are hardly operas.

WEISSENFELS, WEIMAR AND CÖTHEN

'Hunting Cantata' 208 *Was mir behagt, ist nur die muntre Jagd!*
Cantata 134a *Die Zeit, die Tag und Jahre macht*
Cantata 173a *Durchlauchtster Leopold*
Cantata 249a *Entfliehet, verschwindet, entweichet, ihr Sorgen*

Cantata 208 is Bach's first surviving secular cantata, written for the extensive birthday celebrations of Duke Christian of Saxe-Weissenfels on 23 February 1713. It is known as the 'Hunting Cantata' and was adapted and plundered several times, so it must have remained fresh in Bach's mind. It is based on a libretto by the Weimar poet Salomo Franck, and uses the characters of Diana and Pales, Endymion and Pan to tell a simple tale praising the Duke. There are echoes of hunting horns in Diana's staccato repeated notes, and of courtly pomp in the bass's dotted rhythms. The movements are short and attractive, and among them are two of Bach's most famous arias – the one known as 'Sheep may safely graze' and the original of 'My heart ever faithful' from Cantata 68. The rocking motion of the former and its memorable melody have led to countless transcriptions over the years, both for orchestra and (especially) for piano. The latter is in a much simpler form here, providing an object lesson in Bach's ability to create a new melody over constant harmony. The inspired trio sonata movement which springs from the continuo bass line is here added separately in the score. The final chorus, like the first in triple time, is exhilarating.

Cantata 134a (for New Year's Day, 1 January 1719) provided the model for Cantata 134 for Easter (see above, p. 236). Apparently Bach used the actual parts of the secular work in preparing the sacred version, so the form of the original was in doubt for some time. But all the music exists and can be attached to its secular libretto, a hymn of praise to Leopold of Anhalt-Cöthen. Cantata 173a was written for Leopold's birthday on 10 December, probably in 1722, and is the only other one of this period that survives in a complete form. The eight movements praise the Prince, and there is a delightful and quite complex G major duet in the tempo of a minuet, and cheerful soprano and bass arias before the final 'chorus' – which is, however, clearly for the two soloists. This later became a Whitsun sacred piece, Cantata 173.

A slightly later connection with the court at Weissenfels (although it originated in Leipzig) is Cantata 249a, the Pastoral Cantata for another birthday of the Duke on 23 February 1725. The characters are Doris and Sylvia, Damoetas and Menalcas, and though the music is lost, it can be almost entirely reconstructed from the Easter Oratorio, where it was later reused. Many have felt with Dürr that it works better in this secular context where its cheerful exuberance works well: the final ensemble for the four named soloists and the full instrumental forces disproves the feeling that Bach had any problem setting single-voice ensembles against a full orchestral ensemble.

LEIPZIG IN THE 1720S

Cantata 36c *Schwingt freudig euch empor*
Cantata 205 *Zerreisset, zersprenget, zertrümmert*
  die Gruft
Cantata 249b *Verjaget, zerstreuet, zerrüttet, ihr Sterne*
Cantata 36a *Steigt freudig in die Luft*
Cantata 207 *Vereinigte Zwietracht der wechselnden*
  Saiten
Cantata 204 *Ich bin in mir vergnügt*
Cantata 198 *Lass, Fürstin, lass einen Strahl*
Cantata 201 *Geschwinde, ihr wirbelnden Winde*

The sequence of secular cantatas associated with Leipzig
begins with Cantata 36c from April or May 1725, but we are
not sure for what occasion it was written. The text implies
praise of an elderly teacher who wears 'the silver trappings of
age', and the music is more familiar as the rather late Cantata
36 for Advent, but this version has a gavotte as the finale, like
the end of a Handel opera.

Cantata 205 is the first of the occasional Leipzig pieces
written for special events, in this case the name-day of the
teacher August Friedrich Müller on 3 August 1725, and
this one is elaborate enough to be a mini-opera. It is indeed
described as a *dramma per musica* and shows Pallas Athene
celebrated on Mount Helicon with the muses; there are vivid
pictorial treatments of the wind, the laughter of the gods, and
the cracking of the roofs. A striking instrumental combination
is that of viola d'amore and viola da gamba in the aria for
Zephyr, and the final chorus is marked with cries of 'Vivat'
from the whole ensemble.

Cantata 249b is 'a celebration of genius' for the Count
Joachim Friedrich von Flemming on 25 August 1726, and the
music is lost but can be reconstructed from the Easter Oratorio and the Pastoral Cantata 249a, mentioned above. (It
reflects Schmieder's view of Bach's priorities that these cantatas are catalogued under the Easter Oratorio, rather than as
separate pieces.) Cantata 36a is for the birthday of Prince Leo-

pold's second consort on 30 November 1726; this music too is lost, but can be pieced together from Cantata 36 and 36b.

Cantata 207 celebrates another Leipzig teacher, Dr Gottlieb Kortte, of whom it was said that he gave his inaugural lecture as Professor of Jurisprudence from memory as he had left his text at home. It was given on 11 December 1726. The opening is an adaptation of the third movement of Brandenburg No. 1; Malcolm Boyd argued that it points to the original source of that music, as both derived from an earlier cantata. There is a clever reuse of another section from Brandenburg Concerto No. 1 as a trio, where the horn passage from the concerto is replaced with trumpets, but with the addition of staccato, pizzicato strings plucking rhythmically underneath – a wonderful and quite funny stroke to which we might surely object, if we did not know it was by Bach. The cantata ends with a secular chorale movement; this Cantata was reworked as 207a in 1735.

Cantata 204 is a completely different type of piece, a domestic cantata for soprano solo from 1726 or 1727 called 'On contentedness', which conjures up the happiness and devotion of a life dedicated to God: it is worthless to build on friends. 'Pleasure is of no value' and other worthy sentiments are set to light, attractive music in which the soloist duets in turn with two oboes, violin and flute. Perhaps it was sung around the fireside in the Bach family, after a hard week's work composing and copying cantatas.

The *Trauer Ode* Cantata 198, described as the 'Tombeau de S. M. la reine de Pologne', is a beautiful and restrained piece: we have a newspaper report that Bach himself played in the first performance on the 'Clave di Cembalo', with organ, violas da gamba, lutes, violins, recorders, traverse flutes, etc. 'half being heard before and half after the oration of praise and mourning'. (In fact there are no recorders, but there are oboes d'amore.) For those interested in how quickly Bach wrote, we know that the death of Christiane Eberhardine, Electress of Saxony, occurred on 5 September, after which there was a dispute about the writing of the commemorative work between Bach and Görner (see above, p. 93); the Ode was completed on 15 October and performed on 17 October, leaving only two days for copying and rehearsal. There is something old-fashioned about the work, from the courtly double-dotted rhythms of the opening chorus (which was reused in another mourning cantata in 1729), to the old-style fugue that ends part one. The opening of the second part has a tenor aria with long-held notes for 'Ewigkeit' (eternity); the final chorus is in 12/8, as is the earlier alto aria with two violas da gamba and two lutes. We believe that much of this music was reused in Bach's St Mark Passion, but because of its incompleteness that work has never satisfactorily established itself: this fine cantata of mourning should be more frequently heard.

A major work in Bach's output is Cantata 201, 'The dispute between Phoebus and Pan', whose mythological clothing should not conceal that it is a paean in praise of music, to a text by Picander loosely derived from Ovid – the nearest Bach came to a St Cecilia Ode. It dates from the autumn of 1729 (and was revived in 1749, as Bach was arguing the case for music against Biedermann). Almost an hour in length, it is a lavish and dramatic work which some have connected with Bach's debut or at least his early period with the Collegium Musicum. The quickness of the whirling winds is depicted in the triplets that stir under the first chorus; then the dispute unfolds between Phoebus and Pan as to whose singing is the more beautiful, with Mercury and Momus joining to confuse the situation – Momus with the jolly aria that used to be sung under the English title 'Ah yes, just so'. Each has an aria, competitors and judges alike: in a recitative, for his misjudgement, Midas is given donkey's ears like Bottom in *A Midsummer Night's Dream*, vividly depicted here by a leap down more than an octave. The best is surely Mercury's biting aria with two flutes, 'Aufgeblas'ne Hitze', which Andreas Scholl recorded unforgettably. The conclusion tells Midas to go and lie down in the forest, and Phoebus to 'take up your lyre again; there is nothing lovelier than your songs'.

There is a strong final chorus: this is a defence of music with a thoroughgoing sense of fun.

𝛺 *BWV 201, 206, 207, 36c* Soloists, Musica Antiqua Köln/
Goebel
Archiv 457 346-2
𝛺 *BWV 201, 205, 213* Soloists, RIAS Kammerchor,
Akademie fur Alte Musik Berlin/Jacobs
Harmonia Mundi France 901544.45

LEIPZIG IN THE 1730S

Cantata 213 *Lasst uns sorgen, lasst uns wachen*
Cantata 214 *Tönet, ihr Pauken! Erschallet, Trompeten*

In Leipzig during the 1730s Bach turned aside from regular sacred cantata composition, but kept up a steady sequence of works for the Electoral royal family, doubtless helped by his position at the Collegium Musicum and stimulated by his great desire, eventually realised, to be recognised as the court composer. (For completeness, the series of courtly tributes actually begins with the birthday visit of Friedrich Augustus on 12 May 1727 for which Cantata Anh. I 9 was written, but that is lost; Cantata 193a for Augustus's name-day on 3 August 1727 is lost, though some music survives in the council election Cantata 193; also lost are Anh. I 11 written for 3 August 1732 and Anh. I 12 for the same day in 1733.)

These two surviving secular cantatas from the 1730s are very familiar, as their music provided material for the contemporaneous Christmas Oratorio: Cantata 213 of 5 September 1733, for the birthday of Crown Prince Friedrich Christian of Saxony, starts with Part IV of the Oratorio, and Cantata 214 starts with the beginning of Part I. Scholars were so reluctant to believe that Bach could have taken a secular work in praise of Augustus and turned it into a sacred work that they said the Oratorio must have been thought of first; the only evidence of planning is that the libretto of Cantata 213 seems to have been conceived to enable the words to be adapted (though in the case of the final chorus they never were). The plot is 'Hercules at the crossroads', the choice that Hercules makes between riches and hardship, which symbolises the choice the Crown Prince himself made, under the guidance of Mercury, god of tradesmen (and so a symbol of Leipzig). Most of the movements of both cantatas are familiar: though they have been extensively reordered they have not been much revised, and in some cases the texts are rather different in mood as well as content.

Cantata 214 is for a different occasion, the birthday of Maria Josepha, Electress of Saxony on 8 December 1733. It has an opening text, 'Sound you drums, ring out you trumpets', more suitable to Bach's music than the more generalised opening of the Oratorio. Four goddesses praise the Queen in turn: Bellona, Pallas, Irene and Fama. There is a delightful A major soprano aria with a pair of flutes not in the Oratorio, but the D major triumph is dominated by the bass aria with trumpet that reappears at the end of Part I of the Oratorio, and the opening chorus of Part II, reworked here as 'Blossom, you lindens, in Saxony like cedars'.

Cantata 215 *Preise dein Glücke, gesegnetes Sachsen*
Cantata 207a *Auf, schmetternde Töne der muntern Trompeten*
Cantata 36b *Die Freude reget sich*
Cantata 206 *Schleicht, spielende Wellen, und murmelt gelinde*
Cantata 30a *Angenehmes Wiederau, freue dich in deinen Auen!*

The Elector Friedrich Augustus sprang a surprise visit to Leipzig between 2 and 6 October 1734, which probably created some panic in the city in view of everything that had to be arranged. Cantata 215 was written, and its circumstances have been well documented (see above). Whether this anniversary celebration had been planned earlier cannot be certain, but we can imagine the rush to make all the preparations in time, especially with such an elaborate surrounding ceremony.

Remarkably, the libretto does not seek refuge in mythology, but directly uses the events surrounding Augustus's election to weave praise in his honour as King of Poland, though as Dürr nicely remarks it 'does not surpass the norm in its use of flattery for the veneration of a baroque ruler'. The opening chorus, for double choir (presumably uniting all the city's musical forces available), became the Osanna in the B minor Mass; the soprano aria with its unusual continuo-less scoring went into the Christmas Oratorio; it's only a pity that as a consequence the biting bass aria against the King's enemies and the exuberant final ensemble are so rarely heard. (In the sequence of Leipzig works in honour of the royal family, Cantata 205a came earlier, as it was written for the King's coronation on 19 February 1734: the music is lost but was drawn from Cantata 205.)

Cantata 207a was for the name-day of the Elector, 3 August, most likely in 1735 but perhaps later, and survives complete, though the music is heavily drawn from Cantata 207 of 1726 (see above) and so the librettist had to fit his verse to that source. There is no reason to prefer this version. Cantata 36b also took this particular form in 1735, probably as a tribute cantata for a lawyer, a member of the Rivinus family from Leipzig. But the sources are sketchy, and all the music exists in the several other versions of the cantata, which are generally more often heard.

Cantata 206 is a splendid cantata written originally for the Elector's birthday in 1734 but not performed until 7 October 1736; it was revived on 3 August 1740 for the name-day of Augustus. It was described as 'a solemn music with trumpets and drums' and is based on the amusing conceit of a debate between the four rivers of the countries under the rule of Augustus, competing for his affection. The Vistula in Poland, the Elbe in Saxony, the Danube and the Pleisse (Leipzig's river) each have their own aria and in the end agree to combine in honouring the monarch. 'Glide peaceful waves,' sings the quiet opening chorus, with slurred notes like lapping waves, and after the aria for each river the final recitative brings all four singers together, rising from bass to soprano, before the final swinging chorus.

Cantata 30a was written for nearby Wiederau, where Johann Christian von Hennicke took possession of his fiefdom on 28 September 1737. The homage libretto by Picander uses the characters of Destiny, Fortune, Time and the River Elster to hymn his praise. Most of the music was then reused in the late Cantata 30 and so is known from that version. There's a consciously up-to-date galant style in many of the movements, and the music is light rather than grand, as befits the pastoral character of the text, which hymns Wiederau as having 'prosperity which lays new firm foundations on which to build you like an Eden'. (After that we know Bach wrote a Serenade Anh. 13 for 28 April 1738 as homage for the royal couple, but this has disappeared; he also – perhaps – wrote a Serenade, now lost, for 7 October 1739, revived Cantata 206 for the Elector's name day on 3 August 1740, and revised his very first secular Cantata 208 for the same day in 1742.)

𝆓 *BWV 205, 214* van der Sluis, Jacobs, Prégardien, Thomas, Orchestra of the Age of Enlightenment/Leonhardt
Philips 432 161-2
𝆓 *BWV 211, 213* Bonney, Popken, Prégardien, Wilson-Johnson, Orchestra of the Age of Enlightenment/Leonhardt
Philips 442 779-2
𝆓 *BWV 206, 207a* Ziesak, Chance, Pregardien, Kooy/ Concerto Köln/Bernius
Sony Vivarte SK 46 492

SOLO SECULAR CANTATAS

Cantata 202 *Weichet nur, betrübte Schatten*
?Cantata 203 *Amore traditore*
Cantata 209 *Non sa che sia dolore*
Cantata 210 *O holder Tag, erwünschte Zeit*

Bach wrote few secular cantatas for solo voice, but one of his loveliest is the wedding cantata *Weichet nur*, whose origin is uncertain: Rifkin and Jones feel it goes back as far as Weimar, and it survives in an old-style copy from 1730. What could be more beautiful than the retreat of the gloomy shadows in the opening soprano aria with oboe obbligato soaring over wafting string chords? Then Phoebus hastens with swift horses over a pictorially clopping bass line, and the spring breezes waft through motley fields in an aria with violin solo. A triple-time aria with dancing suspensions over the bar line hymns the cultivation of love, and a final short gavotte wishes the couple contentment and a thousand bright days of well-being. I recently heard this cantata in the tiny church in Dornheim where Bach married Maria Barbara; there is no necessary connection of the piece with that occasion, but it sounded perfect.

Cantata 203 and Cantata 209 are the only two texts Bach set in Italian, and their authenticity has often been doubted. The former is more doubtful than the latter, and is an insubstantial work for bass solo, using a harpsichord solo in the second aria. Cantata 209 is most likely a mature work of the 1730s with strong links to the idiom of the Orchestral Suite No. 2, for it features the flute alongside the strings, and the solo writing for soprano is up-to-date, harmonious and shapely. The Italian text, depicting the return of a scholar to his homeland, has been criticised, but that hardly seems to matter in the flowing charm of the music which begins with a sinfonia that could be another movement of Suite No. 2, and concludes with a dancing triple-time aria.

Cantata 210 is another wedding cantata, for soprano solo, and may well be from Bach's last decade, though it is derived from Cantata 210a of earlier in the Leipzig years, for Duke Christian of Weissenfels. The high range of this cantata might suggest a link with the singer of *Jauchzet Gott*, and implies a woman rather than a boy; flute, oboe d'amore and strings all complement the singer through the sequence of recitatives and arias.

Ω *BWV 202, 209, 211, 212* Ameling, English, Nimsgern/ Collegium Aureum
DHM GD 77151

🎧 *BWV 204, 210* Röschmann/Les Violons du Roy/Labadie
Dorian 90207

🎧 *BWV 202, 209, 84* Argenta/Ensemble Sonnerie/Huggett
Virgin 45059

🎧 *BWV 202, 210, 51* Schäfer/Musica Antiqua Cologne/
Goebel
DG 459621

🎧 *BWV 209, 1044* Crowe/Florilegium
Channel Classics 27208

Coffee Cantata 211 *Schweigt stille, plaudert nicht*
Peasant Cantata 212 *Mer hahn en neue Oberkeet*
?Quodlibet BWV 524

Almost as a postscript to Bach's vocal work in the secular
sphere, two cantatas stand out as completely untypical yet
well-loved late works in which Bach attempted to capture
the most up-to-date style of the times, and largely succeeded.
Both are funny, if you share Bach's bucolic sense of humour,
but perhaps Bach's sense of fun, never evident from his few
writings, is the aspect of his world (even more than his Pietistic emphasis on longing for death) with which we find it most
difficult to connect. The Coffee Cantata has a libretto mostly
by Picander which satirises the contemporary taste for coffee
drinking. Liesgen is a young metropolitan lady who will not
give up her coffee habit unless her father finds her a husband.
A recitative adds that she had made it clear that no suitor can
come to her unless he approves of her habit. There seems to
be something of a sexist element here, as the final ensemble
suggests that 'girls remain sisters in coffee, mothers love the
habit, grandmother drank it too, so who could blame the
daughters?' There's a dance-like impetus to the music, and
every aria seems to cry out for movement, especially Liesgen's
'Heute noch'; the final ensemble is a bourrée using a flattened
seventh to great effect.

The Peasant Cantata is surprisingly the very last cantata
of Bach's that can be dated as an original work, though he

continued to revise his earlier pieces. Picander called it a 'cantate burlesque' and it was performed for Picander's superior Carl Heinrich von Dieskau on 30 August 1742. At all points Bach seems concerned to link in this cantata with the folk idiom of the time, as in the final Quodlibet of the Goldberg Variations, completed shortly before this. Dürr makes a different comparison, with the Mozart of *The Magic Flute*, where a simple folk-like style is similarly incorporated into highly sophisticated music. The opening instrumental movement is in short sections, going right back to Biber's *Battalia* or Bach's own Capriccio. The music features a popular song directly in one recitative, and a hunting song from Bohemia; all the arias are based on dance forms (sarabandes, polonaises and minuets), and the final chorus seems to fall over itself with a sense of fun. The plot is cleverly based on the oppositions between peasant and upper classes, town and country, and revolves around Molly and her lover, settling accounts with the tax collector, flattering the chamberlain, and eventually deciding to stop and have a drink in the local tavern, where the bagpipe drones cheerfully. There could be no more vivid depiction of the other side of Bach's existence than this unbuttoned depiction of life in his last decade.

The Quodlibet arrangement might be by Bach, of the sort put together for a family gathering, but it is certainly much earlier: see p. 70.

🎧 *Coffee Cantata, Peasant Cantata* Kirkby, Covey-Crump, Thomas, Academy of Ancient Music/Hogwood
Oiseau-Lyre 417 621-2
🎧 *Coffee Cantata, Peasant Cantata* Mathis, Schreier, Adam, Kammerorchester Berlin/Schreier
Archiv Galleria 427 116-2

Instrumental music

Brandenburg Concertos

Brandenburg Concerto No. 1 in F BWV 1046
Brandenburg Concerto No. 2 in F BWV 1047
Brandenburg Concerto No. 3 in G BWV 1048
Brandenburg Concerto No. 4 in G BWV 1049
Brandenburg Concerto No. 5 in D BWV 1050
Brandenburg Concerto No. 6 in B flat BWV 1051

Like many people, I suspect, I was introduced to the whole world of baroque music years ago by the approachable glories of the Brandenburg Concertos; they kept me refreshed for decades in a vast array of contrasted performances, and set a standard of inventiveness and excellence that all too little other music of the era achieves. The Brandenburgs create a sustained sense of well-being and aspiration: there is something supernaturally dazzling in the richness, variety and deliberately virtuosic scope of these six works. Yet we have to admit that, as with so much else in Bach's output, their survival is almost an accident.

On 24 March 1721 Bach sent to Christian Ludwig, Margrave of Brandenburg, 'Six Concerts avec plusieurs Instruments', as they are described on the title page of the meticulously written-out score. In a somewhat obsequious preface, also in French, he wrote:

> As in taking leave of Your Royal Highness, Your Highness deigned to honour me with the command to send your Highness some of my Compositions; I have taken the liberty of rendering my most humble duty to Your Royal Highness with the present Concertos, which I have adapted to several instruments.

The origin of this 'command' may lie in the visit that Bach paid to Berlin in 1719 to acquire a new harpsichord; or it could have been earlier, as the Margrave knew Prince Leopold of Anhalt-Cöthen and might have encountered Bach in that context, visiting the court at Carlsbad in 1718. At any rate we cannot be sure whether the request was made out of genuine enthusiasm or, perhaps more likely, as a polite 'Do send me your work some time' – roughly equivalent to our modern 'Do let's have lunch one day'.

Bach, however, took the request entirely seriously – he may have pointed forward in his dislike of employers who controlled his music, but he was thoroughly baroque in his deference to those whom birth had placed above him. He assembled six concertos that aimed to demonstrate the maximum variety achievable with the forces he had available to him. In several ways they consciously stretch and expand the envelope of baroque instrumental resources – for example, the use of the violino piccolo in No. 1, the puzzling *fiauti d'echo* in No. 4, the soloistic role given to the lower string players in No. 3 and to violas in No. 6, and of course the starring role – the first in baroque music and a harbinger of the future – given to the harpsichord in No. 5. As Christoph Wolff has noted, 'Every one of the six concertos set a precedent in its scoring, and every one was to remain without parallel.' He also warns us against assuming that the concertos were selected from the Cöthen repertory, which the Prince there would have regarded as his own property. Bach might have chosen instead from outside that repertory, looking for pieces that perhaps date further back – a typically stimulating and radical thought about the origin of these works. Michael Talbot goes further and argues that the pieces were newly written for the Margrave.

It is hardly surprising that there is no evidence that the Margrave ever performed these lavish concertos at his court. In fact, there is almost an intimidatory quality in the demands these concertos make, almost as if Bach is daring anyone to meet their demands. (Who would have happened to have all those instruments to hand? Or a keyboard player who could play the solo part in No. 5?) I recall Roger Fiske suggesting years ago in a broadcast talk that Bach compiled the collection as a form of cultural one-upmanship, sending them to Brandenburg with the implied comment: 'Look what we can do that you can't!' We should beware of assuming, however, that the Margrave did not value them, and the surest evidence that he did is that even if they were not played, they were actually preserved, passed down with his legacy, and so survived for generations to enjoy.

Scholars have struggled with the issue of whether the Brandenburgs are 'a meaningful set', whether they have some kind of inner logic as Bach's later compilations demonstrated. They do not explore a consistent pattern of key relationships, for example, as two are in G, two in F, one in B flat and one in D, all in the major. Do they, as Michael Marissen has argued, embody coded social criticism in the emancipation of the violas and violas da gamba of Concerto No. 6? Such arguments may be stimulating, and it would be unwise to dismiss them because they seem to fit ill with our conventional idea of Bach's political and social leanings, but they tend to overlook the chronological place of the Brandenburgs in Bach's compilations. We should not look in the Brandenburgs of 1721 for the profound symbolism that we find in the collections of the 1730s and 1740s. It was only later, for instance, with the first book of the '48' and the first two books of the *Clavierübung*, that Bach became thorough in his coverage of keys. His previous compilation was the *Orgelbüchlein*, where it is the variety of different treatments of the chorale melodies, linked to planned but unachieved liturgical completeness, that provides the key to the collection. It is surely better to consider the Brandenburgs as providing conscious variety and aspirational virtuosity raised to the highest level – and in the emphasis on many diverse instruments, creating a communal rather than a soloistic experience of the concerto. They confound expectations not only in their instrumentation but also in their form, going beyond the conventions of the Vivaldi-style concerto with which Bach had become familiar, to explore a much wider range of shapes and sonorities; as John Eliot Gardiner has put it, 'He teases us, the listeners, by setting up certain expectations of pattern and phrase-length, and confounds them through his unpredictable and unconventional realisations.'

Concerto No. 1 exists in an earlier version (BWV 1046a/1071) which well demonstrates Bach's striving for diversity: this uses normal violin and horns and has fewer movements, whereas for the Brandenburg version Bach changes to the rarer violino piccolo (here tuned a minor third higher, adding brilliance) and corni da caccia (outdoor hunting horns). The scoring is elaborate and rich; horns burble exuberantly at the start and become progressively part of the textures. The Adagio features solo oboe and violino piccolo, while the violino piccolo comes into its own in the third movement Allegro which was reused in secular cantatas of the 1720s and 1730s. The fourth movement moves the concerto from an Italianate work to a French set of dances, but with the deliberate addition of a Polonaise as one of the trios, as if to provide a cosmopolitan air. There is a Minuet with three trios, the first for oboes and bassoon alone, the second the Polonaise for strings alone, and the third for horns and oboes. (This last is a particularly perky movement, and it is a great warning against being too purist about Bach arrangements that when the composer later borrowed it for Cantata 207 – see p. 333 – he added a jaunty pizzicato accompaniment for strings which makes the piece quite hilarious.)

Concerto No. 2 is based around the mixed ensemble of trumpet, recorder, violin and oboe, again surely a conscious demonstration of instrumental variety, and demands great agility on the part of the high trumpet player. (Thurston Dart promoted in the recording with the Academy of St Martin-in-the-Fields the idea of the horn as an earlier option approved by the composer, but the relevant part suggests this is only an alternative, in case the trumpet was not available.) Interestingly the material given to these different instruments is very similar, creating unity out of diversity, and there is a certain four-squareness about the opening exchanges that possibly points to an earlier origin (though Tovey stressed how Bach used this approach not only in early works). The soloists without trumpet but with continuo provide the second movement, which again is simply imitative, but expressive. Then comes the third movement, described as a fugue but not really sounding like one, especially as the trumpet's bright, high initial phrase also cleverly provides the cadential conclusion – a device later developed by both Haydn and Mozart (in the finale of Symphony No. 39).

No. 3, perhaps the best known concerto of the six, is again startlingly original because all nine string players have their own parts. Three violins, three violas and three cellos (underpinned by continuo) throw ideas around the ensemble in the most inventive way. It's always a challenge when the violas and cellos have material to themselves, especially as Bach makes the leaps there as angular as possible. There is a continuing debate about the 'missing' middle movement of this concerto, as there are only two chords in the manuscript. Insertions of a written-out movement seem to miss the point: either Bach meant to establish the possibility for improvisation within the concertos, in which case you can do anything, or he actually meant what he wrote, and there should just be two modulating chords, maybe with a violin or harpsichord flourish. A complete interpolated movement always feels wrong to me. The final movement by contrast is totally direct and clear: a rushing 12/8 of imitative semiquavers, in the two-part form of a gigue.

Concerto No. 4 provides yet another original combination: a solo violin, but complemented (in the spirit of the communal aspiration of these concertos) by two recorders, or what Bach described as *fiauti d'echo*. These have been the subject of probably over-complex speculation: they were definitely not sopranino recorders as has been attempted, and as we know that Bach used many slightly different terms to indicate the use of a recorder; there does not seem to be any need for a specific echo flute here. The wonderfully inventive writing focuses attention on a violin at the height of its virtuosic powers (maybe created for the same player who played Bach's solo sonatas and partitas of around the same period), and the interplay between the pair of recorders and violin is skilfully managed to create continual interplay and interest. The first movement is in concerto form, with a long *da capo* of eighty-three bars at the close. Then the second movement features the recorders against the body of strings, in gently undulating pairs of thirds that surely might have been unequally played: they should certainly be slurred in pairs and not woven into longer phrases. A cadence leads to the final fugal movement. Did Bach ever write a more exhilarating instrumental movement than this Presto? As so often the energy is immediately provided by a syncopation across the bar line in the main theme, and the complementary figuration is active from the start instead of waiting to form a counter-subject. The two recorders have their own lines, creating a five-part texture; the violin dashes and darts through arpeggios and passage work; and as the movement nears its climax the whole thing twice comes juddering to a halt in a gesture of questioning – an effect matched only by the end of Sibelius's Symphony No. 5.

Concerto No. 5 features violin, transverse flute (which had emerged earlier as a solo instrument and was becoming a favoured instrument for Bach), and harpsichord, here assuming a role of such prominence for the first time. Recent scholarship counsels against making the easy link to the 1719 purchase of a new harpsichord, since this part does not require two manuals. It is, however, a dynamic and forward-looking work in which the harpsichord gradually emerges to dominate the texture, and in a final *solo senza stromenti*, as Bach marked it, delivers a coruscating cadenza of huge power and chromatic intensity. Was it designed for him to play himself? Who else could play it? Interestingly there is, as for the Brandenburg No. 1, an extant earlier version (BWV 1050a), in which the first movement has 180 bars compared to the final version's 227, with a less extended (though in some ways more bizarre) solo. The central movement, Affettuoso, is a gentle dotted-rhythm piece of chamber music for the soloists alone.

The finale is a gigue-like fugue led by the violin and followed by the flute; when the harpsichord joins in it elaborates the subject. As the material develops there is a rare moment of prominence for the violas in a singing passage.

Concerto No. 6 is perhaps the most distinctive of this very unusual collection, as it features instruments rarely given solo roles: two violas and two violas da gamba, with continuo. The writing in the first movement is also extremely unusual in that the canonic imitation between the two violas starts in the very first bar, only a quaver apart, as if we tumble into the music, racing after each other. The central movement is a slow *Adagio ma non tanto* with a plunging line for the two violas over a walking bass (the gambas are ignored here), while the finale uses the same opening motif as the first movement, here reworked as a gigue, in which it takes a little longer for the violas to pursue each other through the texture, before returning to unanimity at the close.

♬ *BWV 1046–1051* English Chamber Orchestra/Britten
Decca Serenata 425 725, 726-2
♬ *BWV 1046–1051, BWV 1067–1068* Concentus Musicus
Wien/Harnoncourt
Teldec (Ultima) 18944
♬ *BWV 1046–1051* The English Concert/Pinnock
DG Blue 471 720, 471 220
♬ *BWV 1046–1051* Il Giardino Armonico/Antonini
Teldec 98442
♬ *BWV 1046–1051* Orchestra of the Age of Enlightenment/
Huggett
Virgin Classics 61552
♬ *BWV 1046–1051* English Baroque Soloists, Debretzeni/
Gardiner
Soli Dei Gloria SDG 707

Orchestral Suites (Ouvertures)

Orchestral Suite (Ouverture) No. 1 in C BWV 1066
Orchestral Suite (Ouverture) No. 2 in B minor BWV 1067
Orchestral Suite (Ouverture) No. 3 in D BWV 1068
Orchestral Suite (Ouverture) No. 4 in D BWV 1069

The four Orchestral Suites by Bach that have survived are not part of a collection like the Brandenburg Concertos; their origins are obscure, and their survival somewhat random. There may have been many more that are lost, and there were certainly earlier incarnations of most of the music. They exist as a pinnacle of his achievement and are some of his most often performed works, as they do not throw up the same problems of instrumentation as do the Brandenburgs, and can be (though these days very rarely are) performed by conventional orchestras: Mendelssohn revived Suite No. 3 as early as 1838. Unlike the Brandenburgs, which so often contradict our expectations, the Suites fulfil them and provide the greatest satisfaction. As Werner Breig has put it, Bach's contribution to the form is 'as qualitatively important as it is quantatively limited'.

It always used to be said that these Orchestral Suites, as they are usually called, or Ouverturen as Bach described them, originated during the Cöthen years when his focus was on writing instrumental music. Perhaps there are traces of their origin there, but the most recent research has pushed their origins forward into the Leipzig years – reasonably so, because these are works of great maturity, and perhaps found their final forms only during the concerts of the Collegium Musicum which Bach directed only from 1729 onwards. Suite No. 1 is earlier, as parts exist from his early Leipzig period in 1724–5, while No. 3 was copied and revised in 1731 (Bach copied out a couple of these parts himself). Around the same time Suite No. 4 was revised: it must have been conceived earlier, and its first movement was then used in Cantata 110 for Christmas Day 1725, with trumpets and timpani added to the texture; these were retained in the revision of around 1730.

The most interesting case is Suite No. 2, which with its use of the fashionable transverse flute as solo instrument seems to be the latest of the four, and might even date from as late as 1738–9 when a new set of parts was prepared including input from the composer. It has been shown that its origin is an earlier work in A minor, evidenced by numerous mistakes in transposing the parts, and that this might have been for the violin (or the oboe, as has most recently been proposed).

Suite No. 1 in C opens with a grand French Overture of clarity and majesty. We do not need to suppose that Bach acquired his French habits directly from that country, as such overtures were common in German through Telemann, who wrote literally hundreds of these pieces, and contemporaries such as Graupner and Fasch (who also wrote around a hundred). 'The ouverture takes its name from "to open", because this instrumental piece opens the door, as it were, to the suites of following music,' wrote Bach's relative Johann Gottfried Walther in 1732. Nor was there any necessary connection with opera: Bach could have been writing such pieces from the moment he arrived in Cöthen. This example's open, harmonious style (whose double-dotting alternatives have roused considerable debate over the years) paves the way for a transparent fugue in which the two oboes and bassoon prattle delightfully in episodes. Then there is a Courante, a pair of Gavottes (in which ingeniously fanfaring strings compensate for the lack of brass instruments), and a triple-time Forlane (Bach's only known example; Ravel included one in his *Tombeau de Couperin*). Then three pairs of dances in which the first is repeated: a pair of Minuets (the second for strings only), a pair of Bourrées (the second in the minor for wind only), and finally a pair of Passepieds which though inventive (the melody from the first is repeated but set low in the second and decorated by new counterpoint) do not quite provide the climactic finish one expects.

Suite No. 2 in B minor should perhaps be seen apart from the others, given its possible late origin as a piece of chamber music for the Collegium Musicum. The writing is extremely mature, and tends towards the fashionable style that Bach was to cultivate in the 1730s; it is no accident that it is the flute in the 'Domine Deus' of the Missa that uses modishly unequal rhythms. The fugal section of the first movement is based on a melodic sequence, and the movements then continue with a Rondeau, a very French (almost Rameau-like) Sarabande, but with distinctively Bachian counterpoint between the outer parts: a pair of Bourrées, a Polonaise with double (perhaps using some local melody), a Minuet, and finally the famous Badinerie, one of Bach's greatest hits in the twentieth century, from James Galway to the Swingle Singers. This might have been written specially for the Dresden flautist Buffardin: its agility and perfect balance make it utterly memorable.

Suite No. 3 has remained in the popular repertory since being taken up by symphony orchestras in the nineteenth century, and it contains Bach's single most played orchestral movement. The second movement is the Air which became immortalised as the 'Air on the G string' in the nineteenth-century transcription by August Wilhelmj, intended for the lowest string of the violin; it has since been adapted in an infinity of ways for other forces. However, this Suite is dominated by its magnificent first movement, which is about as long as all the other movements put together. There is a parallel here with the emphasis given in Bach's cantatas to their first movements, which tend to overbalance the rest. The trumpets do not always play fanfares: they have low pedal points under the strings' swirling semiquavers in the first movement. Indeed they may (as in Suite No. 4) have been added later to a work that originally made more prominent use of the solo violin. Those versions of the Air that stress the melody alone have dulled our appreciation of the supremely subtle inner parts, matching improvisatory freedom and the ground-bass line. The pair of Gavottes is contrasted: leaps of an octave in the first are matched by decorated arpeggios in the second. The Bourrée is dominated by offbeat entries of trumpets and drums, while the final Gigue is an exultant movement with the constantly dancing violins and oboes audaciously doubled an octave higher by the trumpets at the very top of their register. Raymond Leppard observed with some relief that the increasing skills of Bach trumpeters meant that these parts did not always have to be played 'with a sense of impending apoplexy'.

Suite No. 4 has another massive first movement: 188 bars compared with 186 in the remainder of the work. Oboe and strings answer each other, whereas in Suite No. 3 they are mainly doubled, and the central section is in 9/8. The elaboration of this movement that Bach made for Cantata 110 is as splendid as that he made of the solo violin Partita in E for Cantata 29. But here he retained the expansion for the Suite, and it leads to a pair of Bourrées featuring oboes and bassoon with a decorated bass line in the second, a Gavotte for all, a pair of quieter minuets with the second featuring the strings, and a final Rejouissance which is entirely jubilant, with the trumpets and drums reinforcing every exciting cadence.

(A fifth suite in G minor, listed as BWV 1070, is sometimes recorded with the four authentic suites, but is certainly not by Bach. His pupil Christian Friedrich Penzel copied it out after his death, and it is more likely to be by an unknown composer or possibly by Wilhelm Friedemann Bach.)

♩ *BWV 1066–1069, 1070* Musica Antiqua Cologne/Goebel
Archiv 415 671
♩ *BWV 1066–1069 (1067 arr. for oboe)* Ensemble Sonnerie,
Ruiz/Huggett
AVIE 2171
♩ *BWV 1066–1069* Tafelmusik/Jean Lamon
Analekta 23134
♩ *BWV 1066–1069* Amsterdam Baroque Orchestra/
Koopman
Erato 0178682

Concertos

Violin Concerto in A minor BWV 1041
Violin Concerto in E BWV 1042
Concerto for two violins in D minor BWV 1043
Concerto for flute, violin and harpsichord in A minor BWV 1044
Movement in D BWV 1045

When Bach took over the Collegium Musicum in Leipzig in 1729, there was an immediate need for repertory for the weekly concerts, and it is clear that Bach gave this a high priority in his activities. Although this was recognised by Bach scholars, there seems to have been a reluctance to propose that any great works were actually written for these occasions, with a consensus that Bach simply drew on earlier music that he had available to him. There is no reason, however, to suppose that Bach gave any less commitment to these concerts than to the Leipzig services for which he wrote some of his finest sacred music. So it is logical that scholars including Andreas Glöckner and Christoph Wolff have now proposed that some of the finest parts of this instrumental repertory were actually conceived for and performed in these concerts.

This conclusion is partly due to the concision and maturity of the music, especially in the case of the two Concertos for solo violin, and the classic Concerto for two violins. All these could have originated around 1730 in a first flush of enthusiasm for the Collegium gatherings that matched the intense period of enthusiasm for Leipzig sacred cantatas following 1723, and the Triple Concerto BWV 1044 could have been revised and assembled at the same time. 'The possibility of a Leipzig origin for these concertos has, I believe, never been given serious consideration,' wrote Wolff in 1985, yet for some of these pieces we have the original and largely autograph performing parts, which can be dated only to the first years of Bach's Collegium Musicum activities.

Unlike, for example, the diversity of the Brandenburg Concertos, the violin concertos explore limited material and limited sonorities with inventive power. The A minor Concerto is for strings alone: the opening movement presents a group of themes which are then thoroughly explored by the soloist. The central Andante proceeds over a repeated motif in the bass, and the final Allegro assai is a sprightly 9/8 gigue in ritornello form, which uses many contrapuntal devices and draws the soloist into a couple of longer episodes before a brief passage of virtuosity propels us to the end. Unlike the A minor, the E major Concerto does not survive in Bach's hand but only in manuscripts copied after his death, including one by Zelter, who must have performed the work in Berlin. It announces a range of material at the start which the soloist then takes up and works with, but it is never quite clear whether this is a *da capo* plan or a ritornello structure, until two expressive Adagio bars mark a return to the opening material. The central movement in C sharp minor is based on an ostinato quietly announced under sustained strings. And the final Allegro is really a rondo, because exactly the same music returns around each of the soloist's exuberant developments. (I recall years ago Hans Keller using this entire movement in his Radio 3 broadcast glossary of musical terms to define Rondo, just speaking over the music the letters A–B–A–C–A–D–A–E–A and saying as the music finished '. . . and it's as simple as that, it really is'.)

The famous, one is tempted to say immortal, Concerto for two violins is one of the tautest and most concentrated of all Bach's works, with a sublime central movement that will surely last as long as music lasts. The opening is Italianate in form but thoroughly Bachian in its counterpoint, and the subject is immediately treated imitatively, as it will be when the soloists enter. But they do so surprisingly, with a different theme that leaps across the strings. The central movement is marked *Largo ma non tanto*, though those last three words have rarely been observed by generations of players. What impresses is the movement's total logical and musical unity, underpinning an expressive flow of melody with a gentle bass line moving up and down in octaves. Yet the unity is achieved through some significant moments of variety: another rarely observed instruction here is that when the two violins have a small rising three-note motif, it is differently articulated in the two parts, one slurred, one separated, just as in the 'Et in unum Dominum' duet of the B minor Mass. There must be a symbolic meaning here, to do with unity in diversity. The final Allegro is titanic, reminiscent of the finale of the D minor Harpsichord Concerto (see below, originally a violin concerto), based on a powerful semiquaver alternation which acquires a quite obsessive character. There are two powerful episodes, where the upper strings repeat battered chords as the bass line plunges sequentially beneath them – an effect so powerful one feels it should actually end the movement, rather than it returning to its first thoughts. (There's nothing quite as scary as the film of the massed hordes of hundreds of young Suzuki violin pupils playing this piece, and being able at a moment's notice from the conductor to transfer between the first and second parts.)

In the case of the Triple Concerto for flute, violin and harpsichord we know where the material came from, since the first and last movements originated from a keyboard work, BWV 894, while the middle movement is that of BWV 527, the D minor organ trio sonata. It never seems to work very well in performance, but perhaps that is only in comparison with the peerless works with which it has to compete. Then, slightly out of place here, there is an isolated work featuring a violin solo, the Movement BWV 1045 which is a late survival from 1743–6, with three trumpets and timpani; it's an effective piece, doubtless intended as the sinfonia of a cantata that is now lost.

BWV 1041, 1042, 1052, 1056 Zehetmair/Amsterdam Bach Soloists/Zehetmair
Berlin Classics 115002
BWV 1041, 1042, 1052, 1056 Huggett/Ensemble Sonnerie/Huggett
ASV 356

🎧 *BWV 1041, 1042, 1056, 1060* Mullova, Leleux/Mullova Ensemble
Philips 475 745

🎧 *BWV 1041, 1042, 1043, 1060* Kennedy, Stabrawa, Mayer/ Berlin Philharmonic
EMI Classics 757142

🎧 *BWV 1041, 1042, 1043, 1060* Shumsky, Tunnell, Miller/ Scottish Chamber Orchestra/Shumsky
Nimbus 7031

🎧 *BWV 1041, 1042, 1043* Poppen, Faust/Bach Collegium Stuttgart
Hänssler Classics 92125

🎧 *BWV 1044, 1041–1043, 1052, 1056, 1060, 1064* Wallfisch, Nicholson, L. Beznosiuk, Bury, Robson, Mackintosh, P. Beznosiuk/Orchestra of the Age of Enlightenment
Virgin Classics 61558 (2 CDs)

Harpsichord Concerto in D minor BWV 1052
Harpsichord Concerto in E BWV 1053
Harpsichord Concerto in D BWV 1054
Harpsichord Concerto in A BWV 1055
Harpsichord Concerto in F minor BWV 1056
Concerto for harpsichord and two recorders in F
  BWV 1057 (after BWV 1049)
Harpsichord Concerto in G minor BWV 1058
  (after BWV 1041)
Harpsichord Concerto in D minor BWV 1059
  (fragment)

It is easy to forget how revolutionary an idea the keyboard concerto was in Bach's day. The model of the Italian concerto, which inspired so many around Europe, was based on the violin as soloist, or in some of Vivaldi's models, multiple violins. The oboe or a pair of oboes featured in Albinoni's popular concertos. Vivaldi diversified the range of concerto soloists, bringing in many different instruments, writing solos for most of them including the bassoon and cello, while Telemann in his concertos brought diverse instruments together. But it was Bach who emancipated the keyboard and gave the status of a soloist, first in his Brandenburg Concerto No. 5, alongside violin and flute, and then in these keyboard concertos of the 1730s. Handel was soon to write and play his organ concertos, and the genre was established, leading to the early keyboard concertos of Mozart and his contemporaries.

Bach's concertos were not original works; his resource-fulness in reusing his music knew no bounds. We know from the announcements regarding the concerts in Zimmermann's coffee house, when they resumed after the period of state mourning for Augustus the Strong in 1733, that 'the beginning will be made ... with a fine concert. It will be maintained week by week with a new Clavicymbel, such as has not been heard here before and lovers of music as well as virtuosos are expected to be present.' Leaving to one side the thought that this new keyboard instrument might have been a fashionable fortepiano (it seems too early for that, though Bach became very involved with the instrument in the 1740s), this would appear to be a mainspring for the collection of keyboard concertos that Bach arranged mainly from earlier works. Kobayashi dates these arrangements as late as 1738, based on the autograph manuscript in which they are compiled, which looks like Bach's composing copy. Are they really as late as 1738, given that Bach started several years before with the Collegium? In any case they formed part of the fascinating mixed repertory of the Collegium Musicum concerts that George Stauffer has now begun to explore with reference to the Leipzig archives. The concertos have suffered from the prejudice of scholars against transcriptions, starting with Albert Schweitzer, who said they were 'often made with quite incredible haste and carelessness' so that 'we are under no special obligation to incorporate these transcriptions in our concert programmes'. Werner Breig, however, has demonstrated the extreme care with which they were adapted. He suggests that Bach started with BWV 1058 and 1059 but broke off dissatisfied, beginning again with

BWV 1052 to create a six-work set ending with the adaptation of Brandenburg Concerto No. 4.

That D minor Concerto is the first in Bach's manuscript, and it is the longest and most impressive of these works, almost certainly based on a lost violin concerto (see below). It is not clear why at one time Bach's original authorship of this concerto should have been doubted. The solo part has had to be adapted downwards as the top note of the violin was higher than the top note of the harpsichord, but Bach did not transpose the work. Its unison opening is strongly profiled, and the harpsichord's writing makes use of much material that would have been cross-string writing for a violin. Bach had already adapted this strong movement for the Sinfonia of Cantata 146 in 1728, and the second movement was also reused in this cantata with vocal parts beautifully added. It unfolds over a unison line in G minor, with an aria that sounds positively operatic. The plunging scale of the final Allegro introduces a movement of terrific power and energy, and it too makes figuration suitable for the violin entirely appropriate and exciting on the (doubtless two-manual) harpsichord that Bach had available, using overlapping hands. That must have made them sit up in Zimmermann's coffee house.

The E major Concerto is probably drawn from a lost oboe (or flute?) concerto, though the arpeggio writing of the opening seems perfectly keyboard-like. Bach has revised this thoroughly, especially in the keyboard's left hand. The central movement is a lilting siciliano in C sharp minor, and the finale is launched by a tumbling figure. The D major Concerto is a reworking transposed down a tone of the E major Violin Concerto (see above). The A major Concerto was probably conceived for an oboe d'amore, and follows the Vivaldi model of the concerto, though the downward rush of the finale is attractive. The F minor Concerto BWV 1056 may well be based on a lost violin concerto probably in G minor, though the original has disappeared, or perhaps on two different works, since the central movement seems different in range, and might have been an F major movement of a D minor concerto. It is a gentler, less demonstrative work than its companions. The Largo central movement in A flat major had already been used as the Sinfonia to Cantata 156; it has become exceptionally popular out of context in film and elsewhere.

The F major Concerto for harpsichord and two recorders is transcription not of a solo concerto but of Brandenburg Concerto No. 4. It provides a fascinating insight into Bach's habits, because not only does he rewrite the violin line for harpsichord, he also uses the opportunity to provide some filling-in of the parts, showing how richly he always realised the inner writing of his compositions. If Breig's hypothesis is correct, this was the climax of the six-concerto set. The earlier G minor Concerto is a transcription of the A minor Violin Concerto, again transposed down a tone, and here Bach reworks the solo line quite extensively and uses the left hand to enhance the texture of the piece, making this a new work in its own right. The incomplete fragment BWV 1059 is a concerto transcription that was never finished. The music is familiar as the opening of Cantata 35, and it has been proposed that the following movement in that Cantata, and the Sinfonia that opens its second half, could make an oboe concerto (for which see below).

Ω *BWV 1052, 1053, 1054, 1055, 1056, 1057, 1058, 1044*
Rousset, Standage, Brown/Academy of Ancient Music/
Hogwood
Oiseau Lyre 460 031 (2 CDs)

Ω *BWV 1052, 1057, 1054, 1044, The Art of Fugue*
Alessandrini, Vicari, Rufa/Concerto Italiano/Alessandrini
Naïve Opus 111 OP 20011 (2 CDs)

Ω *BWV 1052, 1053, 1054, 1055, 1056, 1057, 1058, English Suites, Goldberg Variations* Perahia/Academy of St Martin in the Fields/Perahia
Sony Classical 89890 (3 CDs)

Concerto for two harpsichords in C minor BWV 1060
Concerto (Duet) for two harpsichords in C
  BWV 1061/1061a
Concerto for two harpsichords in C minor
  BWV 1062 (after BWV 1043)
Concerto for three harpsichords in D minor
  BWV 1063
Concerto for three harpsichords in C BWV 1064
Concerto for four harpsichords in A minor
  BWV 1065 (after Vivaldi Op. 3 No. 10)

As well as writing solo harpsichord concertos for the Leipzig
Collegium Musicum, Bach also made these six arrangements
for multiple harpsichords, perhaps for himself to play with
his talented children, Carl Philipp Emanuel and/or Wilhelm
Friedemann, who were still in Leipzig in the early 1730s.
(This is a reason for preferring an early 1730s date for the
arrangements, as Bach's sons left home from 1733.) Friedrich
Konrad Griepenkerl wrote in his preface to the first published
edition that they were written for C. P. E. and W. F., and that
remark probably originated from Forkel and thus from Bach
or C. P. E. The first in C minor is taken from a lost concerto
presumed to be for violin and oboe (see below) and is more
often heard in that form. The second in C major is a brilliant and exciting piece which is almost completely self-contained as a duet for two harpsichords. Forkel said that 'it can
be played entirely without the accompaniment of the bowed
instruments, and is most excellent thus', and the version with
strings, BWV 1061, is doubtfully authentic. The duet is a perfect demonstration of keyboard antiphony, throwing phrases
and figuration back and forth between the two harpsichords,
and then after the A minor Adagio launching into a Vivace
C major fugue whose driving impetus and sense of direction
even Bach never surpassed.

The C minor Concerto is immediately familiar as a version
of the D minor Concerto for two violins, so often performed
that the keyboard version has suffered by comparison: it is of

course difficult for the harpsichord to match the beauty of the violins in the central Largo, though it suggests a different kind of eloquence. The D minor Concerto for three harpsichords is a very successful transcription of an unknown model, maybe for three violins, though Schmieder suggested a group of violin, oboe and flute, which has also been reconstructed. The solid unison opening of the first movement in triple time is here contrasted with the syncopated line that opens the final Allegro, and in the middle is an ornamented Siciliano. The first harpsichord definitely leads, and has an outburst of Brandenburg Concerto No. 5-type virtuosity as the first movement reaches its climax. In the last movement all three have their solo breaks: surely this was for Bach and his two sons.

Equally enjoyable is the Concerto in C for three harpsichords which shows signs of having been written originally for three violins in D major. The model here could be rather early, since the first movement is quite stolid harmonically, rarely veering beyond C major, while the central movement in A minor is built on expressive slurred pairs of notes. The winning movement is the last, an Allegro unfolding over a bold descending bass line, building endless sequences and rising to heights of exuberance. In the case of the Concerto for four harpsichords in A minor, a unique work in Bach's output, the origin is clear, as it is derived directly from Vivaldi's Concerto for four violins in B minor, Op. 3 No. 10; one can also observe the numerous touches by which Bach makes the music suitable for its new surroundings: arpeggiated passages of the central Largo or the left-hand figuration of the keyboards. Particularly striking is the care with which Bach contrasts the articulation in the central movement: plain semiquavers for the fourth soloist, staccato ones for the third, slurred ones for the second, and arpeggiated demisemiquavers for the first, creating a deliciously shimmering effect like a crowd of buzzing bees.

♎ *BWV 1060–1065* Pinnock, Gilbert, Mortensen, Kraemer/ The English Concert/Pinnock
Archiv 471 754 (3 CDs)

♫ *BWV 1060, 1061, 1062* van Asperen, Leonhardt/Melante
Amsterdam/van Asperen
Virgin Classics 45336
♫ *BWV 1063, 1064, 1065, Italian Concerto* van Asperen,
Lohff, Bussi, Klapprott/Melante Amsterdam/van Asperen
Virgin Classics 45204
♫ *BWV 1060, 1061, 1063, 1065* Eschenbach, Frantz, Oppitz,
Schmidt/Hamburg Philharmonic/Eschenbach
DG 415 655

Violin Concerto in D minor from BWV 1052
Oboe Concerto in F/Oboe d'amore Concerto in D
  from BWV 1053
Oboe Concerto in D minor from BWV 1059
Oboe d'amore Concerto in A from BWV 1055
Violin Concerto/Oboe Concerto in G minor
  from BWV 1056
Concerto for oboe and violin in C minor
  from BWV 1060
Concerto for three violins in D from BWV 1064

There has been a dual approach to reconstructing lost works
by Bach: scholars have wanted to recapture the possible original form of music he later adapted, while performers have
wanted to create 'new' music by Bach for concerts and recordings. All these concertos are likely to be encountered on disc
or in performance, and all are reconstructions of one sort or
another; several are the putative originals of the keyboard
concertos listed above.

The Violin Concerto in D minor, based on the harpsichord
concerto of the same key, is included in the *NBA* as a suggested original. It is wholly idiomatic, with the cross-hand
writing of the keyboard transferring easily to the violin: there
are analogous passages in the Fugue of the G minor Partita
for violin; a good performance of this Concerto is as exciting as one of the keyboard adaptations. The Oboe Concerto
in F is more doubtful, but a version by Hermann Töttcher

and Gottfried Muller has been published and recorded, while Arnold Mehl has transcribed it down a third for oboe d'amore in D. The Oboe Concerto in D minor after the incomplete concerto movement BWV 1059 exists in a reconstruction by Arnold Mehl and also one by Joshua Rifkin, both of which draw on the remaining movements from Cantata 35 to make an attractive piece.

The Concerto for oboe d'amore in A has become one of the most familiar of these solo reconstructions thanks to Heinz Holliger's outstanding advocacy: it is reconstructed in the *NBA* by Wilfried Fischer; its gentle lyricism sits well on the oboe d'amore. The Harpsichord Concerto BWV 1056 has been reconstructed as a violin concerto in the *NBA*, and also as an oboe concerto; the famous Largo, however, is more idiomatic for the violin. Both instruments feature in the Concerto for violin and oboe in C minor BWV 1060, reconstructed from the two-harpsichord concerto of the same key and certainly the most popular and frequently performed of these hypothetical originals. It matches the violin concertos in its concision, but probably has its origins earlier. The rocking motif of the first movement is well suited to both instruments, with its humorous little echo of the final two notes of the theme, and the central movement marked *Largo ovvero Adagio* also juxtaposes them well, moving over a triple-time bass line from the same family as the Concerto for two violins. The bouncy final Allegro is a model of tautly constructed Italian concerto style, and here there is a clear difference between the styles of the two solo parts, with idiomatic violin writing which makes the reconstruction more convincing than the harpsichord version. Among the other multiple concertos, the most successful original version is that of the Concerto for three harpsichords in C major, which Christopher Hogwood and others including Wilfried Fischer in the *NBA* have reconstructed as a Concerto for three violins in D: this should be more often heard.

The above list is confined to those works with some justification in history. There are of course many other successful

Bach transcriptions – for instance, the recent version of the solo alto Cantata 54 for oboe d'amore and strings by Albrecht Meyer – but these have no direct connection with Bach.

♩ *BWV 1055, 1053, 1060, 1059* Ponseele, Terakado/ Ensemble il Gardellino
Accent ACC 24165

♩ *BWV 1055, 1044, 1060* Reichenberg, Standage, Pinnock, Beznosiuk/The English Concert/Pinnock
Archiv 413 731

♩ *BWV 1060, 1041–1043* Ponseele, Terakado/Bach Collegium Japan/Suzuki
BIS 961

♩ *BWV 1060, 1041–1043* Mayer, Kennedy/Berlin Philharmonic
EMI Classics 757142

♩ *BWV 1064, 1041–1044, 1052, 1056, 1060* Wallfisch, Mackintosh, P. Beznosiuk, Bury, Robson, Nicholson, L. Beznosiuk/Orchestra of the Age of Enlightenment
Virgin Classics 61558 2 CD

♩ *Concerts avec plusiers instruments* Café Zimmermann/Valetti
Vol. I BWV 1042, 1052, 1050, 1055; Vol. II BWV 1043,1060, 1048, 1066; Vol. III BWV 1049, 1053, 1064, 1067; Vol. IV BWV 1041, 1044, 1047, 1061
Alpha 13, 48, 71, 137

♩ *Orchestral and Chamber Music: Brandenburg Concertos, Orchestral Suites, BWV 1070, Triple Concerto; Violin Sonatas BWV 1014–1019, 1091a, 1020–1025, Fugue BWV 1026, Viola da Gamba Sonatas; Flute Sonatas, Partita BWV 1013* Goebel, ter Linden, Hazelzet, Staier/Musica Antiqua Cologne/ Goebel
Archiv 471 656 (8 CDs)

Violin partitas, suites and sonatas

**Sonata for unaccompanied violin No. 1 in G minor
  BWV 1001**
Sonata No. 2 in A minor BWV 1003
Sonata No. 3 in C BWV 1005
Partita No. 1 in B minor BWV 1002
Partita No. 2 in D minor BWV 1004
Partita No. 3 in E BWV 1006

To look at the fair copy that Bach prepared in 1720, headed *Sei Soli a Violino senza Basso accompagnato* (adding the unfulfilled promise 'Libro Primo') is a moving experience. Bach's fluent, dramatic, poised musical calligraphy is perfectly laid out on the page; as was his custom, every page of manuscript is used to the utmost, with extra staves to complete the movements added at the bottom of the page where necessary; new works start in mid-page rather than waste any space, even after the great Chaconne. The writing is impeccably clear – doubtless Bach was copying from existing manuscripts and probably modifying and refining as he copied, but there are very few signs of erasures or alterations. The manuscript communicates beautifully, beyond mere notation, the expressive intent of the music. The promise of 'Libro Primo' may have meant only that Bach followed this collection with the cello suites below, but Werner Breig has suggested that perhaps Bach was thinking of a 'Terzo libro' for the flute, and many other instruments might have followed; it seems unlikely that Bach would have neglected the oboe, for example, so prominent is it in his other music.

We know Bach played the violin skilfully, and used also to play the viola, as C. P. E. Bach recalled: 'As the greatest expert and judge of harmony he liked best to play the viola, with appropriate loudness and softness. In his youth, and until the approach of old age, he played the violin cleanly and penetratingly, and this kept the orchestra in better order than he could with the harpsichord.' He said that Bach understood to perfection the possibilities of all stringed instruments, and that is certainly evident from these six perfect works. Were they written for him to play himself? The only music in his output that seems to match the demands here is Brandenburg Concerto No. 4, and even the later cantata obbligatos for violin are not as demanding. (However, the originals of the keyboard concertos discussed above, especially the D minor Concerto, might well have been as challenging for the violin.) It has been suggested that they were conceived for particular players: Joseph Spiess was the leader of the Cöthen orchestra, and at Dresden there were two famous players, Pisendel and Volumier, who might have tackled these pieces (one of the manuscripts of Bach's works survived in a Dresden collection). Significant as a precursor to these works are the remarkable violin pieces of Heinrich Ignaz von Biber, whose unaccompanied Passacaglia in G minor at the climax of his 'Rosary' Sonatas for violin and continuo surely stands directly behind Bach's Chaconne, and the unaccompanied music of the violinist Johann Westhoff, who played at Weimar when Bach was there.

The many technical and musical problems posed by the multiple-stopping in these sonatas and partitas have been a huge challenge to modern performers. The strangest misconception that flourished for some time was that on a violin of Bach's period it would have been possible to play all four strings at once, so that Bach's written-out four-part chords would have been heard in glorious organ-like harmony. Strenuous efforts were made to invent a 'Bach bow' which could do just this on a modern violin, with ludicrous results – a monstrous arc with a huge curvature which bent its way over all the strings. In fact on a period violin the effect is quite different, the short bow and flattened bridge of Bach's time giving far greater agility and subtlety in moving from string to string, making it easier to touch in the harmonies.

Three of the six pieces are Partitas, in the free form of the *sonata da camera*; three are sonatas in the slow–fast–slow–fast mould of the old *sonata da chiesa* (there is nothing to suggest they were used in church, though one eccentric recent recording superimposed sung chorales on the pieces to prove their melodic origins). Though the works were written down in 1720, they would have been brought together earlier, and might include Weimar material as well as Cöthen music. Sonata No. 1 in G minor opens with a florid Adagio, full of decoration over a quite simple harmonic basis, leading to a massive fugue, which Bach liked so much that he adapted it for organ. Its hammer-stroke chords perfectly illustrate the kind of resonance Bach expected from his instrument, with the fugal line supported by accompanying chords either above or below. There is a Siciliano written like a trio with a melody at the bottom and accompanying thirds and sixths above. As will happen often through this set, the complexities of multiple-stopping are swept away by a final Presto of brilliant perpetual motion in a single line. (A notational oddity is that though Bach writes in bars of 3/8, every second bar is drawn only as a half-bar, which gives the impression of longer bar-lengths.)

Sonata No. 2 in A minor also includes a fugue, which found favour even with Bach's contemporary Johann Mattheson (who mocked the word-setting in Bach's Cantata 21). He quoted the fugue's subject: 'Who would believe that these short notes would be so fruitful as to bring forth a counterpoint of more than a whole sheet of music paper, without unusual extension and quite naturally?' The resourcefulness is indeed incredible, alternating between two-, three- and four-part writing within a perfectly constructed scheme. The opening Grave is a highly decorated line; the Andante by contrast sings its Vivaldi-like melody over gently pulsing repeated notes on the lower strings. The final Allegro is a driven single line full of echo effects.

Sonata No. 3 in C major presents the most amazing of the three fugues in this set, at over 350 bars said to be the longest Bach ever wrote. Its subject clearly refers to a Lutheran chorale, *Komm heiliger Geist*, with a descending chromatic line as counter-subject; its plan includes three separate expositions, the second in stretto and the third in the middle in inversion.

(It was this clear chorale reference which led to the misguided attempt to perform sung chorale melodies with various movements of these pieces.) The cross-string writing pushes down onto the low G of the violin to create a remarkably sustained effect. The Adagio that precedes this fugue, with its dotted rhythms and angular quadruple-stopping, creates a high tension from which the succeeding Largo and Allegro assai have to relax. Though the final movement is again a single line, the cross-string writing cleverly gives the impression of continual harmonies.

The three Partitas are more varied in plan: the first in B minor has an Allemanda, Corrente, Sarabande and a final Tempo di Borea each with double (or variation). No. 3 in E major opens with the brilliant Prelude which Bach later elaborated in his Sinfonia to Cantata 29 – one of the most creative pieces of orchestration he achieved. Then there is a Loure, the well-known Gavotte en Rondeau, a pair of Minuets, a Bourrée and a final Gigue. At first the D minor Partita, the second of the three, looks as if it will have the same plan as No. 1. It opens with a sturdy Allemanda and a Corrente, both unusually free of multiple-stopping, a short Sarabanda and a powerful Giga with arching lines. Then comes the overwhelming surprise: a massive Ciacona or Chaconne over the traditional old descending four-note bass line, which Biber had used in his unaccompanied Passacaglia. In a hint of criticism, Malcolm Boyd says that the variations 'may labour the four-bar chord progression on which they are based', but surely the fundamental nature of that sequence gives the elaborated variations their sense of universality, their grounding in daily reality. As the movement unfolds you feel an increasing sense of total inevitability: the plan is not unfamiliar from the keyboard chaconnes of Fux and Muffat, with two sections in the minor enclosing a central section in the major. Bach manages to make those transition points unforgettable: the gentle F sharp touched at the first point, and the renewed B flat at the second. Arpeggiated playing is required which the composer leaves to the player to realise, so different performances vary greatly in sound, while in one D major passage the fanfare-like orchestral writing of the Suites is captured. The sense of infinite power released in the final passages of this Chaconne points forward to the variation movements in Beethoven's late piano sonatas.

Musicians throughout history have revered this Chaconne: Brahms, with a keen sense of self-imposed limitation, transcribed it for piano left hand only. Busoni, refusing any limitations but understanding its musical substance, transformed it into a virtuoso Romantic piano piece. I have heard it realised successfully in all sorts of ways, including by John Williams on guitar. Spitta claimed that this work was the triumph of the spirit over substance, but it is surely the very challenge of matching the transcendent spirit with the human, fallible substance of the performer that gives the Chaconne its unique place in musical history.

🎧 *BWV 1001–1006* Christian Tetzlaff
Hänssler Classics 98250
🎧 *BWV 1001–1006* Viktoria Mullova
ONYX 4040
🎧 *BWV 1001–1006* Rachel Podger
Channel Classics CCS 12198

Sonata No. 1 in B minor for violin and harpsichord BWV 1014
Sonata No. 2 in A BWV 1015
Sonata No. 3 in E BWV 1016
Sonata No. 4 in C minor BWV 1017
Sonata No. 5 in F minor BWV 1018
Sonata No. 6 in G BWV 1019

Though it is the unaccompanied violin works that have found a place in musical history, it is Bach's sonatas for violin with obbligato keyboard that provide a more significant pointer to the future. These are the first important members of a musical family whose offspring was to dominate the first years of the classical violin school. In these works Bach raises the importance of the keyboard to a level it had never previously been given. His method is to write trios for two instruments, as it were: the right hand of the keyboard and the violinist making a duet on equal terms, while the left hand of the keyboard player (possibly reinforced by another bass instrument) provides the continuo lines. The keyboard would also have filled in the continuo harmonies where appropriate. Some of these pieces may indeed have originated as trio sonatas and been adapted for the more 'modern' medium. One copy by Altnickol describes the pieces as 'Sechs Trios für Clavier und die Violine'. The earliest source seems to be a keyboard part written out by Johann Heinrich Bach and the composer around 1725; they give every sign of having been carefully planned as a set.

The sharing of the material varies in the different sonatas. In the B minor Sonata No. 1 the violin's opening line is quite distinct from the harpsichord's; only later does it adopt the same six-note quaver pattern. The following fugue is in three equal parts; the next Andante is cleverly written so the harpsichord avoids the long sustained notes of the violin part; then there's a three-part final Allegro. Sonata No. 2 in A opens with a lovely canon in two parts in Bach's habitually pastoral use of this key, marked *dolce*; the second Andante is also a canon worked over a staccato walking bass. The fast movements are concerto-like in structure and idiom, the violin's arpeggios contrasted with the harpsichord's block chords. The final Presto attempts an up-to-date, cheerful folk-like theme.

The opening Adagio of Sonata No. 3 reverts to a solo line for the violin with realised chords for the keyboard, while the following Allegro is based on an untypical, really rather clunky theme which might have come from the Peasant Cantata. The third movement enables the harpsichord to emerge from its written-out chordal opening to share the violin's triplets. The long final Allegro sparkles with mutual exchanges, so enjoyably extended that it seems as if Bach did not want to finish it. Sonata No. 4 in C minor opens with a Largo that is a siciliano; in both this and the second slow movement the harpsichord has continuous figuration in its accompaniment. The first Allegro is fugal; the second is in the C minor world of the second keyboard Partita. Quite the oddest movement in this set – perhaps intended as a conscious compilation of different techniques – is the opening of No. 5, where the violin just touches in a few additions to a complete keyboard piece, as if making a few comments – and anticipating the 'accompanied sonata' of the classical era. After a fugal Allegro there is an Adagio in which the violin now provides a chordal underpinning to the keyboard figurations. (There is an alternative version of this movement BWV 1018/3a, as there is of the last sonata BWV 1019a.)

Sonata No. 6 exists in three distinct versions. It opens with a splendid, open G major concerto movement, and after an E minor Largo with dotted rhythms, the keyboard has a movement entirely to itself (in an earlier version this is the same as the E minor Corrente in the Partitas, but the later one is a new movement which deserves to be better known, and could easily have found its way into a published keyboard suite). The elaborate B minor Adagio sounds like a flute solo transcribed for keyboard or violin in the mould of the Benedictus of the B minor Mass, while the final bouncing Allegro is very much in the violinistic idiom, with a jumpy syncopated bass line. As so often, Bach brings the art of his own time to perfection, while also looking forward decisively to the future.

🎧 *BWV 1014–1019*; *1019a, 1021, 1023* Viktoria Mullova, Ottavio Dantone
ONYX 4020
🎧 *BWV 1014–1019, 1019a, 1021, 1023* Rachel Podger, Trevor Pinnock, Jonathan Manson
Channel Classics CCS 14798
🎧 BWV *1014–1019, 1019a* Monica Huggett, Ton Koopman
Philips 410 401

?Sonata in G minor BWV 1020
Sonata in G BWV 1021
Sonata in E minor BWV 1023
?Sonata in C minor BWV 1024
?Trio in A BWV 1025
Fugue in G minor BWV 1026

Some of the other violin works attributed to Bach pose problems of authenticity, and the G minor Sonata is probably by C. P. E. Bach. The G major Sonata BWV 1021, in the old-style violin and continuo model, has an introductory Largo, gigue-like Vivace, eloquent E minor Largo and a well-worked final fugal Presto. The E minor Sonata unfolds over a single bass pedal note for a whole movement, and then has an Adagio, Allemanda and Gigue. The C minor Sonata which some violinists have recorded as Bach's is much less certain, and the Trio in A in the style of the accompanied violin sonatas is a version of a piece by Silvius Leopold Weiss, though C. P. E. attributed it to his father and kept the work in his collection. The Fugue in G minor for violin and keyboard was copied by Walther and probably belongs to a lost early Weimar work (*c.*1712): it is an impressive movement, with double-stopping and idiomatic violin writing, and Wolff suggests this is the earliest extant piece of Bach's chamber music.

🎧 *BWV 1024, 1025, 1026* Goebel, ter Linden, Bouman, Hill
Archiv 471 656

Flute sonatas and chamber pieces

**Sonata in B minor for flute and harpsichord
  BWV 1030
Sonata in A for flute and harpsichord BWV 1032
Sonata in E minor for flute and continuo BWV 1034
Sonata in E for flute and continuo BWV 1035
?Sonata in E flat for flute and harpsichord BWV 1031
?Sonata in C for flute and continuo BWV 1033
Partita in A minor for solo flute BWV 1013
?Sonata in G for flute, violin and continuo BWV 1038
Sonata in G for two flutes and continuo BWV 1039
Trio in F for violin, oboe and continuo BWV 1040**

Bach's music for flute is an especially problematic area, which has been admirably surveyed by Hans Eppstein and Robert Marshall, but let not that distract us from one of the greatest pieces he wrote. The B minor Sonata BWV 1030 is a masterpiece of the highest order, and it is revealing that the earliest copy is from the mid-1730s, so its maturity might reflect an origin in that period, as Marshall has convincingly argued. (There is a version of the harpsichord part in G minor, however, and the piece sounds superb when played in that key on the oboe; I vividly remember being completely knocked for six by it in a recital by Heinz Holliger.) Wolff supports this view on the grounds that the first movement 'has no parallel in any pre-Leipzig instrumental composition'. Indeed, that first movement is one of the finest he ever conceived, with winding chromaticisms and urgent triplets building what could be heard as a keening lament: there are clear analogies in the Kyrie of the B minor Mass of 1733. The *Largo e dolce* has a fully realised accompaniment to the flute's theme, showing how Bach filled out his continuo parts to keep the motion of the piece going, and then a unique final movement or pair of movements: the usual fugal finale surprisingly cadences and leads to a two-part gigue of great brilliance.

None of the other flute sonatas claimed as Bach's reaches this level, but the *Neue Bach Ausgabe* was too severe in initially excluding so many of them, and a more recent volume has made amends. The A major Sonata is found (incomplete) in the same autograph as the C minor Concerto for two harpsichords, placing it firmly among the works used for the Collegium Musicum in Leipzig in the 1730s. It is odd that the central *Largo e dolce* is in A minor, but it cadences in E to lead to the final A major Allegro, which is an extended concerto-like movement. It might originally, as Michael Marissen has suggested, have been a trio sonata.

There are two Sonatas for flute and continuo: one is in E minor from a source in the late 1720s from Leipzig. The E major is found only in a source of 1800, long after Bach's death. But it has an inscription saying that it was composed for the royal chamberlain, Federsdorff, thus connecting it with Bach's visits to Berlin in the 1740s. It seems to attempt an up-to-date style in the first movement, with florid triplets that will recur in the *Musical Offering* trio sonata, but the Siciliano, which has become known separately, is canonic. The E flat Sonata was at first excluded by *NBA*, though Grove accepts it and it is a perfectly respectable work which might derive from a Dresden trio by Quantz. The C major Sonata was copied out by C. P. E. Bach during the Collegium years and attributed to his father, but it may have been cobbled together from various sources.

Bach's one work for unaccompanied flute might possibly have been the start of a series of works along the lines of the violin and cello suites, following in the footsteps of Telemann's successful series of such works, but it feels less idiomatic: in the Allemande there is not a single space to breathe up to the high A at the end; the Corrente and Sarabande are followed by the last movement, a Bourre Anglaise (or angloise).

The Trio Sonata in G is a version of the G major Violin Sonata which is included in *Grove*, but Ulrich Siegele has suggested it is by C. P. E. Bach – another arrangement for the Collegium. BWV 1039 is an authentic trio sonata which then became the Gamba Sonata BWV 1027, but it works well in this form. Though two other trio sonatas are definitely inauthentic (BWV 1036 is by C. P. E. Bach and 1037 by Bach's pupil Johann Gottlieb Goldberg), they may well have been used by Bach. The greatest trio sonata of all is in *The Musical Offering* (see p. 427). The trio BWV 1040 does not really need a number of its own since it is the wholly delightful trio sonata that springs as a postlude from Cantata 208 and then Cantata 68, after the famous aria 'My heart ever faithful' (see p. 331).

🎧 BWV *1030–1035* Wilbert Hazelzet, Jaap ter Linden, Jacques Ogg
Glossa 920 807
🎧 *BWV 1013, 1020, 1030–1035, 1039* Lisa Beznosiuk, Paul Nicholson, Tunnicliffe, Brown, Kenny
Hyperion 67264/5 (2 CDs)
🎧 BWV *1030–1035* Emmanuel Pahud, Trevor Pinnock, Jonathan Manson
EMI Classics 17443
🎧 *BWV 1029, 1037, 1030, 527, 530* Rare Fruits Council
Naïve Astree 8804
🎧 *BWV 1037, 1038, 1039, BWV 1079* Florilegium Ensemble
Channel Classics 14598

Cello Suites

Suite No. 1 in G BWV 1007
Suite No. 2 in D minor BWV 1008
Suite No. 3 in C BWV 1009
Suite No. 4 in E flat BWV 1010
Suite No. 5 in C minor BWV 1011
Suite No. 6 in D BWV 1012

The Cello Suites represent an important part of the Bach revival, since it was Pablo Casals's espousal of them and his recording that was a key influence in making Bach's music well known in the twentieth century; they have continued to inspire interpreters, for example Yo-Yo Ma, who based a series of six films by different artists around them. They are more varied and diverse as a collection than the Violin Partitas and

Sonatas, as their keys are not so logically ordered, and indeed a different tuning is needed for the fifth suite, and a different instrument for the sixth; nor are they so consciously virtuosic as the violin solos. But they have an inward concentration that has made them both popular and revered, and that is demonstrated by their extensive use in films (see pp. 29–31).

Spitta suggested that the suites were written for Christian Ferdinand Abel, who played at the Cöthen court, but this is unlikely. They were not written out until much later by Anna Magdalena Bach (BWV says 1720, though others give 1727–31), presumably copying them from the now lost autograph, so there must have been someone who wanted to play them then – perhaps beyond Leipzig. The title page was written out by Georg Heinrich Ludwig Schwanberg and says 'Suites a Violoncello Solo senza Basso composees par Sr. J.S. Bach Maitre de Chapelle', which has led Schulze to suggest a possible link with Wolfenbüttel. The suites all have the same basic form, with preludes added to the normal sequence of dance movements, and extra pairs of dances added in. The well-known G major Prelude announces Suite No. 1 in swinging, ritualistic style; it is beautifully paced, rising to a fine climax at the top of a chromatic scale; there is an Allemande, Courante and Sarabande with multiple-stopping; then a simple pair of Minuets and a final Gigue. The Prelude of Suite No. 2 in D minor is mainly a single line until the final arpeggiated chords, and generally there are touches of harmony rather than long passages in the Allemande, Courante and Sarabande; the Minuets, at least the first, have more cross-string writing, while the Gigue bounces with some of the only sustained two-part writing in the set.

The Prelude of Suite No. 3 in C plunges down to the bottom note of the instrument, and then rises to some strongly arpeggiated writing before coming to a dramatic close full of pauses. After an Allemande, Courante and Sarabande (again only the last has multiple stopping), this time there is a pair of Bourrées, and a Gigue where the two-part writing includes some notable passing dissonances of the minor ninth and major seventh. For Suite No. 4 in E flat the Prelude sweeps repeatedly down the instrument in arpeggios, breaking out in the central section, and the Allemande, Courante and dotted-rhythm Sarabande follow. Here the pair of Bourrées are very stripped down (John Butt says that we almost hear the dance in the second as a skeleton), and the final Gigue runs along in 12/8.

Suite No. 5 has a note saying that the top string of the cello, usually A, should be tuned down to G, though not everyone is agreed that this is either an advantage or changes the character of the work: maybe it is linked to the fact that a version was written for lute in G minor (BWV 995) in around 1730. After the Allemande, Courante and an especially beautiful single-line Sarabande moving with great eloquence across the strings, there is here a pair of Gavottes (the second rather unusual in its flowing triplets) and a final dotted Gigue. Suite No. 6 presents an additional complication: a note says 'à cinq cordes', meaning a cello with five rather than four strings, adding an E string a fifth above the A string (as the violin has, but an octave lower). Cellists can and do play it on a normal instrument, however, but doing so makes the extensive cross-string writing more demanding. The Prelude is one of the best, with bariolage repeated notes across the strings propelling the music, then a very expressive and elaborate Allemande, a bouncy Courante, and a Sarabande. This movement for the first time demands sustained writing across the strings, sometimes in three and four parts (perhaps a cello with more strings and a flat bridge was easier to sustain across the strings in slow writing); there follows a pair of Gavottes and a final Gigue.

♪ *BWV 1007–1012* Pablo Casals
EMI 9659212
♪ *BWV 1007–1012* Truls Mørk
Virgin Classics 45650
♪ *BWV 1007–1012* Anner Bylsma
Sony Classical S2K 48047

♎ *BWV 1007–1012* Pierre Fournier
DG The Originals 449 771
♎ *BWV 1007–1012* Steven Isserlis
Hyperion CDA 67541
♎ *BWV 1007–1012: 'Inspired by Bach'* Yo-Yo Ma
Sony Classical 7464-63203-2
♎ *'Inspired by Bach'* DVD Sony Classical 58785 (3 discs)

Viola da gamba sonatas

Sonata No. 1 in G for viola da gamba and keyboard BWV 1027
Sonata No. 2 in D BWV 1028
Sonata No. 3 in G minor BWV 1029

The three Sonatas for viola da gamba and continuo may have been written quite late: Laurence Dreyfus has argued for an origin in Leipzig rather than in Cöthen as had previously been thought; they are as forward-looking as the Violin Sonatas but in a rather different way, since the viola da gamba part naturally lies between the right-hand and left-hand part of the keyboard. Bach must have had a fine gamba player in Leipzig, as the instrument features so prominently in the Passions, as well as in some cantata movements. These sonatas could have been written for Carl Friedrich Abel (whose father Christian Ferdinand had played the gamba at Cöthen during Bach's time); according to Burney the younger Abel studied with Bach in Leipzig before working in Dresden, and later went to London, setting up a concert series with Johann Christian Bach. Bach wrote both for instruments with six strings and seven strings, of which there are examples extant; though it might be assumed, we do not know to what extent if at all bass viol and cello players overlapped.

Sonata No. 1 survives in Bach's own autograph from around 1742, and though it has been described as a transcription of the Trio Sonata BWV 1039, Wolff prefers to regard it as 'a different means of expressing the same idea'. There are four movements, the first in triple time with the gamba in between the harpsichord top line and the walking bass line; then a fugal Allegro ma non tanto, a flowing Andante and then a final Allegro moderato. The Second Sonata in D, written for the seven-string viola da gamba also used in the St Matthew Passion, is also in four movements, with concerto-like Allegros as the second and fourth movements (it would be possible to create a Bach cello concerto from this piece), and a lyrical B minor Andante. The very fine Sonata No. 3 in G minor maintains the level of inventiveness of the others, but the equality between the keyboard upper part and the gamba has led some to suggest an earlier origin in a double concerto. This piece has always been noted, and Spitta called it 'of the greatest beauty and most striking originality'; recently Laurence Dreyfus has both analysed and played this sonata, pointing out its progressive aspects, and giving it a new status among Bach's works.

Ω *BWV 1027–1029* Jordi Savall, Ton Koopman
Alia Vox AV 9812
Ω *BWV 1027–1029* Mischa Maisky, Martha Argerich
DG 415 471
Ω *BWV 1027–1029* Laurence Dreyfus, Ketil Hausgand
Simax Classics PSC 1024
Ω *BWV 1027–1029* Pieter Wispelwey, Richard Egarr, Daniel Yeadon
Channel Classics 14198
Ω *Arr. of BWV 1027–1029, Organ Sonatas BWV 525 and 527*
Camerata Köln
CPO 777 359-2

Lute music

Suite in G minor BWV 995
Suite in E minor BWV 996
Partita/Suite in C minor BWV 997
Prelude, Fugue and Allegro in E flat BWV 998
Prelude in C minor BWV 999
Fugue in G minor BWV 1000
Suite in E major BWV 1006a

A small group of works related to, if not all directly written for, the lute show Bach's keen interest in the instrument, which he featured in the St John Passion, the early version of the St Matthew Passion, and the *Trauer Ode* (with its two lutes). Bach was certainly friendly with the most famous lutenist of his generation, Sylvius Leopold Weiss, who was employed at the Dresden court and visited Leipzig. There are considerable issues around playing these pieces on the lute, at least as we know the instrument, and they may have been intended for a keyboard instrument called the lute-harpsichord which was described by Fleischer in 1718 and has been reconstructed.

The Suite in G minor is a version of Cello Suite No. 5. The Suite in E minor is inscribed by Walther in his mid-1710s copy 'aufs Lautenwerk' – perhaps a reference to the keyboard version of the instrument. According to the lutenist Tim Crawford, it is challenging for a conventional lute, and adaptations for guitar alter the music to make it more effective. The Partita or Suite in C minor has fine music in it, and looks like a work of the 1730s (Weiss's documented visit to Leipzig was in 1739). The Sarabande recalls the end of the St Matthew Passion, but there are problems for the instrument again in the final double of the Gigue. The Prelude, Fugue and Allegro might also relate to Weiss's visit, or could be a little earlier, but it is mature work whose Prelude relates to the E flat of Book II of the '48'; the concluding Allegro is in triple time. The C minor Prelude is often played as a keyboard work and its patterning naturally suggests the C major version at the start of the '48'. The Fugue in G minor is an arrangement of the fine fugue from the Violin Sonata BWV 1001, while the Suite in E major is a transcription of the complete Violin Partita in E, starting with the favourite Prelude which Bach adapted more than once.

🎧 *BWV 1006a, 995, 997, 1000* Rolf Lislevand
Naïve 8807
🎧 *BWV 1006a, 995, 1001* Paul O'Dette
Harmonia Mundi HMU907438
🎧 *BWV 1000, 1001 etc.* Konrad Junghänel
Accent 77801 D

Keyboard music

From his earliest years Bach must have absorbed with great attention the keyboard music that he heard around him as he was growing up: there was a North German tradition of considerable interest and variety, shown him by his elder brother Johann Christoph, 'under whose guidance he learnt the fundamentals of keyboard playing', as the Obituary relates. Our understanding of Bach's early music is still evolving, and two major developments in recent years have been influential in this: the discovery and identification of the Neumeister Chorales (see the section on organ music) and the identification of Bach's eldest brother Johann Christoph as the scribe of two key early manuscripts, the Möller manuscript and the Andreas Bach Book. (The latter collection acquired its name because Andreas Bach owned it from 1754.) As Richard Jones observes in his recent study of Bach's early music, this strengthens the attributions to Bach made in these two collections, and enables us to understand his earliest keyboard style better. Stephen Crist writes that 'now that the authenticity of these pieces is secure, they can be used as a base line against which to judge many others in manuscripts whose connection with Bach are less certain'. This has begun a process of re-admitting to the Bach canon some pieces that, though included in the Bach Gesellschaft and the first edition of BWV, were progressively excluded as inauthentic.

For the listener these earliest works are likely to be of secondary interest, at least until we reach the Toccatas, which have been frequently recorded. But there are some quirky gems among this repertoire, and they enable us to understand how very quickly Bach learnt and developed.

🎧 *Glenn Gould Plays Bach: Goldberg Variations (1955, 1981), English Suites, French Suites, Partitas, Overture in the French Style, Chromatic Fantasia and Fugue, Italian Concerto, Inventions*

and Sinfonias, Toccatas, Preludes BWV 924–929, Little Preludes, Aria 'in the Italian Style' BWV 989, BWV 906, 917, 919, 950, 951, 974 Glenn Gould
Sony Classical 518509 (12 CDs)

🎧 *English Suites, French Suites, Well-tempered Clavier Book I excerpts, Inventions and Sinfonias, Preludes BWV 925–932, 994, 841–843, etc.* Christophe Rousset
Naïve 196 (6 CDs)

🎧 *Partitas, French Overture, Italian Concerto, Goldberg Variations* Trevor Pinnock
DG Archiv Trio 474 3372 (3 CDs)

Early works

Fantasia in G minor 'duobus subjectis' BWV 917
Prelude and Fugue in A BWV 896
Praeludium and Partita in F 'del tuono terzo' BWV 833
Suite in A BWV 832
Suite in B flat BWV 821
Suite in F minor BWV 823
Sonata in A minor BWV 967
Sonata in D BWV 963

These earliest keyboard pieces (probably) by Bach to have been preserved are full of interest, though none is fully formed. Some are found in the hand of his elder brother in the Möller Manuscript, and so must pre-date 1707 or so. The short G minor Fantasia starts with a toccata-like flourish and proceeds to explore a rising fugal subject against a descending chromatic line. The Prelude and Fugue in A has a gently flowing little prelude and uncomplicated fugue, possibly his first preserved piece in this genre which was to become so important, with a pastoral lilt that recurs in the Missa in A. The Partita in F is a primitive suite with Praeludium, Allemande, Courante, Sarabande with double, and triple-time Air, not really a patch on what Bach would soon achieve in this form.

The three early suites may be fragmentary in transmission, and they show Bach's North German style with traces of early French influence: for example the 'Air pour les trompettes' in the A major Suite. The writing here is a little more advanced: the Suite in B flat was previously doubted as it is not in the Möller manuscript, and so was relegated to the BWV Anhang, but its attribution is secure. The Suite in F minor has only three French-type movements of which the middle is a 'Sarabande en Rondeau' and the last a Gigue; it has been argued by Pieter Dirksen that it is a lute-inspired work from much later. The Sonata in A minor is again in the Möller Manuscript, and feels like a sonata transcription, as if Bach was already hearing Italian music. Can the Sonata in D really be by Bach? It all feels very simplistic and its fugue with a theme 'all'imitatio Gallina Cuccu' particularly silly, but no more naïve, I suppose, than the posthorn imitation in the famous Capriccio below.

♫ *BWV 823, 832, 818a, 819, 847, 851, etc.* Oliver Baumont (harpsichord and clavichord)
Erato 8573-80224-2

Capriccio in B flat on the departure [absence] of his beloved brother BWV 992
Capriccio in E in honorem Johann Christoph Bachii Ohrdrufiensis BWV 993

The first of Bach's pieces to have become famous is included in the earliest collection that includes his work, and dates from around 1704–7. This Capriccio has established itself because of its programmatic nature, like Biber's *Battalia* or Kuhnau's Biblical Sonatas, but it is not by any means a fully formed (or even great) piece. The story is told in six movements: Arioso; Adagio, a coaxing by his friends to deter him from his journey (in harmonious sixths); Fugato, an envisaging of various calamities that could befall him in foreign parts; Lamento; Adagissimo, a general lament of his friends (over the traditional descending chromatic bass); Accompagnato, the friends arrive, since they see that it cannot be otherwise, and take their leave of him; Aria di Postiglione. Allegro poco, leading to Fuga all' imitatione di Posta: fugue in imitation of the post-horn. The lament is especially notable as belonging to the Froberger tradition which reached Bach through Kuhnau; the music is however quite crude, particularly in the final Fugue where the repeated notes of the post-horn inhibit fluid development of the subject. Malcolm Boyd stressed that the title could refer to absence rather than departure. But to whom does it refer? Although identification of the brother with Bach's real brother Johann Jakob who left in 1707 has long been assumed, the word does not only mean brother, and hence the departure could refer to any close friend, possibly his school-friend Georg Erdmann, to whom Bach would later write. The companion Capriccio in E is a bouncy fugal piece honouring his relative in Ohrdruf, and so is a teenage work dating from around this period, but it has never found the same favour, maybe because of its lack of programmatic elements.

♩ *Capriccio BWV 992, BWV 912, 914, 916, 767, 818a*
Andreas Staier
Harmonia Mundi 901960
♩ *Capriccio BWV 992, BWV 914, 996, 998* Gustav Leonhardt
Philips 41614
♩ *Capriccio BWV 992, BWV 971, 911, 807, 808* Friedrich Gulda
DG 477 8020

Overture (Suite) in F BWV 820
?Overture in G minor BWV 822
Prelude (Fantasie) in C minor BWV 921
Fantasia in A minor BWV 922
Aria variata in A minor BWV 989
?Sarabande con partite in C BWV 990
Fugue in A BWV 949
Fantasia and Fugue in A minor BWV 944

The second collection to preserve Bach's earliest work is the Andreas Bach Book which contains several of these pieces.

Both the F major Overture and the G minor Overture have French-style opening movements; the G minor is more consistently French, though other hands are suspected in this piece. The Prelude in C minor of around 1707–13 is really interesting: a bold and eccentric piece, entirely of differently arpeggiated chords and sequences with a prestissimo conclusion – just the last three bars are written in Bach's own hand. The Fantasia in A minor, perhaps a little later (1710–13), is in the mould of the North German sectional toccata, with a hectic beginning, a jerky middle section with a rhythmic pattern too often repeated, and a bold conclusion. It was copied by both Krebs and Preller with added ornaments, and must have been used for teaching.

Aria variata, in the Andreas Bach Book which also contains music by Reincken, and similar variations by Pachelbel, consists of ten variations in a violin-like style, with simple ornamental variations in two voices. It's a pleasant but undemanding work. The *Sarabande con partite* BWV 990 has been consistently doubted as Bach's, but has recently been recorded again, and still sits as his in *New Grove*, though without date; it's a secular version of a chorale partita, quite dull. The Fugue in A is an early work with a couple of indications of pedal towards the close and shows Bach developing an unpromising theme towards a climax. The Fantasia and Fugue in A minor is included in some anthologies and dates from around 1707–13: a brief arpeggio prelude leads to an A minor fugue of running semiquavers, rhythmically unvaried and over-extended, apparently after Torelli. Preller's copy of the fugue includes many ornaments and fingerings.

♩ *Aria variata BWV 989, Sarabande con partite BWV 990, Goldberg Variations* Matthew Halls
Linn CKD 356

Sonata in A minor BWV 965 after Reincken
Sonata in C BWV 966 after Reincken
Sonata in A minor BWV 967
Prelude and Fugue in B minor BWV 923/951 and
  Fugue BWV 951a
Fugues on themes by Albinoni BWV 946, 950 and
  951a, Reincken BWV 954, Erselius 955
Fugue in A BWV 949
Fugue in C BWV 952
Fugue in A minor BWV 959
Fugue in D minor BWV 948
Fughetta in C minor BWV 961

Now that we know that a transcription of a Reincken piece
is Bach's earliest surviving keyboard manuscript (see above),
it is not surprising that he then arranged some of Reincken's
trio sonatas for keyboard. When Bach played to Reincken
in Hamburg in 1720 the aged composer said to the young
virtuoso, 'I thought this art was extinct, but I see that it still
lives in you.' The Sonatas in A minor and in C arrange two
of his sonatas from *Hortus musicus*, published in 1687, while
BWV 967 has an unknown model. The elaboration Bach
added to the slow movements, and the fact that Walther
copied them, has suggested to Richard Jones a 1714–17 date,
much later than the pre-1707 suggested in *Grove*. The Sonata
in A minor BWV 967 is definitely by Bach. The B minor
Prelude and Fugue prefaces with bold harmonies (which may
be by Wilhelm Heironymous Pachelbel) a fugue described as
'ovvero Thema Albinonium elaboratum et ad Clavicimbalum
applicatum', extended by Bach but somewhat overlong. (A
shorter elaboration of the Fugue exists on its own as BWV
951a.) Bach's study of Albinoni and others resulted in several
fugues, the C major using a nicely syncopated subject, while
the Fugue in A equally makes good use of offbeat entries,
something Bach learnt to master, though the working is again
overlong. Nothing is known about the dates of the pleasing
but insignificant Fugue in C BWV 952, while the A minor

Fugue looks like a comparatively mature work with a leaping conclusion to its theme. The Fugue in D minor (1709–11, or perhaps later: 1726–7?) is an example of the elongated fugue subject using a solid motive, sequences and a conclusion that Bach would develop, and ending in flourishes and block chords. The C minor Fughetta is a two-part invention in 12/8 time. These pieces show Bach learning and practising his craft, but it is difficult to urge performing them when there are so many greater pieces clamouring for attention.

◔ *Bach a la maniera Italiana BWV 903, 823, 992, 812, 951a, 989, 913, 968* Rinaldo Alessandrini (harpsichord)
Opus 111 30-258
◔ *Preludes BWV 901–902, 924–931, 933–938, 939–943, 999, BWV 998* Kenneth Gilbert
Archiv 419 426

Prelude and Fugue in A minor BWV 894
Prelude and Fugue in A minor BWV 895
Fantasia on a Rondo in C minor BWV 918

The Prelude and Fugue in A minor of some time after 1715 is a strong piece whose first movement provided the material for the Triple Concerto BWV 1044: the material is exhaustively worked out; the Fugue is a gigue-like invention that foreshadows the Partitas. The Prelude and Fugue in A minor BWV 895 is short and effective, with some interesting fingerings written into Preller's copy, then a four-square fugue subject of the sort Bach would have rejected for the '48'. The C minor Fantasia on a Rondo looks like an early sketch for the two-part invention section of the Partita No. 2, but Jones believes it to be a mature work perhaps dating after the Partitas, and *Grove* for some reason suggests a very late date of after 1740; it might be thought earlier as it has a long working-out that is ingenious but does not achieve much sense of climax.

◔ *Clavierfantasien BWV 922, 904, 921, 919, 894, 902, 901, 903, 917, 906* Andreas Staier
DHM RD 77039

Toccatas BWV 910–916

These keyboard toccatas (which Robert Marshall tried to claim as organ pieces, though pianists and harpsichordists have held on to them) cannot be described as a cycle, but they are collected and sometimes performed together. They are characterised by dramatic gestures and inventive but very over-extended fugues, as if Bach was beginning to relish the possibilities of counterpoint but did not know quite where to stop.

The D minor BWV 913 may be the first of the group, as it is described as 'Toccata Prima' and inscribed to Johann Christoph Bach; its four movements are clearly related to North German organ models – surprises and shocks in the first and third (originally marked 'adagioissimo'!) sections contrasting with long fugues in the second and fourth. The E minor BWV 914 has as its second section a shorter fugue which does not outstay its welcome, and then a most dramatic third section with recitative passages and showy figuration. The fugue that follows, meanwhile, is marked by sequences in constant semiquaver movement, as if based on a violin piece: though it does not always escape dullness it rallies to a terrific finish with intensified chordal writing. The G minor BWV 915 is relatively primitive and does not quite succeed: the long gigue fugue at its close is harmonically odd. Probably from a slightly later period and in the Andreas Bach Book, the G major BWV 916 is much more harmonically secure, with a concerto-like opening, an E minor adagio and a skipping fugue to which the J. C. Bach manuscript adds many ornaments. The F sharp minor BWV 910 has opening flourishes which lead to a solemn triple-time section and a busy and elongated fugue. The C minor BWV 911 is tauter, more successfully negotiating the move from opening gestures to reflective adagio and a crisp fugue which gains energy from syncopations in the subject. The D major Toccata BWV 912 is the most often played, and the most exuberant – an early version is contained in the Möller manuscript. (The central Adagio there has some chords marked 'trem' – a reference to clavichord performance?

The later version expands them.) After a free passage marked *con discrezione*, the final gigue-like section maintains an extraordinary level of energy – especially in the later version where, as the bass line skips up the scale towards the end, the music explodes in demisemiquaver figuration.

♩ *Toccatas BWV 910–915* Angela Hewitt
Hyperion 67310
♩ *Toccatas BWV 910–916* Glenn Gould
Sony 804920
♩ *Toccatas BWV 910–916* Bob van Asperen
Teldec 81237 (Bach 2000)
♩ *Toccata BWV 911, Partita BWV 826, English Suite BWV 807* Martha Argerich
DG The Originals 463 604

Miscellaneous pieces

Chromatic Fantasia and Fugue in D minor BWV 903
Fantasia and Fugue in A minor BWV 904
Fantasia and Fugue (incomplete) in C minor BWV 906

The remarkable Chromatic Fantasia and Fugue is the most important of Bach's earlier keyboard works based on North German models. Though many copies circulated, it has no secure attribution in the earliest copy of 1730, and was published only in 1802. From its style it was perhaps conceived around 1714, but may have reached in its present form before 1723. It is clearly a piece Bach thought worth preserving, though it was not included in any of his published collections. It has been taken up by many keyboard players from Wanda Landowska onwards because of its vivid drama and power. Alberto Basso has written of its 'stormy passagework, the overwhelming force of the dissonant arpeggios, the unprecedented insertion of recitative-like episodes, and the use of the chromatic genre to liberate the music (almost as if trying to defy harmonic gravity)'. Swirling arpeggios and passagework lead to a recitative (related to that in the organ G minor Fantasia?) The fugue is an implacable triple-time chromatic line which is fully worked out, but in a distinct advance over many of the early pieces, this one builds to a genuine climax over a dominant pedal and crashing doubled octaves in the bass. (The *Neue Bach Ausgabe* recognises the evolving nature of the piece by printing three different versions, the last copied by Krebs.) George Stauffer makes the valid point that this piece was attractive to later generations because of its links with *Sturm und Drang* ('storm and stress') effects in the music of Bach's sons Carl Philipp Emanuel and Wilhelm Friedemann. Its D minor tonality thus acquired a pre-echo of Mozart's D minor Concerto. When Wilhelm Friedemann sent a copy of this piece to Forkel he added a little poem, which may be translated:

> Herewith dear man
> some music by Sebastian
> also known as Fantasia Chromatica
> a thing of beauty and a joy in saecula.

The A minor Fantasia and Fugue is one of my favourite pieces of neglected Bach: a highly mature piece (of around 1727 or later) with a sustained organ-style opening – which is specifically marked 'Fantasia pro Cembalo' – and a recapitulation that is beautifully arrived at. The double fugue I have always thought one of Bach's very finest, unlike any in the '48' because of its two-section structure: a first section based on a rising subject in which movement and rest are in equilibrium, and then a second based on a descending chromatic line; the long-delayed combination of the two is a superb moment.

The Fantasia and incomplete Fugue in C minor would be much better known if complete, though the dramatic hand-crossing triplets of the Fantasia have ensured it is performed on its own. In the form it has come down it is a mature piece of the 1730s, and sits alongside the concerto arrangements of those years. There is surely enough of the chromatic fugue to encourage someone to make a completion.

Concertos after Vivaldi and others
BWV 972–987

Bach arranged several concertos by Vivaldi and his patron Prince Johann Ernst for organ (see p. 296) and harpsichord around 1713–14, following Johann Ernst's return from studies in Holland. The Harpsichord Concertos are effective solo pieces which can be heard as pre-echoes of the later and famous Italian Concerto in *Clavierübung II*. They make good recital pieces, without too much subtlety but with great extrovert power. The models for harpsichord are by the Marcello brothers (BWV 974 and 981), Torelli (BWV 979), and Telemann (BWV 985), but most are derived from Vivaldi (BWV 972, 973, 975, 976, 978, 980) and Prince Johann Ernst (BWV 984, 987), leaving a few with unknown sources (BWV 977, 983, and 986).

☊ *8 Concerto Transcriptions from BWV 972–984* Ivor Bolton (harpsichord)
ASV GAU 116
☊ *Concertos: BWV 973–975, BWV 979, 981, 590, 596, Italian Concerto* Alexandre Tharaud (piano)
Harmonia Mundi 901871

?Sonatas BWV 964 and 968, arrangements of
BWV 1003 and 1005/1

We do not know whether the keyboard transcriptions BWV 964 and 968 of movements from the solo violin Partitas are by Bach or his pupil Altnickol, but we have the word of another pupil Agricola in 1775 that 'the composer played them often himself on the clavichord and added as much harmony to them as he found necessary'. A clear example of this is the transcription of BWV 1006, perhaps for keyboard or lute, in an autograph dated 1737 (and the much grander version of that Partita's first movement in Cantata 29). The reworking of BWV 1005/1 is beautifully done, with the creation of a virtually new bass line underpinning the violin's figuration.

☊ *Transcriptions of BWV 1001, 1005, 1012* Gustav Leonhardt
(harpsichord)
DHM GD77014
☊ *Original and Transcription: after BWV 1004, 964, 968,
1006a, 966, 965, 954* Robert Hill (lute-harpsichord,
harpsichord, clavichord)
Hänssler Bach Edition 110

Six Little Preludes BWV 933–938
?Five Little Preludes BWV 939–943

Familiar from many early piano lessons and a much-used book
of Bach preludes published by the Associated Board, these
six are each short but mature and perfectly balanced pieces.
Their origin is uncertain because they were grouped together
only during the 1770s in the circle of C. P. E. Bach. The first
is concerto-like, in C; the second a two-part invention in C
minor, the third a two-part piece in D minor, the fourth a
beautifully logical piece over a walking bass in D which looks
forward to the Goldbergs (the right hand's expressive canonic
imitation is saved for the second half), the fifth is a two-part
toccata in E major, and the sixth is a triple-time invention in E
minor. Then there are five more, which seem to date from the
mid-1720s, but are perhaps not all reliably Bach's.

Clavierbüchlein for W. F. Bach (including Preludes
BWV 924–932, Fugue BWV 953, Minuets
BWV 841–843, Applicatio BWV 994)
Clavierbüchlein for Anna Magdalena Bach
(including BWV 573, BWV 991, BWV Anh. 113–132)

The book that Bach compiled for his son Wilhelm Friedemann from 1720 contains the two-and three-part inventions,
for which see below, early versions of preludes from the '48'
and nine excellent little preludes that show how refined and
concise his style had become by the early 1720s: the first in
C anticipates the first of the '48', the second in D is a rising,
flowing movement, the third in D minor is in lute style, while

the fourth is a toccata in F, and the fifth a splendid little movement in F, a perfect piece of imitative writing. Then there are three minuets BWV 841–843, a Prelude in G minor and an A minor Prelude, and a good Fugue in C BWV 953. The volume starts with an explanation of clefs and an *Applicatio* BWV 994 which shows how to finger.

In Anna Magdalena's two music books there are many pieces that have become the best known of Bach's works, even though some of them are not by him. In the first, there are early versions of the French Suites; also a fragment of an Air and Variations in C minor BWV 991. In the second there are versions of two Partitas and another two French suites, with the famous Minuet in G (BWV Anh. 114) which is now known to be from a suite by Christian Petzold, organist at the Sophienkirche in Dresden, and the Musette in D (BWV Anh. 126), equally familiar to young players. Among the remaining keyboard music there is some Hasse, some Couperin, and other pieces added later, including the Aria from the Goldberg Variations. David Schulenberg raises the possibility that Anna Magdalena might herself be the composer of some of the pieces whose origin we do not know: an encouraging thought.

◯ *Music in the Bach Household* Capella Fidicinia/Hans Grüss
Capriccio 10 031
◯ *Notenbüchlein für Anna Magdalena Bach* Ameling, Leonhardt, Linde, Tölzer Knabenchor
DHM GD 77150

Two-part Inventions BWV 772–786
Three-part Sinfonias BWV 787–801

Bach's desire to bring his works to their best possible form is well illustrated by the surviving versions of these teaching pieces. They appear towards the end of the *Clavierbüchlein* for his son Wilhelm Friedemann, begun around 1720 (see above), where they are described as *praeambula* and fantasias. But they were then revised and copied out again in 1723, changing the order of the pieces so they rose through the scale from C through to B, in the sequence C, C minor, D, D minor, E flat, E, E minor, F, F minor, G, G minor, A, A minor, B flat, B minor. Their didactic intention is made clear in the prefatory note to the new version, where they are described as *aufrichtige Anleitungen* (upright instruction), 'which lovers of the keyboard, especially those who desire to learn, are shown in a clear way not only 1. to learn to play two voices clearly, but 2. to deal correctly and well with three obbligato parts, moreover at the same time to obtain not only good ideas, but also to carry them out well, and most of all to achieve a cantabile style of playing and thereby to acquire a strong fore-taste of composition'. Bach probably meant to demonstrate his practical skills at teaching in the light of the decision to apply for the Leipzig post, where keyboard instruction was an important part of the cantor's duties.

The pieces have absolute rigour while maintaining great expressiveness; each is compact and concise, while being differentiated in character. A crisp invention in C, a more elegiac one in C minor, a flowing one in D (with Bach's own phrasing), then one in D minor based around the scale and diminished seventh. Then a concerto-like, not strictly imitative E flat invention, a syncopated one in E (like the Corrente from Partita No. 6), a strict E minor, the famous arpeggio-based F, the aria-like F minor, a gigue in G, a chromatic G minor, and 12/8 roulades in A, a prelude-like A minor, the well-known bouncy B flat and the final invention in B minor.

The sequence of Sinfonias also starts with the open clarity of C, an arpeggio-based C minor, a sequentially based D, and a D minor with trio sonata texture. Then a dotted-rhythm sarabande in E flat, a flowing triple-time sinfonia in E, and a reflective trio in E minor. A cheerful, open F sinfonia is strongly contrasted with a beautifully expressive and heavily chromatic F minor, and a clear and logical G, which leads to the G minor with its yearning arpeggios and suspensions. The A major sinfonia is sharp and decisive, and the A minor more severe, leading to the final two in B flat and then, with a virtuoso flourish to finish, in B minor. (Another arrangement could be to put the inventions and sinfonias in the same key next to each other, as Glenn Gould recorded them.)

🎧 *Inventions BWV 772–786, Sinfonias BWV 787–801, Preludes BWV 939, 940, 999, Little Preludes BWV 933–938, Fughetta in C minor BWV 961, Prelude and Fugue in A minor BWV 895*
Bob van Asperen (harpsichord)
Aeolus 10034
🎧 *Inventions and Sinfonias* Angela Hewitt (piano)
Hyperion CDA 66746
🎧 *Inventions BWV 772–786, Sinfonias BWV 787–801* Glenn Gould (piano)
Sony Classical 82876 78766 2

French and English suites

Six French Suites BWV 812–817
Six English Suites BWV 806–811
Suite in A minor BWV 818
Suite in E flat BWV 819

There is no reason to call either of these groups of suites English or French, and indeed there is perhaps more French-style writing in the English Suites. It seems clear that the English Suites came first, but they are more weighty on account of their Preludes in each suite, whereas the French launch immediately into a sequence of dance movements. Bach called the latter 'Suites pour le clavessin', and the title French Suites appears only after his death. The first five suites appear in Anna Magdalena's music book begun in 1722; the first and part of the second reappear in her second book begun in 1725. Perhaps they were used as teaching material for Bach's pupils and sons: some of these movements are among his most approachable, and one senses him keeping the range of the music in close, natural patterns for the small hands of pupils. The scheme of the suites is unusual, grouping minor keys first, moving stepwise down from D minor to C minor to B minor, and then into the major for E flat, G, and E (the longest and a later addition to the set). In contrast with Bach's earlier keyboard music, but developing the concision of the inventions and sinfonias, the French Suites are mature, compact and eloquent.

The flowing Allemande of the French Suite No. 1, with its lute-style writing, sets the tone for the whole suite with its tonic pedal that lasts a bar; the same applies to the following Courante, the Sarabande and the first Minuet, while the second Minuet is a trio that could be for two oboes and bassoon, contemporary with Brandenburg No. 1; the final Gigue uses busy dotted rhythms. Suite No. 2 in C minor starts with an Allemande full of melody, with secondary parts touched in, and after the two-part Courante the Sarabande is also in that same melodic style. There's a two-part Air, a minuet and a two-part canonic gigue in triple time. Suite No. 3 in B minor has a more canonic two-part Allemande, a flowing Courante, and a yearning Sarabande where the emphasis flows freely between the treble melody and the bass elaboration in the second half. The Gavotte is called an Anglaise in some sources, and the two-part Minuet in the broken-chord style of that in Partita No. 1 has a Trio with some nice chromatic touches; the Gigue is a closely imitative two-part invention.

Suite No. 4 in E flat begins with a broken-chord Allemande that clearly suggests an origin in lute-style music, followed by a Courante and a Sarabande with the traditional emphasis on the second beat of the bar, and then an unusually imitative Gavotte, flowing Air and skipping Gigue. (There is another, probably later version BWV 815a which adds a Prelude and second Gavotte but omits the Minuet and Gigue – the second Gavotte has particularly attractive counterpoint.) Suite No. 5 in G has always been the most popular of these works, and it is easy to see and hear why, for it is beautifully accomplished within a relatively narrow range of expression. Bach never achieved a more simply euphonious progression of harmonies than in the opening Allemande, and the mainly two-part Courante that follows is as clear as day. A Sarabande, the famously striding Gavotte (those bass octaves recur in the

Air from Orchestral Suite No. 3 and in the Sanctus of the B
minor Mass!), a busy Bourrée and relaxed 6/4 Loure lead to
the hectic final Gigue, which while creating a dazzling effect,
is not nearly as difficult to play as some pieces in this form
and reinforces the feeling that Bach was here writing highly
practical music for his pupils and children. Suite No. 6 in E
major (like the last violin Partita) dates from later, perhaps
1725, and is not so interesting; after the Allemande and
Courante there is a Sarabande which rises up the keyboard,
a perky Gavotte, Polonaise, Bourrée and Menuet before the
final running Gigue, though some sources have the Menuet
incongruously after the Gigue. A later version of this Suite
places a prelude from the '48' as a first movement. You can
take your pick from a wide variety of differently ornamented
and arranged versions of these suites based on early or late
copies; as the pianist András Schiff puts it, it is just a question
of *buon gusto* (good taste).

One accepts the view that the English Suites pre-date the
French Suites, and probably date from the 1710s, but to me
they sound more ambitious than the French Suites, perhaps
less consciously designed for teaching and more for performance. Their big opening movements certainly suggest a
public style; they were called 'Suites avec Préludes'. The only
reason for the title 'English' is a note by the young Johann
Christian Bach on his copy, 'fait pour les Anglois', with the
mysterious explanation by Forkel that 'the composer made
them for an Englishman of rank' – but for whom we may
never know.

The key sequence is descending: A, A minor, G minor,
F, E minor, D minor (it has been pointed out correctly but
coincidentally that this outlines the melody of the first phrase
of the chorale *Jesu, meine Freude*). The English Suite No. 1
is the lightest, with a flowing 12/8 Prelude introducing the
Allemande, two Courantes in 3/2 time 'avec deux Doubles'
and plenty of ornaments, a Sarabande in the French mode, a
pair of two-part Bourrées and the final imitative Gigue. Suite
No. 2 in A minor immediately ups the ante with a thoroughly

worked Prelude bearing all the hallmarks of Bach's interaction
with the Italian masters, with long, hypnotic, Vivaldi-like
sequences building skilfully (and much more powerfully than
in his early works) to a climax. Then an Allemande, Courante,
and an eloquent chordal Sarabande, which starts its second
half in C but sounds for once ineffably sad, and is followed by
a decorated version that might be an alternative; then a pair
of Bourrées and a Gigue in two parts for which Bach indicates
a double repeat.

With Suite No. 3 in G minor the scale of the Prelude
expands again with one of Bach's finest concerto movements,
starting from a single note but expanding to crashing four-
part block chords and running passages right down to the
bottom C and A of the keyboard – a magnificently sonorous
effect. The Allemande and Courante are followed by one of
Bach's greatest Sarabandes, with elaborate decorations as an
alternative or for the repeats, and a contrasted simple pair of
Gavottes, sounding very French, especially as the second is
a Musette over a pastoral drone. The three-part fugal treatment of the Gigue is demanding, difficult, and tremendously
effective.

A full-scale concerto launches Suite No. 4 in F, with the
sustained energy and sequential passagework Bach learned
from the Italian sources he encountered in Weimar (David
Schulenberg references BWV 978 after Vivaldi's Op. 3 No. 3),
building to a climax and finishing abruptly. Some sources add
staccato or accent marks to the opening phrase, so it should
not be warmly slurred. The Allemande, Courante, Sarabande
and a pair of Minuets are all in a relatively popular style and
the Gigue is based on leaping arpeggios. Suite No. 5, says
Schulenberg, 'is somewhat rough around the edges', but its
first movement is tremendous – a fugue in *da capo* form, which
is very unusual, a little over-extended like the toccatas, but
richly worked. Allemande, Courante and Sarabande follow
(once again staccato articulation marks are written into the
latter), and then there's an attractive pair of Passepieds. The
gigue has a weird chromatic shape that recalls the 'Wedge'

Organ Fugue in the same key, and is worked as a three-part fugal texture. Suite No. 6 in D minor begins with a Prelude built on sustained chords that look as if they might need an organ but are actually well suited to the sonority of the harpsichord. The flowing opening section leads through an adagio pause to a concerto Allegro – the whole movement is nearly two hundred bars long. The Allemande is richly worked, the Courante is mainly in two parts, and the Sarabande has a wonderfully developed double where the slow minims of the simple version turn into flowing quavers. The Gavottes are a trio in the minor and a high-lying duet over a tonic pedal in the major. But then comes the clinching movement of this whole set: the 12/16 Gigue, which explores all manner of invertible counterpoint in the context of a propulsive, chromatic line. This shows Bach's art evolving inexorably towards the preoccupations that will result in *The Art of Fugue*.

A pair of suites, BWV 818 and 819, have a similar shape, but though some date them together around 1722, others differentiate, with the first being part of the early works of around 1705 and the second around 1725.

Ω *English Suites BWV 806, 811, French Suites, Clavierbüchlein für W. F. Bach* Christophe Rousset
Naïve 196/Ambroisie AM196 (6 CDs)
Ω *English Suites BWV 806–811, Partitas* Gustav Leonhardt
Virgin 62379 (4 CDs)
Ω *English Suites BWV 806–811* Murray Perahia
Sony Classical 88697 31050-2 (2 CDs)
Ω *French Suites BWV 812–817* Angela Hewitt
Hyperion CDA 67121/2 (2 CDs)
Ω *French Suites BWV 812–817* Bob van Asperen
Aeolus 10084

Clavierübung I *and* II

Clavierübung Book I: Six Partitas BWV 825–830

While many keyboard players treat the '48' Preludes and Fugues (see below) as their daily bread, I have always – perhaps because of the more approachable sequence of keys – been drawn to the six Partitas as works for recreation: the constant variety of their dance movements is inexhaustible, and there is a distinctive fluency and singing quality throughout the set. They were clearly a most important milestone for Bach, for they were his first keyboard works (and almost his first works of all) to be printed and published, first individually between 1726 and 1730, and then as a set in 1731. He was following in the footsteps of his Leipzig predecessor Johann Kuhnau, who published two volumes of *Clavierübungen* in 1689 and 1692; these had seven works, which is the number Bach originally planned, before settling on six. Bach's title page says they were 'composed for music-lovers, to refresh their spirits', and Forkel claimed that 'This work made in its time a great noise in the musical world. Such excellent compositions for keyboard had never been seen or heard before.' Bach organised the sale carefully, with colleagues in Dresden, Halle, Lüneburg and Brunswick acting as agents for him. The key scheme is unusual: B flat, C minor, A minor, D, G, E minor. (It has been suggested that Bach then completed the key scheme in *Book II* by adding the Italian Concerto in F, and the French Overture specially transposed to B minor.) Performers have experimented with different orders when playing the complete set: András Schiff uses 5, 3, 1, then 2, 4, 6; Murray Perahia 1, 5, 6 and 2, 3, 4.

Early versions of Partitas Nos. 3 and 6 open the Anna Magdalena notebook of 1725, so they had existed for a while. Wolff believes that the four *Clavierübung* books were consciously planned as a set to demonstrate the widest possible variety of keyboard styles, genres, forms and categories, and to set 'new performance standards that match the rigorous principles of compositional organisation'. However the Goldberg Variations, though published as *Clavierübung*, were never described as Part Four of a set.

Partita No. 1 in B flat was made most famous to modern listeners by the pianist Dinu Lipatti; the calm perfection of its opening Praeludium, gently rising through mordents and turns, is unmatched, expanding from a single-octave span on the keyboard at the start to no fewer than four octaves at the end. The Allemande dances through arpeggios but has some darker moments; the Courante is propelled by skipping dance rhythms. The Sarabande is a model of Bach's highly decorated cantilena style; the Minuets contrast two-part writing (with much implied harmony) in the first with a musette-like second. Then comes the famous hand-crossing Gigue, a challenge for players of the day, in which the melody is buried within the texture; Gluck so admired this piece he turned it into an operatic aria in his *Iphigénie en Tauride*.

Partita No. 2 in C minor opens with a Sinfonia in which a massive but brief introduction in dotted rhythms quickly gives way to a two-part Andante with quite a florid melody and then a busy, leaping triple-time final section. The Allemande is in close imitation, while the Courante makes effective use of the resonance of the harpsichord to sustain suspensions and dissonances. The Sarabande is relatively simple two-part writing, and then there is a French-style Rondeau which makes witty use of falling sevenths in sequence. The leaps are extended to tenths in the terrific final Capriccio, whose Bachian energy is continually driven by the bass line's agile jumps. It is certainly 'one of Bach's more unbuttoned keyboard pieces' (Schulenberg), and great fun too.

Partita No. 3 in A minor has an opening Fantasia, evenly worked in two parts, a more florid Allemande and a dotted-rhythm Corrente. The Sarabande is unusual, based on triplets without the usual second-beat emphasis, while the following movement is a skittish Burlesca, maybe after some Italian model, with weird harmonies. Then there is a short Scherzo, and a final Gigue with a really complex chromatically leaping theme which Bach seems to have revised after its publication –

particularly in its second half when it jumps downwards rather than upwards.

Partita No. 4 in D starts with a truly magnificent French Overture at the heart of the collection (each of the *Clavier-übung* volumes has an Ouverture at this point), the flourishes of the opening giving way to an extended 9/8 section whose dancing grace Bach never surpassed and whose almost hundred-bar length has total and perfectly paced logic. The Allemande is heavily decorated, with aching rising sequences in each half; the Courante is driven forward by rising figures which then descend in the second half; and then there is an Aria which uses syncopation and a dominant pedal to motor along. The beautiful Sarabande sounds like a flute or violin arioso; then there is a short Minuet. The final Gigue is again Bach at his most inventive: a surprisingly jerky theme based on arpeggios and followed by a sudden pause and sequences is developed so that very soon all the gaps are filled by relentless activity; the second half, contradicting expectation, starts with a new running theme which is then immediately combined with the original theme, and the movement tumbles to a conclusion over a bass line which excitingly touches the dissonant seventh of the scale on its tumultuous way.

Partita No. 5 in G is more modest, but no less appealing; there was a two-year gap before it was published in May 1730. It opens with a Praeambulum which does indeed seem to walk, while stopping to admire the view every so often, eventually gaining the energy to continue. The Allemande flows in triplets, while the Corrente is a clear and simple two-part invention whose second half is ingeniously semi-inverted. The Sarabande is in very French dotted style, with singing thirds like a trio for oboes and bassoon. The witty Tempo di Minuetta plays with the triplet-time minuet rhythm but imposes a duple-time accent on top of it. There is a Passepied and a final Gigue which develops some of the same effective tricks as that in the Fourth – pauses, sequences, and a new theme at the start of the second half, more rigorously treated here.

Partita No. 6 in E minor is on the very highest level of Bach's inspiration: a towering masterpiece, but unusually sombre. The opening Toccata immediately announces with its block chords and dissonances a serious undertaking, and from its musings emerges a fugue theme in the bass voice of yearning and supplication. The mood is sombre but then the E minor theme suddenly turns to G major, a glimpse of sun among the clouds (there is a similar D major moment in the violins during the Kyrie of the B minor Mass); the sighs of the theme are treated in close, dissonant imitation, and then the opening chords return to interrupt the proceedings and rising chromatic figures drive it up to its emotional conclusion. The Allemande maintains stately reserve amidst all its elaboration, while the Corrente (which also occurs as an alternative movement in a violin sonata) is propelled by nervous syncopated energy. The Air provides straightforward contrast, then the Sarabande is one of the most elaborate Bach ever wrote, dense and unremittingly powerful, with many embellishments. We need a simple two-part Tempo di Gavotta at this point, and the final Gigue is a tour de force of angular counterpoint, with a dotted theme that never loses its awkwardness in the course of its sustained development: a 'strange but compelling movement indeed' (Schulenberg).

♫ *Partitas BWV 825–830, English Suites* Gustav Leonhardt (harpsichord)
Virgin Classics 62379 (4 CDs)
♫ *Partitas BWV 825–830* Trevor Pinnock (harpsichord)
Hänssler Classic 92115 (2 CDs)
♫ *Partitas BWV 825–830* András Schiff (piano)
ECM 476 6991
♫ *Partitas BWV 828, 826, 829* Richard Goode (piano)
Nonesuch 79483-2
♫ *Partitas BWV 825, 829, 830* Murray Perahia (piano)
Sony Classical 88697443612

Clavierübung Book II: **Overture in the French Style**
BWV 831
Italian Concerto BWV 971

Following the success of the *Clavierübung I* in its full publication of 1731, one might have thought Bach would have
followed it up immediately, but a publication of the '48' Book
I, by then complete, would have been too large, too expensive
and also perhaps too impractical for wide sale, owing to its use
of some unusual keys. Instead he waited another four years,
and published in 1735 this shorter second book containing
just two works, the Italian Concerto and the French Overture,
probably with a conscious desire to demonstrate his ability
to capture the cosmopolitan breadth of national styles in his
music. 'A Concerto in the Italian taste and an Overture in
the French Manner, for a Harpsichord with Two Manuals,
Dedicated to the appreciative, for the Pleasure of the Spirit.
Composed by J. S. Bach,' says the title page. The first two
books of the *Clavierübung* seem to be deliberately linked: their
key schemes are complementary, for the F and B minor here
complete the circle of keys started by the Partitas. And for
those of a numerological bent, the Partitas contain forty-one
movements, and this book contains fourteen, expressing both
J. S. BACH and BACH in numbers; add the *Clavierübung Book
III*, whose Trinitarian symbolism is clear in its twenty-seven
movements (three times three times three), and the total
number of movements is eighty-two – or twice forty-one!

It was of the Italian Concerto that Scheibe, a fierce critic of
some aspects of Bach's work, wrote:

> Who is there who will not admit at once that this clavier
> concerto is to be regarded as a perfect model of a well-
> designed solo concerto? At the present time we shall be
> able to name as yet very few or practically no concertos of
> such excellent qualities and such well-designed execution.

The Italian Concerto, familiar to generations of pianists, is
indeed a splendid though not especially adventurous example

of Bach's art as he developed it from Vivaldian models: a bold, driven first movement (which exists in an earlier version on its own), a long eloquent central melody like an endless operatic scene, and then one of Bach's continuously energetic finales, marked Presto, powered by its initial leap and upward scale in the bass. The French Overture, perhaps specially transposed into the awkward key of B minor from a pre-existing and more idiomatic version in C minor in Anna Magdalena's autograph, I have always found less inviting, perhaps because of the angularity of the key. After the French Overture opening (again at the middle of the volume) there are varied dances including pairs of Gavottes, Passepieds and Bourrées, interleaved with a Courante, Sarabande and Gigue, with a final Echo movement making the most the two manuals of the harpsichord.

𝅘𝅥 *French Overture in B minor BWV 831, French Suite BWV 816* Piotr Anderszewski
Harmonia Mundi HMC1951679

𝅘𝅥 *French Overture in B minor BWV 831, Italian Concerto BWV 971, Prelude, Fugue and Allegro BWV 998, Duetti BWV 802–805* Davitt Moroney
Virgin 7592722

𝅘𝅥 *Italian Concerto BWV 971, BWV 590, 596, 973–975, 979, 981* Alexandre Tharaud
Harmonia Mundi HMC901871

𝅘𝅥 *BWV 903 Chromatic Fantasia and Fugue, Italian Concerto, French Overture, Duetti, BWV 802–805, Goldberg Variations, Partitas* Christophe Rousset
Decca 000639402 (4 CDs)

𝅘𝅥 *BWV 903 Chromatic Fantasia and Fugue, Fantasia and Fugue BWV 904, 906, Italian Concerto, BWV 972, 973, 965, 994* Richard Egarr
Harmonia Mundi HMU907329

The Well-tempered Clavier

The Well-tempered Clavier (24 Preludes and Fugues)
  Book I BWV 846–869

The '48' have become so central a part of Western music-making and especially of teaching that it is difficult to recapture the full impact they must have made when new. The pieces were not necessarily conceived as joint preludes and fugues, and indeed the preludes seem to have been evolving for a while before the fugues were joined to them. The origin of the idea for a set in all twenty-four keys seems to have come from J. C. F. Fischer's *Ariadne musica* of 1702, republished in 1715 when Bach may have been beginning to think about this collection. Early versions of some preludes appeared in the book he complied for his son W. F. Bach. It is significant that the versions in W. F. Bach's book are of the preludes on the 'white-note' scale. Presumably the idea of filling in the chromatic notes came later, to create the full sequence of twenty-four, and we can trace the evolution of the preludes from simple arpeggio structures like the famous first in C to fully elaborated ventures like the magnificent multi-sectional E flat prelude.

Bach's inscription to Book One reveals the purpose of the collection: 'For the use and profit of the musical youth desirous of learning and for the pastime of those already skilled in this study.' We know that Bach used the collection to teach, and played it through three times for his pupil Gerber in the 1720s. Schumann said, 'Let the Well-tempered Clavier be your daily bread' – and so it has been for generations. A question remains as to how completely well tempered was the tuning that Bach expected for these pieces. We can safely assume it was not like the totally equal temperament expected from today's keyboards (although even their degree of equal tempering is determined by their tuning methods). The tuning system employed must necessarily have been one that enabled all the keys to sound plausibly harmonious, but not identical. Andreas Werckmeister was the great German organ builder who experimented with different tuning systems in close proximity to Bach, and we can expect the debate about tuning to have taken account of his varied and changing approaches to the subject. Such writers as Mattheson (whom Bach admired) and Johann Kuhnau, his predecessor in Leipzig, were active in the theory and practice of writing for all the keys, just around the 1719 and 1720 dates when Bach begins to conceive his collection. J. C. F. Fischer's *Ariadne musica*, meanwhile, contains twenty preludes and fugues in different keys; Bach's subjects sometimes seem indebted to Fischer, though his working-out is immeasurably superior.

The first Prelude and Fugue in C: is there a more famous piece of classical music? Arranged by Gounod with an added melody as a vocal *Ave Maria*; it is formed from an utterly simple and repetitive pattern like lute music, creating a harmonic sequence that in revision Bach extended and clarified. The fugue is a model of clarity, rhythmically shaped (and refined by Bach when revising it) to allow constant quaver motion, building over stretto entries to a long tonic pedal over which the right hand rises to its highest note (echoing Froberger's famous *Lament for Ferdinand IV*). The Prelude and Fugue in C minor is a driving toccata, clearly an exercise for Wilhelm Friedemann, followed by a perfectly paced fugue of four short phrases that answer each other. Then the Prelude and Fugue in C sharp, with another prelude based around split chords, and a strict fugue subject based on leaping sixths. The Prelude and Fugue in C sharp minor matches a triple-time flowing prelude with an old-style fugue of the type to which Bach returned later, worked with great nobility as if to provide a climax to this first quartet of pieces.

The Prelude and Fugue in D is entirely a running treble over a detached bass (good for practising right-hand finger control), until the very end where a cadence passage (added in the revision) intervenes. The French overture-style fugue was one of the battlegrounds about Bach's double-dotting, going back to the theories of Arnold Dolmetsch: how the notes should be co-ordinated is perhaps less important than the superbly gestural, noble strides of this great concentrated fugue with its chordal finish. The Prelude and Fugue in D minor is another lute-type piece with a bass line that becomes more melodic and then a fugue which plays with inversions and finds a route to a culmination at the end. The Prelude and Fugue in E flat is one of the very grandest in the set, pointing forward to the organ 'St Anne' fugue: it begins with an improvisatory set of flourishes, followed by quiet and logical counterpoint, then the same but overlaid with semi-quaver counterpoint, very thoroughly worked out. The fugue here seems rather an anticlimax, a light sorbet after the main course; but that is not to agree with Busoni who replaced it with the Book Two fugue in this key.

The Prelude in E flat minor is a uniquely expressive sara-bande over arpeggiated chords, which sounds distant and remote, with a long Fugue that could well have been con-ceived in D minor. The Prelude and Fugue in E David Schulenberg feels is 'one of the less imposing pairs', but it is surely a deliberate respite: a flowing pastoral in triplets is followed by a lyrical fugue with a witty pause in the subject. The Prelude and Fugue in E minor has a prelude designed to train the left hand in even motion, though Bach added more counter-melody in the right hand in his revision. The fugue is the only two-voice fugue in the set: it has an active, busy subject which is one of the most chromatic in outline, with a throwaway ending. The Prelude and Fugue in F has a two-part invention prelude in 12/8, while the fugue is one closely related to Fischer's model but with Bach's inexorable logic. The Prelude and Fugue in F minor brings the first half of the book to a close with a flowing prelude in which the bass note of each arpeggio is held to weave an expressive counterpoint. The fugue is a full-scale treatment of a chromatic subject that looks forward to the Kyrie of the B minor Mass.

The Prelude and Fugue in F sharp might have been con-ceived separately, a simple two-part prelude in a tricky key, followed by a fugue in trio-sonata texture which uses repeated notes in such a way as to suggest an adaptation of an early work. The Prelude and Fugue in F sharp minor is based on a finger exercise for fourths provided by Couperin, eloquently developed, and then there is a fugue of intense learned power, slowly unpacking its unusual subject. The Prelude and Fugue in G returns to simple openness with a two-part arpeggio idea, followed by a three-part fugue of deceptive symmetry (bar one has the same rhythm as bar four, bar two the same as bar three). The Prelude and Fugue in G minor has a prelude based on a rocking rhythm and a fugue subject characterised by two semitones with a leap of a sixth in the middle. The Prelude and Fugue in A flat has been often transcribed by the Swingle Singers and others – it derives endless subtlety and variety, as Ledbetter notices, from only ten notes. The four-part fugue, whose subject is based around an arpeggio, is relaxed in style.

The Prelude and Fugue in G sharp minor has a gentle and lilting prelude and then a dense and complex fugue. The Prelude and Fugue in A has a three-part invention over a chromatically falling bass, and a perky triple-time fugue with a detached initial note which causes great fun throughout. The Prelude and Fugue in A minor has caused problems for scholars because of the imbalance of prelude, a skipping invention mainly in two parts, with the vast fugue, which reminds one of those in the violin sonatas which explore every possible nuance of the theme. Ledbetter is unforgiving about 'near-objectionable parallel fifths' and Spitta thought it was based on a very early work; it seems to demand a touch of pedals at the splendidly climactic close. The Prelude and Fugue in B flat starts with a toccata of great brilliance interrupted by chords as in Partita No. 6; it evaporates up to the top of the keyboard – which did not stop Czerny adding a plonking bass note at this point in his edition. The fugue is delightful and harmonious, shaped by a descending sixth and down a tone to make a seventh, and repeated semiquavers which almost lose their way. The Prelude and Fugue in B flat minor is one of the greatest in all the literature, a Passion chorus of great intensity, rising to a huge dissonance before subsiding. The fugue is in strict old style, sober and severe, but very impressive. The Prelude and Fugue in B lifts the tension with a simple dancing prelude, and a lyrically singing fugue. Finally the superb Prelude and Fugue in B minor, which Schulenberg rightly calls a masterpiece. The prelude is a trio sonata over a walking bass which looks forward as far as the Goldbergs in its euphony and logic. Then the fugue, as close as Bach came to the Kyrie of the B minor Mass, unusually with the same marking Largo (which at that time meant quicker than Adagio) with chromatically falling semitones that include all twelve notes of the chromatic scale – surely deliberately – and a despairing shape which is fully developed over a massive seventy-six-bar length, punctuated by passages of easeful falling sequences that bring euphonious balm to the ear; the final entry of the subject in the alto perfectly heralds the close.

Is it one's imagination that what Bach is striving for here, especially with his remarks about a cantabile style, is a fugally melodic idiom, moving away from the sometimes brittle brilliance of the early works to a more inward, vocal style? You could surely argue that Bach found a melodic style here, when the music was under his fingers, more readily than in the vocal idiom of many cantata arias from around the same period.

The Well-tempered Clavier (24 Preludes and Fugues) Book Two BWV 870–93

The second book of the '48' presents something of a puzzle: it was not assembled until much later in Bach's life, between 1739 and 1742, when his preoccupations would appear to have moved on rapidly, as evidenced by the Goldberg Variations and then The Art of Fugue. It was unusual for Bach to do something twice, at least to this extent – perhaps he did not want to waste the huge body of material he had accumulated for teaching purposes; possibly he thought the collection might be published in the wake of the Clavierübung? At any rate, the set survives on separate sheets written out partly by

Anna Magdalena and corrected by her husband, assembled together; it was only copied out and entitled 'The Well-tempered Clavier Book 2' by his pupil Altnickol in 1744. The 'London autograph' of 1740 and after is one of the most precious possessions of the British Library; this has no title.

The preludes in particular have a greater variety and expansiveness than those in Book One, and Schulenberg points out that more are in the two-half structure that points towards the sonata and maybe shows Bach's acquaintance with Scarlatti's sonatas recently published in his *Essercizi*. It is possible to analyse how the collection was built up from the simpler pieces in the basic keys, and gradually added to as the collection was assembled. This is essentially a collection of music from the second half of the 1730s, following the period when Bach was concentrating on assembling his sacred Oratorios, and also working towards the third part of the *Clavierübung* for organ.

The Prelude and Fugue in C is thought to be a late addition to the set: Bach originally seems to have thought of beginning with what is now the C sharp minor Prelude, but maybe its lute style was too close to the C major prelude of Book One. This fine prelude creates an imposing drawing-aside of the curtains with perfect voice-leading and pacing, and the galant fugue in three parts has a strongly profiled subject with a pause that makes for effective development. The Prelude and Fugue in C minor, copied by Anna Magdalena Bach, has a toccata-like two-part prelude, and a majestic fugue in which the subjects appears in augmentation (i.e. at half speed) as well as in stretto (i.e. at close distance). The Prelude and Fugue in C sharp begins with a prelude in two halves that is really a mini-prelude and fugue in itself, though the concluding Allegro is very short; the fugue proper has a bouncy subject whose third voice enters in inversion; the development, which Bach expanded in the final version, is really witty. The Prelude and Fugue in C sharp minor are well matched: a flowing 9/8 prelude leading to a 12/16 fugue which is a Gigue that could have come from the Suites or Partitas, with added contrapuntal sophistication.

The triumphal Prelude and Fugue in D is one of the finest in the set: the leaping fanfares of the prelude have often been rhythmically reduced, but Tovey insists 'if a theme sounds like a trumpet, play it like a trumpet', and the tension is between those fanfares and flowing thirds which he says are 'like a vocal duet'. The contrast between prelude and fugue has been aptly compared with that in the maybe contemporary Cantata 29, a *stile antico* fugue following a demonstrative prelude. The astonishing, wonderful fugue lies perfectly under the hands and yet allows all manner of contrapuntal variety to be drawn from its tiny subject, strettos piled on top of each entry, accumulating tension and crowding the texture with entries right up to the echo of the subject in the final bar: surely one of the finest fugues ever written?

The Prelude and Fugue in D minor starts like a torrent and surely shows evidence of acquaintance with Scarlatti, with hand-crossings and sequences; the companion fugue has busy triplets and a chromatic end to the subject. The Prelude and Fugue in E flat starts with a lovely flowing 9/8 prelude with a pastoral feel and a lute style (like the opening movement of BWV 998) and then has a noble fugue whose sober subject and inexorable development point forward right to the end of Bach's life, and the 'Fuga a 3 soggetti' which is a disputed part of *The Art of Fugue*. (I have always loved the way the fugue subject emerges stealthily from the middle of the texture eighteen bars from the end, which must be deliberately hidden, as it cannot be heard unless you unmusically bang out the first note.) The Prelude and Fugue in D sharp minor, one of the trickiest keys for well-tempering, is a two-part toccata-like prelude and a densely worked fugue which may have been written originally in D minor. The Prelude and Fugue in E comprises an improvisatory prelude almost playing with imitation in the treble, followed by a fugue in the old style. This is closely related to a subject used by J. C. F. Fischer in his *Ariadne musica*, but Bach seems determined to show how many combinations of the subject are possible, while searching for maximum expressiveness; after the complexities, the final cadence has an odd sense of bathos, perhaps because the formula was so often copied in later, lesser music. The Prelude and Fugue in E minor combines a binary-form prelude with a fugue subject whose rhythmic profile is especially varied, triplets, semiquavers and detached crotchets creating quite a jerky structure.

The Prelude and Fugue in F opens with a prelude that builds on sustained sonorities, and could be effective on harpsichord, house organ or a clavichord with sustaining power. (It's difficult to agree with Tovey that they 'sound clearest on the pianoforte'.) You marvel at how Bach combines logical power of development with sudden fantasy and unexpected twists in the harmony. The scherzo-like fugue is much lighter, and the pair do not balance. The Prelude and Fugue in F minor has become famous through the Swingle Singers' gently swung version of the prelude. The fugue, which keeps its entries simple and then develops episodes and cheery sequences between them, is the perfect complement. The Prelude and Fugue in F sharp combines a dotted-rhythm prelude with a quasi-gavotte fugue in three parts that starts halfway through the bar. The Prelude and Fugue in F sharp minor present what Tovey called a 'magnificent stream of lyric melody'. Both are indeed shaped so their subjects could be sung, and the fugue's entry in the tenor, taking a long time to rise above the stave in the soprano, is very expressive. This is an early pair in the London autograph.

The Prelude and Fugue in G opens with perhaps the most extrovert and harmonically simple of the preludes, and the fugue is equally open, based around the outlines of simple chords – there is a whoosh of sudden gestural figuration towards the final statement of the theme. There is then a sudden contrast with the lamenting Prelude and Fugue in G minor: the dotted prelude is like a Passion aria, and the fugue makes unusual use for this late date of seven repeated notes, which are however soon surrounded by eloquent counterpoint; the substantial fugue builds to an unusually chordal climax with several cadence points. The Prelude and Fugue in A flat starts with a very late prelude from around 1741, on a rocking figure which recurs through the piece, followed by a fugue on another beautifully vocal theme which seems to be an earlier piece originally in F. The Prelude and Fugue in G sharp minor is difficult to get the fingers around: the prelude is a binary-form sonata-type movement, while the fugue in 6/8 is slightly more restrained than a gigue, containing little contrast but strongly concentrated material.

The Prelude and Fugue in A, as so often with this key, has a pastoral and rustic feel, with running triplets and a light mood, which is maintained in the fugue; this is relatively short and uncomplex, with rhythmic suspensions that are cleverly used in the working-out. (Some have linked this fugue subject to the chorale *Allein Gott in der Höh sei her*, but this feels like a coincidence.) The Prelude and Fugue in A minor opens with a highly chromatic prelude: the composer Casella pronounced it the disintegration of tonality! Yet the odd thing is that the piece feels very rooted in its key because the lines are directed within the tonal framework. The second half starts as an inversion of the first, beautifully done. The fugue subject has four crotchets, a pause, eight quavers, and a rush of quicker notes, which makes for maximum rhythmic contrast in what follows. David Ledbetter claims this 'can only be intended in the spirit of parody'. The Prelude and Fugue in B flat has the most extended of the sonata-type preludes, flowing down from a height and including some hand-crossing. It's interesting that in revising the fugue Bach improved the contrast of quavers against quavers in the counter-subject, reducing one part to crotchets to create greater contrast; again the mood is serene.

The Prelude and Fugue in B flat minor has a busy prelude which is free of strict counterpoint but wends its way agreeably through a maze of trio-sonata figuration to reach an expressive climax that goes steadily upwards (with the bass on tenor F) and then winds downwards. The big fugue is marked with accents and has a chromatic counter-subject, which is developed over a hundred bars. The Prelude and Fugue in B starts with a brilliant toccata and is followed by a *stile antico* fugue of some severity, which is however expressive because the counter-subject unusually overlaps and jumps above the subject at one point, making the player's voice-leading very important. The final Prelude and Fugue in B minor does not provide the same sense of climax as in Book One, but each is an effective movement: the prelude is a busy two-part invention, and the fugue a light triple-time essay with dancing octaves in the theme, taking Bach's idiom towards the fashionable galant just as the set ends.

∩ *Book I BWV 846–869, Book II BWV 870–893* Kenneth Gilbert
Archiv 474 221 (2 CDs), Archiv 9502(2 CDs)
∩ *Books I and II BWV 846–893* Angela Hewitt
Hyperion 67741 (4 CDs)
∩ *Book I, BWV 846–869* Maurizio Pollini
DG 477 8078 (2 CDs)
∩ *Book I, BWV 846–869* Till Fellner
ECM New Series 1853 (2 CDs)
∩ *Books I and II BWV 846–893* Edwin Fischer
Great Recordings of the Century EMI Classics 91951 (3 CDs)

Goldberg Variations

Aria with variations ('Goldberg Variations') BWV 988

. . . a devil in the person of an elegantly dressed gentleman wearing two waistcoats spotted the Bach variations lying under my hat in the anteroom; he thought they were just any variations . . . and wants me to just sit down and play . . . 'All right then, and be bored to death,' I said to myself, and started to play. By the third number, several women get up and leave, pursued by their mop-headed escorts . . . out of exaggerated politeness the Baron stayed till number 30, guzzling all the punch that Gottlieb had placed on the piano for me. I would happily have stopped there, but

this number 30, the theme, tore me irresistibly onwards.
Suddenly the quarto leaves spread out to a gigantic folio,
on which a thousand imitations and developments of
the theme stood written, which I had to play. The notes
became alive, glimmered and hopped all around me – an
electric fire flowed through the tips of my fingers into
the keys, the spirit, from which it gushed forth, spread
his broad wings over my soul, the whole room was filled
with a thick mist in which the candles burned dim . . .
And thus it came to pass that I was left alone with my
Sebastian Bach . . .

E. T. A. Hoffman, *Kapellmeister Johannes Kreisler*

The Goldberg Variations, one of the unassailable peaks of
Bach's output, stands unchallenged in the eighteenth century
as a set of variations – indeed not until Beethoven's Diabelli
Variations of over eighty years later, to which it is related, is
there any attempt to match its scope, and the work inspired
the romantic imagination of E. T. A. Hoffmann (above) as
well as later transcribers and arrangers. It seems to me the
work in which Bach's ingenuity and technical skill combines
most perfectly with the exuberance and communicativeness
of his writing. It was published, as Gregory Butler has established, in the autumn of 1741 for the Leipzig Christmas Fair,
under the title 'Aria with diverse variations for the harpsichord with 2 manuals' by Balthasar Schmid of Nuremberg.
The story of its origins has given it one of the most famous
titles in music, and yet also one of the most unreliable. Forkel
claimed that the variations were written to a commission by
Count Keyserlinck, and that they were written for Johann
Gottlieb Goldberg, to provide pieces 'which should be of such
a soft and somewhat lively character that he might be a little
cheered up by them in his sleepless nights'. It is certainly true
that Bach visited Keyserlinck in the autumn of 1741, when
the Variations had been completed, and that at some point
they were played by his young pupil Goldberg. But Goldberg
was only thirteen or fourteen at this time; we might imagine

– especially now we have evidence of Bach's phenomenal activity at that exact age – that Bach saw the young boy as a brilliant pupil in his own image. Even so, the variations would have been very demanding: is this a case of wishful thinking becoming myth?

Forkel says of Bach's wish to provide a flexible form for the count that 'this wish could best be fulfilled by means of variations, which he [Bach] had until then considered to be an unrewarding labour on account of the unchanging basic harmonies'. The closest predecessors with separate sections are the *Aria variata* BWV 989 and the questionable Sarabande con Partite BWV 990, but also in a single-movement structure the great organ Passacaglia in C minor and the violin Chaconne. There's another phrase in the story worth pausing on: Keyserlinck's request to Goldberg to 'play me one of my variations'. Were the variations always to be played as a set, or is that a fetish of the modern age? We should be able to choose a few of them to include in recitals (as happens, more often, with extracts from *The Art of Fugue* in concert). The first extracts to appear in England, as it happens, were just two variations which appeared in Sir John Hawkins's *History of Music*, given to him by a traveller from Leipzig. In the canon at the third, there is an untypically chromatic bar near the start of the second half which unmistakably includes the notes B–A–C–H in the texture. Did the composer regard this variation as a particularly personal signature when he gave it to a friend?

The aria appears in the second volume of the Anna Magdalena Book, started in 1725, and its origins have been questioned, but there is no reason not to regard it as Bach's. (John Butt says it was added to the book only after the appearance of the Goldbergs.) The underlying bass theme matches in its first eight bars the theme of Handel's huge Chaconne with sixty-two variations, which it is believed Bach would have known through its Amsterdam and/or London editions in the 1730s, and also the Passacaglia with twenty-eight variations by Gottlieb Muffat from the *Componimenti musicali* (as well as a Ciacona with twelve variations on a shorter bass line by his father Georg Muffat). Another influence on Bach could have been the *Essercizi* of Domenico Scarlatti which appeared in 1739, with their highly original keyboard techniques, and the predecessors of Pachelbel's *Hexachordum Apollinis* of 1699, six sets of variations. The origin of the rising canon sequence could be Fux, and further back, though Bach could not have known this work, there is Ockeghem's *Missa prolationum* which has a similar sequence of canons. Probably more significant is Buxtehude's *Partita la capricciosa*, which also has thirty-two variations and which was based on the theme 'Kraut und Rüben' that appears in Bach's final Quodlibet. Werner Breig has suggested that the work was built up in stages, and that an initial stage perhaps included only eight canons and twenty-four variations. Although it has been claimed that variations could be moved around without loss, they are surely paced to provide a sense of culminating power and force – especially in the second half, where the music takes off after variation 24 in a new way to provide a sense of climax: perhaps this sequence does indeed represent a later layer of the composition.

Symmetry is everywhere evident. The thirty-two-bar structure of the aria, in two sixteen-bar halves, is mirrored by the thirty-two movements of the work, again divided at the mid-point. The canons increase by an interval each time they appear, from the second to the ninth. A cross-symmetry is provided by the French Overture which stands at the beginning of the second half of the variations. (Commentators have pointed out that this links the collection to the other volumes of the *Clavierübung*, but this may be a coincidence.) The two little fugues are 10 and 22, six variations away from the centre. The basic structure, very satisfyingly for the listener, is in groups of three variations of character-piece, study and canon. Whether the publication in 1741 under the title *Clavierübung* was designed consciously to link the volume with the preceding series is doubtful, for it is nowhere described as Book IV, only under its generic title.

*

The Aria unfolds with considerable elaboration over its slowly moving bass line. After the first eight bars the bass line too enters into the conversation, and its second half ends with even quaver movements, creating a sense of anticipation. Variation 1 is a two-part toccata with hand-crossing for a single keyboard; the intensification at the close as the bass line strides upwards is notable. Variation 2 is a trio-sonata texture with free imitation that prefigures the canon but does not attempt one; the bass line achieves greater momentum in the second half. Variation 3 is the canon at the unison, heard a bar apart, running in 12/8 over a bass line that soon joins in the chase. Variation 4 is a sturdy, imitative four-part texture, with the number of bars halved so giving a sense of real concision. Variation 5 is another dazzling toccata, marked for one or two manuals with extensive hand-crossing. Did Bach know Rameau's keyboard writing as well as Scarlatti's? Variation 6 is the canon at the second, over a continuously flowing bass line: the sense of culmination is superbly managed, using the suspensions of the opening to create a passage where the canonic parts overlap each other to create extra tension before the end. Variation 7 was thought of as a siciliano, but is marked in Bach's own copy as a gigue, which adds to its dotted-rhythm vitality. Variation 8 flows, scarcely taking breath; it is in two parts, with every semiquaver filled. Variation 9 is the canon at the third, one of the most expressive, which you can hear for two oboes and bassoon; note the unusual twist and intensification in the third bar of the second half, where B–A–C–H can be heard in the middle of the texture. Variation 10 is a cheerful fughetta, *alla breve*: its logic is inexorable as there is an entry every four bars, but the second half adds a lovely suspension to highlight the final entry and turn it to a cadence. Variation 11 is a flowing two-part triple-time invention, where the overlapping parts are best heard on two manuals. Variation 12 is the canon at the fourth, in triple time, trying something new because the answer is the mirror of the subject. Variation 13 is a lyrical decorated aria in the mould of Bach's most gracious writing for flute. Variation 14 springs another virtuoso trick: a whirl with trills, mordents which dance up and down the keyboard, and a headlong rush towards the end of each half. Variation 15, the last of the first half, is a beautifully intricate canon at the fifth: for the first time the music moves into the minor and the subject and answer are in inversion. The second half ingeniously takes the theme into the bass, so the canonic parts duet with new syncopated material, before the final evaporation where the answering part rises to a high D and stops.

Variation 16 is the magnificent French Overture, mirroring those in his orchestral suites, with a triple-time fast section. Variation 17 is another *moto perpetuo* for the two manuals, a two-part invention full of thirds and sixths, less harmonically varied than other movements. Variation 18, the canon at the sixth, is an imperious, totally confident movement which must be among the most supremely logical pieces of music ever written, with the strict imitation to the half-bar providing ideal impetus and a sense of climax. Variation 19 is in 3/8, a sort of pastoral, perhaps a gentle minuet, perhaps more energetic than that. Variation 20 takes virtuosic hand-crossing to a new level, with bounding figures that jump all over the keyboard, making it hard to disentangle one's fingers even on two manuals. Variation 21 is the very expressive canon at the seventh, in the minor and for the first time over a chromatic version of the bass line, which also then changes the canon. Variation 22 reverts to the original bass line, and is the second fugal movement, six away from the centre, an *alla breve* that is equally logical and well paced. Variation 23 dances down the keyboards and then works its way up again; alternating thirds and sixths in the second half make this a witty and exuberant variation. Variation 24 is the canon at the octave, this time two bars apart, dancing in 9/8 time.

Then comes the extraordinary Variation 25, a G minor aria of such intensity that it appears to come out of nowhere like a lost Passion aria, and raises the whole set onto a new level of feeling. The aria is elaborate, and the two-part accompaniment worked out in detail. As if the music has been suddenly liberated, Variation 26 races away with new-found freedom, with a dual time signature: 18/16 for the running semiquavers in groups of sixes, and 3/4 for the chords beneath that sound the harmonies; halfway through each section the time signatures (and the musical material) change hands. Variation 27 is the innocent canon at the ninth which needs no support at all, just the two voices pushing each other along. Variation 28 ushers in a new level of virtuosic power in the writing with trilling inner parts, leaping octaves and dazzling display; the events of the second half are the same, but ingeniously in a different order. Variation 29, with its battering block chords and toccata-like triplets, creates a phenomenal sense of climax and excitement. The second half cascades down the keyboard and ends with the block chords again. Variation 30 – then, when we might expect a canon, at the tenth, we get instead a Quodlibet, one of the most humane, moving and wistful movements Bach ever wrote: just at the point when his music has driven wildly into the future, creating new worlds which others would have to explore, he pulls back and brings together some old folksongs, tying the work back to his family, to history and tradition, with an earthy sense of reality and warmth. It is as effective as it is unexpected. Then the Aria returns and we are back where we started: or perhaps not, for in the potential of that innocent sequence a whole new world has been uncovered.

Ralph Kirkpatrick's pioneering edition of the Goldberg Variations of 1938 includes this apt quotation from Sir Thomas Browne's *Religio medici* of 1643: 'There is something in it of Divinity more than the ear discovers; it is an Hieroglyphical and shadowed lesson of the whole World, and creatures of God . . . it is a sensible fit of that harmony which intellectually sounds in the ears of God.'

🎧 *Goldberg Variations* András Schiff (piano)
ECM 000106302
🎧 *Goldberg Variations* Gustav Leonhardt (harpsichord)
DHM 77149

♩ *Goldberg Variations* Glenn Gould (piano)
Sony 52594 (1955 mono) Sony 37779 (1981 stereo)
Released together on *A State of Wonder* SM3K 87703
♩ *Goldberg Variations* Tatiana Nikolayeva (piano)
Hyperion CDA66589
♩ *Goldberg Variations* Trevor Pinnock (harpsichord)
Archiv 415 130-2
♩ *Goldberg Variations* Christophe Rousset (harpsichord)
Decca 475 7080

Canons

Canon a 4 perpetuus BWV 1073
Canon a 4 BWV 1074
Canon a 2 perpetuus BWV 1075
Canon super fa mi a 7 BWV 1078
Canon Concordia discors BWV 1086
Canon trias harmonica BWV 1072
Canon triplex BWV 1076
Canone doppio sopr'il soggetto BWV 1077
14 Verschiedene Canones BWV 1087

Throughout his life Bach, as a master of counterpoint, was fascinated by the challenge of the canon, the strictest form of musical imitation. We may regard this as a dry-as-dust preoccupation, but for Bach it demonstrated the underlying philosophy of his art. Puzzle canons (that's to say those written without a solution, so that the recipient has to work it out) were very familiar in Bach's time, and formed a common genre in dedications and autograph books. The earliest one we have dated is BWV 1073 from 2 August 1713, written in Weimar for an unknown recipient, which is a perpetual Canon in four voices. It's written as one melody line with four different clefs and four entry points indicated, so you have to work out the pitches and intervals and take it from there; it actually works starting from the bass and working up the parts. A similar conceit underlies the Canon a 4 BWV 1074 for Ludwig Friedrich Houdemann written in Leipzig in 1727 with four clefs and a single line, but this one starts with the soprano and works down at close imitation. The perpetual Canon in two parts from Leipzig 10 January 1734 BWV 1075 is simpler, more like what we would call a canon, with the second voice entering at the same pitch as the first.

Much more elaborate, from the end of the period when Bach was increasingly concerned with these devices and was using them in his music, is BWV 1078 dated 1 March 1749, which survives only in a copy by Kirnberger. Over a repeating ground bass of the notes F–A–B (i.e. B flat)–E, which with the letter 'R' for 'repetatur' (meaning repeated) spells the name of the dedicatee (perhaps Benjamin Faber who was godparent to Altnickol's son in 1749), a seven-part canon unfolds 'super Fa Mi post Tempus Musicum'. The inscription to this canon also clearly shows Bach playing with the letters of his name in the inscription Bonae Artis Cultorem Habeas – 'you have someone who cultivates good art'. Indeed. The Canon 'Concordia discors' (which had no BWV number when first added to the *NBA*, but is now BWV 1086) is a two-part canon which works by inversion, written out after Bach's death on 16 March 1778 in the hand of Bach's pupil J. G. Müthel. (There is also a missing canon for which only the inscription survives in Bach's hand, dated 2 November 1725.)

Christoph Wolff devotes one of the most penetrating and original passages in his great Bach biography to the tiny 'Canon trias harmonica' BWV 1072, a piece scarcely noted by scholars, which was recorded in Marpurg's *Abhandlung von der Fuge* of 1754. Wolff's discussion shows how this incredibly simple two-bar theme, when realised for two choirs and eight voices, demonstrates the basis of Bach's intersecting horizontal and vertical contrapuntal art. 'In his modest canon, Bach subjects the concepts of space and time and their complex interrelationship (a main philosophical theme of the late seventeenth and early eighteenth centuries) to a treatment that actually captures both natural phenomena in a single musical event. Surprisingly, this little canon turns out to offer a profound lesson in music theory, composition, philosophy, theology and above all in the unity of knowledge . . . a true mirror of the well-ordered universe.' Its effect is like sound suspended in timeless space: a forerunner of minimalist music.

Quite an exciting shock was caused in the musical world when Bach's own copy of the Goldberg Variations was identified in Strasbourg in 1974. Not only did this copy contain corrections to the printed edition of the work, which was known since

Forkel had mentioned that Bach 'had carefully corrected his copy', but it included a whole new page at the back, of fourteen varied canons on a shortened eight-note version of the bass line of the work. (I was working for the English Bach Festival at the time of the discovery, and we were able to put on the first performance in the UK of the newly discovered set with the English Concert in May 1976.) Two of these canons were already known: No. 11 is BWV 1077, 'Canone doppio sopr' il soggetto', the canon written out on 15 October 1747 'for Fulde', a theology student in Leipzig, and No. 13, BWV 1076 is the famous 'Canon triplex' which Bach holds in his portrait by Elias Haussmann. The whole set has a distinctly theoretical aspect, and it is very likely that there was a link to Lorenz Christoph Mizler's Societät der Musikalischen Wissenschaften and its periodical *Neu-eröffnete musikalische Bibliothek*, perhaps for presentation to the society. But they were overtaken by the more practical demonstration of contrapuntal technique in the Canonic variations on 'Vom Himmel hoch' for organ. They are best characterised by Marpurg, who said that Bach was not interested in dry, wooden and pedantic products of some modern contrapuntists as he was 'a composer who (so to speak) shook all kinds of paper intricacies out of his sleeve, any one of which would make many a man sweat for days, and most likely in vain'. The early ones are simple and theoretical, but have been worked into a sequence in several recordings: then follow some more expressive one: No. 12, a canon duplex using the theme in three different tempi, and No. 14, a four-part canon in augmentation and diminution. There is a clear symbolism in the fact that there are fourteen canons, moreover arranged 4–1–4–1–4 to draw in the reference to J. S. BACH as well as BACH. In the canonic parts of the Canon triplex there are also fourteen notes, and keen numerologists have spotted fourteen buttons on Bach's coat in the portrait – an allusion which can be confirmed with reference to the cover of this book . . .

Ω *BWV 1072–1078, 1086, 1087, The Musical Offering*
Behringer, von der Goltz, Kaiser, Müllejans
Hänssler 92.133

The Musical Offering BWV 1079

Not many exciting things happened to Bach during his long life. Compare Mozart, taken around Europe from his earliest age to meet kings and emperors, demonstrating his art for money. Bach worked within a narrow geographical area for a small number of employers, and apart from his youthful journey to encounter Buxtehude, did not travel widely. But one of the most memorable encounters of his life came towards the very end, in March 1747, when he visited Frederick the Great. This story was retold recently as the subject of an entire book, *Evening in the Palace of Reason* by James Gaines, which places the visit in its cultural and personal context. It is worth quoting the original description of this visit from the contemporary press, since it is an immediate report not coloured by the legends of time:

> We hear from Potsdam that last Sunday the famous
> Capellmeister from Leipzig, Herr Bach, arrived with the
> intention to have the pleasure of hearing the excellent
> Royal music there. In the evening, His Majesty was
> informed that Bach had arrived in Potsdam and was
> waiting in His Majesty's antechamber for His Majesty's
> most gracious permission to listen to the music. His
> August self immediately gave order that Bach be
> admitted, and went, at his entrance, to the so-called
> Forte e Piano, condescending also to play in His Most
> August Person and without any preparation, a theme
> for Capellmeister Bach, which he should execute in a
> fugue. This was done so happily by the aforementioned
> Capellmeister that not only His Majesty was pleased to
> show his satisfaction therat, but also all those present
> were seized with astonishment. Mr Bach found the
> theme propounded to him so exceedingly beautiful that
> he intends to set it down on paper as a regular fugue and
> have it engraved on copper.

He was accompanied by his son Wilhelm Friedemann, who amplified the account for Forkel, and then went to Berlin to visit his other son, C. P. E. Bach, who showed him the new opera house in Unter den Linden. Once back in Leipzig, with a verve we recall from the Brandenburg Concertos, he immediately started work on *The Musical Offering*, which was published in Leipzig barely two months later. As a quite recently discovered newspaper advert in Leipzig put it: 'The elaboration consists of 1. two fugues, one with three and one with six obbligato parts 2. a sonata for transverse flute, violin and continuo and 3. diverse canons, among which is a fuga canonica.' Endless scholarly ink has been spilled on the correct order, meaning and purpose of *The Musical Offering*; but now we have escaped from the prejudice that this is just 'paper music' of little value for the performer, and from the earlier judgement of Spitta and others that the set was a jumble which had no logic or uniformity. (He called it 'a strange conglomeration of pieces, lacking not only internal connection but external uniformity'.) It is actually completely logical, and for the listener the work makes a direct appeal and is not even very controversial in its form. It is all playable by quite a small ensemble of five people, and the confusing layout of the print seems to derive from the fact that some pieces are for keyboard, others for instrumental ensemble. Really it is a musical tool kit, and you can assemble it in various ways: however you order them, the three groups of movements mentioned in the advertisement above are the essence of the work. You can play the Ricercars, the Trio Sonata and then all the Canons, but that gives too little sense of progression and climax. Most practical versions (starting with the edition by that great Bach scholar Hans T. David) split the canons around the central trio sonata, placing the first Ricercar a 3 at the start, and the great six-part Ricercar at the end. The Ricercar is announced with an acrostic:

Regis
Iussu
Cantio
Et
Reliqua
Canonica
Arte
Resoluta

which means 'the music asked for by the king, and the rest worked out in canonic art'.

The first Ricercar must be the nearest to that which Bach improvised on the piano at the court of Frederick the Great, and indeed its florid style is in the most up-to-date style that Bach managed, with sighing thirds and expressive chromatic moments. Bach was surely attempting here something particularly suited to Silbermann's fortepiano and its idiom. The second Ricercar, printed next but most appropriately played at the close of the collection, is an astonishing demonstration of old-style counterpoint echoing such works as the G major Fantasia BWV 572. But it has an expressive grandeur which makes it an exceptional event in Bach's output. This six-part Ricercar stands alongside the Credo of the B minor Mass as the culmination of one whole strand of Bach's art: in this case the keyboard fugue, realised with ultimate richness and skill. C. P. E. Bach said it was his father's proudest boast that he could write a fugue in six parts playable by one player: this is it, and Bach's autograph manuscript is one of the beautiful documents to have survived, showing as much about Bach the musician as we know correspondingly little about Bach the man.

The trio sonata is also an elaborate essay in the galant style: rather more tricky to play, one might guess, than the King would be comfortable with. The opening Largo is especially expressive, with drooping figures, while the first Allegro is a sparkling movement still in galant mode with many trills and flourishes, which suddenly makes room after forty-six bars of development for the royal theme to enter in the bass. It takes even longer, 118 bars, for the theme to be allowed onto the violin; the flute only gets the theme in the home key after a pause in the 161st bar! Back in the bass the royal theme is reinforced before the end. Then the central Andante, mostly in thirds and full of forte–piano contrasts (Kirnberger provided an interestingly full realisation of the continuo part for this movement), and the last Allegro in 6/8, based on a variant of the royal theme but not quoting it directly.

The canons, 'canones diversi super Thema Regium', grouped here together for ease, are more expressive and effective variants on the types explored in the Goldberg canons:

1 In two parts, cancrizans (i.e. backwards).
2 For two violins at the same pitch over the theme.
3 In contrary motion under the theme in the treble.
4 By augmentation in contrary motion, that is two tempi sounding at once; this is headed 'Notulis crescentibus crescat Fortuna Regis' (may the king's fortune augment like the augmented notes).
5 Perhaps the most ingenious of this group: a canon that rises 'per tonos' a tone higher each time, marked 'Ascendentque Modulatione ascendat Gloria Regis' – obsequiously, Bach observes that as the modulations rise so does the glory of the king.
6 Fuga canonica in Epidiapente, featuring the royal theme a fifth apart over a new bass line.
7 The 'Canon perpetuus super Thema Regium' places the royal theme in the middle of the texture, with a dotted descending theme treated in canon above and below it – incredibly clever and effective.
8 Canon perpetuus for flute and violin with continuo.

Finally two canons headed 'Quaerendo invenietis'. Seek and ye shall find, which like a few of the instructions here has theological overtones. 9 is a canon a 2, inverted, and 10 a canon a 4, which given that it has three equal treble parts and a bass line, seems as if it should be played by four instruments – remarkably impressive in effect.

Although the whole set could be theoretically played by three players, harpsichord, violin and flute (if the keyboard took two parts of the four, for instance in canon 10) – and that is what the *NBA* puristically suggests – it would be wrong to exclude the cello, and sensible to give some of the material to a second violin, which is required in canon 2, making a coherent group of five players for the whole work. Of course, many have wanted to orchestrate the piece further. The six-part Ricercar is often heard on massed strings or string ensemble; and it prompted one of the greatest Bach orchestrations of all, the forensic dissection by Webern in which the lines are shared between orchestral solo instruments, which manages to be both completely transparent and deeply expressive at the same time. Inspired by that, Paul Dessau orchestrated five of the canons for East German Radio in 1972.

☊ *BWV 1079* Le Concert des Nations/Savall
Alia Vox AV 9817
☊ *BWV 1079* Ensemble Sonnerie/Huggett
Virgin Classics 545139
☊ *BWV 1079, 1072–1078, 1086, 1087* Behringer, von der
Goltz, Kaiser, Müllejans
Hänssler 92.133
☊ *BWV 1079* Moroney, See, Holloway, ter Linden, Cook
Harmonia Mundi France 90260
☊ *BWV 1079, 1031, 1035* Hazelzet/Musica Antiqua
Cologne/Goebel
DG Eloquence 469680

The Art of Fugue BWV 1080

> I often imagine him in the year of his death, in the exact
> middle of the eighteenth century, bending with clouding
> eyes over *The Art of Fugue*, a composition whose aesthetic
> orientation represents the most archaic tendency in Bach's
> oeuvre (which contains many orientations), a tendency
> alien to its time, which had already turned completely
> away from polyphony toward a simple, even simplistic,
> style that often verged on frivolity or laziness.
>
> Milan Kundera, *Testaments Betrayed*

Some of the greatest achievements in music occur late in the
life of particular forms. Just as these forms might be about
to become extinct, composers find in them new possibilities
and new depths. The viol consorts of Purcell, the English
madrigal, the Elgar symphonies are all part of this rich tradition. So too is Bach's collection *The Art of Fugue*, written just
as the tide of baroque counterpoint was about to be swept
away by new galant and rococo classicism. Bach demonstrated
for anyone with eyes to see and ears to hear the immense rich
musical possibilities of fugal form, just as it was becoming
unfashionable. But he did so in a form that caused posterity
endless trouble.

The Musical Offering, published in 1747, has caused
speculation and uncertainty to generations of Bach scholars,
yet it was published under Bach's guidance and during
his lifetime. The case of *The Art of Fugue* is even more
problematical, because the first publication of the work took
place in 1751 only after Bach's death, and the origination
of the work is surrounded by myth. The belief that it is
incomplete has placed it in the same category as such works
as Mozart's Requiem, or Elgar's Third Symphony, around
which argument and discussion have raged. But if one
sets aside the complications, the result is one of the most

profound and significant works in musical history, which makes a direct appeal to audiences prepared to engage with its complexities. Donald Tovey wrote an unrivalled listener's guide whose object was 'to direct the listener's attention to what is immediately enjoyable, whether on first listening or intimate acquaintance' – a noble aim.

It used to be thought that compiling *The Art of Fugue* was the last thing that Bach did, but recent research has almost completely overturned that notion. The studies of Bach's handwriting in his last decade have shown conclusively that the work of composing and compiling the first version of *The Art of Fugue* was complete by around 1742, shortly after the publication of the Goldberg Variations. That manuscript does not have the title *Art of Fugue* (which was however first written on it by his trusted son-in-law Altnickol, so it may well represent Bach's intentions). So the work greatly pre-dates *The Musical Offering* of 1747, of which it had been thought a successor. However it is now clear that the autograph manuscript and the published edition of 1751 present two different strands of the work, which have to be reconciled in making decisions about performance. In the autograph manuscript there are, perhaps not coincidentally, fourteen pieces, twelve fugues and two canons. These are evidently fair copies of previously existing fugues, written on paper from around the same time as the Peasant Cantata, 1742. Then there are some supplementary sheets whose purpose is doubtless related to the publication of the work, but whose function is not clear. On these Bach's handwriting is much later than in the body of the autograph, and it is here that an element of incompleteness enters the picture.

For the preparation of the print it seems that Bach revised his old fugues (adding new conclusions to the first three, for instance) and prepared some new pieces, one of which was inserted as Contrapunctus 4 and is an especially important and innovative work. Then there were two extra canons (which might naturally have resulted from work on that special form during the 1740s). He reshaped the order of the work creating a five-part introduction to the art of the fugue: simple fugues, counter-fugues, multiple-theme fugues, mirror fugues and canons, as Wolff says 'remarkably predating any theoretical textbook on the subject'.

Finally there are two controversial pieces whose links with the remainder of the work are not clear, but were published in the print. The first is headed 'Fuga a 3 soggetti' and is the famous fugue where Bach introduces his own name as a subject, and breaks off soon afterwards. C. P. E. Bach wrote later on the manuscript: 'NB while working on this fugue, in which the name BACH appears in the countersubject, the author died.' The fugue does not actually contain the *Art of Fugue* theme, but it has been shown, starting with Nottebohm in the nineteenth century, that the theme can be combined with the three presented, and the assumption has been that this was presumably what Bach was working towards. The second is the so-called 'deathbed chorale' with the text 'Wenn wir in höchsten Nöten sein' – a revised version of BWV 668.

The form of the work can therefore be summarised most clearly by taking the order of the published print on the left, with the numbering in the earlier autograph collection on the right; this does not exactly tally with the movement numbers in the original BWV, though the Kleine Ausgabe adopts the numbering below:

Print		Autograph
1	Contrapunctus 1	1
2	Contrapunctus 2	3
3	Contrapunctus 3	2
4	Contrapunctus 4	–
5	Contrapunctus 5	4
6	Contrapunctus 6	7
7	Contrapunctus 7	8
8	Contrapunctus 8	10
9	Contrapunctus 9	5

10	Contrapunctus 10	–
11	Contrapunctus 11	11
12a	Contrapunctus inversus a 4	12a
12b	Contrapunctus inversus a 4	12b
13a	Contrapunctus inversus a 3	13
13b	Contrapunctus a 3	14
14	Contrapunctus a 4	6*
15	Canon per augmentation	(15)**
16	Canon alla Ottava	9
17	Canon alla decima	–
18	Canon alla duodecima	–
19/1	Fuga (inversa) a 2 clav	–***
19/2	Alio modo fuga a 2 clav	–***
20	Fuga a 3 soggetti	–***
21	Wenn wir in höchsten Nöten sein	–

*   actually an early version of 10 included in the print by mistake
**   added later to the autograph at an intermediate stage
*** also included in the manuscript additions to the autograph

Taking each group in turn, the wealth of demonstration of fugal techniques is quite unparalleled; the fundamental key of D minor gives a Dorian modal feel to the whole collection.

1 A sober presentation of the theme, which Bach revised with dramatic pauses at the end.
2 The theme moves to the bass with a dotted counter-subject.
3 The theme is inverted, already making it more expressive, with a chromatic counter-subject.
4 This remarkable fugue, added at the end of Bach's life, has what Tovey called a new idea very late in the life of the fugue: allowing the subject to modulate and so acquire greater harmonic freedom. Wolff has convincingly pointed out the very close similarity of this new technique to the 'Et incarnatus',

the last movement that Bach added to the Credo of the B minor Mass.

5 Now the theme is varied with a dotted rhythm and treated in inversion, the final bars adding more voices. 5–7 are all counter-fugues where the subject is answered by its inversion.

6 'In Stylo Francese' refers to the ceremonial dotted rhythms; this is a diminution fugue in which the subject is answered by the inverted subject at double the speed, which is then answered by the subject at the same speed; this incredible combination is developed over eighty bars with stretti at varying intervals, normal and double and even treble.

7 'Per Augmentationem et Diminutionem': in parallel with the last fugue, this starts with the quicker subject and is answered in inversion by it at half speed, followed by the inversion at the quicker speed; the expressiveness and beauty with which this is developed through the various stretti is remarkable.

8 A three-part triple fugue in which new themes appear. The first has a chromatic twist that leads to a new counter-subject recalling the 'crucify' choruses from the Passions; after a dramatic flourish in the middle the main theme is heard inverted, anticipating the way it will be heard in 11, with which it is linked. This is a passionate and powerful fugue.

9 By contrast this is an enormously enjoyable double fugue made popular by the Swingle Singers. Scuttering scales develop their counterpoint for thirty-four bars until the main theme is magically planted on top of the texture, and the cheerful sequences continue to alternate with the theme through 130 bars of blissful counterpoint.

10 'Alla decima' is a complex four-part double fugue, introducing a new theme with pauses, combined with a version of the main theme and its inversion, which are then ingeniously combined, and the main theme in the bass ends the fugue.

11 This is a four-part triple fugue with a version of the theme already used in 8, with a chromatic counter-subject. In this massive fugue of 184 bars Bach unusually signals some structural points, especially where the chromatic 'crucify' line

gets going, and tries very many different combinations of the themes, built up with extreme intensity over the following passages and unrelentingly sustained to the end.

12 The pair of Contrapuncti rectus and inversus bring a new variety through their use of triple time; the second is the direct mirror of the first, as can easily be heard by the little flourish in the bass at the end of the first, echoed by the same flourish inverted in the treble at the end of the second.

13 Another pair which does the same with a leaping theme with triplets.

Omitting *14* which was added by mistake (BWV relegates this and calls it 10a, thus changing its numbers for the following pieces) . . .

15 This begins the sequence of canons – it's a rather unattractive piece, awkwardly cast, by augmentation in contrary motion and called 'in Hypodiatesseron'.

16 A canon at the octave, in a dancing 9/16 in a style not unfamiliar from the Partitas and Goldbergs, but breathtakingly assured.

17 The Canon alla decima 'Contrapuncto alla Terza' is a two-part canon a third (or actually a tenth) apart, whose pace gradually increases so that one is dazzled by the command it shows. At the end the player is allowed a little cadenza.

18 The Canon alla Duodecima 'in Contrapuncto alla Quinta', which has a long eight-bar theme before the answer enters at an octave and a fifth distance. To celebrate the arrival home there are a couple of bars marked Finale to add at the end.

19 Two fugues which require two keyboards in rectus and inversus, arrangements of the three-part mirror fugues of No. 13.

20 Then we come to the incomplete fugue included at the end of the original print. It is a serene and beautiful piece, but does it belong here? The arguments have been long and inconclusive: Spitta believed that it had no place because it did not use the *Art of Fugue* theme, and purist performers such as Gustav Leonhardt have supported that view, excluding it from their performances and recordings. However, since it was demonstrated by Nottebohm and others that the theme would fit with the three themes used here it has usually been played, and many people have completed it, from Donald Tovey to Davitt Moroney in his excellent practical keyboard edition. In a bold hypothesis, Wolff famously argued that the completion of the fugue must have been written but lost, because Bach would have had to have worked it out before writing the earlier sections.

However, the latest twist in this fascinating saga is the essay by Gregory Butler in *About Bach* (ironically a tribute book to Wolff). He draws attention to the little-noticed comment on the back of this fugue – 'und einen anderen Grund Plan' (another ground plan) – and suggests that it formed part of some *other* plan, arguing quite forcibly that 'there is not a shred of evidence that this work belongs in the collection'. It is not based on the *Art of Fugue* theme, it is written in key-board score unlike the other fugues and the title was 'fuga' rather than Contrapunctus. This is a revolutionary turning of the tables. It implies that Bach at the very end of his life was still not content with what he had achieved and was straining towards yet another creation, which was destined to remain unfulfilled.

Yet should this actually lead us not to perform the fugue in this context? For everyone who has heard it, this incomplete music touches a vein of serenity, moving beyond technique, that pushes it further than the rest of *The Art of Fugue*; and how are we then to experience it? In the confusion that followed Bach's death, with his sons and pupils trying to come to terms with and understand his legacy, this great piece formed part of their understanding, as did the 'deathbed chorale'. In performance it should surely not be excluded: even if it is not part of the concept of *The Art of Fugue*, writing the 'Fuga a 3 soggetti' was one of the last things that Bach did, and with it he planned 'another ground plan' that was to be yet another demonstration of his art, one that remained incomplete on his death. The fullest way we can associate ourselves with the dilemmas of Bach's sons and heirs is to include in performance the incomplete fugue which introduces the theme B–A–C–H. We could equally include the final chorale arrangement in which, unmistakably, by means of his final revision Bach signed his own name.

The Art of Fugue has inspired many different orchestrations and versions over the years since it began to be revived, but performance on a single keyboard, whether harpsichord or organ, is increasingly preferred. C. P. E. Bach emphasised that 'everything has been arranged for use at the harpsichord or organ'. However a string quartet (which Tovey preferred, to demonstrate the contrapuntal lines) is perfectly possible. Extracts from the work have been interleaved in performance with music by Kurtág, Stravinsky and others. It has been arranged for brass ensemble, saxophone quartet, even a viol consort. The version for full orchestra by Fritz Stiedry, a conductor who gave some Schoenberg premieres, was made in 1941 and had become established, but now sounds rather dated. Solo keyboard performances allow all the detail of Bach's remarkable inspiration to be heard.

♉ *BWV 1080* Fretwork
Harmonia Mundi 2907296
♉ *BWV 1080, 1044, 1052, 1057, 1054* Concerto Italiano/ Alessandrini
Naïve 20011
♉ *BWV 1080* Hesperion XX/Jordi Savall
Alia Vox AV 9818
♉ *BWV 1080* Davitt Moroney (harpsichord)
HMC 2901169-70
♉ *BWV 1080* Pierre-Laurent Aimard (piano)
DG 001076502
♉ *BWV 1080 arr. Fritz Stiedry* Radio Symphony Orchestra Berlin/Zender
Koch CD 311 032 H1

I am in the front row of the balcony. A murmur fills the
hall. I look down on the heads of the crowd below . . .
She enters, looks at them and smiles. For a moment,
for more than just a moment, she casts her eyes around,
troubled, searching, then sits down at the piano.

She plays without the music, her eyes sometimes on
her hands, sometimes closed. What she hears, what she
imagines I do not know. There is no forced gravitas in her
playing. It is a beauty beyond imagining – clear, lovely,
inexorable, phrase across phrase, phrase echoing phrase,
the incomplete, the unending 'Art of Fugue'. It is an equal
music . . . .

Vikram Seth, *An Equal Music*

As the materials of the BACH theme were suddenly
broken off by the last note of Bach's overpowering quad-
ruple fugue, the celestially gentle final chorale entered to
usher us in to the realm of eternity. Audience members
stood transfixed, while they listened to the pulsating
sounds of painful sadness that hovered over them. There
was no sound of applause. Only a foreboding sense of
mysticism prevailed, which groped its way, in the shadow
of death, after the secretive form of the dead master . . .

Description of *The Art of Fugue* at the 1928 Bach
Festival in Kassel

Further reading

Books about Bach are, to adapt the German pun on his name, an ocean rather than a brook. Scholarly work shows no signs of abating, and it is currently moving into new areas of contextual and political studies, alongside the source studies and musical analysis that have been the recent favoured subjects. The volumes recommended here are reasonably up to date and have all provided material for this book. They are all in English: those with German may wish to tackle the detailed introductions and critical commentaries to the *Neue Bach Ausgabe* (*NBA*), and read the documents relating to Bach in *Bach-Dokumente* published between 1963 and 1972. However, there is a fine English selection in *The New Bach Reader* (see below), and Volume 4, of pictorial documents, has a good English translation. Research about Bach is published annually in German in the *Bach-Jahrbuch*. The new catalogue called *The Bach Compendium*, edited by Christoph Wolff and Hans-Joachim Schulze, is still in progress: meanwhile the most useful catalogue remains the 'Kleine Ausgabe' of Schmieder's BWV catalogue, published in 1988, and the updated summary of *The New Grove* work-list in *Grove Music Online*, now part of *Oxford Music Online*.

GUIDES

Oxford Composer Companions: J. S. Bach, ed. Malcolm Boyd (OUP, 1999)
The most useful single-volume multi-entry guide to all Bach's output, arranged alphabetically, with encyclopaedic coverage of his works: there is no narrative, but each major piece or collection is covered and (for example) every cantata has its own separate entry by writers including Nicholas Anderson. It is currently out of print, but indispensable.

The New Grove Bach Family, ed. Stanley Sadie, Christoph
Wolff and others (Macmillan, 1983)
A model example of Grove's major biographies, with a fine
narrative from several hands including the neglected English
scholar Walter Emery, lucid and well judged, plus coverage by
Christoph Wolff and others of the main members of the Bach
family. However, the work-list especially is now showing its
age, and needs to be compared with the updated version in
Oxford Music Online.

*The New Bach Reader: A Life of Johann Sebastian Bach in Letters
and Documents*, ed. Hans T. David and Arthur Mendel,
revised and expanded by Christoph Wolff (Norton, 1998)
This seminal collection of documents first appeared in 1945,
and is established as a classic in its field. Much of its original
text remains in this new version, which also adds over a hundred documents that have come to light since. It brings Bach
directly to life as no other book.

The Cambridge Companion to Bach, ed. John Butt (CUP, 1997)
This is the most up-to-date survey of current thinking on
Bach from many authors, with important pieces by Ulrich
Siegele on the politics, Stephen A. Crist on the seventeenth-
century background to Bach's early works, and Robin Leaver
on the liturgical context. The sections on reception history
are disappointing, and some repertories, especially the cantatas and motets, are under-represented, but an important
book.

The Worlds of Johann Sebastian Bach, ed. Raymond Erickson
(Amadeus, 2009)
The newest entrant on the Bach scene is this attractively
presented and well-illustrated book of varied essays, including such reliable writers as Wolff, Leaver and Marshall; the
volume is good on political background, but that outstanding scholar Hans-Joachim Schulze is sadly intolerant of Bach
interpretation today.

An Introduction to Bach Studies, Daniel R Melamed and
Michael Marissen (OUP, 1998)
As the authors rightly say, 'a small book about a big subject',
but an ideal guide to further reading on Bach and where to
find key scholarly articles on major topics.

Bilddokumente zur Lebensgeschichte Johann Sebastian Bachs
(Pictorial Documents of the Life of Johann Sebastian
Bach), Bach-Dokumente Vol. 4, Werner Neumann (VEB
Deutscher Verlag für Musik, 1979)
A most valuable compilation of pictorial sources, portraits,
places, letters and autograph manuscripts, with a good
English translation.

BIOGRAPHY

J. S. Bach, Malcolm Boyd (Master Musicians, third edition,
OUP, 2000)
In its thoroughly revised form, this is the most sensible,
concise and reliable of all short Bach biographies, a well-
balanced narrative which signals uncertainty where that exists.
Inevitably not all works are covered but Boyd's assessments
were always acute.

Johann Sebastian Bach, the Learned Musician, Christoph Wolff
(OUP, 2000)
This is the major biography of our time, a new and rounded
portrait drawing on the author's extensive research (see
Studies, below) to create a picture of a composer who continually strove for perfection. The author's range and knowledge is astonishing; the information and judgement is superb,
though the view of Bach is arguably idealised. We eagerly
await his full treatment of Bach's music.

Johann Sebastian Bach: Life and Work, Martin Geck trans.
John Hargraves (Harcourt, 2006)
Not to be confused with his smaller volume (see below), this
solid book covers the field impressively, is up to date with
German scholarship and is especially good on reception
issues; Geck says more about the music than Wolff.

J. S. Bach: A Life in Music, Peter Williams (CUP, 2007)
The most recent Bach biography takes a detailed and often
sceptical look at the history, based on a re-examination of the
Obituary published four years after Bach's death. Williams is
pro-rhetoric, anti-numerology, and full of interesting queries
and quirky comments, but often sidesteps the big picture in
examining the detail.

J. S. Bach, Martin Geck (Haus, 2003)
Derived from his larger-scale biography which had not at that
point been translated from German, this somewhat dour but
thorough portrait of Bach by a noted German scholar covers
key issues with a strong sense of cultural background.

Bach: An Extraordinary Life, Davitt Moroney (Associated
Board, 2000)
This unpretentious little book is full of good insights from
a player and scholar who knows the music intimately: a fine
short introduction.

Nekrolog or Obituary Notice of Johann Sebastian Bach, trs.
Walter Emery (Travis and Emery, 2009)
Back in 1942 the Bach scholar Walter Emery embarked on
a new translation of the Obituary, supplemented by notes
reflecting the state of knowledge at the time. His impeccably
handwritten (!) copy has now been published in facsimile
by his family firm, and it makes a touching and beautiful
document.

Evening in the Palace of Reason, James Gaines (Harper
Perennial, 2005)
Written from enthusiasm and with understanding, this com-
pelling narrative of the events around the creation of *The
Musical Offering* by a former *Life* and *Time* editor is subtitled
'Bach meets Frederick the Great in the Age of Enlightenment'.

CULTURAL BACKGROUND

The Late Baroque Era, ed. George J. Buelow (Macmillan 1993)
Linked to the television series *Man and Music*, this fine set of volumes was, like the programmes that inspired it, never finished; but this one includes excellent cultural background by Bernd Baselt on Central Germany, George Buelow on Hamburg, Lübeck and Dresden, and George Stauffer on Leipzig.

The World of Baroque Music: New Perspectives, ed. George B. Stauffer (Indiana UP, 2006)
A slightly random collection of essays, worth searching out for Stauffer's 'Bach and the Bounds of Originality', Daniel Melamed on the St John Passion and David Schulenberg on North European keyboard music.

Bach among the Theologians, Jaroslav Pelikan (Fortress Press, 1986)
A thoughtful little book by a theological scholar who does not claim to be a musical expert, about Bach's relation to Lutheranism, including much about the chorale texts he set.

Music and Society: The Politics of Composition, Performance and Reception, ed. Richard Leppert and Susan McClary (CUP, 1987)
A stimulating collection, including Susan McClary's fiery polemic, 'The Blasphemy of Talking Politics during Bach Year'.

SCHOLARLY STUDIES

Bach: Essays on his Life and Music, Christoph Wolff (Harvard, 1991)
This prequel to Wolff's major Bach biography was described by him as 'a book about a book the author doesn't feel quite ready to write'. Yet it is in some ways even better than the biography that followed: closely argued and shedding new light on an astonishing range of issues in Bach's life and music, from the Buxtehude, Reincken and Vivaldi background to the publication puzzles of the last years. Wolff's incisive analysis and acute judgement have redefined Bach scholarship.

About Bach, ed. Gregory Butler, George Stauffer, Mary Dalton Greer (Illinois, 2008)
This recent book of essays in tribute to Wolff contains some radical new thoughts: Butler on rethinking *The Art of Fugue*, Mary Greer on why Bach started to study his family when he was fifty, and Douglass Seaton on Schumann's use of the B–A–C–H theme.

Bach and the Patterns of Invention, Laurence Dreyfus (Harvard, 1996)
This innovative, prize-winning book pushes forward our understanding of Bach's creative methods, discussing his way of composing and suggesting that his work criticises the conventions of his age at the same time as rising above them.

Early Music: J. S. Bach Tercentenary Issue (OUP, May 1985)
A collection of major articles for the anniversary, including Wolff's seminal article on 'Bach's Leipzig Chamber Music' and Robert Marshall on 'Bach's Orchestre'. The cover shows a possible Bach family portrait, now doubted, but inside there is a less often remarked, but vivid, silverpoint drawing said to be of the composer.

The Creative Development of Johann Sebastian Bach, Vol. 1: 1695–1717, Richard Jones (OUP, 2007)
The most important English-language Bach study to have appeared in recent years, from a leading British scholar; this book boldly tackles the chronology of the early works, and suggests how his style was formed. The second volume is awaited.

Essays on J. S. Bach, Gerhard Herz (UMI Research Press, 1985)
Herz's moving autobiographical introduction about his time in 1930s Germany begins a collection of his pioneering essays on Bach reception history and the B minor Mass.

*The Compositional Processes of J. S. Bach: A Study of the
Autograph Scores of the Vocal Works*, Robert Marshall (2 vols,
Princeton UP, 1972)
An ambitious and acclaimed attempt to reconstruct the
methods by which Bach conceived and realised his compositions, tracing the process of conception and correction
through the materials of his autograph scores. Hypothetical
but fascinating.

MUSIC
The Cantatas of J. S. Bach, Alfred Dürr, trans. Richard Jones
(OUP, 2005)
The standard work on all the cantatas, including a wealth of
detail, texts, translation, and musical and liturgical commen-
tary by the leading Bach scholar. Richard Jones has performed
a splendid, meticulous labour of love by making it available in
English.

*The World of the Bach Cantatas, Volume 1: Early Sacred
Cantatas*, ed. Christoph Wolff (Norton, 1997)
The first of a projected series linked to Ton Koopman's cantata
recordings for Erato. As that series moved from Erato to
Challenge Classics, only this volume was published in English,
though there are two more available in German (and Dutch).

Analysing Bach Cantatas, Eric Chafe (Oxford, 2000)
Developing themes from his earlier book, *Tonal Allegory in
Bach's Cantatas*, this prize-winning book explores some cantatas in detail, showing how tonal schemes, musical detail and
theological themes intertwine. Not an easy read.

Bach: The Choral Works, Stephen Daw (Fairleigh Dickinson
UP, 1981)
A pioneering work treating the cantatas and other works
chronologically, with many detailed observations on performances and recordings: a model of musicology rooted in
practice.

Cantata No. 140, Wachet auf, ruft uns die Stimme, ed. Gerhard Herz (Norton Critical Scores, 1972)

It might seem odd to include a single score in this list, but Herz's exemplary introduction includes the most easily available (and by far the cheapest) version of the new chronology of the cantatas, as well as surveying the critical comments of others about this masterpiece.

Bach: The Mass in B minor, The Great Catholic Mass, George Stauffer (Yale Music Masters, 2003)

A fine monograph, exploring the work in detail and looking for possible occasions for its use. The subtitle seems a misnomer, since Stauffer leaves the denominational allegiance of the Mass open.

Hearing Bach's Passions, Daniel R. Melamed (OUP, 2005)

A penetrating and exceptionally clear introduction to the issues surrounding Bach's Passion settings, not only the famous two but the complications of the others; revelatory on the two-choir structure of the St Matthew Passion and strongly supporting small-scale performance.

The Keyboard Music of J. S. Bach, David Schulenberg (second edition, Routledge, 2006)

A thorough and detailed treatment of the keyboard music, always bearing in mind the needs of performers as well as scholars; somehow lacks enthusiasm for the music.

Bach's Well-tempered Clavier: the 48 Preludes and Fugues, David Ledbetter (Yale 2002)

Not only a detailed guide to all the music in the '48', but a comprehensive background covering tuning, teaching, theory and instruments.

The Organ Music of J. S. Bach, Peter Williams (3 vols, Cambridge, 1980)

The essential work on all Bach's organ music, with detailed source notes, analyses and descriptions of each separate work, gathering a lifetime's work together. The first two volumes have been revised and reissued in one volume.

J. S. Bach as Organist: His Instruments, Music and Performance Practices, ed. George Stauffer and Ernest May (Indiana/Batsford, 1986)

A symposium of views on Bach's organs, his playing, and his organ music.

CAMBRIDGE MUSIC HANDBOOKS

Bach: The Goldberg Variations, Peter Williams (2001)
Bach: The Brandenburg Concertos, Malcolm Boyd (1993)
Bach: Mass in B minor, John Butt (1991)

PERFORMANCE

The Essential Bach Choir, Andrew Parrott (Boydell, 2000)

Here is all you could want to know, and perhaps more, about the explosive arguments around the performance of Bach's choral music, including the first publication of Joshua Rifkin's full 1981 lecture that ignited the controversy. There is endlessly fascinating documentation, and Parrott is especially good on the background and pre-history; his own performances have been some of the best demonstrations that undogmatic solo-voice-led accounts are musically convincing.

Bach Performance Practice, 1945–1975: A Comprehensive Review of Sound Recordings and Literature, Dorottya Fabian (Ashgate, 2003)

Comprehensive indeed, this is an extremely detailed investigation of changing performance styles, informed by a proper doubt about the revival of 'historical' styles but bogged down by a dense unidiomatic style and an inability to see the musical wood for the trees. There is a fascinating, if bitty, CD of extracts.

BACH ON THE INTERNET

Among the endless resources on the web, which constantly change, among the most useful currently are:

www.bach-cantatas.com

comprehensive documentation of all Bach's works and many recordings, with extensive discussion threads

www.bach-leipzig.de
the official site of the Bach Archiv Leipzig, the Bach Museum Leipzig, and the annual Bach Festival

www.bach-digital.de
the beginnings of an invaluable digital archive of Bach manuscripts

www.bach-institut.de
the site of the other leading Bach study centre in Göttingen

www.bachnetwork.co.uk
scholarly work by a British-led group of experts, including an on-line journal

www.music.qub.ac.uk/tomita/bachbib
Yo Tomita's comprehensive on-line Bach bibliography

www.jsbach.org
an informative site by Jan Hanford and John Koster

Alphabetical index of Bach's works

The main entry for each work is in **bold** type. All works with German titles are listed under their first letter, even if they begin with the definite or indefinite article.

Index of Bach's works, ordered by BWV number

Following the second edition of BWV (1990) updated in the *Kleine Ausgabe* (1998)